When Law Fails

The Charles Hamilton Houston Institute Series on Race and Justice

The Charles Hamilton Houston Institute for Race and Justice at Harvard Law School seeks to further the vision of racial justice and equality through research, policy analysis, litigation, and scholarship, and will place a special emphasis on the issues of voting rights, the future of affirmative action, the criminal justice system, and related areas.

When Law Fails

Making Sense of
Miscarriages of Justice

EDITED BY

Charles J. Ogletree, Jr.,
and Austin Sarat

New York University Press

NEW YORK AND LONDON

NEW YORK UNIVERSITY PRESS
New York and London
www.nyupress.org

Library of Congress Cataloging-in-Publication Data
When law fails : making sense of miscarriages of justice / edited by
Charles J. Ogletree, Jr. and Austin Sarat.
p.   cm. — (Charles Hamilton Houston Institute series on
race and justice)
Includes bibliographical references and index.
ISBN-13: 978-0-8147-4051-4 (cl : alk. paper)
ISBN-10: 0-8147-4051-0 (cl : alk. paper)
ISBN-13: 978-0-8147-4052-1 (pb : alk. paper)
ISBN-10: 0-8147-4052-9 (pb : alk. paper)
1. Justice, Administration of—United States.   I. Ogletree, Charles J.
II. Sarat, Austin.
KF8700.W44 2009
347.73—dc22   2008031464

New York University Press books are printed on acid-free paper,
and their binding materials are chosen for strength and durability.
We strive to use environmentally responsible suppliers and materials
to the greatest extent possible in publishing our books.

Manufactured in the United States of America

c   10 9 8 7 6 5 4 3 2 1
p   10 9 8 7 6 5 4 3 2 1

To my son Ben, with love and hope (A.S.)
To the survivors and descendants of the 1921 Tulsa Race Riot (C.O.)

Contents

Acknowledgments

We are grateful for the enthusiastic participation and insightful contributions of the distinguished scholars whose work is included in this volume. Their work was first shared at a workshop sponsored by the Charles Hamilton Houston Institute for Race and Justice on November 17–18, 2006. We gratefully acknowledge the help of the institute's dedicated and talented staff. We continue to find great satisfaction in our continuing collaboration and the pleasures of a shared intellectual venture.

Introduction

Charles J. Ogletree, Jr., and Austin Sarat

Perhaps it is in the confluence of DNA testing, the commercial boon of reality TV drama, and a natural inclination for redemption stories that we find "miscarriages of justice" more and more the stuff of popular culture. The successful off-Broadway production of *The Exonerated* tells the story of six death-row inmates who get freed before their executions. The play evolved into a Court TV movie that *Entertainment Weekly* called "Searing Drama." The entertainment world has provided the groundwork for academics and theorists who have long labored to advance the view of miscarriages of justice not as aberrations but as deeply revealing, central features of our legal system. The natural, narrative arcs, the theme of "a second chance" may make for searing drama, but the broader significance of miscarriages of justice demands a close and careful examination that does not lend itself to happy and easy resolutions.

In America and elsewhere, law fails often and becomes a tool of injustice. Political theorist Judith Shklar argues that, in the study of law, "injustice should not be treated intellectually as a hasty preliminary to the analysis of justice." According to Shklar, "the real realm of injustice is not in an amoral and prelegal state of nature. It does not appear only on those rare occasions when a political order wholly collapses. It does not stand outside the gate of even the best known states. Most injustices occur continuously within the framework of an established polity with an operative system of law, in normal times."[1] Indeed, this book, *When Law Fails,* examines the nature of injustices in such terms—not as errors but as organic outcomes of a misshaped larger system.

The most dramatic and best-known examples of miscarriages concern conviction and sentencing of innocent people in capital cases. Exonerations from death row have become increasingly common: since 1973, more than 125 people in 25 states have been released from death row by evidence of their innocence.[2] These exonerations possess enormous power in the debate around the death penalty. In particular, exonerations played a strong role in moratoria on executions in Illinois and New Jersey, among other states. Widely publicized exonerations spurred introduction of congressional legislation, including the Innocence Protection Act, a comprehensive package of criminal justice reforms aimed at reducing the risk that innocent persons are executed. The bill would ensure that convicted offenders have the opportunity to prove their innocence through DNA testing. It would assist states in providing competent legal services at each stage of a death penalty prosecution and compensate people who prove they had been unjustly incarcerated.[3]

Miscarriages of justice in the United States are a repeated staple of our history. From the largely unknown Tulsa Race Riot of 1921,[4] to the infamous 1930s case of the Scottsboro Boys,[5] to the lynching of the young African American teenager, Emmitt Till,[6] to the 1983 case of Rolando Cruz,[7] and through the 1977 conviction of Leonard Peltier[8] and the 1984 conviction of Darryl Hunt,[9] the twentieth century witnessed more than its share of miscarriages of justice. Faulty eyewitness identifications, false confessions, and biased juries, as well as the politicization of prosecution and the pervasive fact of racial bias in the criminal justice system, make error a legal commonplace not only in capital cases but throughout the legal system. In a 2006 Gallup Poll, 63 percent of Americans believed that an innocent person was executed in the past five years.[10] Perhaps the dramatizations and popularization of such miscarriages has led more people in the United States to reconsider their views on the death penalty.

A notably wide range of men and women have forced the matter of real-life miscarriages of justice onto public agendas in recent years. In several cases, their party affiliations and personal backgrounds would not predict their commitment to reversing injustice. The power of this collective voice provides a wide, new opening for us to analyze miscarriages of justice. To understand how wide this opening just might be and the potential for shifting public opinion, consider the case of the former governor of Illinois, George Ryan. Born and raised in Iowa, Ryan pursued a career in pharmacy and later entered politics. After serving terms in the Illinois House of Representatives, then as lieutenant governor, and later as the Illinois secretary of state, Ryan was elected governor of Illinois in 1998.

At the time of his election, Governor Ryan was a firm supporter of the death penalty. He presided over death penalty cases and did not appear to have difficulty in using his executive authority to affirm the convictions of people who had been tried, sentenced, and had their appeals exhausted. In a 2001 article about Ryan in *The Nation*, Bruce Shapiro wrote: "[I]f you sent to central casting for a Midwestern conservative, they'd send back Governor George Ryan of Illinois. With his white hair, plain business suit and heartland directness, Ryan is nobody's image of a crusading criminal-justice reformer." That all changed dramatically in the year 2000, when Governor Ryan learned the history of the imposition of capital punishment in his state. Of 25 jury cases in which people had been convicted and their appeals completed, 13 of those on death row were actually *innocent*.[11] After reviewing the numerous errors in life and death decisions, Governor Ryan appointed a Capital Punishment Commission to examine how the Illinois death penalty was applied and to make recommendations for changes. While waiting for the commission's report, Ryan declared a moratorium on executions.[12]

The Commission on Capital Punishment studied the matter for several months and made more than 80 recommendations for change to the capital punishment system. The commission report noted sentences imposed on the mentally retarded and the inappropriate use of race in sentencing and trial outcomes. It also revealed that ultimately police brutality was rampant.[13]

Governor Ryan commuted the death sentences of 167 people on death row. "I will sleep well tonight knowing I made the right decision," Ryan said following the blanket commutations. In explaining his decision, Ryan noted some of the myriad ways that a legal system, with supposed procedural and substantive protections, can fail:

> Thirty-three of the death row inmates were represented at trial by an attorney who had later been disbarred or at some point suspended from practicing law. . . . Of the more than 160 death row inmates, 35 were African American defendants who had been convicted or condemned to die by all-white juries. . . . Forty-six inmates were convicted on the basis of testimony from jailhouse informants.[14]

While Governor Ryan's actions in 2000 and 2003 were celebrated by death penalty abolitionists both domestically and abroad,[15] they did not wipe the slate clean. Seven years earlier, the U.S. Supreme Court had taken a different approach, and those decisions still stood. In *Herrera v. Collins*, then-Chief Justice William Rehnquist held that the Court did not need to grapple with the question of whether a person facing execution might be innocent. The Court, Rehnquist said, need only be concerned with the question of whether a defendant had received a fair, technically efficient, and procedurally sound trial. In recounting the procedural history of Herrera's case, Chief Justice Rehnquist wrote:

> In February 1992, petitioner lodged the instant habeas petition—his second—in federal court, alleging, among other things, that he is innocent of the murders of Rucker and Carrisalez, and that his execution would thus violate the Eighth and Fourteenth Amendments. In addition to proffering the above affidavits, petitioner presented the affidavits of Raul Herrera, Jr., Raul Sr.'s son, and Jose Ybarra, Jr., a schoolmate of the Herrera brothers. Raul Jr. averred that he had witnessed his father shoot Officers Rucker and Carrisalez and petitioner was not present. Raul Jr. was nine years old at the time of the killings. Ybarra alleged that Raul Sr. told him one summer night in 1983 that he had shot the two police officers. Petitioner alleged that law enforcement officials were aware of this evidence, and had withheld it in violation of *Brady v. Maryland,* 373 U.S. 83 (1963).[16]

The question of innocence was irrelevant, however. As Chief Justice Rehnquist wrote:

> Petitioner asserts that the Eighth and Fourteenth Amendments to the United States Constitution prohibit the execution of a person who is innocent of the crime for which he was convicted. This proposition has an elemental appeal, as would the similar proposition that the Constitution prohibits the imprisonment of one who is innocent of the crime for which he was convicted. After all, the central purpose of any criminal justice is to convict the guilty and free the innocent. See *United States v. Nobles,* 422 U.S. 225, 230 (1975). But the evidence upon which petitioner's claim of innocence rests was not produced at his trial, but rather eight years later. In any system of criminal justice, "innocence" or "guilt" must be determined in some sort of judicial proceeding. Petitioner's showing of innocence, and indeed his constitutional claim for relief based upon that showing, must be evaluated in light of the previous proceedings in this case, which have stretched over a span of 10 years.[17]

In a breathtaking denial of Herrera's claim of actual innocence, Chief Justice Rehnquist observed:

All of these constitutional safeguards, of course, make it more difficult for the State to rebut and finally overturn the presumption of innocence which attaches to every criminal defendant. But we have also observed that "[d]ue process does not require that every conceivable step be taken, at whatever cost, to eliminate the possibility of convicting an innocent person." *Patterson v. New York*, 432 U.S. 197, 208 (1977). To conclude otherwise would all but paralyze our system for enforcement of the criminal law.[18]

It may be that law without failure, perfect justice, is not attainable or that it is not attainable at a price Americans are willing to pay.

Justice Rehnquist's views in *Herrera* invited outrage. Justice Harry Blackmun, in a stirring dissent, gave voice to such outrage, which may find its roots not merely in American culture but in an even more universal, human inclination toward fairness. He wrote: "Nothing could be more contrary to contemporary standards of decency or more shocking to the conscience than to execute a person who is actually innocent."[19] It is exactly this kind of outrage that helped shift the position of a tough-on-crime conservative like George Ryan. As Blackmun put it:

I have voiced disappointment over this Court's obvious eagerness to do away with any restriction on the States' power to execute whomever and however they please. . . . I have also expressed doubts about whether, in the absence of such restrictions, capital punishment remains constitutional at all. . . . Of one thing, however, I am certain. Just as an execution without adequate safeguards is unacceptable, so too is an execution when the condemned prisoner can prove that he is innocent. The execution of a person who can show that he is innocent comes perilously close to simple murder.[20]

Nearly one year later, in *Callins v. Collins*, Blackmun, frustrated by the increasing number of examples of miscarriages of justice in the American legal system, concluded that he could no longer support *any* decision affirming a death penalty sentence. He said:

From this day forward, I no longer shall tinker with the machinery of death. For more than 20 years, I have endeavored—indeed I have struggled —along with a majority of this Court, to develop procedural and substantive rules that would lend more than the mere appearance of fairness to the death penalty endeavor. Rather than continue to coddle the Court's delusion that the desired level of fairness has been achieved and the need for regulation eviscerated, I feel morally and intellectually obligated simply to concede that the death penalty experiment has failed. It is virtually self evident to me now that no combination of procedural rules or substantive regulations ever can save the death penalty from its inherent constitutional deficiencies.[21]

This moral certainty is nothing new of course. But, the fact that it is increasingly common and found increasingly in uncommon places provides inspiration and urgency for this book. In *When Law Fails*, we examine various shortcomings of our legal system, their history and origin, and some of the ways in which law's built-in practices and mechanisms contribute to miscarriages of justice.[22] We bring together a distinguished group of scholars to try to make sense of miscarriages of justice. Whatever their cause, miscarriages of justice have more than just political, personal, and made-for-TV consequences. They reveal something about a society and a legal system where not all is well. They force us to articulate the value of "justice" in our society.

There are, of course, numerous books about particular, infamous cases, as well as research on factors that contribute to miscarriages of justice, such as prosecutorial misconduct. But we think that much work of an interpretive and historical nature remains to be done: the work of figuring out how we should make sense of miscarriages of justice. What are the legal, cultural, and political meanings of a miscarriage of justice? Is this concept useful for talking about ways in which the law fails, or does it impose too narrow a parameter for discussion and debate? Are miscarriages of justice systemic or symptomatic, or are the problems that lead law to misfire idiosyncratic? What theoretical frames are most productive in illuminating this problem? What are the broader implications of miscarriages of justice for the ways we think about law? Are there ways of reconceptualizing miscarriages of justice that are particularly useful for illuminating the phenomena and other ways that are less fruitful? Together, the research collected in this book takes an important step to address these questions, offering some answers and some avenues for future inquiry.

Part I, "On the Meaning and Significance of Miscarriages of Justice," begins with a dramatic story of injustice and the larger national narrative implicated by the process of responding to that injustice. Indeed, in Mary Dudziak's view, miscarriages of justice play significant roles in an

American story of progress, a story that has importance for America's standing in the world. When law fails, what may matter most is not the initial failure but the story that gets told of the nation's response.

But Dudziak suggests that even when an error is recognized as meaningful, significant, and deserving of redress, mechanisms of forgetting often ensure that both the person subject to a miscarriage of justice and the broader significance of their case are lost to history. Dudziak writes that this erasure helps the United States project a desired national identity to the rest of the world. When miscarriages are redressed, they can be represented as part of the nation's "march of principle." Redress helps to both excuse past injustices and legitimize present decisions in the name of progress. Dudziak argues that America projects this teleological legal image in order to legitimize its status as a progressive leader of the free world. The law's power to resolve issues, Dudziak says, often acts as glue to restore the image of America. Thus, she contends, "What happens to the person at the center of the story is, at best, secondary."

To illustrate her argument, Dudziak recounts the case of Jimmy Wilson, set in 1957 in highly segregated Marion, Alabama. Wilson was a middle-aged African American man who had done yardwork for an elderly widow named Estelle Baker. One night, after having consumed a fair amount of alcohol, Wilson arrived at Baker's house to ask for money. According to her testimony, he broke into her house, demanded cash, and, when he was not satisfied with the amount she gave him, choked her in an attempt to elicit more. She also claimed that he tried to rape her, but a noise from a nearby house scared him away. Wilson claimed that Baker had advanced him money before and that he had had no intention of scaring her into giving him money. He said that she had invited him into the house and that he did not touch her.

In 1950s Alabama, fear of the black man in the white woman's bedroom overwhelmed due process of law. Wilson's trial took only four and one-half hours, and the all-white jury deliberated for less than an hour. He did not testify, and his lawyer made virtually no effort to defend him. The jury sentenced Wilson to death for robbing Baker of $1.95. The Supreme Court of Alabama affirmed this decision following its automatic appeal.

During the 1950s, Dudziak notes, because of the Cold War, the United States tried to project an international image of superiority and progressive liberalism. "But," Dudziak writes, "superior values were not always on display in the United States. And as the United States. positioned itself as the leader of the 'free world' in the early years of the Cold War, the nation found itself under increasing global scrutiny. Racial incidents were no lon-ger local news." Thus Jimmy Wilson's story was publicized throughout the world, and in many nations people began to protest the Alabama court's decision. The Wilson case thus became an issue of diplomatic importance, so important that the State Department began to track the story's global impact.

Eventually, Wilson's new lawyer, Fred Gray succeeded in convincing the governor of Alabama to commute Wilson's sentence to life in prison. As a result, the international outcry quickly diminished, and the Wilson case enfolded into a narrative of progress. And Jimmy Wilson could be forgotten. What mattered in this case and others was not individual in-justice, only that America visibly demonstrated its advanced rule of law to the world. Dudziak writes, "Stories of *domestic* American law, stories of justice and injustice among Americans, have been part of a global nar-rative that defines the meaning of America in the world. Erasing Jimmy Wilson helped protect a narrative about America that American leaders had self-consciously tried to construct."

In chapter 2, Charles Ogletree, Jr., recounts another story of law's fail-ure. But this story did not easily fold itself into a national narrative of injustice and redress. This chapter focuses on a race riot that took place in Tulsa, Oklahoma, in 1921. Ogletree contends that the devastation caused by the riot, coupled with the state's ongoing refusal to compensate the vic-tims, constitutes an instance in which the law has proven unable or un-willing to provide justice and redress.

The trouble began when Dick Rowland, a young African American man, was riding the elevator up to a "colored" restroom in a building in segregated Tulsa. Rowland accidentally stepped on the foot of the eleva-tor operator, who happened to be a white teenage girl; she consequently slapped him. Although that was the extent of the incident, rumors of black-on-white sexual assault began almost immediately. Eventually, Row-land was arrested and taken to jail to await a hearing. When it became obvious at the hearing that no rape or sexual assault had taken place, the charges were dismissed.

Unfortunately, rumors to the contrary had already spread throughout the white community, and a lynch mob was waiting outside the jailhouse when Rowland was released. A fight ensued between the white lynch mob and a group of black residents who had come to protect Rowland. After the fight, the blacks returned home to Greenwood, the "colored" area of Tulsa. However, the altercation did not end when the blacks withdrew.

The sheriff "deputized dozens of white men and gave them orders to 'invade' Greenwood." Heavily armed, the white mob rioted in Greenwood that night.

Before the riot, Greenwood was a thriving area, full of successful business and other establishments. The mob burned down many of these businesses and over a thousand homes; they killed numerous black residents and held others as "prisoners" in detainment camps. Though the death toll still remains unknown, estimates range from dozens to hundreds. After the riot, local African American attorneys filed lawsuits on behalf of the victims, who sought compensation for the devastating physical, emotional, and monetary losses they had suffered. Those suits did not succeed. Ogletree writes that "it was not simply the court of law but the court of public opinion that crushed hope of reparations" as the efforts toward compensation were hindered by widespread belief in the white community that blacks had instigated the riot. In addition, the membership of many of Tulsa's law enforcement officials in the Ku Klux Klan created yet another roadblock to legal redress.

It was not until decades later that the victims of the riot received any recognition. In 1999, the Oklahoma State Legislature created the Tulsa Race Riot Commission. The commission's purpose was to investigate and evaluate the events of the 1921 riot and to recommend what actions should be taken, if any. The commission's 2001 report stated that the riot was, in fact, initiated by the white mob and that "the black community and their descendants were entitled to restitution." Despite this recommendation, compensation was not provided. There was no way to enforce the commission's recommendation, and once again the victims were left without recourse. While some of the victims had flourished in spite of (or perhaps because of) the riot and had built exemplary, extraordinary lives, everyone involved had been greatly affected, and the state and city seemed unwilling to acknowledge this impact.

In 2002, Ogletree himself became involved in the struggle for reparations. Ogletree assembled a group of lawyers who agreed to work pro bono for the Greenwood group. Their legal strategy was to argue that the Tulsa Race Riot Commission's should be considered "newly discovered evidence," thus "start[ing] the clock running again" on the statute of limitations, which normally expired after two years. Ogletree and his colleagues filed the new lawsuit in 2003. While the judge agreed that a miscarriage of justice had occurred, he was not convinced by the plaintiffs' legal argument. In what he referred to as "strictly a legal conclusion," the judge ruled that the statute of limitations prevented the victims from receiving compensation. On appeal, a circuit court again denied relief; thereafter, the Supreme Court refused to hear the case. As of this moment, the victims have still not received restitution, but they have filed a petition in an international court and have proposed legislation to extend the statute of limitations.

Toward the end of his chapter, Ogletree explains how this specific miscarriage of justice can be used as a tool to examine law's limits and failures in a broader sense: "Beyond telling the story about the miscarriages of justice in Tulsa in 1921, the Tulsa race riot also tells us something about law and its relevance to justice. . . . [It] illustrates a number of ways that the rule of law was ineffective in protecting the interests of its citizens." Ogletree points to several different failures of law in Tulsa: its powerlessness in the face of the mob, its failure to protect citizens against violence, and its continuing inability to redress obvious wrongs. Ogletree argues that the story of the Tulsa race riot "makes apparent the fact that courts of law are not always the most appropriate or ideal places to resolve disputes. Indeed, the limits on what claims may be raised, the time at which they may be raised, and the scope of the issues that may be raised leave many persuasive and powerful matters outside the walls of the court."

In chapter 3, Robert Weisberg examines one of the devices that prevent courts from taking up miscarriages of justice, the so called harmless error doctrine. Under this rubric, "a reviewing court agrees with a defendant's claim of legal error at trial," yet by finding the error harmless provides no redress. The question the courts must ask under the harmless error doctrine is "whether . . . error so materially undermined the fairness of the trial as to require reversal."

Weisberg asks us to "imagine how the state answers the defendant who rightly or concededly says that he is the victim of error by the legal system." He acknowledges that "[f]or much of our legal history, we followed the 'Exchequer Rule,' whereby trial error that took the form of wrongful admission of evidence always required reversal. We do not know quite how rigorously the Exchequer Rule was enforced or whether its paradoxical effect was to discourage appellate courts from even finding error. By early in the twentieth century, states started passing laws requiring some proof of harmfulness of error . . . while automatic reversal seemed to remain the norm for errors of constitutional magnitude."

He pays particular attention to the Supreme Court's decision in *Chapman v. California*, where the prosecutor violated the Fifth Amendment by allowing the prosecutor to comment on the defendant's failure to testify: "[T]he Court held that the standard on appeal was that the state had to prove harmlessness beyond a reasonable doubt . . . (and) by holding that the question of harmless error is part of the federal question, the Court suggests that the necessity of self-correction of injustice was in a sense part of the very definition of constitutional justice." Yet *Chapman* is, Weisberg reminds us, "hardly the end of the story. [T]here are softer versions of harmless error in such areas as the defendant's due process right to discovery of exculpatory evidence and her Sixth Amendment effective assistance of counsel. And softer still are the rules that apply on federal habeas corpus review of state convictions."

As Weisberg sees it, this doctrine is one place in which law figures its own relationship to and responsibility for injustice: "In this incredibly nuanced and complex area of doctrine," we can see "when and how the institutions we lump under the term 'legal system' view themselves in regard to the occurrence of incorrect legal outcomes in criminal cases." Weisberg suggests that the harmless error doctrine invites us into the mundane world in which legal institutions draw "the boundary between justice and nonjustice." He argues that "as dryly technical as the harmless error doctrine appears, it may give us some new revealing clues as to how the legal system distinguishes what lies within itself and its powers of self-redress and what lies without." Attending to harmless error rules, Weisberg argues, "forces us to define what factors we view as exogenous to, and therefore unavoidable or uncontrollable by, our legal system, even if these mistake-producing forces sometimes manifest themselves symptomatically within the system and thereby seem to constitute 'miscarriage of justice.'"

In Part II, "Miscarriages of Justice and Legal Processes," we examine different actors and stages in the legal process (including the police, the jury system, sentencing, and punishment) at which breakdowns—failures of the kind often addressed in harmless error cases—occur, and we analyze why those points are so error prone. In chapter 4, Jonathan Simon analyzes miscarriages of justice and error during police investigations. Simon writes that from the 1960s to the present, academic discussion of American policing has focused mainly on rights enforcement and crime control. Earlier discourse focused on methods of improving the police "craft" to eliminate conviction of the innocent. Simon associates this change with the advent of the "war on drugs."

While before the 1960s and the war on drugs police were seen as corrupt, brutal individuals, police have now come to be associated with the interests of the victims of crime and, by extension, the interests of the entire public. Simon writes, "The conventional wisdom is that police are much more professional than they were a generation or two ago, largely a result of a decline in discretion and investment in better management, training, and technology." This new perception of police has insulated them from regulation seeking to improve the reliability and visibility of investigatory techniques.

In addition, Simon argues that "[u]nlike burglary or robbery, drug crime produces an almost limitless population of available arrestees." The only real limiting factor governing the number of arrests is the amount of police resources. This fact creates an environment in which police can wrongly convict someone more easily, hold them in jail without much evidence, and prosecute them with less effort and based on faulty testimony. As a result of mass incarceration, the police have a pre-made list of suspects—a list made before any specific crime is committed—from which a police officer can pick and choose rather than having to search for a suspect from scratch. Also, given the number of technical violations of parole, persons recently freed from jail "can be easily taken into custody and held without the burdens of proof that would normally fall on the prosecution."

Since suspects have prior criminal records, police can more easily use faulty testimony such as jailhouse informants and can more easily force confessions since the suspect is already in a weak position. The ease of finding and capturing a suspect allows what Simon calls "tunnel vision: "the police only look for evidence pointing to a specific suspect they have already targeted." Thus, "[w]hile the rhetoric of the war on crime celebrated police, the tactics emphasized rounding up low-value suspects through relatively easy low-grade surveillance and seizure."

In Simon's view, "the war on drugs may have helped reduce internal normative checks on manipulating evidence against suspects by promoting a view that law enforcement is engaged in a wholesale war against a criminal underclass (framed by race, age, and gender) rather than retail struggle against individual wrongdoers." Simon suggests that to decrease false convictions, police should return to an individualistic approach to law enforcement. Rather than being vigilantes or robo-cops, police officers should insinuate themselves into a community so that they can use local knowledge and cooperation to catch individuals, as well as guard themselves against stereotyping.

In chapter 5, Daniel Givelber examines the fallibility of the jury system in criminal courts. Givelber writes that in the twentieth century, the common concern about the criminal justice system has been whether we let too many guilty people go free rather than whether we accidentally convict the innocent. Since the mid-1990s, as DNA testing has shown the frequency with which innocent people have been convicted, academics have recognized the shortcomings of the system of adjudication. Previously, only newly discovered evidence of guilt against a third party or a witness recanting his testimony could prove a convicted person to be innocent.

Givelber describes the classic jury study by Kalven and Zeisel, which showed "that juries were seven times as likely to acquit when the judge would have convicted as they were to do the opposite—to convict when the judge would have acquitted." Recently, the National Center for States Courts attempted to replicate the Kalven and Zeisel study. They found that "[u]nlike 50 years earlier, judges and juries in the 2000s are more likely to disagree about when an acquittal is appropriate than they are about when a conviction is appropriate." Juries still acquit more than judges would, but at a much lower rate. The study also found that "[j]uries convict at a higher rate than judges (46% vs. 27%) when the judge evaluates the evidence of guilt as weak . . . and judges convict at a higher rate than juries (41% to 17%) when the jury evaluates the evidence as weak."

So what, Givelber asks, has changed since 1966? He believes that the change has resulted from the due process revolution of the late twentieth century. Today, defendants have the right to competent counsel and a trial by jury, Fifth Amendment rights have been strengthened, the state must now provide exculpatory material in court, and the jury must reflect the makeup of the community. Yet, Givelber contends, these improvements have not improved the inaccuracy of the system. If anything, Givelber writes, these "improvements" have restricted the amount of information juries hear about a case. He writes, "The juries determining guilt or innocence in the 1950s and 1960s were considerably more likely to hear from the defendant, to hear from more than one defense witness, and to hear *any* defense witness than the contemporary juries in the NCSC study."

Givelber notes that another reason contemporary juries get less information arises from the bureaucratic limitations of the public defender system. The NCSC data show a link between public defenders, private attorneys, and the number of witnesses called to testify during a trial. Public defenders, because they have more cases, less time, less money, and often less skill than private attorneys cannot put the same effort into each case. The data show that private attorneys call in multiple witnesses much more often than public defenders and that defendants with private attorneys are convicted at a much lower rate.

Givelber concludes that since the mid-1990s the "constitutional rights of criminal defendants have increased while the evidence relating to guilt or innocence presented to the jury by criminal defendants has decreased." In effect, the courts have sacrificed factual accuracy for due process values. While the law has broadened the constitutionals rights of defendants, at the same time, it has meant that juries get less information about both the crime and the person accused of committing it.

In chapter 6, Douglas Berman moves from law enforcement and adjudication to consider the resulting problem of what he calls "overpunishment." While Simon and Givelber focus on the falsely convicted innocents, Berman is more interested in the fates of all convicts, including the guilty. Berman is concerned with the injustice of what he calls the "American affinity for punishment," which is rarely seen as a source of miscarriage of justice. Moreover, he believes that the recent focus on traditional miscarriages of justice may even worsen the problem of severe punishments.

As is widely known, there has been a tenfold increase in imprisonment levels since 1970. America incarcerates at a rate five to ten times higher than most other industrialized western countries. There has also been a huge growth in the number of criminals serving life sentences, even juveniles. Modern prisons are extremely unsafe and overcrowded. Berman also describes a new type of prison called the "supermax," which keeps prisoners completely isolated from one another and kept in their cells 22½ hours a day.

Rarely does the public see images of extreme punishment, and even when such punishment is documented, it does not garner much media or political attention. This is because most people view themselves as innocents and so do not create an empathic bond between themselves and a criminal. In addition, legislators only consider criminals in the abstract, not as individuals. Also, "because criminal codes are rarely created anew, legislatures typically contemplate crime and sentencing laws only in response to a perceived 'crime problem,'" which causes legislators to enact progressively tougher laws to solve each new perceived problem.

Any subsequent dips in crime serve to validate those tougher laws, and any increase in crime merely causes an increase in the harshness of the laws.

Berman believes that the focus on the "innocence problem" has taken attention away from the problem of extreme punishments. We are desensitized to other forms of injustice because of our excessive focus on wrongful convictions. In addition, focusing on the injustice of the death penalty also distracts us from other forms of extreme punishment. Berman notes, "I view the death penalty as an extreme punishment distraction because most people enduring unjust sentences are not on death row, and the possibility of unjust capital punishment for murderers is not the best reason for reforming the harshest aspects of federal and state criminal justice systems." In his conclusion, Berman argues that "tough on crime" policies are "costly and often ineffectual." Most important, he wants to refocus the conversation about when law fails to include the way we punish the guilty.

The way we respond to the guilty is also at the heart of the chapters by Linda Ross Meyer and Austin Sarat. In chapter 7, Meyer takes up the issue of responding to the guilty in the context of military justice. She is interested, in particular, in the place of mercy in that system. She begins with some general observations of the relationship of mercy to justice. While some believe that mercy is incompatible with justice, Meyer disagrees. She believes that justice is not merely impersonally treating like cases alike. Cases are related analogously and are subject to interpretation; therefore, different sentences in two similar cases do not necessarily mean the justice system has failed. "In other words," Meyer writes, "there is a metaphysical crack in the law that requires unrule-bound discretion and judgment that leaves room for the kind of inarticulable experience that is mercy."

Yet, in her view, mercy is not always appropriate. It is inappropriate when we cannot experience a connection between us and the criminal other than our shared humanities, whereas "[a]ppropriate mercy . . . is an experience of recognizing another as a second self." Mercy is appropriate when grounded on "mutuality of temporal limitation," "mutual vulnerability," "mutual dependency," and "recognition of mutual guilt." The only way to repair the "experience gap" between judge and defendant is "to make the defendant's narrative richer and more compelling, rather than restricting the judge's vision to a few facets of the case." Like Dudziak and Givelber, Meyer suggests that in order to adjudicate fairly, the judge (or jury) needs to understand the complete narrative of the individual, not merely pieces of the story.

Contrasting the federal court system to military tribunals, Meyer observes that in the latter, more information may be presented about the character of the defendant, whether or not the information is related to the specific crime. This more complete picture of the individual creates a stronger bond between the military judge and the accused, leaving more room for mercy. The military also has a structural hierarchy of responsibility, so blame for crimes is often placed on more than one person.

The place of mercy becomes more problematic when crimes are committed by military personal against "outsiders" or "enemies." Meyer notes that sentences for soldiers convicted of crimes against nonmilitary persons (i.e., civilians and prisoners) seem more lenient than sentences for soldiers who committed crimes against other soldiers. Meyer argues that since we require our soldiers to be tough, to dehumanize and racialize the enemy, and to use violence, we are partially responsible for their actions; by showing them mercy, then, we are taking part of the blame on ourselves. They are partially what we made them. Thus, "[t]he great emphasis in military trials on character evidence and the offender's prior service record, while often mystifying to civilian commentators, may be the framework for a possible non-cynical account of appropriate mercy in sentencing war-related crimes." Leniency is often appropriate in military cases because we need to recognize that war cannot be fought honorably. This is not to say there should be no judgment or sentencing of accused servicemen, merely that mercy does and should have a place in the process.

Returning from the military to the civilian justice system, in chapter 8, Sarat takes up the clemency process in capital cases. Noting the rarity with which capital sentences are commuted, he contends that the clemency process becomes a way of memorializing miscarriages of justice in the death penalty system. In recent years, politicians like Bush and Clinton have reserved clemency only for cases with "undisputable truth" of innocence. Since the courts have already considered the question of mercy during the sentencing phase of a death penalty trial, governors are able to say that they are merely respecting the judgments of the courts.

In this context, Sarat explores ways of understanding the meaning of clemency petitions: (1) petitions as prophetic or as a form of what Robert Cover dubs "'redemptive constitutionalism.' . . . [T]hose documents refuse to recognize the violence of the present moment as the defining totality of law and carry a vision of a future in which Justice prevails over that violence," and (2) petitions as a bridge between narrative and history, as a record of an unjust death which cannot be silenced even if the petition is not heard. Sarat argues that clemency petitions "are both a kind of testimony and a way of recording a history of injustice."

Most clemency petitions address legal faults rather than directly requesting mercy. Thus, while executive clemency is less restricted by legal rules, appellants frame their stories mainly in legal terms. Clemency petitions, he argues, fall into five categories, or "genres": Insistence on Innocence; Ineffective Assistance of Counsel; Mitigating Circumstances; Religion, Family, and Contrition; and Systemic Bias in the Criminal Justice System. In all clemency petitions, Sarat writes, "law (appears to be) two things at once: the social organization of violence through which state power is exercised in a partisan, biased, and sometimes cruel way, and the arena to which citizens address themselves in the hope that law can, and will, redress the wrongs which are committed in its name." Thus, he suggests, these petitions expose an extreme tension in law between violence and progress. Petitions serve to confront and memorialize this tension.

The two chapters in Part III, "Reconceputalizing Miscarriages of Justice," conclude the book by asking us to consider whether miscarriages of justice need to be retheorized, if we are to understand their broadest significance in both law and society. In chapter 9, Markus Dubber argues that we can analyze the penal process from two perspectives, which he labels the police and the law: "From the standpoint of police, the penal process is a system for the identification and elimination, or at least reduction, of human risks to the state's police, understood in the traditional sense of good order or welfare. . . . By contrast, if one regards the penal process from the perspective of law, it appears as a 'criminal justice system' designed to do justice, meting out punishment to offenders for injuries inflicted on victims." Most scholarship on miscarriages of justice, including most the authors in this book, adopt the law model.

Dubber believes the penal process, in actuality, is a police institution. As he observes, "[t]he problem with miscarriages of justice is not that they are miscarriages or that they are miscarriages of justice. They are not miscarriages because the system does not seek to do justice in the first place. At best, they are miscarriages of police, false positives in a system of risk incapacitation." What follows, then, is Dubber's examination of whether these "miscarriages of police" should be normatively titled injustices or merely administrative problems: "Just how out of place talk of miscarriages of justice is will depend on just how irrelevant considerations of justice are in the operation—as opposed to the ideological apparatus—of the penal process."

When states enact criminal laws, they are exercising the police power, a power that facilitates their independence as sovereign governments. Police power is thus inherent in the very concept of government. This power is not only essential but also essentially unlimited, since "[i]t encompasses any measure that might be appropriate to advance the goal of good police, where the assessment of appropriateness is a matter for the discretion of the entity wielding the power." Legislators and courts have historically shied away from restricting police power, preferring to allow the penal system free reign.

Dubber provides a few examples of the police power in action. (1) Jurisdiction is based on the police notion that the main victim of crime is the sovereign state. Crime in a certain area gives the ruler of that area the power to demand retribution. (2) The concept of double jeopardy is also based on the notion of the state as the paradigmatic victim of crime: "The violation of a state-issued norm amounts to an act of disobedience, literally an offense against the sovereign (so that the prohibition of placing someone twice in jeopardy for "the same offense" does not apply)." (3) This sovereign as victim concept also legitimizes police penalty because under this conception there are no victimless crimes, "not because every offense can be connected to the possibility of someone suffering some harm sometime in the future but because every offense is a victimful crime for the simple reason that the notion of a victimless crime is an oxymoron in a system of penality that regards every crime as an offense against the state insofar as it violates a state command."

Any attempt to "legalize" state punishment by regulating it through law is at best only an effort to create a more efficient government. Regulations of policing are purposely kept vague so that the police may wield all the power they need to eliminate criminal threats. Any errors in the system are merely errors rather than miscarriages of justice, since the system is actually not concerned with justice: "An error of penal classification is harmful only insofar as it is so egregious as to undermine the state's effort to assert its authority because the only relevant harm is harm to the state, the paradigmatic victim of the penal police process." In an effort to maximize efficiency, it might be *prudent* to minimize errors, but not *necessary*. He concludes that "[w]ithout a fundamental reorientation of the penal process, pointing out miscarriages of justice nibbles at the irrelevant margins of an unjust police regime."

In chapter 10, Patricia Ewick suggests that the phrase "miscarriage of justice" denotes "spectacular, singular, and exceptional failings" of the law. Drawing us back to Dudziak and Ogletree's opening chapters, Ewick says that "[w]hen we speak of a 'miscarriage of justice' we imagine lives are shattered and destroyed, freedoms lost, and cherished ideals undermined." But Ewick suggests we need to pay attention to smaller injustices, which, she suggests, occur often indirectly and cumulatively. Because of their size and mundane character, these events are difficult to label "unjust" and are therefore often ignored.

"Justice" has been studied thoroughly by moral philosophers but, according to Ewick, "injustice" has been largely ignored because it has only been considered as the breakdown of justice, or merely "not justice." And "[w]hile moral philosophers have failed to adequately examine the meaning of injustice, socio-legal scholars have been curiously silent in regard to the meaning of justice." Their silence is most often attributed to the fact that justice is a moral, normative entity that falls outside the "value-free realm of so-called objective science." Instead, socio-legal scholars study the notion of power as a stand-in for justice simply because power is more compatible with methods of socio-legal study since power leaves a physical trail that can be studied empirically. To these scholars, injustice is merely the inevitable consequence of law as power, rather than being the abnormality it is considered to be by moral philosophers. In either case, Ewick writes, injustice has been an insufficiently studied concept.

To understand injustice more clearly, Ewick explores Shklar's distinction between injustice and misfortune. Misfortune is a result of fate, change, nature, or any other nonhuman agent. Injustice requires a specific human agent who causes "pain, indignity, or injury" and who thereby breaks a mutually acknowledged obligation between the two parties: "Injustice is, therefore, inherently a social phenomenon. Outside of a constellation of roles, and the relationships and responsibilities they define, injustice could not exist." Recognition of injustice both names and empowers the victim who can then make a claim on the responsible party. The victim of injustice can *demand* reparation while a victim of misfortune may only *request* it. Often, though, an injustice is not named or protested. Ewick ascribes this to the fact that "[s]ociological research has consistently shown that relatively powerless persons are able to express critical views of dominant values as they encounter them in their daily lives, but they are less able to translate that skepticism more generally and even less to convert it into a politics of protest."

Another difficulty in creating this "politics of protest" is that "many of the conditions of the late modern era make such counterhegemonic claims of injustice increasingly difficult to generate or sustain." In particular, since modern social, economic, and political power is now exercised on a global scale, individual injustices are often too small to be addressed. The relationship between a government and its people is more unstable as national boundaries become more permeable. Paradoxically, "[f]orms of postmodern power not only incapacitate ideological revisions by effacing the everyday through the diminishment of scale, they simultaneously operate by *enlarging* the scale of local action such that the everyday, the mundane, the personal and the immediate myopically conceal the context in which power operates. . . . '[M]oral individualism' has replaced the constraints and limitations previously exercised by family, community, and state and thereby the possibilities of injustice as defined by their roles and relationships." Thus the government is both distant and very close. As governmental power becomes globalized, individuals seek empowerment by privatizing their lives, which, in turn, keeps them from being able to enact large-scale social changes to address structural injustice.

Taken together, the essays collected in *When Law Fails* show both the drama and the daily reality of miscarriages of justice, of law's inability to deliver justice, and of its breakdowns and missteps. They call on us to notice the ways our responses to the injustice which law does, or which it condones, are conditioned by our deeply engrained cultural expectations. They call on us to see beyond the headlines, to see the embeddedness of law's failures in the very fabric of legality itself. They call on us to see in law's failures lives shattered but also systemtic problems left unaddressed. And, importantly, they remind us that the effort to make sense of miscarriages of justice must go hand in hand with the effort to end them.

NOTES

1. Judith N. Shklar, *The Faces of Injustice* (New Haven: Yale University Press, 1990), 19.

2. Death Penalty Information Center, *Innocence and the Death Penalty*, available at http://www.deathpenaltyinfo.org/article.php?did=412&scid=6 (accessed November 19, 2007).

3. S. 486, The Innocence Protection Act of 2001, available at http://frwebgate. access.gpo.gov/cgi-bin/getdoc.cgi?dbname=107_cong_bills&docid=f:s486is.txt.pdf (accessed November 19, 2007).

4. See, for example, "Tulsa Race Riot: A Report by the Oklahoma Commission to Study the Tulsa Race Riot of 1921," February 28, 2001, available at http://www.ok-history.mus.ok.us/trrc/freport.htm.

5. The Scottsboro Boys are a group of nine African American teenagers who were charged with allegedly raping two white girls on a train in Tennessee in 1931. See Clarence Norris and Sybil Washington, *The Last of the Scottsboro Boys* (New York: Putnam's, 1979); Dan T. Carter, *Scottsboro: A Tragedy of the American South* (Baton Rouge: Louisiana State University Press, 1979).

6. Emmett Till traveled from Chicago to visit relatives in Mississippi in 1955 and was lynched for allegedly whistling at a white woman. See Stephen J. Whitfield, *A Death in the Delta* (Baltimore: Free Press, 1988); Mamie Till Mobley, *The Death of Innocence* (New York: Random House, 2003); Clenora Hudson-Weems, *Emmett Till: The Sacrificial Lamb of the Civil Rights Movement* (Troy, MI: Bedford Books, 1994).

7. Rolando Cruz was wrongly convicted of the kidnapping, rape, and murder of a 9-year-old girl in Illinois. Cruz was pardoned in 2002 by Governor George Ryan.

8. Leonard Peltier was convicted of the murder of two FBI agents during a shoot-out in South Dakota in 1975. He is currently serving two consecutive life sentences.

9. Darryl Hunt was wrongly convicted of the 1984 murder of a newspaper reporter, Deborah Sykes. He was later exonerated by DNA evidence.

10. Gallup News Service, June 1, 2006. For more statistics about changing public opinion on the topic of the death penalty, see Death Penalty Information Center, *Innocence and the Death Penalty.*

11. Bruce Shapiro, "A Talk with Governor George Ryan," *Nation,* January 8, 2001.

12. Governor's Office, "Governor Ryan Declares a Moratorium on Executions, Will Appoint Commission to Review Capital Punishment System," press release, January 31, 2000. See also Executive Order Number 4 (2000) by Governor George Ryan creating the Commission on Capital Punishment, May 4, 2000, available at http://www.idoc.state.il.us/ccp/ccp/executive_order.html (accessed November 19, 2007).

13. Report of the Commission on Capital Punishment, April 15, 2002, available at http://www.idoc.state.il.us/ccp/ccp/reports/commission_report/index.html (accessed November 19, 2007).

14. George Ryan's Commutation Announcement, Northwestern University, January 11, 2003, available at http://www.law.northwestern.edu/depts/clinic/wrongful/RyanSpeech.htm (accessed November 19, 2007).

15. Barry James, "Clearing of Illinois Death Row Is Greeted by Cheers Overseas," *New York Times,* January 14, 2003.

16. *Herrera v. Collins,* 506 U.S. 290 (1993).

17. Ibid.
18. Ibid.
19. Ibid. at 430.
20. Ibid.
21. *Callins v. Collins*. 510 U.S. 1141 (1994).
22. Our book builds on the work of others, including the late Judith Shklar's previously mentioned book, *The Faces of Injustice*. Shklar examines not just human failure but cultural factors that influence the way injustices occur, are addressed, or ignored. Ultimately, she considers our ability to discern the difference between mere misfortune and true injustice. At the same time, an important forbearer to this work is Austin Sarat and Thomas R. Kearns (eds.), *Justice and Injustice in Law and Legal Theory* (Ann Arbor: University of Michigan Press, 1999). Most notably, in a far-reaching essay in that volume, Robert W. Gordon considers tools for undoing injustice that have been used historically, including their ability to address the structural, deeply entrenched, often invisible mechanisms through which injustice occurs in society. Gordon's analysis guides our current work, warning us not to look narrowly at the agency of injustices perpetrated by individuals on specific victims but to perceive these injustices as emerging from a tangled mix of structural, cultural, and historical forces that are often difficult to tease apart. See Robert W. Gordon, "Undoing Historical Injustice," in Austin Sarat and Thomas R. Kearns (eds.), *Justice and Injustice in Law and Legal Theory* (Ann Arbor: University of Michigan Press, 1999), 35–77.

Part I

||||||||||||||||||||||||||||||||||||||||||||||||||||||||

On the Meaning and Significance of Miscarriages of Justice

Chapter 1

The Case of "Death for a Dollar Ninety-Five"

Miscarriages of Justice and Constructions of American Identity

Mary L. Dudziak

One July night in Alabama in 1957, a story began that would capture, for a moment, the attention of the world. That it involved a man, a woman, and a small amount of money, all could agree. The man was black, the woman was white, the criminal charge was robbery. The penalty was death. About the remaining details, there were different stories, but one thing was clear: at stake in the case was not just the life of Jimmy Wilson but the meaning of America.

This is a story about a case long forgotten. It was, as it turns out, the point of the case for Jimmy Wilson to be forgotten, so that America might emerge unsullied.

Jimmy Wilson is not the first disappearance to be noted in American legal history, of course. Others have written about the ways that human beings disappear in law. Cases come to stand for principles and legal concepts, but the human whose life story gave rise to a legal dispute fades from the page. The detachment of legal idea from life story has often been described as an absence that affects our understanding of the true meaning of law and justice. John T. Noonan, Jr., has suggested that "neglect of persons . . . led to the worst sins for which American lawyers were accountable."[1] The absence of the person has also been described as imposing a false or incomplete narrative. Kendall Thomas has written that the absence of the person in legal history leaves an "ordered image that the historical narrative of constitutional progress imposes on an unruly past." Angelo Herndon, an unjustly imprisoned African American labor organizer, was not forgotten by legal history, but Thomas describes the "dissection" and "dismemberment" of this human being's encounters with the law, with episodes fitting into different doctrinal categories, obscuring the whole.[2]

But the erasure of the person from the law is more than a hole, an absence, an incompleteness. It also aids in the forward-looking construction of ideas about the nature of American justice.[3] When legal principle is detached from human person, American justice is measured through the march of principle. Ambiguities and injustice in the individual case do not get in the way of the story. The nation can be identified with certain legal ideas, with the idea of a rule of law itself. The messiness of life stories does not disrupt this construction of national self-identity.

The Jimmy Wilson case illustrates this. The case captured attention at home and abroad, feeding a global debate about the nature of American democracy. This helps us to see the way narratives of justice and the rule of law aid conceptions of American identity.[4] It is not simply the law but the nation that is constructed when we form legal narratives. When the image of American justice is fractured, resolutions of miscarriages of justice often serve to repair a breach in American identity, making America whole again. What happens to the person at the center of the story is, at best, secondary. In fact, for America to be whole, Jimmy Wilson needed to disappear. In this way, forgetting Jimmy Wilson did not simply leave a void in our understanding, as Noonan might suggest but, instead, aided the formation of a particular national narrative. In this case, for the story to turn out right, the nation is restored, and the person is forgotten.

Death for a Dollar Ninety-Five

The case of "Death for a Dollar Ninety-Five" began in Marion, about 80 miles northwest from Montgomery, Alabama, the state capital. Montgomery "remained one of the most rigidly segregated cities of the South," in the 1950s, historian Patricia Sullivan has written. The urban South had been energized by World War II, and the city's population had increased by nearly 50 percent during the 1940s. Though many new migrants were white, Montgomery remained 37 percent African American in 1951, but "only 3.7 percent of eligible black voters were registered."[5] Alabama was also home to the city of Tuskegee, the site of the legendary Tuskegee Institute and the location of a notorious 1960 voting rights case, when the city redrew its boundaries to exclude nearly all African Americans from the city limits to ensure that they could not vote in city elections.[6] Events in Birmingham and elsewhere in the state would move the conscience of the nation and the world in the 1960s.[7] But in 1950s Alabama, Jim Crow's hold remained firm: nearly all elected officials, judges, police officers, and jurors were white.[8]

Alabama was in the news in the 1950s, ground zero in what was still a fledgling civil rights movement. Martin Luther King, Jr., was a new, 26-year-old pastor at the Dexter Avenue Baptist Church when the Montgomery bus boycott catapulted him to civil rights leadership in 1956. The year-long struggle by the African American community against segregation in Montgomery captured the attention of the nation and the world.[9] But the full impact of this effort, and the course of the movement, could not be known in 1957 when Jimmy Wilson found himself in a jail cell. That the nation was on the cusp of change held out promise for an African American defendant in Alabama, but also trouble.

"I Speak for the White Race," was the headline in a weekly column in the leading local newspaper by a local judge in March 1957. Judge Walter B. Jones cut to the heart of the issue, as he saw it:

> I speak for the White Race, my race, because today it is being unjustly assailed all over the world. It is being subjected to assaults here by radical newspapers and magazines, Communists and the Federal Judiciary. Columnists and photographers have been sent to the South to take back to the people of the North untrue and slanted tales about the South. . . . Their real and final goal is the intermarriage and mongrelization of the American People.
>
> His race would "never submit," Jones insisted. "The white race shall forever remain white."[10]

Linking equality with miscegenation had been a central theme for some time. Virginia Durr wrote that, for the White Citizens Councils that had "flowered all over the Black Belt" after *Brown v. Board of Education,* "their slogan is that 'the end of segregation will mean unlocking the bedroom doors of our white women to Negro men.'"[11] Other Southern leaders would famously stand at the schoolhouse door, drawing a line there for white supremacy.[12] Alabama state judges drew the line where they could, in the cases in their courtrooms.

It was in this context that Jimmy Wilson walked into Estelle Baker's bedroom one night. The *Montgomery Advertiser* reported the story on August 2: "A 53-year-old Negro is charged with burglary, robbery and robbery with intent to ravish of an elderly widow last Saturday night." The widow, Mrs. E. B. Baker, "said the robber ordered her to give him money, and was given a few dollars from her purse. He was not satisfied with the amount, she said, and choked and threatened her until he was frightened away by a noise from a nearby home."[13]

This was not, however, an encounter between strangers. Baker testified at trial that Jimmy Wilson had worked for her in her yard. On the evening of July 27, he arrived at her home, "and said he had come to do some work. She replied that it was too late."[14] Wilson asked for some water, and Baker told him to go outside, to the back of the house, and get water there, as he had before. Wilson went outside and then entered the house again through the back door: "She asked him what he wanted and he said he wanted her money. She said she had none and he said, 'Yes, you have too.' She went to her wardrobe and got her purse and he told her to 'pour it out on the bed.'" Baker said that she poured about $3.95 onto the bed, and that he took most of it. Then, she said, "He threw me on the bed, pulled off my stepins, and attempted to rape me, that is what he did."[15] Baker testified that Wilson threatened to kill her if she moved. Then, "a light flashed outside. . . . He jumped up and told her he would kill her if she opened her mouth and then ran out the door." Two days later, Baker picked Wilson out of a five-man lineup at the Perry County Jailhouse. At trial, however, when asked if she saw him in the courtroom, "she said that she did not know and she then stated that she did not want to see him."[16]

Wilson's court-appointed lawyer was State Representative Judson C. Locke. He moved unsuccessfully for a mistrial when Baker testified about the alleged assault, arguing that it "infuriates the mind of the jury." But he did not crossexamine Baker or any other witness. He did not call Wilson to testify in his own defense and did not call any other defense witnesses. "Wilson was actually being tried for touching a white woman," a University of Alabama law professor later told a reporter. "His lawyer still could have attempted a defence. It doesn't sound as if he did anything but appear in court."[17] The entire trial took four and one-half hours. The all-white jury took less than an hour to convict Wilson of the only crime he was charged with at trial: robbery.[18]

Only three people had ever been sentenced to death before in Alabama for robbery, all African American men. Wilson became the fourth. The Alabama Supreme Court heard his appeal. Wilson's lawyer argued that it was impermissible to admit evidence of the alleged attempt to "ravish" Baker since it happened after the offense of robbery had been committed. The court upheld the conviction, finding the evidence part of the context of the crime and finding that the trial as a whole did not result in unfairness.[19]

Even seeing the events of that night from the perspective of Baker's testimony, how could a jury sentence Wilson to death? Virginia Durr thought of it this way, writing to a friend as her husband, Clifford Durr, assisted Fred Gray in Jimmy Wilson's defense:

> This is the FOURTH death sentence this summer. One was electrocuted, he was a fifteen-year-old boy accused of rape. The second was commuted, he was a seventeen-year-old boy accused of rape. In neither instance were the women harmed in any way and both stories were terribly phony. The third was commuted, that was simply murder so no wild emotion over that, and murder of a policeman, and now the Wilson case which is on the face of it a robbery case but in reality is a rape case or attempted rape. I sometimes feel we southern white women are some kind of obscene goddesses that they make these burnt offerings to. "Burn the Nigger, burn the Nigger" is what you hear when one of them comes up and there is something so awful and horrible about it, especially when no white man ever gets the death penalty for rape in any case and of course when it occurs with a Negro woman they never even believe it is rape. A little thirteen-year-old Negro girl who was babysitting got raped by the man of the house when he took her home and the proof was positive and she was terribly torn and harmed and yet nothing was ever done to the white man.[20]

Others have chronicled the role of ideas of black male sexuality and white female purity in conceptions of white Southern culture and in the policing of race and gender.[21] A death sentence, carried out by the state within the walls of a prison was, in some ways, a civilizing gesture, removing the power to directly police the lines of race and sex from the community. That lynching remained the preference of many was underscored by the report that Wilson was held in prison in another county "for safekeeping."[22]

In this context, it was, of course, a breach for Jimmy Wilson to be in Estelle Baker's bedroom or simply to be inside with her, alone, after dark. Whether or not they touched, whether or not the "stepins" came down, Wilson had crossed a line running straight to many unmarked graves in Alabama.[23] That his path toward death was through a courtroom, with the aid of a lawyer and appellate review, was simply a sign that the New South was modernized and civilized.

Jimmy Wilson would tell his own story of the case to a Toronto reporter. Marty Goodman described Wilson this way: "His cheeks sunken,
his eyes haggard, he perspired during our hour-long interview, though
the warden's office was air-conditioned." He was five foot seven and 135
pounds. "He crossed and uncrossed his arms, patted his shoulders and
scratched his short, gray fuzzy hair while puzzling two syllable words. He
is fully aware he must die for the crime he committed although, he says,
he realized this only recently." According to Goodman, he said "over and
over again . . . 'They never asked me anything,' . . . 'The policeman that
arrested me . . . he didn't ask. He says 'that's how it happened, wasn't it?' I
say 'no.' He cuffed me until I say 'yea . . . that's how.'"[24]

Wilson admitted to drinking the night of the alleged crime: "That was
bad . . . an old man like me." He ran out of money and thought of Baker,
who had advanced him money before against future wages. "So I went
back. She refused. I thought about it all day and went back again. She
must have been scared because she gave me some—about $1.50. . . . I'm
not sure because I paid it all to the taxi when I left." When Wilson arrived
at the house the second time, Baker "told me to come in. I went in. I ain't
lying . . . before God I ain't." Wilson admitted that he and Baker argued.
Then "[s]he reached inside her purse and threw the change on the bed. I
asked for more but she said she didn't have no more. I never touched her.
I never broke in. I know I shouldn't have been drinking . . . but I'm telling
the truth. I don't want to die."[25]

The Alabama Supreme Court ruled against Wilson following an automatic appeal. Newspapers then reported: "Court upholds death penalty
in $1.95 theft," and the case became known as the case about death for
$1.95.[26] After reading of the story in a New York paper, Louis Kousin, a
Cranford, New Jersey, social worker, sent a check for $1.95 to Alabama
Governor James Folsom. He wanted to "dramatize what he called the 'un-
believable fact' that Wilson was scheduled to die for stealing $1.95."[27]

By early September, while a motion for rehearing was pending in the
Alabama Supreme Court, Wilson had a new lawyer and a new chance.
Fred Gray was just four years into his law practice in Montgomery, but
he had already become a fixture in the civil rights movement, representing Rosa Parks and Claudette Colvin before her, in their challenges to bus
segregation that led to the Montgomery Bus Boycott.[28] Wilson's first lawyer, a white man, had said that "no effort would be made as far as he
knew to appeal to the federal courts." In contrast, although Gray declined
to discuss his plans, he "told a newsman asking about a possible habeas

corpus petition in [state] court that it could also be filed in federal court." This simple answer was enough for a local news story: "Fred Gray May Take Wilson Case into Federal Court."[29] The best course for his client, however, was not clear.

In a letter, Virginia Durr wrote that the "big question" for the lawyers in the Wilson case was "what to do, try and get clemency of which there is a very good chance or to go to the courts with a weak case under Alabama law and there seems no federal question of any significance and take a chance on [John] Patterson coming in and not giving him clemency."[30] Governor Folsom had said that he would always grant clemency in death penalty cases "if I can find some excuse."[31] Patterson would take office in January 1959, and Gray said, "Patterson was a racist," and "I'd already had trouble with him."[32] The question of strategy, Durr thought, "will have to be settled by Wilson himself, whether he wants to take a chance on his life or accept what looks like a good chance for clemency, and life imprisonment! The poor fellow is perfectly ignorant," she thought, "and seems almost in a daze and it is hard to know if he knows what he is saying or if he just says what he thinks the 'white folks' want to hear."[33]

Publicity did not always help in a death penalty case. Public outcry over fifteen-year-old Jeremiah Reeves's death sentence had seemed to put pressure on Governor Folsom, who then did not grant clemency.[34] So the lawyers did not seek to publicize Wilson's case.[35] Nevertheless, publicity was just what Jimmy Wilson received.

The World Takes an Interest in Jimmy Wilson

On June 27, 1958, a small article appeared on the front page of the *Listener Daily* in Monrovia, Liberia. "American Negro May Die for $1.95," was the headline. The story reported that Wilson "will go to the electric chair" unless the governor intervened. The *Listener Daily* article was nearly identical to a story in the European edition of the *New York Herald Tribune,* which had circulated in Monrovia a few days before. A dispatch from the American Embassy in Monrovia to the U.S. Department of State reported on this development. "It hardly seems necessary to point out," wrote Richard L. Jones at the embassy, "that one small news item of the above type does considerable damage to the United States in this area of Africa. Although this sort of thing is by no means a new problem, nevertheless it is unfortunate when it occurs."[36]

By 1958, race in America had become a regular story in newspapers around the world. The United States was the leader of the free world during the Cold War, and differences between the nation and its Soviet adversary were regularly described as the difference between a regime of rights and a regime of oppression. If America was the land of the free, governed by a rule of law, treating all with dignity, then how, foreign commentators often wondered, did American values square with racial segregation and discrimination? Race was widely thought to be the nation's Achilles' heel, and it was a vulnerability easily exploited by the Soviet Union, which used this issue relentlessly in anti-American propaganda. In this environment, American diplomats were sensitive to the way any episode of racism could further erode the image of the nation in the world.[37]

But the world took an interest in the Jimmy Wilson case. The Monrovia *Listener Daily* article was just the beginning. The U.S. Consulate General in Toronto reported to the State Department on August 25 that two front-page stories about the Jimmy Wilson case had appeared in the Toronto *Star*. The *Telegram* had carried a "screaming headline" on the story and reported Canadian efforts to intervene in the case: "Prime Minister Diefenbaker had been asked by a member of the Canadian Parliament to try to prevent the execution," but "the question was ruled out of order and never answered." A Toronto woman acquainted with Kwameh Nkrumah "pleaded by overseas phone with Ghana's prime minister to intercede with President Eisenhower to prevent the execution and urged him to lead a world protest against it." In an editorial, the *Telegram* argued that the punishment should fit the crime and pointed out that "people of the South should remember that these cases are reported around the world and give excellent propaganda material to those wishing to criticize the United States for tolerating barbaric, obsolete laws."[38] Numerous news stories were followed by extensive radio and television coverage of the Wilson story in Canada.[39]

Although Ghana's Prime Minister Nkrumah declined to become personally involved, by August 30, the U.S. Embassy in Accra reported that Wilson's death sentence was "being strongly denounced by every newspaper in Ghana," with each emphasizing that "the severity of the sentence can be accounted for only because Wilson is a negro." Archie Lang, the second secretary of the U.S. Embassy, thought that "it seems likely that the goodwill which exists here towards the US will be seriously compromised if the execution is carried out. Even if the sentence is commuted, it will probably still leave a mark."[40] Soon diplomatic posts around the world cabled the State Department for assistance. A telegram from Dublin asked for "facts and instructions how to handle inquiries regarding Wilson Alabama case,"[41] and the U.S. Embassy in Montevideo asked for the same.[42] More than 400 high school students in Switzerland sent a letter to the U.S. ambassador to that nation, expressing "friendship for the United States, but shock at this particular case."[43] Student groups in Tunis and Copenhagen also protested, as did the rector of a university in Uruguay.[44]

In sentencing Wilson to death, the State of Alabama poured salt onto a wound that American diplomats had worked hard to heal. American race relations had long been viewed as central to American identity. Gunnar Myrdal famously called the "Negro problem" an "American Dilemma" in 1944.[45] Around the world, as well as at home, many believed that the way the nation treated the race it had formerly enslaved was a reflection of the true nature of American democracy. During World War II, a broader civil rights consciousness within the United States developed, as many viewed American racism in a new light in the context of the war with Germany. This was a war against Nazi racism. It seemed hypocritical for the United States to wage a war that was in part an ideological battle against Germany when in the United States itself racial intolerance of a different kind continued to reign.[46]

This issue took on particularly urgent global implications after World War II. The Cold War was seen by American leaders as a struggle of apocalyptic proportions. The United States and the Soviet Union were seen as representing different ways of life. President Truman warned the nation in 1947:

> At the present moment in world history nearly every nation must choose between alternative ways of life. . . . One way of life is based upon the will of the majority, and is distinguished by free institutions, representative government, free elections, guarantees of individual liberty, freedom of speech and religion, and freedom from political oppression. The second way of life is based upon the will of a minority forcibly imposed upon the majority. It relies upon terror and oppression, a controlled press and radio; fixed elections, and the suppression of personal freedoms.[47]

American world leadership was needed to maintain the freedom of Americans, and of other peoples of the world. The two were linked: "If we falter in our leadership, we may endanger the peace of the world—and we shall surely endanger the welfare of our own nation."[48] To meet this challenge,

American leaders turned not only to buildup in strategic arms but also to the battle of ideas. In this battle, the U.S. could simply put its superior form of government on display. As a crucial 1950 National Security Council report suggested, "the potential within us of bearing witness to the values by which we live holds promise for a dynamic manifestation to the rest of the world of the vitality of our system."[49]

But superior values were not always on display in the United States. And as the United States positioned itself as the leader of the "free world" in the early years of the Cold War, the nation found itself under increasing global scrutiny. Racial incidents were no longer local news. When African American soldiers returned home from World War II, Southern communities reminded them, violently, of their place. Beatings, maimings, and killings of veterans were news throughout the nation and the world. Many foreign readers wondered what the nature of American democracy was if such things could happen in America. News of battles of school segregation and voting rights reinforced the international concern about race in America.[50]

The strategic consequences of this issue heightened when the Soviet Union featured race in America as a principle anti-American propaganda theme by the late 1940s. Soviet propaganda was often overblown, of course, but was also easy to write. Sometimes the most inflammatory news was simply a reprint of an article from a U.S. news source about something that had really happened, such as the time Macio Snipes of Georgia was shot to death by four whites after being the only African American in his district to vote. U.S. allies worried about the impact of civil rights problems on the image of American democracy around the world. While Soviet propaganda was often dismissed, many found propaganda on race and America to be uniquely effective because there was so much truth to the stories. For this reason, the U.S. ambassador to India in the Truman administration, Chester Bowles, among others, hammered away at the importance of the issue, arguing that the United States had a limited amount of time in which to address its civil rights problems in order to maintain the nation's global standing. Secretary of State Dean Acheson went as far as to provide material to the Justice Department to include in its brief in *Brown v. Board of Education*, to emphasize to the Supreme Court that a ruling against segregation was essential to protect the nation's global prestige and Cold War allegiances.[51]

The State Department and the Voice of America tried hard to protect the image of America in the face of continued negative press, hoping to turn the story of race in America into a story of enduring racial progress. The *Brown* ruling was a success for American diplomats. The 1957 crisis in Little Rock was a great challenge, but with the secretary of state's involvement, by sending in federal troops to integrate Central High School, President Eisenhower turned a devastating drama of American racial intolerance into a story for the world that the force of American government was behind equality.[52]

And then came Jimmy Wilson. For Secretary of State John Foster Dulles, the Wilson case was certainly unwelcome, though not entirely a surprise. There were the big cases like Little Rock, of course, but there were also periodic eruptions, like small flare-ups in a forest fire. They would emerge, demand attention, and then, if addressed, hopefully recede from view. When the Wilson case first captured the world's attention, the State Department began to track its global impact, at times pestering U.S. embassies around the world for information.[53]

The U.S. embassy in London received over 1,000 protests about Wilson, "a much greater volume of mail than the Embassy has had on any other specific incident in America over the past two years," which would have included the widely covered Little Rock crisis. This was in part, the embassy counselor for public affairs thought, "because the case of one individual has a greater dramatic appeal than broad or abstract issues; and partly because the present case involves what appear to the British as the various evils of color prejudice, capital punishment, and lack of a just trial."[54]

When the Alabama Supreme Court denied Wilson's petition for rehearing, the news was carried in Dutch papers, prompting two telephone calls to the U.S. Embassy at The Hague that threatened the life of the U.S. ambassador, claiming that the ambassador "would not survive day after Wilson execution."[55] In Jamaica, the *Pittsburgh Courier* reported, "hundreds of shouting men and women, carrying anti-American slogans, marched to the consulate in protest." They chanted: "If Jimmy Wilson goes to the electric chair, no American white man nor woman can remain in Jamaica." This protest followed a meeting that had been attended by "thousands of Negroes."[56]

Secretary of State Dulles wrote to Governor Folsom to inform him of the international reaction. In mid-September, according to Dulles's aide, "approximately 600 letters a day are being received protesting the sentence at the London Embassy and . . . about 400 daily are being received in Ireland." Other protests went directly to the White House.[57]

Much of this worldwide attention bore down directly on the governor of Alabama. Folsom "received an average of 1000 letters a day from all over the world, some of them containing one dollar 95 cents."[58] The case prompted the secretary of the British Labour Party to send a letter to the governor urging clemency, which was widely covered in the British press.[59] The Presbyterian Church of Jamaica sent a telegram urging that clemency would "forstall an act that would . . . bring an eternal blot on a great and generous nation."[60] A telegram from the International Commission on Jurists at The Hague drew attention to "'world legal concern regarding the Wilson case' and urgently requested clemency 'in the interests of the prisoner as well as the high legal reputation of the United States in and outside of the free world.'"[61] From *Telemark Arbeiderblad,* an influential, normally pro-U.S. newspaper in Oslo, Norway, 700 protest petitions from readers poured in.[62]

In reaction, Folsom told the press: "I admit that we have got the worst penal system in the world, including Dark Africa. . . . I hope the next Legislature will do something about improving the situation."[63] On September 13, he held a press conference "to announce he was 'snowed under' with mail from Toronto demanding clemency." Over 3,000 letters had arrived that day alone. "I've been Governor for two terms and I've never seen anything like it," he said. "I am utterly amazed." Folsom "hinted broadly," the *New York Times* reported, "that he would commute the death sentence to life imprisonment whenever a clemency hearing is requested."[64]

Even the *Birmingham Post-Herald* came down in favor of clemency. In an editorial, the paper emphasized that "the decision is for Governor Folsom to make," but clemency "would serve not only justice but the best interest of Alabama as well. . . . So much world-wide interest has been centered in this case and misunderstanding of it is so widespread the sentence of death, if carried out, could never be satisfactorily explained much less justified before world opinion." It was "abhorrent" that in a Mideastern country, a person convicted of petty theft could be "dragged into the public square and there have his right hand severed at the wrist. . . . How much more difficult it must be for the people of many countries to understand a penalty of death in a theft involving $1.95."[65]

With Wilson's execution date set for October 24, Fred Gray was now "'exploring every possibility' to save [his] life."[66] When he asked for a clemency hearing in front of Governor Folsom, the governor quickly granted it, saying: "I want to put an end to this international hullabaloo."[67]

At the hearing, Solicitor Blancard McCleod, for the State of Alabama, strongly objected to clemency. He argued that Wilson had made "complete and deliberate plans to rob and rape an 82-year-old woman." This was, he shouted, "the most vicious, heinous and contemptible crime man is capable of."[68] The *Post-Herald* reported that Gray argued that Wilson was "a victim of a 'prejudiced jury' and that he would never have been given the death penalty if he had been a white man." Gray also urged that clemency be granted "to protect the prestige of Alabama and the United States abroad." The governor listened silently, asked Wilson a few questions about his background, and then said, "hearing dismissed." The proceeding lasted half an hour.[69]

Jimmy Wilson would not die in the electric chair. Folsom announced his decision on September 29. He was now finished with a case that had plagued him. "I have given him clemency," he said. "It will be up to the Pardon-Parole Board to see how long he has to serve."[70] Folsom sent a message to Secretary Dulles advising him that he had commuted Wilson's sentence to life imprisonment. "Knowing of your interest in the matter I thought you would like to have a formal notice of the decision," he wrote.[71] The international media reaction to this decision was euphoric. In Nigeria, Jeremy Blunt, in his *Daily Telegraph* column, called Folsom "God's own Gentleman, No 1 Citizen of the State of Alabama!! What a name! What a divine use of one's position!! What a heart!!! What humanity!!!!" There remained more work to be done in Alabama, Blunt thought: to remove the statute under which Wilson had been sentenced from Alabama law.[72] *Telemark Arbeiderblad* in Oslo celebrated its own role, noting that over 1,200 readers had sent in appeals. "No one knows the role of our readers in this event," the paper said of the commutation decision, "[b]ut ten thousands of other people, most of them probably Americans reacting as we did, did the same, so perhaps we were a little whirl in a large stream?" The paper's editor wrote to the embassy that the turn of events and the U.S. Embassy's handling of the protest ultimately "strengthened my reader's confidence in the U.S.A."[73]

In England, the reaction was tempered. Twelve hundred British Labour Party delegates cheered when they received a cable with the news that Wilson's sentence was commuted, but then jeered when they learned that he would serve a life sentence.[74] Fred Gray agreed with this sentiment. "I still feel that life imprisonment is extreme and harsh punishment for what Jimmy Wilson did," he said.[75] Gray considered filing a petition for habeas corpus in federal court, but this course was never pursued. A new trial would have posed risks. Gray lost touch with Wilson not long after. "We lawyers, people call us when they need us," he later said. "They usually don't."[76]

Under Secretary of State Christian Herter sent out a helpful form letter for embassies to use in replying to Wilson-related correspondence. It said that Folsom had commuted Wilson's sentence and that "[t]he Pardon and Parole Board of the State of Alabama has the authority to determine when Jimmy Wilson may be released from prison."[77] Meanwhile, dispatches from U.S. embassies around the world on the case quickly dropped off. As if overnight, Jimmy Wilson was forgotten.

A blot on the American image had been removed. But Jimmy Wilson was still in prison, serving a life sentence for stealing a handful of change.

The image of America would endure other rough patches during the Cold War and the civil rights movement, until civil rights acts passed by congress in the 1960s and other evidence of civil rights progress helped to convince the world that the U.S. government was behind civil rights reform, not racial inequality.[78] What of Jimmy Wilson? According to the Alabama Department of Corrections, Jimmy Wilson was paroled on October 1, 1973.[79] He would have been 70 years old and had served 16 years in prison. From that point, the historical record is silent.

In the Wilson case, when the crisis was passed, it seemed important in the celebrating that the person at the center of the story be forgotten. A wrong had been righted, but Wilson's punishment remained obviously excessive. This should cause us to ask just what the miscarriage was that was set aright, what the harm was that had so surely been undone. If justice had arrived, but not quite for Jimmy Wilson, then just who, or what, was justice serving?

Forgetting the "Scottsboro Boys"

Wilson's fate was not unlike that of many other subjects of miscarriages of justice. The "Scottsboro boys" were, perhaps, the most notorious examples. Scottsboro involved nine African American teenagers falsely accused of gang rape of two white women on a freight train in Alabama in 1931. After perfunctory trials with minimal representation before all-white juries, eight defendants were quickly convicted and sentenced to death.[80] In various appeals, their cases led to landmark rulings in the U.S. Supreme Court.[81] But victories on appeal would lead to new trials and new injustices. Through it all, the Scottsboro defendants remained in jail. While charges against some of the young men were eventually dropped years later, others were convicted on subsequent retrials and served long prison terms before being paroled. Andy Wright, the last, was not released until 1950. Arrested when he was 19, Wright was then 38 or 39.[82]

The lives of the "Scottsboro boys" were shattered, but their cases were landmarks in American justice. The first Supreme Court case, *Powell v. Alabama*, established the right to adequate counsel in capital cases. Justice Sutherland wrote for the Court in a widely quoted passage:

> The right to be heard would be, in many cases, of little avail if it did not comprehend the right to be heard by counsel. Even the intelligent and educated layman has small and sometimes no skill in the science of law. If charged with crime, he is incapable, generally, of determining for himself whether the indictment is good or bad. He is unfamiliar with the rules of evidence. Left without the aid of counsel he may be put on trial without a proper charge, and convicted upon incompetent evidence, or evidence irrelevant to the issue or otherwise inadmissible. He lacks both the skill and knowledge adequately to prepare his defense, even though he had a perfect one. He requires the guiding hand of counsel at every step in the proceedings against him. Without it, though he be not guilty, he faces the danger of conviction because he does not know how to establish his innocence. If that be true of men of intelligence, how much more true is it of the ignorant and illiterate, or those of feeble intellect. If in any case, civil or criminal, a state or federal court were arbitrarily to refuse to hear a party by counsel, employed by and appearing for him, it reasonably may not be doubted that such a refusal would be a denial of a hearing, and, therefore, of due process in the constitutional sense.[83]

In *Powell*, "the ignorance and illiteracy of the defendants, their youth, the circumstances of public hostility, the imprisonment and the close surveillance of the defendants by the military forces, the fact that their friends and families were all in other states and communication with them necessarily difficult, and above all that they stood in deadly peril of their lives —we think the failure of the trial court to give them reasonable time and opportunity to secure counsel was a clear denial of due process." In this case, "the necessity of counsel was so vital and imperative that the failure of the trial court to make an effective appointment of counsel was likewise a denial of due process."[84]

Powell v. Alabama was lauded at the time it was decided. "A Notable Decision: The Supreme Court Writes a Chapter on Man's Rights," was the headline of a *New York Times* op-ed on the case by Harvard law professor Felix Frankfurter. "Even lay comment upon the Scottsboro decision was alive to a significance that went beyond a respite from death for seven illiterate Negro boys," he wrote. "In truth, the Supreme Court last Monday wrote a notable chapter in the history of liberty." The significance of the case lay especially in the return of the Fourteenth Amendment's due process clause to its more appropriate purposes, Frankfurter argued. Due process rights had been used by the Court to protect property rights; "[n]ow . . . they return to their more immediate purpose of protecting black men from oppressive and unequal treatment by whites."[85]

Powell's holding has been remembered. It is widely cited in contemporary legal casebooks. While the contributions of the case to constitutional criminal procedure are noted, usually there is no discussion of the fate of the Scottsboro defendants after the ruling was announced.[86] For Frankfurter, the transcendence of the ruling lay, in part, in its failure to provide specific relief for the defendants themselves. "Thus the judgment of the court transcends the fate of the seven pitiful defendants concerned," he wrote. "It leaves that fate ultimately untouched. Upon the question of guilt or innocence it bears not even remotely."[87] The "Scottsboro boys" made their mark on American law largely by appearing in the Supreme Court and then, at some point, dropping out of notice.[88]

In Scottsboro, the image of American justice was remedied, but the defendants' lives remained shattered. Milestones in American law reinforced faith in American justice, in spite of the fact that the Scottsboro defendants themselves continued to live tortured lives. These cases paved the way for fairer treatment of others; but if American justice and constitutional rights rest on personal harms and remedies, it remains troubling that resolution benefits the future but not the present, the nation but not the person at the heart of a case.

Constructing America

When Governor Folsom commuted Jimmy Wilson's sentence, the case of "death for a dollar ninety-five" that had infuriated the world disappeared from the global radar screen. It no longer interrupted a narrative that mattered to an American self-concept and also, it was thought, to U.S. national security.

When someone is forgotten, we often think of this as an absence. The missing story results in a void. From this standpoint, forgetting people in the law results in misunderstandings and incomplete narratives. But the act of exclusion is also a creative act, an act of making a particular narrative.

In *Powell v. Alabama* and the Jimmy Wilson case, what is remembered is the rectification, the workings of the rule of law. What is left out is the failure of the law to put an end to wrongs inflicted within the legal system to the humans whose stories had been the occasion for the rule of law to demonstrate itself to the world. That demonstration depended on the erasure of the defendants' continuing stories.

What has been set right, what has been accomplished, in cases like this? We often think of American legal narratives in domestic terms.[89] But there is another narrative space for law's stories. Stories of *domestic* American law, stories of justice and injustice among Americans, have been part of a global narrative that defines the meaning of America in the world.[90] Erasing Jimmy Wilson helped protect a narrative about America that American leaders had self-consciously worked to construct.

During the Cold War years, the story of race in the United States did not stand alone. Instead, for foreign audiences and Voice of America copywriters, it was part of a broader narrative about U.S. national identity. In the story promoted by the U.S. government, American democracy was superior to Soviet communism—not because America had always been pure of heart but because American democracy was on a path of moral progress. The structure of government itself aided this onward movement toward realizing an American ethos, which was imagined to be a true, essential characteristic.[91] The nation's shameful past of slavery and discrimination served a useful purpose in this narrative. As U.S. information programming became more sophisticated in the 1950s, American diplomats learned not to deny the past but to embrace it. A troublesome past helped to illustrate the extent of progress.

In an important pre-*Brown* circular for foreign audiences on race in America, the message was that the nation had made so much progress in a mere 100 years from slavery to freedom that surely American democracy was a superior form of government to an authoritarian structure like the Soviet Union.[92] This narrative provided an explanatory framework for the state of American injustice in the 1950s. Inequality could be explained as a stage in the inevitable path of racial progress. But it was crucial to this narrative for "progress" to remain on display. Eruptions like the Wilson case threatened to disrupt the progress narrative. To preserve the narrative, and the image of America, a resolution was required that would keep Jimmy Wilson alive and get him out of the Ghana papers.

Clemency plays an interesting role in the making of an American Cold War image. Austin Sarat places clemency on the borders of law. By showing us an outside, a fissure, it helps us see what law is.[93] If "America" is thought of as defined by the "rule-of-law," then clemency, by drawing a border between American legal identity and what is on the outside, helps us see what America is.

Once Governor Folsom granted clemency, the harm that had been driving this case—the harm to the American image—was rectified. Wilson's sentence remained unjust, but there was no audience for his story. And for there to be closure, it mattered that his story seemed to come to an end. In the global arena, a chapter had been closed. America was all right again.

Restoring the image of America required two things: Jimmy Wilson could not be executed, and the governor's act must be seen as the end of the story. And so, it was the nation that was saved when the death sentence was commuted. What happened to Jimmy Wilson was simply beside the point.

NOTES

For comments on an earlier draft, thanks to Austin Sarat, Ron Garet, and participants in the colloquium Making Sense of Miscarriages of Justice, Harvard Law School, October 2006. For exemplary assistance with research, I am grateful to Janet Katz, senior reference librarian, Harvard Law Library, and Rebecca Haffajee, J.D., Harvard 2006. Special thanks to Fred Gray, Jimmy Wilson's lawyer, who is still practicing law in Tuskegee, Alabama.

1. John T. Noonan, Jr., *Persons and Masks of the Law: Cardozo, Holmes, Jefferson, and Wythe as Makers of the Masks* (New York: Farrar, Straus Giroux, 1976), vi.

2. Kendall Thomas, "*Rouge et Noire* Reread: A Popular Constitutional History of the Angelo Herndon Case," *Southern California Law Review* 65 (September 1992): 2602–3, 2704. See also Margaret E. Montoya, "*Mascaras, Trenzas y Grenas:* Un/Masking the Self While Un/Braiding Latina Stories and Legal Discourse," *Harvard Women's Law Journal* 17 (1994): 185; Toni M. Massaro, "Empathy, Legal Storytelling, and the Rule of Law: New Words, Old Wounds?" *Michigan Law Review* 87 (August 1989): 2099–2127. Thomas finds that discussions of the Angelo Herndon case (with Angelo Herndon himself left out) keep the case as "a stage in the historical unfolding in constitutional law of an inexorable logic of progress, . . . a vision of constitutional history with the history left out." Ibid., 2599. For a critique of the progress metaphor in legal history, see Mary L. Dudziak, "*Brown* and the Idea of Progress in American Legal History: A Comment on William Nelson," *St. Louis University Law Journal* 48 (Spring 2004): 851.

3. In this sense, law is a form of memory. As Marita Sturken has written, the construction of memory requires forgetting, as selected past events are formed into the narrative that we remember. Marita Sturken, *Tangled Memories: The Vietnam War, the AIDS Epidemic, and the Politics of Remembering* (Berkeley: University of California Press, 1997).

4. Mary L. Dudziak and Leti Volpp, introduction to Dudziak and Volpp, eds., *Legal Borderlands: Law and the Construction of American Borders* (Baltimore: Johns Hopkins University Press, 2006), 6.

5. Patricia Sullivan, ed., *Freedom Writer: Virginia Foster Durr, Letters from the Civil Rights Years* (Athens: Georgia University Press, 2006), 27.

6. *Gomillion v. Lightfoot*, 364 U.S. 339 (1960). See also Fred Gray, *Bus Ride to Justice* (Montgomery: NewSouth Books, 2002), 111–23.

7. Diane McWhorter, *Carry Me Home: Birmingham, Alabama—The Climactic Battle of the Civil Rights Revolution* (New York: Touchstone, 2001).

8. Gray, *Bus Ride to Justice*, 124–25, 142, 155.

9. Taylor Branch, *Parting the Waters: America in the King Years, 1954–63* (New York: Simon and Schuster, 1988), 16, 144–203.

10. Quoted in Gray, *Bus Ride to Justice*, 26.

11. Quoted in Sullivan, *Freedom Writer*, 78. See also Renee C. Romano, *Race Mixing: Black-White Marriage in Postwar America* (Cambridge, MA: Harvard University Press, 2003), 146–60.

12. Dan T. Carter, *The Politics of Rage: George Wallace, the Origins of the New Conservatism and the Transformation of American Politics*, 2nd ed. (Baton Rouge: Louisiana State University Press, 2000), 137.

13. "Marion Negro Man Held in Robbery of Widow, 70," *Montgomery Advertiser*, August 2, 1957, p. 6A. Papers would later report that Baker was 82.

14. *Wilson v. State*, 28 Ala. 86, 105 So. 2d 66, 67 (1958).

15. Ibid., at 68.

16. Ibid.

17. Marty Goodman, "Robs White Widow, Can't Read, Write, Aware He'll Die," *Toronto Daily Star*, August 20, 1958; Attachment to Consulate General, Toronto, to Department of State, August 25, 1958, Despatch no. 22, Records of the Department of State, RG 59, Central Decimal File, 811.411/8-2558, National Archives, College Park, Maryland (hereafter cited as National Archives).

18. "Negro Doomed for Robbery of Widow, 70," *Montgomery Advertiser*, October 23, 1957, p. 1.

19. *Wilson*, 105 So. 2d at 69–70. There is a long history of imposition of the death penalty for robbery and burglary dating from the colonial period in North America. By the early twentieth century, the death penalty was reserved for murder in Northern states but retained for other crimes in the South. Stuart Banner writes that, as of 1954, burglary remained a capital crime in four states: Alabama, Kentucky, North Carolina, and Virginia. Stuart Banner, *The Death Penalty: An American History* (Cambridge: Harvard University Press, 2002), 228–29.

By 2008, the death penalty was reserved for murder except in four states that authorized it for rape of a child and a fifth, Montana, that authorized it for repeat rape with serious injury. Louisiana is the only state in recent years to sentence a defendant to death for a crime other than murder. The United States Supreme Court struck down the Louisiana law allowing the death penalty for rape of a child in 2008, finding the death penalty unconstitutional when the crime did not result in death of the victim. *States Allowing the Death Penalty for the Sexual Assault of a Child,* Death Penalty Information Center, available at http://www.death penaltyinfo.org/article.php?did=2612#statesw; *State of Louisiana v Kennedy,* No. 95-KA-1981 (2007), available at http://www.lasc.org/opinions/2007/05KA1981.opn. pdf.

20. Quoted in Sullivan, *Freedom Writer,* 165.

21. Wilbur Cash, *The Mind of the South* (New York: Vintage, 1991); Lillian Smith, *Killers of the Dream* (New York: Norton, 1994), 116–20, 134–49; Glenda Gilmore, *Gender and Jim Crow: Women and the Politics of White Supremacy in North Carolina, 1896–1920* (Chapel Hill: University of North Carolina Press, 1996), 37, 68, 72–73, 82–84, 88.

22. "Perry Negro Accused of Rob-Assault," *Birmingham Post-Herald,* August 2, 1957, p. 1.

23. Stewart E. Tolnay and E. M. Beck, *A Festival of Violence: An Analysis of Southern Lynchings, 1882–1930* (Champaign: University of Illinois Press, 1995); W. Fitzhugh Brundage, ed., *Under Sentence of Death: Lynching in the South* (Chapel Hill: University of North Carolina Press, 1997).

24. Goodman, "Robs White Widow."

25. Ibid.

26. "Court Upholds Death Penalty in $1.95 Theft," *Birmingham News,* June 12, 1958, p. 1; "Execution Faces Alabama Negro, 55, in $1.95 Robbery," *Jacksonville Times Union,* August 17, 1958, p. 10.

27. "Theft Case Stirs Furor," *Montgomery Advertiser,* August 19, 1958, p. 1.

28. Gray, *Bus Ride to Justice,* 36–52.

29. "Fred Gray May Take Wilson Case into Federal Court," *Montgomery Advertiser,* September 10, 1958, p. 34.

30. Quoted in Sullivan, *Freedom Writer,* 167.

31. Quoted in "Wilson Reprieve Believed Certain," *New York Times,* August. 29, 1958, p. 12.

32. Fred Gray, telephone interview by Mary L. Dudziak, November 4, 2006.

33. Quoted in Sullivan, *Freedom Writer,* 167. While serving as Alabama Attorney General, Patterson brought suit against the NAACP to enjoin the organization from doing business in Alabama. His 1958 campaign for governor was openly supported by the Ku Klux Klan. When Patterson defeated the more moderate George Wallace, he promised to maintain segregation in the schools and threatened to shut the schools down if anyone attempted to integrate them. Ibid., 97–98, 167; Gray, *Bus Ride to Justice,* 174.

34. Sullivan, *Freedom Writer,* 166.

35. Gray, telephone interview.

36. Amembassy Monrovia to Department of State, July 1, 1958, Despatch no. 3, Records of the Department of State, RG 59, Central Decimal File, 811.411/7-158, National Archives.

37. Mary L. Dudziak, *Cold War Civil Rights: Race and the Image of American Democracy* (Princeton: Princeton University Press, 2000), 12–13, 18–46, 113–45.

38. Consulate General, Toronto, to Department of State, August 25, 1958, Despatch no. 22, Records of the Department of State, RG 59, Central Decimal File, 811.411/8-2558, National Archives.

39. Amembassy Ottawa to Secretary of State, August 28, 1958, Airgram no. G-69, Records of the Department of State, RG 59, Central Decimal File, 811.411/8-2858, National Archives.

40. Amembassy Accra to Department of State, August 30, 1958, Despatch no. 126, Records of the Department of State, RG 59, Central Decimal File, 811.411/8-3058, National Archives.

41. Dublin to Secretary of State, August 26, 1958, Telegram no. 42, Records of the Department of State, RG 59, Central Decimal File, 811.411/8-2558, National Archives.

42. Montevideo to Secretary of State, September 16, 1958, Telegram no. 126, Records of the Department of State, RG 59, Central Decimal File, 811.411/9-1658, National Archives. While reaction was widespread, it did not occur in all countries. There was little reaction, in French West Africa, for example, which was attributed by consular officials to the lack of English-language users in the region. Amcongen, Dakar, French West Africa, to Secretary of State, September 19, 1958, Airgram no. G-28, Records of the Department of State, RG 59, Central Decimal File, 811.411/9-1958, National Archives.

43. Embassy, Bern to Department of State, September 16, 1958, Despatch no. 176, Records of the Department of State, RG 59, Central Decimal File, 811.411/9-1658, National Archives.

44. Amembassy Tunis to Department of State, September 16, 1958, Despatch no. 208, Records of the Department of State, RG 59, Central Decimal File, 811.411/9-1658, National Archives; Amembassy Copenhagen to Department of State, August 29, 1958, Despatch no. 153, Records of the Department of State, RG 59, Central Decimal File, 811.411/8-2958, National Archives; Embassy of Uruguay to Department of State, September 19, 1958, Records of the Department of State, RG 59, Central Decimal File, 811.411/9-1958, National Archives.

45. Gunnar Myrdal, *An American Dilemma: The Negro Problem and Modern Democracy,* 2 vols. (New York: Harper and Row, 1962; first published in 1944).

46. Peter Kellogg, "Civil Rights Consciousness in the 1940s," *Historian* 42 (November 1979): 18–41; Jonathan Seth Rosenberg, *How Far the Promised Land? World Affairs and the American Civil Rights Movement from the First World War to Vietnam* (Princeton: Princeton University Press, 2006), 315–16.

47. President Harry S. Truman, Address before a Joint Session of Congress, March 12, 1947, Avalon Project website, Yale University, at http://www.yale.edu/lawweb/avalon/trudoc.htm.

48. Ibid.

49. Ernest R. May, ed., *American Cold War Strategy: Interpreting NSC 68* (Boston: Bedford/St. Martin's, 1993), 42; Michael Hogan, *Cross of Iron* (Cambridge: Cambridge University Press, 1998), 295–301.

50. Dudziak, *Cold War Civil Rights,* 29–46.

51. Ibid., 26–27, 29, 33–36, 37–39, 45–46, 99–102.

52. Ibid., 48–54, 107, 144–45.

53. Dulles to All AF Posts, September 12, 1958, Department of State Instruction no. 1073, Records of the Department of State, RG 59, Central Decimal File, 811.411/9-1258, National Archives.

54. AmEmbassy to Department of State, September 23, 1958, Despatch no. 717, Records of the Department of State, RG 59, Central Decimal File, 811.411/9-2358, National Archives.

55. The Hague to Secretary of State, September 12, 1958, Telegram no. 469, Records of the Department of State, RG 59, Central Decimal File, 811.411/9-1258, National Archives.

56. "West Indians Storm U.S. Consulate on Wilson Case," *Pittsburgh Courier,* September 20, 1958, p. 7.

57. "Wilson Case May Go to U.S. Court," *Baltimore Afro-American,* September 20, 1958, p. 1. Dulles's executive secretary, Ralph Hammond, indicated that Dulles was "very emphatic that he was not trying to interfere with the judicial or court system of Alabama, but just wanted to inform the Governor of what was occurring throughout the world." "Dulles Sends a Letter to Folsom Dealing with Condemned Negro," *New York Times,* September 6, 1958, p. 7.

58. "World-wide Appeals for Negro," *Rhodesia Herald,* September 8, 1958, p. 9; Enclosure to AmConGen Salisbury to Department of State, October 3, 1958, Despatch no. 171. RG 59, Central Decimal File, 811.411/10-358; AmEmbassy to Department of State, September 23, 1958, Despatch no. 717.

59. AmEmbassy to Department of State, September 23, 1958, Despatch no. 717, Records of the Department of State, RG 59, Central Decimal File, 811.411/9-2358, National Archives.

60. AmCongen Kingston, to Department of State, September 25, 1958, Despatch no. 96, Records of the Department of State, RG 59, Central Decimal File, 811.411/9-2558, National Archives.

61. "Jurists Urge Clemency for Negro Facing Death," *Washington Post and Times Herald,* September 2, 1958, p. A3.

62. AmEmbassy Oslo, to Department of State, September 29, 1958, Despatch no. 213, Records of the Department of State, RG 59, Central Decimal File, 811.411/9-2958, National Archives.

63. "Dulles Sends a Letter to Folsom Dealing with Condemned Negro," *New*

York Times, September 6, 1958, p. 7. The governor added: "I want to say to the world that I have fought for four years of my first administration to reduce the Alabama prison population. . . . As a result, my administration was prosecuted and persecuted." "Dulles Tells Folsom of World Concern over Negro's Fate," *Birmingham Post-Herald,* September 6, 1958, pp. 1–2.

64. "Folsom Swamped by Pleas for Negro," *New York Times,* September 14, 1958, p. 56.

65. "The Wilson Case," *Birmingham Post-Herald,* September 5, 1958, p. 12.

66. "Jimmy Wilson Loses Appeal for Rehearing," *Birmingham Post-Herald,* September 12, 1958, p. 1.

67. "Wilson Death Sentence Commuted to Life," *Washington Post and Times Herald,* September 30, 1958, p. A3; "Gov. Folsom Saves Negro from Chair," *New York Times,* September 30, 1958, p. 22.

68. "Folsom Delays Ruling on Wilson," *Birmingham Post-Herald,* September 27, 1958, p. 1.

69. Ibid.

70. "Wilson Escapes Death Sentence, New Appeal Hinted," *Birmingham Post-Herald,* September 30, 1958, p. 3.

71. Folsom to Dulles, September 29, 1958, Records of the Department of State, RG 59, Central Decimal File, 811.411/9-2958, National Archives.

72. AmConGen Lagos, Nigeria, to Secretary of State, October 3, 1958, Airgram no. G-21, Records of the Department of State, RG 59, Central Decimal File, 811.411/10-358, National Archives.

73. Amembassy Oslo to Department of State, October 13, 1958, Despatch no. 243, Records of the Department of State, RG 59, Central Decimal File, 811.411/10-358, National Archives.

74. "Folsom Move Cheered," *New York Times,* October 1, 1958, p. 22.

75. "Attorney Plans Renewed Fight for Jim Wilson," *Pittsburgh Courier,* October 11, 1958, p. 2.

76. Gray, telephone interview.

77. Department of State to American Embassy Canberra, October 20, 1958, No. A-51, Records of the Department of State, RG 59, Central Decimal File, 811.411/10-2058, National Archives.

78. Dudziak, *Cold War Civil Rights,* 240–41.

79. Rebecca Haffajee, telephone conversation with Alabama Department of Corrections, Records Department, spring 2006.

80. James Goodman, *Stories of Scottsboro* (New York: Pantheon, 1994), 5–6. The lone exception was defendant Roy Wright, the youngest at age 13. According to James Goodman, because of Wright's age, "the state, mindful of public opinion, asked only for life in prison." But when 11 jurors "held out for the death penalty, the judge declared a mistrial." Ibid., 41.

Scottsboro gained a more sustained international audience than the Jimmy Wilson case, though without the Cold War edge. See James A. Miller, Susan D.

Pennybacker, and Eve Rosenhaft, "Mother Ada Wright and the International Campaign to Free the Scottsboro Boys, 1931–1934," *American Historical Review* 106 (April 2001): 387.

81. *Powell v. Alabama,* 287 U.S. 45 (1932); *Patterson v. Alabama,* 294 U.S. 600 (1935); *Norris v. State of Alabama,* 294 U.S. 587 (1935).

82. *Patterson v. State,* 234 Ala. 342 (1937); *Norris v. State,* 236 Ala. 281 (1938); *Weems v. State,* 236 Ala. 261 (1938); Goodman, *Stories of Scottsboro,* 308–9, 370, 378, 380–81; "Scottsboro Timeline," *Scottsboro: An American Tragedy,* American Experience, PBS Online, at http://www.pbs.org/wgbh/amex/scottsboro/timeline/timeline2.html. Wright had previously been released in 1943 but escaped north, in violation of his parole. When he returned, he appeared before the Parole Board and was ordered to return to his job. When he complained to his boss about work conditions, his boss placed him in handcuffs and sent him back to prison. Wright was finally released in 1950. Goodman, *Stories of Scottsboro,* 370–73.

83. *Powell,* 287 U.S. at 68–69.

84. Ibid., 71.

85. Felix Frankfurter, "A Notable Decision: The Supreme Court Writes a Chapter on Man's Rights," *New York Times,* November 13, 1932, p. E1.

86. Two paragraphs from Sutherland's opinion follow a quotation from the Sixth Amendment at the opening of chapter 4, on "The Right to Counsel and Other Assistance," but there is no information about the fate of the Scottsboro defendants, in Ronald J. Allen, Richard B. Kuhn, and William J. Stuntz, *Constitutional Criminal Procedure: An Examination of the Fourth, Fifth, and Sixth Amendments and Related Areas,* 3rd ed. (Toronto: Little, Brown, 1995), 141–42. See also Yale Kamisar, Wayne R. LaFave, Jerold H. Israel, and Nancy J. King, *Modern Criminal Procedure: Cases, Comments and Questions,* 11th ed. (St. Paul, Minn.: Thompson/West, 2005), 28, 59–60, 81–87, 153, 184–85, 760, 769, 771, 847; Marc L. Miller and Ronald F. Wright, *Criminal Procedures: Cases, Statutes and Executive Materials,* 2nd ed. (New York: Aspen, 2003), 676–77, 679; Stephen A. Saltzburg and Daniel J. Capra, *American Criminal Procedure: Cases and Commentary,* 6th ed. (St. Paul, Minn.: Thompson/West, 2000), 779–83; Joel Samaha, *Criminal Procedure,* 2nd ed. (Minneapolis: West, 1993), 57–61. At the time this essay was written, a few casebooks included information about what happened to the Scottsboro defendants. The most extensive treatment in a casebook appeared to be Joshua Dressler and George C. Thomas III, *Criminal Procedure: Principles, Policies and Perspectives,* 2nd ed. (St. Paul, Minn.: Thompson/West, 2003), 1–14, with a long excerpt about the historical context from Goodman, *Stories of Scottsboro,* and a short note on the aftermath of the case. A fuller story of *Powell* is covered in a new collection, Michael J. Klarman, "*Powell v. Alabama:* The Supreme Court Confronts 'Legal Lynchings,'" in Carol S. Steiker, ed., *Criminal Procedure Stories* (St. Paul, Minn.: Thompson/West, 2006).

87. Frankfurter, "A Notable Decision."

88. Another Scottsboro case was *Norris v. Alabama,* 294 U.S. 587 (1935). The Supreme Court overturned Clarence Norris's conviction on the ground that where "all persons of the African race are excluded, solely because of their race or color, from serving as grand jurors in the criminal prosecution of a person of the African race" the defendant is denied the equal protection of the laws. African Americans had to be listed on the jury roll for a defendant's due process rights to be satisfied. The case was remanded; Norris was tried again and convicted again. His death sentence was commuted to life in 1938, and he was finally paroled in 1944.

The Scottsboro defendants would later be the subject of important historical works, including documentary films, and their story informs our understanding of the history of race and American criminal justice. See, for example, Goodman, *Stories of Scottsboro;* Dan T. Carter, *Scottsboro: A Tragedy of the American South,* rev. ed. (Baton Rouge: Louisiana State University Press, 1979); PBS, *Scottsboro: An American Tragedy,* at *http://www.pbs.org/amex/scottsboro;* Michael J. Klarman, "The Racial Origins of Modern Criminal Procedure," *Michigan Law Review* 99 (2000): 48–97.

89. Austin Sarat (chapter 8 in this volume), drawing on Drucilla Cornell, brings our attention to two audiences of legal interpretation: the present and the future. Writing about legal interpretation usually proceeds on a domestic terrain. This is, after all, where law's violence is often realized. See Robert M. Cover, "Violence and the Word," *Yale Law Journal* 95 (1986): 1601. But there is another way to bifurcate the audience: the local and the global.

90. Understandings of American identity are, of course, informed by U.S. actions overseas, as well as perceptions of international threats. David Campbell, *Writing Security: United States Foreign Policy and the Politics of Identity,* rev. ed. (Minneapolis: University of Minnesota Press, 1998). For recent treatments of the way "America" is understood, see Michael Kazin and Joseph A. McCartin, *Americanism: New Perspectives on the History of an Ideal* (Chapel Hill: University of North Carolina Press, 2006); Dudziak and Volpp, *Legal Borderlands.*

91. Essentializing the American character is at work in Myrdal, *The American Dilemma,* and other classic writings on race in America. Rogers Smith's critique of the Myrdalianism embedded in American political science can be seen as a critique of this essentialism. Rogers Smith, *Civic Ideals: Conflicting Visions of Citizenship in U.S. History* (New Haven, Conn.: Yale University Press, 1999).

92. "The Negro in American Life" (circa 1950), folder 503, box 112, series II, Chester Bowles Papers, Manuscripts and Archives, Yale University; Dudziak, *Cold War Civil Rights,* 49–55.

93. Austin Sarat, "At the Boundaries of Law: Executive Clemency, Sovereign Prerogative, and the Dilemma of American Legality," in Mary L. Dudziak and Leti Volpp, eds., *Legal Borderlands: Law and the Construction of American Borders* (Baltimore: Johns Hopkins University Press, 2006), 611.

Chapter 2

When Law Fails

*History, Genius, and Unhealed Wounds
after Tulsa's Race Riot*

Charles J. Ogletree, Jr.

On January 25, 2007, the esteemed American historian John Hope Franklin turned 92. Dr. Franklin has led a rich and storied life and continues to win great acclaim and success in the academy and as a tireless public servant. Even as he celebrates the astonishing accomplishments of his 92 years, though, he cannot help but be haunted by events of May 31, 1921, when he was just six years old and living with his family in Oklahoma. That year, a virulent racism triggered what might now best be defined as one of the twentieth century's clearest examples of a miscarriage of justice. The white-led race riot in Tulsa, Oklahoma, changed the course of the Franklin family's life and thus is one of the defining moments in Dr. Franklin's personal history. For the most serious students of America's racial history, Tulsa 1921 also represents a defining moment and spot of shame for the nation.

It is what happened—or more precisely what did not happen—*after* Tulsa that provides one of our clearest and most compelling narratives about a miscarriage of justice and wounds left unhealed. It is a story best told through the lives of real survivors and their descendants. It is a miscarriage that many times the mechanisms of American law had the power to make right, but chose not to.

No one in John Hope Franklin's family was physically injured in the race riot, but the course of their lives was altered forever. What his father saw and what he dedicated himself to after the Tulsa riots stand as a potent symbol of both gross injustice and a remarkable triumph of the human spirit.

John Hope Franklin was born in 1915 in Rentiesville, Oklahoma, and spent his earliest years there with his older sister, Anne, born in 1913; his mother, Mollie; and his father, Buck Colbert Franklin. In the early twentieth century, Buck Franklin was one of the most successful and well-known African American lawyers in the nation. He had launched his practice in Rentiesville but soon set up a law office 70 miles away in Tulsa. His family remained in Rentiesville while Buck rented an apartment in a segregated and highly prosperous, culturally exciting section of Tulsa called Greenwood. He planned to move his family there in June 1921.[1]

Let us now fast forward from the image of young John Hope Franklin, about to reunite with his father, to the newer picture of the distinguished, vastly accomplished 80 plus-year-old Franklin in 1997. That was the year President Bill Clinton appointed Franklin chairman of "One America," an ambitious effort to discuss and illuminate matters related to race and justice in the United States of America. Franklin's committee developed plans of action and made recommendations to the president for the achievement of broader understanding, equality, and justice in America.[2]

In 2005, John Hope Franklin published his memoir, *Mirror to America: The Autobiography of John Hope Franklin*. This best-selling book tells the life story of an American treasure. A reader can easily see the straight line of connection between the events of Tulsa 1921 and the recommendations of Franklin's "One America" committee seven and a half decades later.

The 1921 Tulsa Race Riot

On May 31, 1921, Franklin, Anne, and Mollie were in Rentiesville, eagerly awaiting the day when they would officially move to Tulsa. Buck's law practice was flourishing, and the time had come for the family to be reunited.

However, as Franklin writes in his autobiography, "news of the violence [in Tulsa] reached us [in Rentiesville] well before news of [Buck Colbert Franklin]."[3] He and his family read of the destruction, violence, and unknown number of deaths in a local African American paper, the *Muskogee News*. Days passed without any word from Franklin's father. Finally, the Franklin family received a letter in the mail from Buck that verified his safety, told the story of what happened in Tulsa, and informed them that their departure from Rentiesville was delayed indefinitely.

The riot and its aftermath changed the lives not only of Buck Franklin but of all the citizens in the segregated black neighborhood in Tulsa called Greenwood, named for the main artery, Greenwood Avenue and dubbed by many as "The Black Wall Street" for the notable financial success of the black community in a segregated American town.[4] The Stradford Hotel and the Dreamland Theatre were just two of the flourishing black establishments in Greenwood at that time. Doctor's offices, law firms, numerous retail stores, and a library lined busy sidewalks full of families and workers.[5] At the time, 15,000 people lived in Greenwood and 191 businesses operated there.[6]

Then, on May 31, a 19-year-old African American shoe shiner and Greenwood resident named Dick Rowland took a bathroom break from his station on Main Street in Tulsa. Rowland was not permitted to use the whites-only bathroom on the first floor of the building next door. So he had to ride an elevator to the "colored" restrooms on the top floor. A white teenager named Sarah Page worked as an elevator operator in the building. This is where the trouble purportedly began. Accounts differ about the details of Rowland's and Page's exchange, but in at least one report, Dick Rowland accidentally stepped on Sarah Page's foot and she slapped him.[7] Not wishing to cause a scene or trouble for himself, Rowland then left the elevator and exited the building. As happened in so many cases and so many places after disputes or seeming disputes between blacks and whites and especially when gender was in the mix, rumors flew. The local newspaper fueled false reports that a black man had sexually assaulted a young white woman in an elevator.[8] Even though the reports were untrue, Police arrested Dick Rowland and took him to the local jail to await a hearing.[9] Then, more news spread. The word on the street was that there would be a lynching that night and that the victim would be young Dick Rowland.[10]

Following the hearing, charges against Dick Rowland were dismissed. There was no proof that a crime had been committed.[11] He had never assaulted and certainly had not raped Sarah Page. However, the facts did not impress the white mob gathering outside the local jail to lynch Dick Rowland. The mob grew loud and unruly. Meanwhile, a group of African American residents, including several veterans of World War I, caught wind of the gathering and impending lynching. They decided to go down to the jail and protect Rowland, and they were armed to protect themselves, too, as members of the white mob carried their own guns. The far smaller group of African Americans attempted to prevent whites from entering the jail, but a sheriff told the African Americans to go home. They refused to leave, understanding that they were all that stood between innocent Dick Rowland and a lynch mob. A gunshot went off. A fight broke out between the blacks and the whites. The fight was short-lived, though, and the black residents retreated to the Greenwood section of Tulsa where they lived. Then, the local sheriff deputized dozens of white men and gave them orders to "invade" Greenwood. The white "deputies" walked into gun shops, acquired more weapons, and marched into Greenwood well armed.[12]

The white mob, ostensibly going after the black men who had been at the jailhouse trying to protect Dick Rowland, incited a racial riot as they stormed through Greenwood that night. They left inexplicable destruction in their wake. They burned the Stratford Hotel and the Dreamland Theatre and many other black businesses, including Buck Colbert Franklin's thriving law office. The mob went door to door, torching an estimated 1,115 black homes. They sought out black boys and men. They killed them or forced them into detainment camps created to hold black prisoners.[13]

The devastation was staggering.[14] Rioters destroyed more than $1.5 million worth of property, a figure that equates to more than $17 million today. Newspaper reports claim that the mob killed "dozens" of African Americans that night and into the next morning. But reports from African American witnesses suggest that hundreds of African American citizens were never found.[15] On June 2, 1921, Adjutant General Charles F. Barrett of the Oklahoma National Guard announced that all funerals would be banned because of, among other reasons, "the emotional stress that still prevailed." Numerous witnesses say that many people killed in the riot were taken away on trains and buried outside of Tulsa, or that some are buried in sacred grounds in Tulsa that have never been uncovered.[16] The number of lives taken by rioters on the night of May 31 and early morning of June 1 remains unknown.[17] Having suffered such devastating losses, Tulsa's African Americans scattered across the country with no homes, no ability to rebuild, and the threat of harm if they continued to challenge whites in Tulsa.[18]

The riot fires claimed not only Buck Franklin's law office but also the boarding house where he had rented a room and where he had kept the money he had saved to pay for his family's relocation. All he had left were a few books that had not been fully destroyed by the fire. Eventually, he, too, was rounded up by the white mob and detained, even though he tried to urge calm that might prevent the riot.[19]

Despite having lost his home, being separated from his family, and having had his law office destroyed, Buck Franklin joined forces with his law partners and set up a tent as a temporary office. Immediately after the riot, he found his typewriter, and with the few law books he had recovered, he and his partners began to file lawsuits to get compensation from insurance companies for the losses that African Americans had suffered as a result of the race riot.[20] The lawsuits went all the way to the Oklahoma Supreme Court, which denied them. This left the African Americans who had resided within a 10-block area and had suffered the loss of more than 1,000 homes and properties no recourse under the law.[21]

It was not simply the court of law but also the court of public opinion that crushed hope of reparations for the victims of the 1921 Tulsa race riot. A perception pervaded Tulsa's white community that African Americans were the cause of the riot and that whites were the victims. On June 25, 1921, a grand jury was convened to investigate the cause of the riot. In its final report, the grand jury wrote:

> We find that the recent race riot was the direct result of an effort on the part of a certain group of colored men. . . . There was no mob spirit among the whites, no talk of lynching and no arms. The assembly was quiet until the arrival of the armed negroes, which precipitated and was the direct cause of the entire affair.[22]

Indeed, the erroneous belief that Tulsa's African American citizens had caused the violence of May 31 and June 1, 1921, would persist for generations.[23] For some white Tulsans, the destruction of Greenwood, which was sometimes called "Niggertown," was viewed as a positive outcome of the riot. In a 1921 article, Amy Comstock wrote:

> It was in the sordid and neglected "Niggertown" that the crooks found their best hiding place. It was a cesspool of crime. There were the low brothels where the low whites mixed with the low blacks. There crimes were plotted and loot hidden. One city administration after another . . . let "Niggertown" pretty much alone. . . . The cause of the Tulsa race riot was the cause that is common to all race riots plus a city too busy building to give thought or care to the spawning pools of crime that indifferent citizens thought did not really matter because it was "over there." Now they know better. Most such disasters bring their resultant good.[24]

In the immediate aftermath of the tragedy, there were some public demands for restitution on the part of the city of Tulsa and the state of Oklahoma. In a 1921 *New York Times* article, Judge Loyal J. Martin, a former Mayor of Tulsa and the head of the commission formed to coordinate relief efforts after the riot, is quoted as stating:

Tulsa can only redeem herself from the country-wide shame and humiliation in which she is today plunged by complete restitution of the destroyed black belt. The rest of the United States must know that the real citizenship of Tulsa weeps at this unspeakable crime and will make good the damage, so far as it can be done, to the last penny.[25]

Even as money was donated from private citizens and from other parts of the country to help the city of Tulsa in providing reparations to the victims of the riot, it was refused. An article in the *Tulsa Tribune* stated:

Tulsa is going to take care of this problem herself. That was made certain at the reconstruction Board hearing this morning. The $1,000 offered by the Chicago Tribune will be sent back at once with the courteous statement that the city is able to take care of its own problems here. Private funds are to be stopped at once.[26]

The Tulsa victims never had a day in court to present their claims. They were not able to address these matters in any court for decades. Indeed, many of those who lost their homes and property in 1921 died during the first half of the twentieth century, and still more passed away by the end of that century. The survivors who remained assumed that there would never be a day of reconciliation. Mary E. Jones Parrish, a black Tulsan who wrote about the riot in its immediate aftermath, observed:

The Tulsa disaster has taught great lessons to all of us. . . . Some of our group who have been blest with educational or financial advantages are oftimes inclined to forget ourselves to the extent that they feel their superiority over those less fortunate, but when a supreme test, like the Tulsa disaster comes, it serves to remind us that we are all of one race; that human fiends, like those who had full sway on June 1st, have no respect of person. Every Negro was accorded the same treatment, regardless of his education or other advantages. A Negro was a Negro on that day and forced to march with his hands up for blocks.[27]

Additionally, Tulsa in 1921 was a community where many of the public officials were members and active participants in the Ku Klux Klan. According to Professor Alfred Brophy, "the entire bench of the Tulsa district court, the court clerk, the county sheriff, and all the jury commissioners" were known members of the Klan. Because the Ku Klux Klan "was inextricably linked with law enforcement in riot-era Oklahoma," the survivors knew that the idea of seeking remedies was a waste of their time.[28]

The irony of this miscarriage of justice is that many who were born in the latter half of the twentieth century and grew up in Tulsa never knew that there was a race riot in Tulsa in 1921. Brent Staples describes the experience of Representative Don Ross, the Greenwood district's representative in the Oklahoma State Legislature. Although he is a Greenwood native, Ross did not hear about the riot until he was a 15-year-old sophomore at Booker T. Washington High School in 1956. Staples writes of Ross's experience:

> The news came from a teacher, W. D. Williams, who had watched the early stages of the invasion from his family's apartment on Greenwood Avenue—and seen his family's real estate holdings reduced to ruins. When Williams revealed this in class, Ross leapt to his feet. "I thought he was lying," Ross recalls "I challenged him almost with my finger in his face—something that got you kicked out of school in those days. I thought my community was a proud community that would never have let whites get away with burning us down." But Williams settled the matter with a collection of photographs showing scenes from the riot, including corpses with arms and legs burned away and wicker coffins stacked on the backs of trucks, being borne away to anonymous graves.[29]

Even when there was awareness, many had no sense of the devastating impact it had on Tulsa's African American community.[30] As Brophy writes, they "rarely heard the black story. Meanwhile, white Tulsa presented its sanitized version of the story."[31]

Hope of Relief

The first glimmer of hope for the 1921 Tulsa race riot survivors and their descendants came in 1999. Finally, the Oklahoma State Legislature agreed to create the Tulsa Race Riot Commission and to ask it, a bipartisan group, to engage in a comprehensive and extensive evaluation of what occurred in Tulsa in 1921 and to make whatever recommendations they deemed appropriate in light of what they found.[32]

In February 2001, the Commission issued a comprehensive report analyzing the events from 80 years earlier, and the stinging report had a clear and unequivocal conclusion: despite the public reports from 1921 to the present and despite the image of African Americans being the cause of the riot on May 31, 1921, the cause was, in fact, a white mob that overpowered the African American group trying to defend their property and their persons. The ultimate conclusion was that the black community and their descendants were entitled to restitution.[33] This bipartisan report was timely in that it highlighted a gross miscarriage of justice and set the table for what many hoped would be reconciliation and resolution of the most tragic example of domestic terrorism in America's history.

Despite the recommendation of the Tulsa Race Riot Commission, Governor Frank Keating concluded that neither the state of Oklahoma nor the city of Tulsa would provide any compensation in 2001 to the victim of the 1921 race riot.[34] It was a stinging rebuke of the victims of the 1921 race riot and left them with few options.

In 2002, I had the honor of giving the Buck Colbert Franklin Memorial Civil Rights Lecture at the University of Tulsa School of Law. During the course of that event, I was asked to attend a private meeting with a group of "Greenwood citizens." I agreed to go to the Greenwood Cultural Center and met with a group of African American women and men for several hours. The youngest person there was in his late 80s. The oldest was 105 years old.

When I asked why they were there, they told me that they were all survivors of the 1921 Tulsa race riot and that they were looking for a way to receive restitution for their losses from more than 80 years earlier. This seemed an incredible task to ask, even of someone who might have creative legal theories, but it was a stunning reminder of how a matter of race had been swept under a rug and virtually eliminated from our nation's history for nearly a century. It is no accident, then, that John Hope Franklin would dedicate his life to ensuring not only that such a history never be forgotten but that it be widely understood with the hope that understanding might lead to improvement, even transformation.

By the time that events had brought me to that room in Tulsa, John Hope Franklin's perseverance, intelligence, and deep humanity had brought him physically far from the state of his birth. However, in all his pursuits, I would learn later, Tulsa was seared in his memory. It was a kind of launching pad helping lead him to insight, inspiring socially concerned scholarship for a higher purpose.

John Hope Franklin eventually attended the segregated Booker T. Washington High School in Tulsa and graduated at the top of his class. He earned a degree in history from Fisk University in 1935 and a Ph.D. in history from Harvard University in 1941. At Harvard, he was not allowed to live in the dormitories or eat in the cafeteria with the white students. Franklin was not just a great student at Harvard; he was an extraordinary one. This was viewed as a contradiction, as there were few black students during this period. The black students there faced low expectations and visceral bias. Franklin went on to teach at the North Carolina College for Negroes, Fisk University, Howard University, and the University of Chicago. In 1982, Duke University named him James B. Duke Professor of History.[35]

Back in the auditorium in Tulsa, I agreed to look into the matter further. Then, I assembled some of America's greatest lawyers to work pro bono on behalf of the victims of the 1921 Tulsa race riot. We had a strong legal hook. Even though the statute of limitations, the city and state's strongest defense, would have normally expired after two years, the newly discovered evidence by the Tulsa Race Riot Commission in 2001 would, we would argue, start the clock running again. This would give the victims until 2003 to file a lawsuit.

With this theory in hand, we filed a lawsuit in February 2003 on behalf of 150 survivors and more than 200 descendants of men and women who had since died. We filed the claim in the Western District of Oklahoma in Federal Court and presented evidence before Judge James Ellison and demonstrated why the victims were entitled to trial and compensation. In a stunningly sympathetic and technically narrow ruling, Judge Ellison agreed that the Tulsa race riot victims had a right to sue but that the statute of limitations prevented them from being granted relief. Judge Ellison's statements affirmed that there had indeed been a great miscarriage of justice in 1921 and afterward. His words provide comfort in that he clearly recognizes the harm the Tulsa race riot victims suffered. But the judge's conclusion is deeply disappointing:

> The Commission Report is a valuable tool in understanding and documenting the Race Riot of 1921. It also brings attention to an extremely tragic event in our City's and State's history, and, hopefully, will be a tool for

healing and uniting communities. Although Plaintiffs urge that it should also be the foundation for the application of equitable doctrines to prevent the barring of claims by the statute of limitations, the Court is unable to find any legal basis for using the Report in this way. There is no comfort or satisfaction in this result, and there should be none to Defendants. That Plaintiff's claims are barred by the statute of limitations is strictly a legal conclusion, and does not speak to the tragedy of the Riot or the terrible devastation caused.[36]

With Judge Ellison's denial of relief, our hope lay with the 10th Circuit Court of Appeals. We argued that Ellison's conclusion was incorrect. But a three-judge panel again denied our claim.[37] We sought a rehearing before the same court, asking the entire court to consider this travesty. Though a rehearing was denied, four justices dissented.[38] It is worth noting what four of the judges determined to be the facts and the balance of the evidence, even though it was not enough to give us an additional day in the 10th Circuit. On behalf of four dissenting judges on the 10th Circuit, Judge Carlos Lucero, wrote:

> No case in my tenure on the court could be more compellingly described as meeting . . . standard of presenting a "question of exceptional importance" deserving the attention of the entire court than this. In one of the more shameful events in our nation's history, over two hundred African-Americans were slaughtered and a whole section of the City of Tulsa was burned in an uncontrolled riot in 1921. Official government action by the City of Tulsa and the State of Oklahoma fueled this carnage by deputizing and arming the mob, and authorizing the National Guard to detain the victims while their forty-two square block community was razed to the ground.
>
> All subsequent claims raised by the victims fell upon the deaf ears of the courts at the time, and most languished without even a cursory glance at the merits. None of the over one hundred lawsuits filed were successful. In a perversion of justice, a grand jury commissioned by the state exonerated the city and state, and all white rioters, and blamed the victims for the atrocity. This history alone raises a "question of exceptional importance"— the laudable recent investigation of this tragedy by the State of Oklahoma compels us to confront it.
>
> In summary, plaintiffs seek the one thing they could not get in 1921: a court to hear their claims free of official denial of culpability. Because the governments officially denied their guilt for the Riot and instead employed

their judicial powers officially to condemn the African-American community for the tragedy, the district court properly concluded that equity demands tolling the statute of limitations. The district court's dismissal of plaintiffs' claim that those exceptional circumstances merited tolling the statute until the publication of the Commission Report should be revisited. Because the panel erred by affirming that conclusion and by applying an inappropriate legal standard to decide plaintiffs' fraudulent concealment claims, this matter deserves en banc consideration.[39]

Undaunted by the failure of these efforts, we went to Washington, D.C., and filed a petition for a hearing before the U.S. Supreme Court. Disappointingly, without a word or a hearing, the Supreme Court refused to consider the case.[40]

Despite these losses, the fight for the Tulsa race riot victims continues. We filed a petition with the Organization of American States,[41] an international court that has jurisdiction to review claims of "discrimination of people of African descent,"[42] under which we believe the Tulsa race riot victims fall, and to compel the government to consider remedies despite the usual protections of sovereign immunity and statute of limitations.

Wanting to ensure that all the possible avenues are pursued to protect these victims, we have also solicited the U.S. government to create legislation to protect the Tulsa race riot victims. On April 24, 2007, Congressman John Conyers, the first African American to serve as chairman of the House Judiciary Committee, held hearings on the Tulsa riot, and, as a result of that, he and Congressman Jerrold Nadler, a Democrat from New York, introduced the 2007 Tulsa-Greenwood Race Riot Claims Accountability Act of 2007, H.R. 1995, designed to extend the statute of limitations for five years in order to allow the Tulsa victims to have their day in court.[43] Ironically, while this well-intentioned legislation marks an important step forward, it is interesting to note that some members of the Republican House Judiciary Committee articulated arguments suggesting that compensation, rather than extending the statute of limitations, may be the appropriate remedy.[44] In any event, the Tulsa race riot of 1921 may finally be getting its day in court.

Tulsa's Legacy as a Miscarriage of Justice

As the story about Tulsa illustrates a classic miscarriage of justice, it is worth noting the deeper effect of this story on our collective history. While John Hope Franklin thrived and excelled since the 1921 Tulsa race riot, history is littered with hundreds of other African Americans from Greenwood whose pain and suffering seem endless and whose very existence has been all but forgotten.

Among those influenced by the riots in Tulsa was the great African American author Ralph Ellison. Ellison was a native Oklahoman who lived through the era and witnessed Oklahoma's vicious racism.[45] And more than 20 years after Tulsa's riots, in 1944, sociologist Gunnar Myrdal published his classic, *An American Dilemma*, where he describes the challenges of African Americans and Native Americans in their struggle to be a part of a society where race and ethnicity seemed to be a defining mark between who was a citizen and who was considered "the other."[46] In writing about the challenges of people of African descent in the twentieth century, and certainly reflecting his experience as an African American in Tulsa during the riot era, Ralph Ellison in a review of *An American Dilemma* observed:

> But can a people (its faith in an idealized American Creed not-withstanding) live and develop for over three hundred years simply by *reacting?* Are American Negroes simply the creation of white men, or have they at least helped to create themselves out of what they found around them? Men have made a way of life in caves and upon cliffs; why cannot Negroes have made a life upon the horns of the white man's dilemma?[47]

Ralph Ellison not only participated in but described a different dilemma facing African Americans in a post–Tulsa race riot environment. He asked, pointedly: What were the challenges of that community to try to survive and thrive after such blatant and widespread white supremacy? Ellison writes:

> There was an optimism within the Negro community and a sense of possibility which, despite our awareness of limitation (dramatized so brutally in the Tulsa riot of 1921), transcended all of this and it was this rock-bottom sense of reality, coupled with the sense of the possibility to rise above it.[48]

These sentiments voiced by Ellison apply to the indomitable spirit of the Tulsa race riot survivors but also reveal and clearly illustrate the extent of the physical, financial, and emotional damage to a thriving black community through no fault of its own. Ellison also illustrates the agonizing reality of the application of law to the lives of African Americans in the twentieth century in his classic novel, *The Invisible Man*. Ellison places his protagonist, the Invisible Man, tellingly, in Greenwood. In his treatment of the Invisible Man's dilemma of being present and not seen, Ellison illustrates the powerlessness of the faceless and voiceless African Americans in the twentieth century, particularly in places like Tulsa.[49]

In trying to describe the remarkable conflicts of the Invisible Man's experience, Alfred Brophy, a noted historian and one of the most knowledgeable people on the subject of the Tulsa race riot, made the connection between the actual men and women who suffered in 1921 and how their lives might parallel that of the Invisible Man:

> I imagine that the Invisible Man was someone like A. J. Smitherman, the editor of the *Tulsa Star*, whose editorials talked about the importance of taking life if necessary to prevent a lynching, or J. B. Stradford, the lawyer who cooperated with Smitherman in urging the community to take action to protect itself against mob violence. Stradford fled to Chicago after the riot to avoid prosecution for incitement. At least those are the Invisible Man's roots.[50]

But beyond the story of the miscarriages of justice in Tulsa in 1921, the Tulsa race riot also tells us something about law and its relevance to justice, particularly for African Americans in twentieth-century Tulsa. The riot illustrates a number of ways that the rule of law was ineffective in protecting the interests of its citizens.

The rule of law first became a barrier to Dick Rowland, because even though he was simply accused of a crime, the angry lynch mob made it clear that there was no assurance that he would be safe as a matter of law. Thus, the riot emerged from the lawless Oklahoma countryside where the only meaning of the "rule of law" was the rule of "laws"—that is, African Americans were subjected to the arbitrary dictates of law enforcement officers, often in ways that undermined their own integrity.[51]

Second, the race riot itself was an absurd and darkly comical failure of the rule of law to protect against violence. The white mob took the law into its own hands and was officially encouraged to do so by city law enforcement. In so doing, the victims wound up blamed for causing the riot. Despite indictments of the city's police chief for dereliction of duty[52] and investigation of a grand jury into the participation of a number of whites in inciting the riot and for looting,[53] authorities took no meaningful legal action against the white citizens responsible for the destruction.[54]

Finally, in a tragic and inexcusable way, even after the riot, when law should have prevailed, there was no justice for African Americans. The city refused to compensate them for losses caused by the city's police and special deputies. African Americans lost their homes and their businesses, their livelihood. Many lost their lives, their parents, sisters, brothers, friends. Even those who "escaped unharmed" had their lives irreversibly altered. Astonishingly, the city even passed a zoning ordinance designed to move the black section of Tulsa further away from the center of the city.[55] In every conceivable way, law failed the citizens of Greenwood, and what was formerly known as the Black Wall Street became a city under siege of white supremacy.

Even now, law continues to fail the survivors of the 1921 Tulsa race riot. What is perhaps most tragic is the fact that, unlike the general claims made for reparations for the descendants of long-deceased enslaved Africans, we have a twenty-first-century example of survivors of a devastating racial assault who can tell their story from their childhood days, who have been denied the opportunity to do so in a court of law. While there is also compelling documentary evidence that proves the losses suffered by black Tulsans during the riot, it is the eyewitness testimony of the death and destruction that occurred in Tulsa on May 31 and June 1, 1921, that is most precious.[56] The accessibility of this eyewitness testimony and the opportunity to make restitution directly to the victims are dwindling by the second. It is heartrending to look back to 2003 when an effort to address this miscarriage of justice led to a complaint with 150 survivors of the 1921 race riot, and to survey our list of clients in 2007 and see fewer than 80 still alive. If they die, will evidence of this miscarriage of justice simply disappear? Is that what our opposition is hoping for?

As we think about miscarriages of justice and how we address them, the case of the victims of the Tulsa race riot makes apparent the fact that courts of law are not always the most appropriate or ideal places to resolve disputes. Indeed, the limits on what claims may be raised, the time at which they may be raised, and the scope of the issues that may be raised leave many persuasive and powerful matters outside the walls of the courthouse, with victims searching for other ways to address those issues. To explain his understandings of the limits and downfalls of the law, Ralph Ellison wrote:

> The law deals with facts, and down here the facts are that we are weak and inferior. But while it looks like we are what the law says we are, don't ever forget that we've been put in this position by force, by power of numbers, and the readiness of those numbers to use brutality to keep us within the law. Ah, but the truth is something else. We are not what the law, yes and custom, says we are and to protect our truth we have to protect ourselves from the definitions of the law. Because the law's facts have made us outlaws.[57]

It is to vindicate Buck Colbert Franklin, his son Dr. John Hope Franklin, the 150 survivors of the 1921 Tulsa race riot, their descendants, and ourselves that this book addresses a broad range of miscarriages of justice. In this way, such accounts become more than simply a recitation of nightmarish pieces of our history. They also become tools to evaluate how law has failed us and beacons for how we might think of reconceptualizing our society and our values in a way that will make it more sensitive to, aware of, and responsive to the claims of those who have been left outside the canyons of opportunity. It is as well a testament to the resilience of those who have fought valiantly despite setbacks, knowing that there is a higher moral authority when our democratic systems fail to properly exercise their weight. In essence, when law fails, our options may be limited, but our responsibility to pursue matters in other venues with vigor and enthusiasm will only begin.

NOTES

1. John Hope Franklin, *Mirror to America: The Autobiography of John Hope Franklin* (New York: Farrar, Straus Giroux, 2005), 11, 9, 15.

2. For Franklin's discussion of his work with the One America board, see ibid. at 342–64. He went on to write one of the most venerable books in American history, *From Slavery to Freedom.* More than 3 million copies of the book have been printed since it was first published in 1947. It has been distributed in five languages, in many parts of the world. Its ninth edition is scheduled for publication in 2008. In addition to *From Slavery to Freedom,* Franklin has written *In Search of the Promised Land: A Slave Family in the Old South; Runaway Slaves: Rebels on the Plantation; George Washington Williams: A Biography; The Militant South*

1800–1861; Reconstruction after the Civil War; The Free Negro in North Carolina; Racial Equality in America; The Color Line: Legacy for the Twenty-First Century; A Southern Odyssey: Travelers in the Antebellum North; The Historian and Public Policy; Color and Race; and *The Emancipation Proclamation.* John Hope Franklin's scholarship has garnered much recognition. He has received the Presidential Medal of Freedom, the highest civilian award granted in the United States, as well as the Cleanth Brooks Medal of the Fellowship of Southern Writers, the Encyclopedia Britannica Gold Medal for the Dissemination of Knowledge, the W.E.B. DuBois Award from Fisk University, the NAACP's Spingarn Medal, and the Leadership Conference on Civil Rights' Hubert H. Humphrey Civil Rights Award. In addition, Franklin has served as president of the Southern Historical Society, the Organization of American Historians, the United Chapters of Phi Beta Kappa, and the American Historical Association.

3. Ibid., 16.

4. Scott Ellsworth, *Death in a Promised Land: The Tulsa Race Riot of 1921,* foreword by John Hope Franklin (Baton Rouge: Louisiana State University Press, 1982), 14 and 15 (noting that Greenwood was "known by some before the riot as the 'Negro's Wall Street'"). See also Alfred L. Brophy, *Reconstructing the Dreamland: The Tulsa Riot of 1921—Race, Reparations, and Reconciliation,* foreword by Randall Kennedy (New York: Oxford University Press, 2003), 181.

5. According to Ellsworth, *Death in a Promised Land,* "in the early years of the twentieth century, Tulsa became not one city, but two. Confined by law and by white racism, black Tulsa was a separate city, serving the needs of the black community. And as Tulsa boomed, black Tulsa did too" (14).

6. Brent Staples, "Unearthing a Riot," *New York Times,* December 19, 1999.

7. Buck Colbert Franklin, *My Life and an Era* (Baton Rouge: Louisiana State University Press, 1997), 199. According to another account, Rowland stepped on Page's foot, "causing her to lurch back, and when he grabbed her to keep her from falling, she screamed." Ellsworth, *Death in a Promised Land,* 43.

8. Ellsworth, *Death in a Promised Land,* discusses the racial climate in Tulsa in the 1920s and notes the role of the *Tulsa Tribune* as a catalyst in the ultimate occurrence of the riot (100–101).

9. According to Franklin, *My Life and an Era,* the assistant county attorney, Samuel Crossland, reported that the allegation was untrue after "a most thorough and painstaking investigation" (199).

10. Accounts of the events of May 31 and June 1, 1921, vary. For example, see Ellsworth, *Death in a Promised Land,* 46, and Staples, "Unearthing a Riot."

11. Franklin, *My Life and an Era,* 199.

12. Ellsworth, *Death in a Promised Land,* 51–52, 54–55.

13. Ibid., 70, 57.

14. For a description of the extensive destruction in Greenwood, see Franklin, *My Life and an Era,* 197–99.

15. Walter F. White, "The Eruption of Tulsa," *Nation*, June 28, 1921, p. 909.

16. Ellsworth, *Death in a Promised Land*, 67, 69. See also Robert L. Brooks and Alan H. Witten, "The Investigation of Potential Mass Grave Locations for the Tulsa Race Riot" in *Tulsa Race Riot: A Report by the Oklahoma Commission to Study the Tulsa Race Riot of 1921* (Tulsa: Oklahoma Commission, 2001).

17. For a discussion of the various possible figures and the logic behind their determination, see Ellsworth, *Death in a Promised Land*, 66–68.

18. According to Ellsworth, *Death in a Promised Land*, "the dislocation of black Tulsa that the riot caused was immense. One-half of the city's black population was forcibly interned for varying lengths of time. When they gained their release, many of these people found their homes had been destroyed. Most had to live with friends or relatives, or simply make do the best they could. Some left town for good. . . . The erection of tents and shacks in the burned areas of black Tulsa began when blacks were allowed to return, and probably increased considerably by mid-June, at which time most black Tulsans has been released by white authorities" (89).

19. Franklin, *My Life and an Era*, 197.

20. Ibid., 198.

21. For more, see Brophy, *Reconstructing the Dreamland*, 95–100.

22. Ibid., 95.

23. For a mid-twentieth-century account of the causes of the riot, see Ed Wheeler, "Profile of a Race Riot," *Oklahoma Impact Magazine* 4 (June/July 1971): 14–26: "[A]lmost simultaneously the black and white mobs began firing at one another. . . . Pawn shops and hardware stores were immediately broken into, looted by both black and white mobs and stripped of firearms" (19). Here the emphasis was on the fact that the eruption of violence was simultaneous and that looting occurred by the hands of both blacks and whites. It was not until late in the twentieth century and the early twenty-first century that the burden of blame was shifted away from Tulsa's African American residents. See also *Tulsa Race Riot: A Report by the Oklahoma Commission to Study the Tulsa Race Riot of 1921*.

24. Amy Comstock, " 'Over Time': Another View of the Tulsa Riots," *Survey* 46 (July 2, 1921), 460.

25. "Tulsa in Remorse to Rebuild Homes; Dead Now Put at 30," *New York Times*, June 3, 1921.

26. "City to Meet Demands out of Own Purse," *Tulsa Tribune*, June 3, 1921, p. 8.

27. Mary E. Jones Parrish, *Events of the Tulsa Disaster* (N.p.: n.p., n.d.), 21–23, cited in Ellsworth, *Death in a Promised Land*, 103.

28. Alfred Brophy, "Norms, Laws and Reparations: The Case of the Ku Klux Klan in 1920s Oklahoma," *Harvard BlackLetter Law Journal* 20 (2004): 30–31.

29. Staples, "Unearthing a Riot."

30. For a discussion of these silences written into Tulsa's institutional memory, see Ellsworth, *Death in a Promised Land*, 104–7.

31. Brophy, *Reconstructing the Dreamland*, xix.

32. *Tulsa Race Riot: A Report by the Oklahoma Commission to Study the Tulsa Race Riot of 1921*. See also Ross E. Milloy, "Panel Calls for Reparations in Tulsa Race Riot," *New York Times*, March 1, 2001.

33. *Tulsa Race Riot: A Report by the Oklahoma Commission to Study the Tulsa Race Riot of 1921*.

34. Milloy, "Panel Calls for Reparations."

35. For an account of his time at Booker T. Washington High School, see Franklin, *Mirror to America*, 23–37, 57, 59. For his teaching career, see ibid., 206. Franklin describes the discrimination he observed at Harvard as one of the reasons that he wanted to leave Cambridge after passing his oral exams: "I had . . . begun to wonder why I had never been offered a teaching assistantship, especially since I had performed at the very top of both of my seminars and in some of the lecture courses. . . . I needed more teaching experience, which, it was hard for me not to conclude, Harvard had denied me because of my color" (80–81). According to Franklin, the James B. Duke chair was "Duke's highest professorship, and although there were several in the University, no one in the Department of History had ever held one, and no African American had ever held an endowed chair at Duke" (308–9).

36. *Alexander v. State of Oklahoma*, 2004 U.S. Dist. LEXIS 5131 (N.D. Okla., Mar. 19, 2004).

37. *Alexander v. State of Oklahoma*, 382 F.3d 1206 (10th Cir. 2004) at 1220 (holding that "[t]he Tulsa Race Riot represents a tragic chapter in our collective history. While we have found no legal avenue exists through which Plaintiffs can bring their claims, we take no great comfort in that conclusion.").

38. *Id.*

39. *Id.* at 1159–65.

40. *Alexander v. Oklahoma*, 2005 U.S. LEXIS 4132 (U.S., May 16, 2005).

41. Petition available at http://www.alldeliberatespeed.com/OASTulsaPetition. pdf (October 7, 2007).

42. "Brazilian Donation Gives Start to New OAS Office on Rights of Afro Descendants in Americas," Organization of American States, March 1, 2005, at http://www.oas.org/oaspage/press_releases/press_release.asp?sCodigo=#-035/05 (May 6, 2008).

43. H.R. 1995, Tulsa–Greenwood Race Riot Claims Accountability Act of 2007, at http://thomas.loc.gov/cgi-bin/query/z?c110:H. R.1995 (October 7, 2007).

44. During the April 24, 2007, hearing on the Tulsa race riots before the House Committee on the Judiciary, Congressman Mike Pence, a Republican from Indiana, asked: "[A]s we think in this legislation about extending the statute of

limitation, which is not without precedent, [but] would be highly unusual to do, or, as some have suggested, whether a specific relief bill would be more appropriate in this case?" "Tulsa-Greenwood Race Riot Claims Accountability Act of 2007 Hearing before the Subcommittee on the Constitution, Civil Rights, and Civil Liberties of the Committee on the Judiciary House of Representatives," 110th Congress, April 24, 2007, at http://judiciary.house.gov/media/pdfs/printers/110th/34924.pdf (October 10, 2007), 57.

45. A good introduction is Ralph Ellison, *The Collected Essays of Ralph Ellison* (New York: Modern Library, 1995). See also Lawrence Patrick Jackson, *Ralph Ellison: Emergence of Genius* (New York: Wiley, 2002).

46. Gunnar Myrdal, *An American Dilemma: The Negro Problem and Modern Democracy* (New Brunswick: Transaction, 1995).

47. Ralph Ellison, "An American Dilemma: A Review," in Ralph Ellison, *The Collected Essays of Ralph Ellison* (New York: Modern Library, 1995),328–39.

48. Ralph Ellison, "Remembering Jimmy," in Ralph Ellison, *The Collected Essays of Ralph Ellison* (New York: Modern Library, 1995), 273–74.

49. To learn more about Ellison's critique of the law and its burdens on the Invisible Man, see, for example, Alfred Brophy, "Foreword: Ralph Ellison and the Law," *Oklahoma City University Law Review* 26 (2001): 823.

50. Ibid.

51. Ellison wrote extensively in his prose and fiction about the actions of "laws" in this sense. For an overview, see ibid.

52. "Tulsa Race Riot Jury Indicts Police Chief," *New York Times,* June 26, 1921.

53. "Thirty Whites Held for Tulsa Rioting," *New York Times,* June 5, 1921.

54. Ellsworth writes in *Death in a Promised Land:* "The twenty-seven cases that the grand jury initiated too ended for the most part in inaction. . . . Court records reveal that twenty of these cases were definitely dismissed, at least eighteen of them by the motion of the county attorney. . . . Five of the remaining six seem to never have gotten off the ground because the bench warrants which were issued were never served. The final case was also probably dismissed, or simply allowed to die" (97). The twenty-seventh case was that of Dick Rowland's assault on Sarah Page, which was dismissed when Page refused to press charges.

55. Ellsworth, *Death in a Promised Land,* 85–89. Ellsworth quotes the mayor of Tulsa in 1921: "Let the negro settlement be placed farther to the north and east. . . . A large portion of this district [Greenwood] is well suited for industrial purposes rather than for residences" (85). To these ends, the city passed an ordinance requiring that any buildings being rebuilt in the burned area of Greenwood had to be "fireproof," thus barring many African Americans from the possibility of reconstruction because of the prohibitive cost. It was Buck Colbert Franklin who filed the lawsuit that resulted in the overturning of this ordinance.

56. In his testimony before the House Committee on the Judiciary at the

April 24, 2007, hearing, Alfred Brophy eloquently stated: "What I think is so critical is that there are people still alive who suffered the harm. . . . Oftentimes when the subject of reparations, for example, for slavery comes up, people say, 'Well, nobody is still alive who was enslaved.' What is so critical here . . . [is] that direct living connection. We have the ability, I think, to restore something of that dreamland that existed for folks who made their way against the tide in Greenwood. And I hope, either through this legislation or just direct remedial legislation, [we] will do that." "Tulsa-Greenwood Race Riot Claims Accountability Act of 2007 Hearing," 58.

57. Ralph Ellison, "Notes on Juneteenth," quoted inBrophy, "Foreword: Ralph Ellison and the Law," 824–25.

Chapter 3

||||||||||||||||||||||||||||||||||||||||||||||||||

Margins of Error

Robert Weisberg

Is the legal system responsible for miscarriages of justice? The question is odd and full of ambiguities, and that is why I pose it at the start. I would not aspire to take on the great, grand questions about the relationship between positive law or legal institutions on the one hand and justice on the other. But I do want to explore the problem of when and how the institutions we lump under the term "legal system" view themselves in regard to the occurrence of incorrect legal outcomes in criminal cases. If the legal system acknowledges legal *mistakes,* how does it understand their significance in regard to the more heavily fraught notion of *injustice*? In particular, I consider the especially rich ambiguities in the term "responsible" —implying such things as causality, blameworthiness, obligation or aspiration, and remedy. And I do so by examining a set of legal rules not normally associated with such big questions but which, I suggest, lead us to some possible answers. Let me reframe things in terms of recent events.

In a much publicized and controversial 2002 study, James Liebman and colleagues at Columbia Law School reported that almost 70 percent of modern death penalty sentences handed down between 1973 and 1995 were overturned on direct appeal or habeas corpus review for serious legal errors.[1] This study struck many as confirming the incurable injustice of our capital punishment system.[2] This study struck others as deeply flawed. In the view of critics, the Liebman study either lacked technical methodological rigor[3] or exaggerated the significance of the reversals, since many sentences were restored after retrial and no actual case of execution of an innocent person was reported.[4] But perhaps the most interesting debate the study spawned was about what Liebman's findings, if accurate, signified to us about the relationship between legal error and injustice. Some critics insisted that the apparent incidence of legal error was misleading, because the number of legal errors is a function of the number of legal rules. Hence, they argued, it was the very extension of greater due process rights to capital defendants in the constitutional decisions of the 1970s that produced the possibility of legal error in the first place.[5] By this view, in a sense, the legal system "created" more error by virtue of being more just. As a corollary, some argued that the high percentage of reversals decried by Liebman actually portrays a self-critical system that reassuringly diagnoses legal error as a means of preventing or curing unjust outcomes.[6]

Thus, underlying the pro-con passions about the Liebman report are very foundational questions about the relationship between the legal system and injustice: Should the legal system "get credit" for preventing injustice by reversing erroneous convictions or sentences? Is a reversed trial court judgment inherently an injustice at the moment it happens, regardless of the ultimate redress the appellant wins? Is an appellate reversal a cure for an infection of injustice from outside the legal system, such as the prejudice or irrationality of witnesses or jurors? Or is it a mechanical adjustment for technical error that is itself just a product of the system's technical definition of a right? Are state courts an independent sphere of law, so that federal habeas corpus reversal of a state judgment is an exogenous cure for injustice? Or is the federal review part of a larger self-correcting system? And thus the debate reveals that where and how often one sees justice miscarrying may depend on how one draws the relative boundaries of justice and institutional law.

For another perspective on this "boundary dispute" between law and justice, consider the drama of exoneration. Highly publicized exonerations, especially if the exoneree has served a long sentence, lead us to complex and conflicting reactions: we rejoice that a grave moral imbalance has been adjusted, we lament the unredeemable loss of years of life, and we may applaud those whose toil and dedication have overcome injustice. But whether this exoneration should lead us to celebrate that the legal system has finally worked—that is a very complicated question. Indeed, the exoneration may strike us as merely confirming the failure of our institutions of justice, not just because the redress has been delayed but, more important, because so often the saving forces have come from outside the justice system and therefore serve to embarrass it. Most obviously this occurs when unassailable DNA evidence categorically exonerates a convicted prisoner. These cases, of course, often involve lawyers using statutory postconviction protocols, and courts and prosecutors often arrange formal motions of dismissal. But the public image is often that of justice corrected—or condemned—by some combination of extralegal factual investigation and science.[7]

DNA, of course, presents a very special case of the relationship between what is inside and outside law. Consider, for example, what would happen if, some time after a conviction, a prosecution witness took and failed a lie detector test. Even were the legal system to permit the polygraph report, it could absorb it into the overall package of evidence before the decisionmaker, because the polygraph can make no claim of drastically altering the accuracy of the decision. The polygraph would not threaten or embarrass the law with correction, because its own margin of error is not very different from the legal system's sense of its own inherent margin of error. By contrast, DNA's potential for absolute certainty may force the justice system to accommodate it as a superior tool for truth telling. Indeed, it is so superior that it threatens our rules of finality and procedural rigor, because those rules are themselves contingent on our skepticism about accuracy within the legal system. By virtue of this very power, DNA "offers" to make law better than law normally is. But the law can accept this offer only if it can accommodate this superior accuracy without sacrificing other things that the legal system thinks are inherent in, indeed constitutive of, the legal system itself.

So is DNA an offer the legal system cannot refuse? Perhaps so, but early in the DNA revolution, in 1993, the Supreme Court tried hard to refuse it, or at least to delay accepting it. In the famously troubled case of *Herrera v. Collins,* the Court nervously allowed for the possibility that a perfectly accurate exonerating test in a capital case might force it to constitutionally preempt otherwise legitimate rules of finality.[8] There, a state court inmate did not plead some conventional legal error at trial but insisted that newly discovered evidence proved him wholly innocent. The Court ruled that, as a general matter, such a "freestanding" claim of actual innocence does not merit habeas relief; however, the Court did ambivalently allow that a perfectly accurate exonerating case (Herrera's apparently was not) might force it to preempt legitimate rules of finality.[9] But so far it has avoided taking, or not been forced to take, that step.

Yet another recent example of how this "boundary dispute" complicates our understanding of miscarriages of justice involves executive clemency. Clemency has always been a problem for jurisprudence. If we trace its roots to a royal theory of divine grace, it looks like a deus ex machina, nullifying the institutions of law. But if we look at it as a venerable legal power of the executive branch, it appears to fit more comfortably within law. The nature and justification of clemency became a highly public topic in 2003 because of the very politically controversial action of Illinois Governor George Ryan in commuting all death sentences in Illinois. Some applauded the commutations as a noble, if extralegal, act of moral authority redeeming the whole justice legal system from its failures. Others decried it as a reckless coup d'état against all principles of law itself.[10]

The discussion over clemency has reached a very abstract philosophical level. In the 1990s, legal academia saw a revival of interest in working out coherent principles of retributive justice.[11] And as a corollary to that development in jurisprudence, recently academics have been debating anew whether executive clemency is part of justice or something outside it—or, somewhat more precisely, whether mercy is part of the retributivism that grounds our system of justice or part of some philosophical principle external to jurisprudence.[12] The dominant view has been that clemency or mercy breaks the logical retributive link between crime and deserved punishment.[13] But some academics have found the philosophical question an agonizing one, struggling over how to reconcile clemency with the rule of law in modern America and over whether the claims of victims of crime pose an insuperable threat to any harmonization of law and clemency.[14]

Meanwhile, an alternative view holds that if we do not view retribution as merely revenge or retaliation, clemency turns out to have a legally legitimating pedigree, either as the part of the "equity" side of Anglo-American law-equity pairing or, more broadly, as a component of democratic responsibility and accountability. By that view, clemency is built into our legal institutions, representing one of many checks and balances, and sensibly designed like jury nullification or prosecutorial discretion as a necessary safety valve in a larger governmental scheme of self-adjustment.[15] As a corollary, drawing the boundary between justice and such other values as mercy often works within the structure of institutions and along the dimension of separation of powers, though even in this sense it may raise large philosophical questions. Thus, we see legislatures acknowledging past wrongful convictions by engaging in apology and atonement, even though these expressive actions, like mercy, are usually performed retroactively by court or executive.[16] And still another perspective, that of the burgeoning restorative justice movement, relies on a communal model of justice that is completely different from classic retributivism. It uses that model as the very basis of its official legal regime, and so that regime much more comfortably accommodates sentiments of mercy and acts of clemency.[17]

Thus, the debates over the death penalty and the recent spate of official exonerations have provoked deep inquiry into who or what is responsible for the causes or cures of these grave legal mistakes. These questions force us to define what factors we view as exogenous to, and therefore unavoidable or uncontrollable by, our legal system, even if these mistake-producing forces sometimes manifest themselves symptomatically within the system and thereby seem to constitute "miscarriage of justice." And I suggest that one way of examining these issues is to turn away from the high drama of exonerations to ponder a set of extremely technical legal rules that fall under the rubric of the "harmless error doctrine." Under this rubric, a reviewing court agrees with a defendant's claim of legal error at trial but then must ask whether that error so materially undermined the fairness of the trial as to require reversal. "Harmless error" rules play a considerable role in criminal law. Indeed, when the California Supreme Court went from a virtual always-reverse pattern to a virtual always-affirm pattern in death penalty appeals two decades ago, the change manifested itself as a set of harmless error rules more than as a set of changes in underlying legal doctrines.[18]

Just what metric or standard we use to tell whether the error has invalidated the trial court outcome—that is what this surprisingly complex area of law is all about. I suggest that as dryly technical as the harmless error doctrine appears, it may give us some new revealing clues as to how the legal system distinguishes what lies within itself and its powers of self-redress and what lies without. More bluntly, it shows us how the legal system anticipates or responds to charges that it is to blame for miscarriages of justice. In this foray, I generally stay within the conventionally defined legal boundaries of harmless error doctrine. But I necessarily slide around a bit. At times, I look at situations where the state's response to a claim of harmful error is to deny that there was error in the first place. At times, I consider situations not formally denominated harmless error at all but where the state's response to a claim of miscarried justice nevertheless sounds remarkably like "yes, error indeed, but harmless." And at times, I look at situations where the legal system admits both error and serious harm but disclaims any power to offer redress.

I. *The Territory of Harmless Error*

"Harmless error" is so complex and varied a category of legal doctrines that I must take a few brief but incrementally more detailed tries at taxonomy. To begin, of course, we need a very rough cut at how we define "error" in the first place. I first put aside cases where the error can be. traced to egregiously dishonest actions of particular officials who know that their actions target an innocent defendant or are at least reckless as to that possibility. This category—let us call it "malevolent error"—might include, for example, police officers or prosecutors who commit or suborn perjury or destroy evidence they know to be truthfully exculpatory. Sometimes we blame the legal system for these actions—sometimes by virtue of legal doctrines of vicarious or supervisory responsibility, and sometimes as a matter of expressive moral symbolism. But however such questions of agency are conceived, we readily expect the legal system to use its mechanisms to correct these miscarriages. We expect it to use some combination of exoneration of the innocent and civil or criminal sanction of the villainous official, the latter to offer some retributive justice to the defendant but also to deter similar future misconduct.

Of course, my exclusion of malevolent errors is inexact: some "errors" treated under the conventions of harmless error doctrine are actions taken in bad faith by officials who know they are breaking the law but who may actually believe the defendant is guilty. And some "errors" by their very definition at least ambiguously imply bad faith by the state. For example, if a prosecutor's failure to disclose exculpatory evidence violates the due process rule of *Brady v. Maryland,*[19] the prosecutor may have trouble convincing us that the violation was merely accidental. Moreover, as in its treatment of truly malevolent errors, the appellate court's purpose in offering redress to the defendants is in part to deter future error.[20] But whatever the cure for legal villainy, the question of whether and when and how the legal system expresses regret and offers redress to the wronged defendant for what we can comfortably call "error", that is a more complicated matter—legally, ethically, culturally—and that is my concern here.

I focus on nonmalevolent errors as defined by constitutional and statutory rules of procedure. These are the rules governing police investigation (especially searches and seizures, interrogations, and lineups)[21] and practices at trial (versions of the right to counsel, discovery, jury selection, joinder and severance, plea bargaining regulations, reasonable doubt and more specific jury instructions, etc.). These rules can be conceived as prophylactics recognizing some potential for design flaws in the processes of prosecution, flaws that risk mistakes falling outside a reasonable margin of error. Of course, since these rules are enforceable by appellate judges, they can (to recur to the debate over the Liebman study discussed above) be viewed as design *virtues,* at least in the secondary sense of internal corrections for unavoidable design flaws.

Warning: Since I want to imagine how the legal system might be thought to respond to an individual putatively suffering a miscarriage of justice, I exercise a bit of rhetorical license here (I would not dignify it with the term "literary"). I occasionally insert a very contrived dialog between a series of hypothetical aggrieved individuals ("D" for defendant) who will episodically exhibit some knowledge of law, and a monolithic voice somewhat crudely representing the "legal system" ("LS"). So as I go through the varieties of harmless error doctrine in more detail, I try to imagine how the state answers the defendant who rightly or concededly says that he is the victim of error by the legal system. To telegraph a few of my main themes:

Sometimes the state's answer will be:

LS: You have not really suffered injustice in any important sense—you have simply misunderstood what justice is by exaggerating the significance of the personal harm the error has caused you.

When the legal system denies injustice in this way, it often does so because the harm was something short of a conviction in the first place. Or it may be because the harm was not the categorical wrongfulness of the conviction in a binary choice between conviction and acquittal but, rather, a choice of a sentence along a continuum of possible sanctions where that placement is necessarily somewhat arbitrary, so that the claim of error, much less injustice, is misguided.

Sometimes the answer will be:

LS: You may indeed have suffered something that, understandably, subjectively feels like a serious injustice. Were we all omniscient, we might well objectively agree this was injustice. But we cannot take your word for it that you are innocent, and we simply cannot perfect the accuracy-producing machinery of legal system. Therefore, we cannot afford to take the risk that you are indeed guilty. And we have to expect you to bear the risk of error, just as in a myriad nonlegal ways we ask you to accept the risk of undeserved harm in the name of greater social goods, ranging from efficient highway and bridge-building to optimal regulation of food and drugs.

And sometime the answer will be:

LS: Doubtless you have suffered an undeserved harm that the broad ethical principles of our jurisprudence may condemn. But the fault lies outside our power to correct or prevent. True, the legal system was the instrument that carried out that harm. But as it is not the predicate cause, so it cannot be the ultimate cure.

II. The Legal Terrain

A. Error Denied

Now to examine the formal legal rules that constitute harmless error doctrine, we can first elaborate the category in which the legal system, at least by its vocabulary, insists on denying error or finesses the question of error by insisting on some subtlety and flexibility in the definition of error.

D1: I was arrested but then I was released. The police now admit they had the wrong person. Was this not a miscarriage of justice?

LS: There was a mistake but no injustice. Our system makes proof beyond a reasonable doubt the standard at trial, because it believes that the central form of injustice to be avoided is an erroneous conviction. You were never convicted. If you feel abused by the system, that is because (a) the custody itself was unpleasant, or (b) you felt stigmatized by the arrest. We should do all we can to address the former, and you can be able sue if the arresting officers physically or even psychologically abused you. But your innocence in fact does not make custody based on probable cause unjust.[22] As for the latter, we can only cure injustices in the judicial system, not the social system (though we try to mitigate the problem with certain measures to keep the record from becoming too public). Within the realm of law, your case shows that the system worked. To the laity, cases like yours may sound in injustice once any human causal agent is identified in a published narrative of "exoneration" (if the term can be used for revelation of innocence solely after incorrect arrest). But our lawyers, who are more sophisticated, know that the imperfection of human institutions requires us to allow for a margin of "just error."

Actually, if we look at the broader goals of police action, this does not even look like a mistake at all. Admit it: you yourself would feel less safe in a world where more than probable cause is necessary for arrest, because you would not be able to persuade the police to arrest someone you plausibly think has committed a crime against you. The police would just be too risk-averse. In that regard, to borrow from the vocabulary of the criminal law, not only was your arrest *excused*, it was even *justified*. So we ask you to engage in an exercise by imagining yourself as a crime *victim*.

D2: It is one thing if, as you say, you disclaim any responsibility for relieving me of stigma from an arrest. It is quite another thing if, as happened in my case, you explicitly take up that responsibility. I was arrested for a petty misdemeanor; it got knocked down to a minor violation. Later I went through the formal procedure for expungement, and expungement was ordered. I was about to be hired for a wonderful new job. But then the employer called some company called ChoicePoint to do a background check on me. But the arrest showed up. In fact, it showed up as a conviction. I lost the job.[23]

LS: This is regrettable. In fact, now we are beginning to regret ever promising to expunge, because we have thereby created unrealistic expectations.[24] No one anticipated that records that used to be held only in paper form by government agencies are now getting digitized and sold in bulk to the private sector. Commercial databases now contain many many millions of criminal records, and these records are often out of date and even flat-out wrong. Apparently, the problem has increased since September 11. In any event, we suggest you consider suing your employer. Or ask your employer to sue Choice-Point. Or sue ChoicePoint yourself.

D2: But this is *your* fault. And these lawsuits you suggest are within realm of the legal system you represent, so why not take care of the problem through a unitary form of redress?

LS: Our problem is this: We cannot keep what happens in the legal system confidential. Nor should we, given the democratic value of transparency. Of course, as government officials we can control what formal collateral consequences follow from conviction—that is why, for example, we are facing debates over felon voter disenfranchisement. But we cannot prevent the wider social effects of perceptions and misperceptions of what happens in the system, unjust as they seem. The world of civil lawsuits to which we are sending you is only partly within the realm of legal institutions and rules. If you sue in tort, or even under certain employment statutes, the litigation standard often will depend on customary values that law itself does not prescribe. And even if we figured out a rule that ensured your job, there would still be a painful social effect of your arrest that lies in the hearts of people, not in the real of legal regulation.

D3: I was indicted by a grand jury. The prosecutor flagrantly violated rules of grand jury procedure. She allowed two government witnesses in the grand jury room at the same time so they could hear each other's testimony. She allowed extraneous information to get to the grand jurors. She even misinstructed the grand jury about the law.

LS: Well, what then happened to you? Maybe the trial judge should have granted your motion to quash the indictment. But she didn't, and the jury convicted you. And you do not seem to have any good objections to the trial itself. So there is no injustice to complain about, because your conviction beyond a reasonable doubt surely moots any complaint that there wasn't even probable cause.[25] If the motion to quash had been granted, then you would have gotten a fresh start. Of course, I suppose in that case, if you had not been reindicted, you would have complained about the stigma of the original charge. But, again, we cannot control the wider social misperceptions of how the system works. Maybe an indictment is a death knell for a big business enterprise—that is what the people at Arthur Andersen say—but for an individual, it is simply a necessary risk of the system.

D3: But some other poor fellow was indicted by a grand jury whose members were selected in a racially discriminatory manner. The trial judge refused to drop the indictment. This fellow then got convicted and he appealed, and he got his conviction reversed even though the grand jury issue was his only claim.[26]

LS: Yes, an exception is made for *that* kind of legal error involving a grand jury. Exclusion of potential grand jurors on the basis of race "is practically a brand upon them, affixed by the law, an assertion of their inferiority, and a stimulant to that race prejudice which is an impediment to securing to individuals of the race that equal justice which the law aims to secure to all others."[27] It strikes at our fundamental values, not just of our judicial system but of our whole society as well. "It is a grave constitutional trespass, possible only under color of state authority, and wholly within the power of the State to prevent."[28] So for over a century we have believed in only one effective remedy for this grave illegality. Reversing the conviction "is not disproportionate to the evil that it seeks to deter. If grand jury discrimination becomes a thing of the past, no conviction will ever again be lost on account of it."[29] After all, the harm was not only to the wrongly indicted individual but to society as a whole, and "to the jury system, to the law as an institution, to the community at large, and to the democratic ideal reflected in the processes of our courts."[30]

D3: Let me understand this. You have in this instance defined the harm to be the wider effect of a constitutional error, way beyond the harm to the indicted person at trial. So you are acknowledging that the legal system takes account of these wider effects. Well, wider effects result from a lot of other legal errors, including those from the undeserved stigma of an illegally obtained indictment. And they, too, are within the power of the state to prevent through reversal of convictions.

LS: Not quite: Our concern with discrimination in grand jury selection also derives from our concern with the harm of the indictment itself.

The grand jury does not only determine only that probable cause exists to believe that a defendant committed a crime, or that it does not. In the hands of the grand jury lies the power to charge a greater offense or a lesser offense; numerous counts or a single count; and perhaps most significant of all, a capital offense or a noncapital offense—all on the basis of the same facts.[31]

Indeed, "[t]he grand jury is not bound to indict in every case where a conviction can be obtained." So this illicitly selected grand jury may indeed have harmed the proceedings that follow. We must adhere to the rule of mandatory reversal, because "we simply cannot know that the need to indict would have been assessed in the same way by a grand jury properly constituted."[32]

D3: Well, that is fine, but that reasoning applies to the kinds of errors I suffered at the grand jury as well. So what is the rule here? Is "harmfulness" a matter of effect on a conviction or a matter of wider social effects?

LS: You naively ask for a simple answer to a complex question. We weigh many different factors in defining harmful errors, and our doctrines cannot be captured in any single principle.

B. Calibrations of Harm

Now we enter the central legal territory of harmless error, where the Supreme Court has laid out a long and complicated manual of rules for appellate courts to follow. I give a quick picture of the terrain and then map it in some detail.

We can start with the category of acknowledged but at least theoretically redressable errors. And we might begin by noting, and then putting aside, a category we could call "super-redressable error." This is the type of error that requires a reviewing court to order unconditional dismissal without possibility of retrial. One example would be the rare reversal of a conviction on the ground that the statute supporting the charge is categorically unconstitutional (though a trial for the same act under a different statute might be possible). A more mundane, though equally decisive, one would be a reversal on the ground that the charge fell outside the statute of limitations or, in some circumstances, the requirements of a speedy trial.[33] Finally, there is double jeopardy, where the reviewing court holds that the challenged trial should never have taken place. The reason can be that an earlier trial for the same crime came to final judgment,[34] or that in the earlier trial, the court wrongly declared a mistrial, where the mistrial was traceable to prosecutorial misconduct or where "manifest necessity" was lacking.[35]

But almost all legal errors in our system now permit the possibility of retrial with the error corrected. All the complexity concerns what, if anything, the defendant must prove after convincing the appellate court that legal error indeed occurred below. One possibility, of course, at least for errors of constitutional magnitude, would be no further proof at all—that is, a rule of automatic reversal. But nothing so simple has emerged.

The older, pre–Warren Court history of harmless error is itself extremely convoluted, and I sketch it only quickly here. For much of our legal history, we followed the "Exchequer Rule" whereby trial error in the form of wrongful admission of evidence always required reversal.[36] We do not know quite how rigorously the Exchequer Rule was enforced or whether it had the paradoxical effect of discouraging appellate courts from even finding error. By early in the last century, states started passing laws requiring some proof of harmfulness of error—employing a variety of doctrines described below—while automatic reversal seemed to remain the norm for errors of constitutional magnitude. The formulation of such early harmless error rules varied tremendously, but the general federal doctrine captured by *Kotteakos v. United States* might serve as rough average. There, in determining whether an acknowledged misinstruction on a conspiracy charge required reversal, the Supreme Court said:

> If, when all is said and done, the conviction is sure that the error did not influence the jury, or had but very slight effect, the verdict and the judgment should stand, except perhaps where the departure is from a constitutional norm or a specific command of Congress. But if one cannot say, with fair assurance, after pondering all that happened without stripping the erroneous action from the whole, that the judgment was not substantially swayed by the error, it is impossible to conclude that substantial rights were not affected.[37]

Kotteakos remains important as a kind of default standard, a fair proxy for the harmless error rules applied in state and federal courts where the newer constitutional rules (discussed below) do not apply. But it is also thematically important because it captures the weird hyperfastidiousness of harmless error rules generally. *Kotteakos* seems to say:

LS: Even if we choose not to reverse your conviction, notice how obsessively careful we are in respecting your rights as well as the interests of justice more generally. Indeed, you are benefiting from the kind of scrutiny of your verdict that Henry James gave to every tiny social interaction in his novels—as illustrated by our use of thoroughly Jamesian prose, full of passive-voice, double-negative delicacy.

The error in *Kotteakos* was about a misunderstanding of the common law of conspiracy, and, as the Court noted, it involved neither a constitutional rule nor a precise legislative command. As the Warren Court proliferated new rights of criminal defendants under constitutional law, some instances of automatic reversal did arise. Most notably, the category includes such fundamentals as the Sixth Amendment right to counsel under *Gideon v. Wainwright*[38] and to a trial by jury under *Duncan v. Louisiana*.[39] Just how obvious it is that these rights must be put into this category depends on the rationale we choose for defining the category—as discussed below. For now, let us be cautious about assuming that the rationale for the placement is that it is simply too hard to determine how much the violation of one of these rights harmed the defendant. That rationale, though perhaps reasonable, does not have deep roots, because the predecessor case to *Gideon* in fact acknowledged that there was a right to counsel but insisted that the denial of this right was often harmless because of particular circumstances.[40]

So why should not all constitutional errors lead to automatic reversal? The Court did not take that approach, perhaps in part because of a kind of hydraulic equilibrium in the system: the fear that the strong remedy of automatic reversal might induce appellate courts to disingenuously find no error in the first place. But the Court did pick up the hint from *Kotteakos* that the standard for constitutionally harmless error should be a searching one. Hence the rule of *Chapman v. California*.[41]

In *Chapman*, where the prosecutor violated the Fifth Amendment by allowing the prosecutor to comment on the defendant's failure to testify, the Court held that the standard on appeal was that the state had to prove harmlessness beyond a reasonable doubt. This seems a very generous rule for the defendant. And in terms of the larger theme of the relationship between legal error and miscarriage of justice, *Chapman*, an appeal from a state court, is even more striking: by holding that the question of harmless error is part of the federal question, the Court suggests that the necessity of self-correction of injustice was in a sense part of the very definition of constitutional justice.

Now *Chapman* is hardly the end of the story. As discussed below, there are softer versions of harmless error in such areas as the defendant's due process right to discovery of exculpatory evidence and her Sixth Amendment right of effective assistance of counsel. And softer still are the rules that apply on federal habeas corpus review of state convictions. These gravitate toward the opposite extreme from double jeopardy—the principle suggested (ambiguously) in *Herrera* that even a powerful claim of actual innocence by itself might not warrant habeas review. But *Chapman* itself is critical in understanding the larger phenomenon of harmless error. Although *Chapman* seems very generous in setting a higher-than-*Kotteakos* standard for constitutional error, we have to be careful of what it actually says:

D4: So if I can induce any reasonable doubt whatsoever that the jury would have convicted once unbenighted, then I get a retrial for sure?

LS: Well, just to be safe, let us read *Chapman* precisely:

> There is little, if any difference between our statement in *Fahy v. Connecticut*[42] about "whether there is a reasonable probability that the evidence complained of might have contributed to the conviction" and requiring the beneficiary of a constitutional error to prove beyond a reasonable doubt that the error complained of did not contribute to the verdict obtained. We, therefore, do no more than adhere to the meaning of the *Fahy* case when we hold, as we do now, that before a federal constitutional error can be held harmless, the court must be able to declare a belief that it was harmless beyond a reasonable doubt.[43]

D4: Now doesn't that sound like, having proved an error, I have to bear some burden—to show some reasonable probability that the error was harmful? That does not sound like a reasonable doubt standard imposed on the prosecutor like the one at trial. At trial, I wasn't asked to prove any reasonable probability of anything.

How to parse these nuances, and how significant they are—these are matters I return to shortly.

Meanwhile, automatic reversal remains the standard for some errors, but the cases represent quite a medley. Some, like *Gideon* errors, are so symbolically powerful as to lie outside technical analysis. Others have fallen under the powerful but vague rationale that they are similarly "structural." These include denial of the right to public trial,[44] failure to ensure an impartial jury in a capital case,[45] and appointment of an interested party's attorney as prosecutor for contempt charges.[46] Clearly, in all of these cases, the defendant might be told he is the beneficiary of a rule designed to serve some broader institutional purpose, such as the "integrity of the process" or the public perception of fairness of the overall system. But as discussed with grand jury errors, above, sometimes the emphasis subtly shifts toward a case-specific empirical problem.

Thus, when the error is a trial judge's bias, "his actual motivations are hidden from review, and we must presume that the process was impaired."[47] And when a trial jury has been exposed to prejudicial publicity or is selected by improper criteria, "we have required reversal of the conviction because the effect of the violation cannot be ascertained."[48] That last category of jury selection has increased in salience since *Batson v. Kentucky* declared it unconstitutional for a prosecutor to exercise a peremptory challenge for a racially motivated purpose.[49] Even a single peremptory challenge, if the proof of purposeful discrimination is there, violates the equal protection clause. So an appellate conclusion of even a single instance of a *Batson* violation that the trial judge failed to correct —that must lead to reversal.[50] Of course, for all we know, those who decided this nervously worried that the balance would be restruck by appellate reluctance to find the error.

One kind of error is undeniably wholly peculiar because the right it attaches to is wholly peculiar—the *Faretta* right of self-representation.[51] The error of denying a defendant's request to self-represent might be described either as structural (in the sense that it clearly permeates the whole trial) or simply empirically troublesome (because it is hard to say what harm it does). But the real reason is that, in fact, courts are quite confident they know what harm a *Faretta* violation does to the defendant's chance of acquittal—namely, none whatsoever—but the self-representation right stands on such other professed grounds as the "autonomy" of the defendant.

To pursue some of the nuances in the distinctions between automatic and conditional reversal, let us imagine them in the context of the pivotal modern case:

D5: Well, here we are in 1991, and I have proved to the state court's satisfaction that a confession was coerced from me. This was a flagrant violation of due process of law—no technical *Miranda* stuff here[52] —and *Chapman* cited this as a prime example of automatic reversal. Correct?

LS: Well, we have now decided, in *Arizona v. Fulminante*,[53] that even a coerced confession is subject to harmless error. *Chapman* does not mean what it seems to say. Oh, it referred to some older cases indicating what you suggest, but these cases were relegated to a footnote, and, in our view, this citation "is more appropriately regarded as a historical reference.'"[54]

D5: Well, I guess the Supreme Court is as infallible as it cares to be if it can just twist what it said before. But how about a little logic? Surely, the pattern for distinguishing automatic reversal from harmless error cases, if it is to make any sense, would put coerced confessions on the automatic reversal side.

LS: Well, no. Most of those automatic reversal categories involve "structural" rights. They deal with matters preceding the presentation of evidence and pervading the whole process. However bad a coerced confession is, it is an evidentiary matter—something about what information gets to the jury. That is the distinction.[55]

D5: Would you still rule that way if the confession had come from a rubber hose beating?[56] Besides, some of the established cases that are already put on the harmless error side of the line—such as bad prosecutorial argument or instruction—these have nothing do with bad evidence. So the rationale isn't even symmetrical.

LS: Well, all right then, the real rationale is what might be called "durational." We ask whether the error occured during the presentation of the case to the jury.[57] That covers coerced confessions and other matters subject to *Chapman,* like lawyer arguments and instructions. It does not cover *Gideon* rights and all those other structural ones.

D5: When does the "duration" start? The voir dire? And when does it stop or get interrupted? What happens if a juror is bribed when court is not in session?[58]

LS: It all comes down to gradations of miscarriage of justice. *Gideon* is virtually a theological right in our criminal justice system. The same may be true of public trial rights. The other "structural" ones are just unavoidable matters of *stare decisis,* plus a few odd ones like *Faretta.*

Besides, we must admit, it turns out that the good thing about using the theological status of *Gideon* as our benchmark is precisely that there are virtually no more *Gideon* errors now anyway. Aside from a few small technical cases involving low-level punishments,[59] no judge ever commits *Gideon* error. *Gideon* tells us when there has been a categorical absence of justice. You can be cynical and call this a great bargain for the state—an opportunity for profound expressive symbolism at no new incremental cost. Or you can view this expressive symbolism more idealistically, as a way of reinforcing profound values in our system. Apply automatic reversal too often and you dilute those values. So you should stop looking to *Gideon* as a model. Coerced confessions, like other bad things that happen during the course of prosecutions, are only grave miscarriages if they make a difference toward convicting the innocent.

Chapman now applies to the great number of errors, including Fourth Amendment exclusionary rule violations,[60] erroneous admission of defendant's statements because of various Fifth[61] and Sixth Amendment[62] rights or illegitimate lineups violating the Sixth Amendment,[63] confrontation clause errors involving wrongful admission of a nontestifying codefendant's confession,[64] denial of right to be present during trial,[65] a jury instruction involving an illicit presumption,[66] the use of an invalid aggravating factor in a penalty phase,[67] and so on.

But the variations of the harmless error rule are still more nuanced. Whatever distinction one might discern between the *Kotteakos* standard and the *Chapman* standard, there is a different threshold for constitutional discovery errors under *Brady v. Maryland*[68] or ineffectiveness of counsel claims under *Strickland v. Washington.*[69] Those doctrines build a harmful error component directly into the definition of the error and set it at a level roughly described as a "reasonable probability" that without the violation the outcome would have been different. Thus, in the case of *Brady,* the exculpatory information the prosecution must turn over is actually defined as that which, in retrospect, meets the reasonable probability standard. And as for *Strickland,* after finding that the defense lawyer performed below a reasonable level of competence, the reviewing court must also find the level of "prejudice" that is phrased essentially the same as the *Brady* standard. Everyone views this standard as tougher on defendants than *Chapman.* But of course no one has any data, or any reliable method for obtaining data, to determine whether it is indeed tougher or by how much. Trial court decisions are simply not susceptible to the kind of variable-controlling we would need.

D6: I pleaded guilty. I faced a possible sentence of eight years. My lawyer was a fool. He told me the judge would likely give me six years for a gun enhancement, so I cut a deal for four years. But it turns out the enhancement would have given me three years. If I had known that, I would have cut a deal for two years. The court has agreed that this was ineffectiveness of counsel. But it will not give me any relief.

LS: You say that had you been better informed about the sentencing rules, you would have held out for a much better deal. That may be true. But when in applying the constitutional standard for effective assistance of counsel, we apply it differently when the appeal is from a guilty plea. The criterion for prejudice—our special name for harmful error here—is whether with an effective lawyer you would have chosen to go to trial—not that you would have gotten a better deal.[70]

D6: If my lawyer was constitutionally incompetent, how can you dismiss the harm of a wildly excessive sentence?

LS: Well, how do we know for sure what sentence you would have pleaded to if your lawyer had better informed you? More important, who is to say that a sentence is excessive when it is still a sentence you could have gotten had you been convicted? What happens at trial—whether you get convicted or not—implicates fundamental questions of justice. An unjust conviction is a miscarriage of justice. But how much of a sentence you get, at least when it is under the statutory maximum—that cannot be described as right or wrong, much less just or unjust. After all, these sentencing measures are arbitrary. Politicians legislate long maximum sentences, sometimes just for symbolic political gain, and many of them realize that a convicted defendant will get less. Your unfortunate placement along an arbitrary continuum of sentences is not any miscarriage.

D6: But I just read a new case where a lawyer misguided his client about the possible sentence, and the wrongful sentence was held prejudicial enough.[71]

LS: A surprising decision, and maybe it will not stand. But that was about ineffectiveness at trial. What we said about the arbitrary nature of sentencing needs to be underscored when we are talking about the contingencies and unpredictability of guilty pleas. As long as you are not coerced into that plea, you cannot complain that where you show up on the sentencing spectrum is unjust. Who knows what negotiating skills and varieties of human fallibility—moral and intellectual—might go into the bargain? Yes, the sentence is constrained by, and therefore sits under the umbrella of, a legal rule: the maximum sentence. But the outcome is outside the formal rules of law —and therefore outside of justice—because it depends on those human factors outside our control.

D6: Your disavowals are remarkable. You treat legislated sentencing ranges as just arbitrary data points, as if all the legal system does is set a maximum and leave things to chance or these so-called vagaries of human behavior. But the range is itself a legal creation, and all these vagaries are actions not of human behavior in general but of legal actors, especially lawyers in particular.[72] They are part of your world, not the outside world. They are not even like jurors, who supposedly represent the uncontrollable mores of the lay world. These are professionals who operate under the rules you set up, and my lawyer violated a legal standard you yourself have set.

Then there is the still more nuanced distinction between all of the errors described above and the area of attorney conflict. It is close to an absolute truth that if a defendant objects that her lawyer has a conflict of interest—especially because the lawyer represents a codefendant—the trial judge must ensure conflict-free representation. But the Sixth Amendment turns out to be generous even to a defendant who assents to or insists on the possibly conflicted representation and then complains after conviction that the conflict hurt him. But how generous? That is a matter of harmless error.

Under *Cuyler v. Sullivan*,[73] the test in conflict cases offers yet another exquisitely differentiated standard. It is tougher to meet than the clear-cut test of "possible conflict if interest" if the judge tries to *force* counsel on defendant[74]—but easier to meet than *Strickland* prejudice: the defendant must show that the conflict "adversely affected" the outcome. Roughly speaking, the defendant has to identify some clear manifestation in trial strategy or mechanics that the conflict produced, and convince the appellate court that this alteration of tactics or choice of mechanisms may have contributed to the bad outcome. But, if the Court is to be believed, the defendant need not go quite so far as to show a reasonable probability of effect on the outcome.[75]

But we are far from finished with the calibrations.

C. Federalism and Finality

D7: Well, the police coerced a confession from me, and the proof is an explicit decision from the federal courts—the judicial institution most expert in and sensitive to the constitutional rights of criminal defendants. In fact, mine is a habeas corpus case where the federal court explicitly rebuked the state court for failing to recognize this error. So, disappointed as I am that a coerced confession does not lead to automatic reversal, at least I can rely on the *Chapman* standard.

LS: Afraid not. For federal habeas, the best you can hope for is *Kotteakos*

—the standard of a "substantial and injurious effect or influence in determining the jury's verdict."[76] After all, this federal habeas scheme is an extraordinary one. It is a statutory extra protection, an extraordinary remedy whose role is secondary and limited, and special considerations apply. You had a chance for *Chapman*-level review when you pressed your claim in state court. Those courts "are fully qualified to identify constitutional error and are often better situated to evaluate its prejudicial effect on the trial process."[77] As noted in *Brecht v. Abrahamson,* any additional deterrent effect that applying the *Chapman* rule could create pales in comparison with the costs, including the injury to state sovereignty. There would always be

> significant "social costs," including the expenditure of additional time and resources by all of the parties, the "erosion of memory" and the "dispersion of witnesses," and the frustration of society's interest in the prompt administration of justice; and results in retrials that take place much later than those following reversal on direct appeal. . . . [B]ecause the *Kotteakos* standard is grounded in the federal harmless error rule, federal courts may turn to an existing body of case law and, thus, are unlikely to be confused in applying it.[78]

D7: I am losing count of the non sequiturs in that rationalization. First, I understand the general concerns that habeas corpus intervention threatens finality, state autonomy, and so on. That is why, when I filed my habeas petition, I stressed to the federal court how punctilious I was in regard to all those waiver and exhaustion rules and other jurisdictional rules that a habeas petitioner must take care of. The point here is that the federal court has now overcome all these prudential concerns and allowed for the presumptive trust we should have in the state courts' devotion to the constitution. So why should my chance of reversal be lower than it was in the state courts? In fact, it is as if I have suffered a multiple wrong: my confession was coerced, it was admitted at trial, and I had to undergo the indifference or ignorance of a state court and wait until this late appeal to win redress. And by the way, I am impressed by your skill at euphemistic delicacy and evasiveness in your reference to "social costs." I hear from other defendants that you disclaim responsibility for the effects of legal outcomes that manifest themselves outside your self-defined boundaries. Now you seem to measure these costs rather selectively.

LS: You are still treating your claim as having established a constitutional violation and infer therefore that you suffered injustice. Remember, that even under *Chapman,* we are expressing some skepticism that the error made a difference. So please do not speak of the constitutional error as injustice itself. It is a matter of probabilities and prudence and policy, not deontology. If we apply *Chapman,* we might slightly reduce the false positives of harmful error while risking an increase in false negatives. And since most of the action will always remain in state courts, we will be achieving little, if any, effect in inducing the state courts to be more careful. It is not as if reports of your federal reversal would make state court systems much better than they are now.

D7: But why is that *my* problem? I thought harmless error analysis was about identifying injustice in my case, not improving the court system more generally. Am I to suffer injustice because rectifying it might not help others?

D8: At my capital trial, members of the decedent's family sat in the gallery, visible to the jury, wearing buttons with his photograph.[79] This was so prejudicial as to deny me a fair trial. I have cited very relevant Supreme Court cases about jury prejudice—cases involving similar things such as state troopers sitting right near the prosecutor or a defendant being forced to wear jail clothes in court.[80] The state appellate courts said those precedents did not apply to my case. I am sure that is wrong. Finally, I have gotten to federal habeas corpus review. Unlike most petitioners, I did not waive the claim, and I have completed all the procedural requirements. And, in fact, I have no complaint with the *Brecht* harmless error rule applied on habeas. I am willing to prove that the error in my case met that standard.

LS: Things have changed since *Brecht.* In 1996, Congress altered the federal habeas corpus law. Concerned that federal courts had been intruding too much on the state courts, it imposed a new constraint. In the revised habeas corpus law, Congress made clear that it is not sufficient for a petitioner to show that the state court misapplied constitutional law. You have to show that the court *egregiously* violated constitutional law. You have to show that the state court flagrantly contradicted clear Supreme Court precedent or engaged in an egregiously unreasonable application of settled law.[81] So you may indeed have a plausible claim that the buttons in the courtroom violated due process, and were a federal court—indeed, were the Supreme Court —to address that question, you might win. But the federal court should not address that question on federal habeas. Because even if it turns out some day that what the state court did was wrong, what it did was not flagrantly wrong.

D8: So you have come up with a new harmless error rule.

LS: No, this has nothing to do with harmless error, and you should stop invoking that trope. This is just the application of a clear statutory mandate about court jurisdiction.

D8: Oh, I think it is a harmless error rule, because you are saying that a material constitutional error may have occurred at my trial, but that it lies within some constitutional margin of error.

LS: Well if we define the error as a violation of law that was clearly established at the time of the state trial, then it was not even error. You are confusing law and justice with federalism and finality. You are saying that we are allowing the states to misapply the Constitution. Nowhere have we ever said so. Rather, we know how hard it is to read our own precedents, and in the interests of comity and federalism, we must acknowledge that these constitutional issues are matters of probability and uncertainty and efficiency, and this is especially true when you are moving from one realm of justice (the state) to another (the federal).

D8: That may be what the words say, but I stick to my position that this is a harmless error rule, and a most bizarre one. It is one thing to hold that an error in regard to the facts of guilt may be harmless, as a matter of probability and because we cannot fully know the hearts and minds of jurors or the phenomena of nature. But now I am being told that the state court must be forgiven its constitutional trespasses—because it cannot fully know the hearts and minds of the Justices of the Supreme Court. You are allowing the state courts to treat higher federal authority as some unpredictable force of nature.

You engage in this self-division and declare two parts of yourself to be separate realms between which principles of justice do not cross. Worse yet, you engage in the most bizarre form of outward imputation. It is one thing to disavow responsibility for those unpredictable vagaries of juries about evidence or about how human nature assigns stigma. But now you are saying the same thing about judges. Worse yet, you are saying it about the Supreme Court itself—as if the Supreme Court cannot be held responsible for the unforeseeable ways it will change its mind on the meaning of the Constitution.

D9: Now this is going too far. I have an undeniable claim of ineffectiveness and prejudice. It goes like this. I was convicted of felony murder, based on a robbery. Fair enough. But at the penalty phase, the prosecutor charged as an aggravating circumstance that I committed the killing for pecuniary gain.[82] That was double-counting, and it was clearly illegal, because the state court adhered to the clear precedent of a case called *Collins* from the Eighth Circuit.[83]

The problem is that my lawyer was a fool and failed to even mention this precedent to the trial judge. So I got sentenced to death. By the time I convinced the appellate courts that I had been the victim of ineffective assistance of counsel, the *Collins* case had been overruled.[84] But it was good law at the time of the trial. *Strickland* says that prejudice—that harmful error—means that there was a reasonable probability that an effective lawyer would have made a difference. There is no mystery about this here. A minimally effective lawyer would have knocked out that key aggravator. So you have just rewritten the harmless error rule.

LS: But what we really meant in *Strickland* was that you were entitled to a fair shot at a *just* result. Yes, you surely would have knocked out the aggravator, and perhaps would have avoided death. That would have been the "correct" result at the time. But not the *just* result. We know that now. The better outcome you might have won has to be an outcome you were justly entitled to. Call this harmless error doctrine if you wish. The miserable lawyering you suffered caused you no harm.

D9: The law changed. But did justice change? Justice is too big and profound to be captured in any one phase of the vagaries and evolutions of legal doctrine. In retrospect, my victory over the aggravator would have been wrong but hardly unjust. Indeed, it would have been very clearly just because it is surely justice that I be held only to the law at the time of the trial.

LS: Are you saying that you should get a windfall from the luck of timing?

D9: I may have to accept that I am entitled to no more justice than the law allows. But am I entitled to *less* justice than the law allows? Especially when I am relying on the law that certainly applies at the time of my trial, regardless of the vagaries of its future change? And please do not just say that the law never changes—that courts simply discover what it has always meant. That went out the window with the new federal habeas act of 1996. So many other defendants claiming miscarriage of justice are offered the "consolation" that what appears to be miscarriage is just bad luck—because of factors outside the control of the system. Why cannot I benefit from *good* luck when I have it? Indeed, why is this luck and not justice? Especially because the Supreme Court itself has said that ineffectiveness is to be measured at from the moment of the alleged error by the lawyer.[85]

LS: That business about contemporaneous context was about the quality of the performance, not the prejudice. The Court feared that too much hindsight second-guessing about the quality of performance, in light, perhaps, of evolving standards of professionalism, "could dampen the ardor and impair the independence of defense counsel, discourage the acceptance of assigned cases, and undermine the trust between attorney and client."[86]

D9: You are very selective—indeed, whimsical—about who has to suffer for what kind of uncertainties about life and law. Do I not at least deserve some symmetry with the rules of retroactivity? After all, under *Teague v. Lane*,[87] new constitutional rules of criminal procedure cannot be announced on collateral review, lest they then be retroactively applicable to undeserving (and frighteningly numerous) revivable collateral claims by long-term prisoners.

LS: That retroactivity rule was motivated by a respect for the states' interest in the finality of criminal convictions and the recognition that a state should not be penalized for relying on "the constitutional standards that prevailed at the time the original proceedings took place."[88] But as a habeas petitioner, you yourself have no interest in the finality of your state court judgment. Quite the opposite. Nor do you have any claim of reliance on old precedent for your own actions. Please do not try to turn this into an ex post facto claim.

D9: The Supreme Court itself is never sure of where its criminal procedure decisions are headed.

> Changes in the law are characteristic of constitutional adjudication. Prior to 1985, most of those changes were in the direction of increasing the protection afforded an individual accused of crime. Since 1985,

relevant changes in the law often have been in a different direction, affording less rather than more protection to individual defendants.[89]

If supposedly timeless principles of justice and positive Supreme Court law are out of synch, that is not my fault.

LS: It is not a matter of your fault. But you are asking to be the beneficiary of a hypothetical trial court decision that, in retrospect, would have been lawless. Death penalty decisions cannot be based on lawless decisions or arbitrariness, whimsy, or caprice.

D9: That is a remarkably disingenuous invocation of the fear of capricious death penalties. And it is equally disingenuous to call this hypothetical legal-at-the-time trial court decision "lawless."

III. Some Thematic Reflections

In the end, what are we to make of all this? It would be too easily glib and ironic to say that the Supreme Court should be congratulated on its phenomenal verbal—indeed, literary—artistry in fashioning these exquisite nuances of harmless error. It would be easy—too easy—to say that they are not nuances at all but verbal fog-and-smoke disguising an implicit permission for judges to follow their viscera whatever the standard.

A moving response comes from one real state court judge, the Hon. Alfred LeBlanc from Louisiana, who pleads for recognition that judges believe these nuances matter and that they worry—indeed, agonize—over the judicial duty the application of these nuances imposes.[90] His thoughts merit attention. And the state courts are a good place to assess this level of judicial concern, since they have the freedom to be more generous in their own state court appeals than constitutional rules like *Chapman* would require.

Louisiana limits reversal to errors that "affect" the "substantial rights" of the defendant. Judge LeBlanc notes that the term "substantial" only modifies the term "right," so that, one might infer, even a slight error might be reversible, while, conversely, a massive error with respect to some right not itself deemed "substantial" might get ignored. But he notes that in practice the courts have shifted the term "substantial" to modify the violation itself, and, indeed, the state courts have followed *Chapman* for all manner of errors, even though they could use a stingier rule for nonconstitutional errors. He shows that the emphasis is "on the impact of the error rather than the untainted evidence."[91] And, demonstrating even more delicacy in the interest of wronged defendants, Judge LeBlanc recognizes that many believe that the courts "cheat": that they make their own judgment about the defendant's guilt rather than actually reconstructing the jury's decision.

While the philosopher's distinction between the glass half empty and the glass half full may provide subtle commentary about the cognitive role of perspective, it does not alter a shared perception of what the glass contains. Similarly, regardless of whether it is approached from the perspective of the error or the perspective of the "untainted" evidence, the key question in harmless error review is whether, in light of the entire record, the jury relied to some measure on improper evidence in reaching its verdict.[92]

Judge LeBlanc goes on to concede the defense bar's objection that such an analysis does not fully comport with the admonition that the "focus" of harmless error review rests on the error complained of and not on the other evidence of record. But he rightly argues that the *Chapman* standard implicitly assumes a quantitative, and not a qualitative, standard:

> The focus of the *Chapman* standard is upon the error's contribution to the verdict, not upon any quality appurtenant to the error. . . . While Louisiana's State Capitol building may be a breathtaking site upon the alluvial flatlands of the Mississippi, it fades into a meaningless speck against the backdrop of Mount Everest.[93]

Then our judge shows how even the "quantitative" standard is subtly sensitive to experience,

> [i]ncluding the importance of the evidence to the State's case, the presence or absence of additional corroboration of the evidence, and the overall strength of the State's case. . . . Nor does this mean that a reviewing court should attempt to glean the scope of the actual jury's deliberations, for, as any trial judge, prosecutor, or defense attorney can clearly attest, "in the end no judge can know for certain what factors led to the jury's verdict."[94] . . . [I]f a reasonable juror, after considering the error, would find no cause to question his verdict, then the verdict "actually rested upon" the other evidence of record. . . . There is no simple formula or magic incantation that can guide the appellate court's ultimate determination of harmlessness vel non. The key ingredient is an experienced and knowledgeable jurist.[95]

But rest assured that there is an implicitly qualitative aspect to the quantitative, since the court must consider the "impact" of the error and hence the more pervasive or insidious prejudice of some errors in terms of probative effect. Thus, erroneous admission of a defendant's prior crimes requires especially great scrutiny, because "it may corrupt or undermine other properly admitted evidence, or may otherwise alter the dynamics of the trial."[96]

D10: All right then, I am impressed by this sensitivity. But even this fine judge essentially confesses that I as an individual may have to bear the burdens of the cognitive uncertainty of criminal trials. And he expects me to rely on him because he is "an experienced and knowledgeable jurist." I am sure he is, but how does his "experience" bear on my problem, and what is the relevant "knowledge" he possesses? Is he an expert in the cognitive psychology of jurors, so he can hypothesize how they would think under counterfactual circumstances? Or is he, when all is said and done, a super-juror himself, one who relies on a disembodied transcript and who can distinguish the guilty from the innocent?

After all, he finally admits that this is all quantitative. Which means that if a number of us who have suffered flawed trials, say 20, stand before you, you will know that at least one of us is absolutely innocent. And if you give us another trial, maybe two or three others of us would get acquitted, whether guilty or not, because you have accepted the requirement that you must prove guilt beyond a reasonable doubt. By breaking the rules of procedure at trial, didn't you forfeit the right to sacrifice any of us in the name of convicting most of us? And isn't it wholly within your powers to at least restart the process fairly?

LS: You do not appreciate how hard we try to reduce these errors, how rigorously we work to account for all interests, especially yours. This is not just careful judgment on our part. It is as close to science as we can make law. Indeed, a team of social science experts has reviewed the way these harmless error rules are actually working.[97] They have brought into the equation all the crucial variables, such as the probability of error, the probability of harmful error if an error occurs, the probability of conviction at trial without error, the probability of conviction at trial given harmful error, the cost of trial and retrial, the cost of appellate review per appeal, the number of issues addressed by appellate court, the reversal rate for different types of convictions, the cost of retrying defendants whose convictions are reversed, the social benefit from conviction, the social harm from conviction when error is harmful, the utility of prosecutor from conviction, and the prosecutor's cost of trial and cost of preventing error.

This team has drawn some inferences that suggest the rules work in ways both undramatic and perfectly sensible. The experts have not only weighed all the costs and benefits but also have taken into account such criteria as whether the error was intentional and who made it.

It turns out that intentional prosecutor and judge errors are more likely to be found harmful and more often lead the appellate court to reverse the defendant's conviction than inadvertent errors. Prosecutor errors are more likely to be forgiven than judge errors, both because judge errors are likely to have greater influence on jurors and because a

> judge who has failed to correct a prosecutor's error (even an intentional one) has quite likely also failed to correct an offsetting defense error. Errors are less likely to be harmful when defendants face a higher error-free probability of conviction. Appellate courts are more likely to publish an opinion when they are reversing the lower court since the likelihood that the case presents a difficult issue on which precedent would be helpful is greater when there is disagreement among judges.[98]

This should be very reassuring. It shows that we do not condone bad faith actions by prosecutors, and we are especially hard on judges, because they are, of course, the figures you have most in mind when you make your plea to this monolith called the legal system. It is harder for us to control what prosecutors do. We also have to worry about good-faith disagreements among judges themselves.

D10: All this self-division, this self-disavowal, is disingenuous. You, the legal system, include all prosecutors as well as judges. Indeed you, the legal system, include all the legal rules. So your outward imputation to these forces like prosecutorial behavior or to the state of the actual law—these are just evasions.

LS: We also think very hard about how the rule should operate. Let me try again to show you how rigorously we do this. In particular, let me show why what you denounce as dishonest outward imputation or disavowal is really a set of facts about the natural world that you have failed to appreciate. We have learned to attend to the irreducible uncertainties in our ability to determine factual guilt as well as our ability to counterfactually determine how a differently informed jury might have decided a case. And in doing so, we are very sensitive to the costs at stake here. Here is further reassurance from our social science experts:

> Let H be the social harm from error committed by the prosecutor or a prosecution-minded judge when the error raises the probability of conviction and the defendant is convicted at trial. H is likely to be large if the error leads to the conviction of an innocent person. For this means that the guilty person has gotten away with the crime, which reduces the incapacitation benefit of criminal punishment, may reduce deterrence by reducing the expected cost of crime relative to lawful activities, and may spread fear among the law-abiding population of being wrongly convicted. H also includes reputational losses, reduced earnings, and nonpecuniary losses to a person convicted of a crime he didn't commit. The harm is greater for convictions resulting in longer sentences, and so we expect H to be greater the more serious the crime. The effect on deterrence would be small, however, if other potential criminals assumed that the innocent person had actually committed the crime.[99]

Again, it all comes down to a problem the legal system cannot fully solve, and one you cannot deny. In a large group of defendants, I know that at least one of you is likely telling the truth when you deny guilt. I also know that in a fair trial two or three of you would be acquitted. But I do not know who those are among you, and that is because one ultimately cannot do much better than the fallibility of human cognition.

D10: So now you *do* purport to take account of all the harms that a legal judgment, even a false legal judgment, can cause outside the legal system. You nicely describe them under such names as "reputational losses." But the problem is *how* you take them into account. They are simply vague factors in your balance. They argue *some*what in favor of avoiding error. But we end up with the same margin of error that the government tolerates—with the cost on my side.

Please acknowledge that you chose to rely on a particular set or a particular pool of fallible human beings, who remain identifiable, so

we could go back and have them do the case over, with a full explanation to them of what they can now consider and not consider. You
have incorporated those fallible beings into the system by the way
you have selected jurors. They cease to be exogenous forces at that
point.

LS: That will not work:

> Because it is too costly to figure out how whether a particular jury was
> actually influenced by a trial error (not only because it would require a
> costly and inconclusive inquiry but also because it would burden and
> embarrass the jurors), appellate courts ask in effect how an average jury
> would have been influenced, thus ignoring intellectual, emotional, and
> other relevant differences among individual juries. This saving comes at
> a cost, because it makes it more likely that the appellate court will fail to
> detect a harmful error. The likelihood is increased by the fact that the
> prosecutor, being present at the trial, has better information than the
> appellate court about the actual characteristics of the jury. This may give
> him an incentive to induce a harmful error, knowing that it is unlikely
> to be corrected on appeal. It may nevertheless be optimal for the ap-
> pellate court to forgo the costs of assessing the impact of error on the
> particular jury and stick with an average or reasonable jury rule.[100]

D10: So now you expel from the legal system the real human beings you
brought in, in favor of some bloodless abstraction called the average or reasonable jury. By that reckoning, why did you give me a
jury trial at all? Why not just have a judge—or maybe a sociologist
—speak for that abstraction? Was my right to trial by jury just your
begrudging concession to an encrusted constitutional rule, and one
you can evade once we are in this netherworld of hypothetical/retro-
spective trials?

LS: No—our harmless error doctrine is the fairest way to accommodate
all the interests that are implicated once we have a verdict of conviction coming from a jury, which, by your own concession, was fairly
selected. Now we are truly in a different situation. And again, let me
assure you how careful we are:

> Even an error that results in the conviction of a guilty person may im-
> pose a social cost, if either the court doesn't know for certain that the
> person is guilty or if the legal right that the prosecutor infringed is

thought to confer a social benefit even when invoked by a guilty person. But in the latter case H will be small and may be more than offset by the benefit of convicting the guilty. We may assume for the sake of simplicity, and without affecting our conclusions significantly, that all rights of criminal defendants are intended for the protection of the innocent, making H zero (or close to it) if the appellate court knows the defendant is guilty. But of course the court does not "know"; it can only guess. H can therefore be assumed to be positive to the extent that, by reducing the court's confidence in the strength of the prosecutor's case, it reduces the subjective probability that the defendant is truly guilty The costs to the procedural system of errors, mainly the costs to the appellate court of ferreting out errors and the cost of retrying defendants, we consider separately.

Let e be the probability of prosecution error, h the (conditional) probability that the error is harmful, p the probability of conviction at trial in the absence of error or when the error is harmless, and q the probability of conviction when the error is harmful. Given an error, h denotes the probability that $q > p$, since otherwise there is no harm from error. By assumption, therefore, an error that does not increase the probability of conviction is harmless.[101]

D10: Let's get back to prosecutors. Why can't you control them better?
LS: We do, and the way we recommend applying the harmless error rule addresses is the following:

> If the prosecutor's case is going well (say p is high) he will have less incentive to gamble on committing an error that raises the probability of conviction but makes reversal more likely. But if his case is going poorly (p is low), he may be willing to risk such an error because he has little to lose. Thus, we expect a negative correlation between the likelihood of a deliberate harmful error and the error-free probability of conviction. For all these reasons, an appellate court that faces significant information costs should be more willing to reverse a conviction when it believes that an error may have occurred and that the prosecution's evidence at trial was weak rather than strong.[102]

D10: But you are still risking my life and liberty with abstract probabilities. If you agree that sometimes prosecutors deliberately violate my rights, why can't you at least make *that* reversible error? Couldn't you

at least monitor trials to prevent clearly intentional errors by prosecutors and deter those prosecutors by guaranteeing me a retrial?

LS: Well, we are back to where we were before. We lack omniscience.
We cannot control or even accurately observe the vagaries of human
motivation:

> [S]ince it may be as difficult for the appellate court to distinguish be-
> tween intentional and unintentional errors as to determine the influence
> of error on the particular jury, a rule of automatic reversal in intentional-
> error cases may not be optimal. In fact, it may be more difficult to de-
> termine whether an error was intentional than whether it was harmless.
> The court can guess whether the error is the sort that would be likely
> to sway the average jury, but to determine whether the prosecutor had
> committed the error deliberately would require a difficult and usually
> inconclusive inquiry into the prosecutor's state of mind, though we [can
> also] suggest later a possible proxy for deliberateness that is easier to
> observe.[103]

In fact, if you want to see to what lengths you drive us when you
force this question, we have scribbled a little explanation in the margin but let us present it here in the text. Please note that U means the
prosecutor's utility; x is the prosecutor's cost of trial; y is the prosecutor's cost of avoiding error; r is the reversal rate for an error; and B is
the number of errors to be decided by the appellate court.

The prosecutor's utility if he commits an intentional error is

$$(9)\ U^e = hq[(1-r^2)B + r^2(pB-x)] + (1-h)p[(1-r^3)B + r^3(pB-x)] - x - y$$

where y is the prosecutor's cost of committing such an error. That cost
may be either positive (e.g., the cost of hiding exculpatory evidence) or
negative (e.g., the savings from doing nothing to prevent misconduct
by subordinates). To simplify, we assume that these factors cancel out,
so that y equals 0, though we shall point out how the results change if
$y = 0$.

Assuming that both e and h equal 1 in the intentional-error case, (9)
becomes

$$(10)\ U^e = q[(1-r^2)B + r^2(pB-x)] - x$$

Whether the prosecutor commits an intentional error will depend on whether U^e is greater or less than U^{ne}, which in turn will depend on the appellate court's reaction to the error.[104]

D10: Enough with these abstractions. They have nothing to do with what judges really do. Maybe I should just hope for an experienced and knowledgeable jurist.

D11: Well, years after my conviction and after my appeals have run out, I now have terrific new evidence that I am wholly innocent. I can only hope that the Supreme Court will recur to its suggestion in *Herrera* that I have a claim of constitutional error. I can only hope that the Court finally follows the path called for by Justice Blackmun in his passionate dissent there. He recognized that it is indeed unconstitutional to secure an innocent person:

> I have voiced disappointment over this Court's obvious eagerness to do away with any restriction on the States' power to execute whomever and however they please. Just as an execution without adequate safeguards is unacceptable, so too is an execution when the condemned prisoner can prove that he is innocent. The execution of a person who can show that he is innocent comes perilously close to simple murder.[105]

LS: Nice effort to at least bring Justice Blackmun on the side of the deontological and categorical. But the effort does not work, because he, too, put the question in terms of all these probabilities and efficiencies you are otherwise complaining about. He did not reject all the fine verbal parsing and the agonizing over the extralegal uncertainties that plague any effort at absolute justice. He was simply inclined to be somewhat more generous in his own parsing:

> I think the standard for relief on the merits of an actual innocence claim must be higher than the threshold standard for merely reaching that claim or any other claim that has been procedurally defaulted or is successive or abusive. I would hold that, to obtain relief on a claim of actual innocence, the petitioner must show that he probably is innocent. . . .
>
> [C]onviction after a constitutionally adequate trial strips the defendant of the presumption of innocence. The government bears the burden

of proving the defendant's guilt beyond a reasonable doubt, but once the government has done so, the burden of proving innocence must shift to the convicted defendant. The actual innocence inquiry is therefore distinguishable from review for sufficiency of the evidence, where the question is not whether the defendant is innocent but whether the government has met its constitutional burden of proving the defendant's guilt beyond a reasonable doubt. When a defendant seeks to challenge the determination of guilt after he has been validly convicted and sentenced, it is fair to place on him the burden of proving his innocence, not just raising doubt about his guilt. . . .

[T]he court charged with deciding such a claim should make a case by case determination about the reliability of the newly discovered evidence under the circumstances. The court then should weigh the evidence in favor of the prisoner against the evidence of his guilt. Obviously, the stronger the evidence of the prisoner's guilt, the more persuasive the newly discovered evidence of innocence must be.[106]

Justice Blackmun realized that in a world where human decisionmakers make mistakes, and where the legal system requires some finality, it is meaningless to say that it is unconstitutional to execute an innocent person. Not wrong, but meaningless. Such a statement fails to acknowledge the unavoidable fallibility of human decisionmaking and the unavoidable uncertainty about the factual world. So Justice Blackmun was not rejecting the general doctrines of harmless error. He was just disagreeing about the proper metric.

Concluding Note

D12: I do not claim that I am innocent of murder. But I believe my death sentence was nevertheless illegal. I killed a white person. Had I killed a nonwhite, I would not have been charged with capital murder, or if I had been so charged, the jury would have given me life.

LS: So you say. And we agree that if the decisive factor in your death sentence had been this form of racial prejudice—the greater valuation on a white life—you may have had a legal claim. But the way to make that claim is to invoke the equal protection clause, and therefore you would have to show that this bias was fully intentional.

Have you any proof that this is what was in the prosecutor's mind when she charged you—or even the jury's mind when it voted for death? You have to show that some party who acted on the behalf of the state was purposefully prejudiced.

D12: You know very well that such "smoking gun" evidence never arises. But you also know that in some large fraction of death sentences the discrimination is purposive. You know that because in *McCleskey v. Kemp*[107] you accepted the famous statistical study by the David Baldus group. The correlations it showed were so overwhelming that you accepted them as causal significant.

LS: All that shows is that among some large sample of defendants in your situation, the claim is, in theory, good. But we have no way of ferreting out which ones.

D12: So you are admitting that many errors of discrimination have occurred. And in effect you are declaring them harmless.

LS: Yet again a defendant is twisting a constitutional principle into the form of a harmless error issue. We are not saying the error is harmless in your case. Yet again, you are saying that you have not proved error.

D12: You are not blaming me for failing to prove discriminatory purpose. You are even sympathizing with me for the difficulty of my proving so, by your sober tragic recognition of the uncertainties of knowing what goes on in the human heart. But that is what you always do in harmless error cases, where you accept a margin of error because the cost of preventing or rectifying all errors would be to impose too large a burden on law enforcement. So it still looks like harmless error to me, because, just like in the cases that you are willing to call harmless error, you are denying harm by insisting that much of the burden of mistake be put on putatively wronged defendants.

LS: Well, recall that McCleskey did not just make an equal protection claim. He also claimed that the undeniable irrationality of racial prejudice violated the Eighth Amendment by skewing the results of capital trials. And we took that claim seriously. But we had to reject it because his argument, like yours, just goes too far. Justice Powell said that proof of racial discrimination against killers of white defendants could not win legal redress, precisely because that discrimination showed racism insidiously pervading all of criminal justice so that it was beyond the power of the Supreme Court to cure:

At most, the Baldus study indicates a discrepancy that appears to correlate with race. Apparent disparities in sentencing are an inevitable part of our criminal justice system. The discrepancy indicated by the Baldus study is "a far cry from the major systemic defects identified in *Furman*." As this Court has recognized, any mode for determining guilt or punishment "has its weaknesses and the potential for misuse." Specifically, "there can be 'no perfect procedure for deciding in which cases governmental authority should be used to impose death.'" Where the discretion that is fundamental to our criminal process is involved, we decline to assume that what is unexplained is invidious.[108]

We have done our best to guard against discriminatory and irrational exercise of discretion, and, besides, you could just as well have been the beneficiary of this discretion. But more important, look where your argument is leading us:

The Eighth Amendment is not limited in application to capital punishment, but applies to all penalties. Thus, if we accepted McCleskey's claim that racial bias has impermissibly tainted the capital sentencing decision, we could soon be faced with similar claims as to other types of penalty. Moreover, the claim that his sentence rests on the irrelevant factor of race easily could be extended to apply to claims based on unexplained discrepancies that correlate to membership in other minority groups, even to gender. Similarly, since McCleskey's claim relates to the race of his victim, other claims could apply with equally logical force to statistical disparities that correlate with the race or sex of other actors in the criminal justice system, such as defense attorneys or judges. . . . The Constitution does not require that a State eliminate any demonstrable disparity that correlates with a potentially irrelevant factor in order to operate a criminal justice system that includes capital punishment.[109]

D12: Time and time again you allude to the vagaries of human behavior and cognition and disclaim responsibility for the apparent errors they may cause. But here you have a vast amount of egregious "error"—to put it mildly—within the system of capital punishment. In part, you suggest that the source of the errors lies outside the law of capital punishment per se. But just on the other side of that boundary we are still very much within the criminal justice system. You do not deny or minimize the scope of error I have uncovered. In fact, you seem to blame me for embarrassing you by exposing the even wider scope of error. All that lies within your system, not without.

LS: Well, the Supreme Court is still just a court. The solution may lie with the legislature.

D12: That is disingenuous. Even if the principles of separation of power can serve as a rationalization for certain technical legal problems, I am speaking of miscarriage of justice. And for that, the responsible party is the whole system.

LS: Well, Justice Powell, who wrote *McCleskey*, publicly said a few years later, after he retired, that he had come to view the decision as a regrettable error.[110]

NOTES

1. James Liebman, Jeffrey Fagan, and Valerie West, "A Broken System: The Persistent Patterns of Reversals of Death Sentences in the United States," *Journal of Empirical Legal Studies* 1 (2004): 209.

2. Editorial, "Pass a Resolution to Condemn the Death Penalty: Death Penalty Debate Continues," *Syracuse Herald*, July 7, 2000, p. A10.

3. Adam Vangrack, "'Serious Error with "Serious Error': Repairing a Broken System of Capital Punishment," 79 *Washington University Law Quarterly* 79 (2001): 973 (challenging the Liebman report for the vagueness of the category of "serous error" it used as a variable and for not making its data available for replication).

4. Paul G. Cassell, "We're Not Executing the Innocent," *Wall Street Journal*, June 16, 2000, p. A14; Vangrack, "Serious Error," 1005.

5. Cassell , "We're Not Executing."

6. Vangrack, "Serious Error," 1005.

7. Many of the investigators working for the famed Center on Wrongful Convictions at Northwestern are journalism students. At http://www.medill.northwestern.edu/alumni/medillian/summer99/Protess.PDF.

8. *Herrera v. Collins*, 506 U.S. 390 (1993).

9. *Id.* at 417 (except for possibility of "a truly persuasive demonstration of 'actual innocence,'" freestanding claims of innocence based on newly revealed evidence do not warrant habeas corpus order to reopen state capital judgment).

10. John Charles Boger, "Foreword: Acts of Capital Clemency: The Words and Deeds of Goveror George Ryan," *North Carolina Law Review* 82 (2004): 1279.

11. For a critical review of contemporary theories, see David Dolinko, "Some Thoughts on Retruibutivism," *Ethics* 10 (1991): 537.

12. Stephen P. Garvey, "Is It Wrong to Commute Death Row? Retribution,

Atonement, and Mercy," *North Carolina Law Review* 82 (2004): 1319; Daniel Markel, "Against Mercy," *Minnesota Law Review* 88 (2004): 1421.

13. Markel, "Against Mercy," 1454.

14. Austin Sarat, "Putting a Square Peg in a Round Hole: Victims, Retribution, and George Ryan's Clemency," *North Carolina Law Review* 82 (2004): 1345.

15. Markel, "Against Mercy," 1457–59.

16. Robert Weisberg, "Apology, Legislation, and Mercy," *North Carolina Law Review* 82 (2004): 1415 (legislation can serve as expression of atonement even if prospective in legal effect).

17. Erik Luna, "Introduction: The Utah Restorative Justice Conference," *Utah Law Review* (2003): 1.

18. Sam Kamin, "Harmless Error and the Rights/Remedies Split," *Virginia Law Review* 88 (2002): 1, 62–72.

19. *Brady v. Maryland,* 373 U.S. 83 (1963).

20. For example, *United States v. Leon,* 406 U.S. 897 (1984).

21. Some constitutional claims arising from police investigation muddy our definition. This is true of most Fourth Amendment claims of illegal search or seizure and some technical claims under the Fifth or Sixth Amendment involving illegal interrogations. In these cases, the defendant seeks to suppress evidence to vindicate a right of privacy or autonomy or to deter future police violations but cannot credibly claim that the evidence would lead to a factually wrongful conviction. I finesse that set of issues here and generally assume that the harm of a legal error is not just the risk of a conviction that would not have occurred absent the legal error but a conviction of a factually innocent person.

22. Although a person can sue for a civil rights violation under 42 U.S.C. §1983 for a wrongful arrest, generally that arrest is not wrongful as long as the officer had probable cause to believe that the person had committed a crime.

23. Adam Liptak, "Criminal Records Erased by Courts Live to Tell Tales," *New York Times,* October 17, 2006, p. A1.

24. "Thomas A. Wilder, the district clerk for Tarrant County in Fort Worth, said he had received harsh criticism for refusing, on principle, to sell criminal history records in bulk. 'How the hell do I expunge anything,' Mr. Wilder asked, 'if I sell tapes and disks all over the country?'" *Id.*

25. *United States v. Mechanik,* 520 U.S. 461 (1997).

26. *Rose v. Mitchell,* 443 U.S. 545 (1979).

27. *Strauder v. West Virginia,* 100 U.S. 303 (1880) at 308.

28. *Vasquez v. Hillery,* 474 U.S. 254 (1986) at 262.

29. *Id.*

30. *Ballard v. United States,* 329 U.S. 187 (1946) at 195.

31. *Vasquez v. Hillery* at 263.

32. *Id.* at 264.

33. The right to a speedy trial is a problem for harmless error doctrine. As a

general matter, a violation of the Sixth Amendment's speedy trial clause means dismissal with prejudice—that is, immunity from retrial. *Strunk v. United States,* 412 U.S. 434 (1973). Logically, dismissal without prejudice (i.e., automatic reversal but retrial) may undercompensate the defendant. On the other hand, dismissal with prejudice may be too generous to a defendant who has not suffered much prejudice to his chances of a fair trial by reason of the delay. For that reason, violations of a speedy trial *statute* often leave the court with discretion to determine the right remedy. *United States v. Taylor,* 487 U.S. 326 (1988) (federal Speedy Trial Act).

34. *Fong Foo v. United States,* 369 U.S. 141 (1962).

35. *Oregon v. Kennedy,* 456 U.S. 667 (1982).

36. Roger Traynor, *The Riddle of Harmless Error* (Columbus: Ohio State University Press, 1970), 6–8.

37. *Kotteakos v. United States,* U.S. 750 (1946) at 776.

38. *Gideon v. Wainwright,* U.S. 335 (1962) (Sixth Amendment right of counsel at trial guaranteed for indigents).

39. *Duncan v. Louisiana,* U.S. 145 (1968) (Sixth Amendment right to jury trial where more than sixth months' incarceration is possible).

40. *Betts v. Brady,* 316 U.S. 455 (1942).

41. *Chapman v. California,* 386 U.S. 18 (1967).

42. *Fahy v. Connecticut,* 375 U.S. 85 (1963).

43. *Chapman v. California* at 24.

44. *Waller v. Georgia,* 467 U.S. 39 (1984).

45. *Gray v. Mississippi,* 481 U.S. 648 (1987)

46. *Young v. United States,* 481 U.S. 787 (1987).

47. *Tumey v. Ohio,* 273 U.S. 510 (1927) at 535 (reversal required when judge has financial interest in conviction, despite lack of indication that bias influenced decisions).

48. *Vazquez v. Hillery,* 474 U.S 254 (1986) at 263.

49. *Batson v. Kentucky,* 476 U.S. 79 (1986).

50. *Id.* at 100.

51. *Faretta v. California,* 422 U.S. 806 (1975).

52. *Miranda v. Arizona,* 384 U.S. 436 (1966), creates fairly technical rules for interrogations under the rubric of the Fifth Amendment privilege against self-incrimination, and the Sixth Amendment right of counsel supplies some other technical rules governing admissions confessions. *Massiah v. United States,* 377 U.S. 201 (1964). But the old due process rule remains in force—a truly involuntary, coerced confession violates due process. *Spano v. New York,* 360 U.S. 315 (1959).

53. *Arizona v. Fulminante,* U.S. 279 (1991).

54. *Id.* at 308.

55. *Id.* at 307–8.

56. See David McCord, "The 'Trial'/'Structural' Error Dichotomy: Erroneous, and Not Harmless," *Kansas Law Review,* 45 (1997): 1401, 1413.

57. *Arizona v. Fulminante* at 307.

58. McCord, "'Trial'/'Structural' Error Dichotomy," 1414–15.

59. *Alabama v. Shelton,* 535 U.S. 654 (2002) (suspended 30-day sentence can constitute "actual imprisonment" to trigger *Gideon* right).

60. *Chambers v. Maroney,* 399 U.S. 42 (1970).

61. *Miranda v. Arizona,* 384 U.S. 436 (1966).

62. *Milton v. Wainwright,* 407 U.S. 371 (1972).

63. *United States v. Wade,* 388 U.S. 218 (1967).

64. *Schneble v. Florida,* 405 U.S. 427 (1972).

65. *Rushen v. Spain,* 464 U.S. 114 (1983).

66. *Rose v. Clark,* 478 U.S. 570 (1986); *Carella v. California,* 491 U.S. 263 (1989).

67. *Stringer v. Black,* 503 U.S. 222 (1992).

68. *Brady v. Maryland,* 373 U.S. 83 (1963).

69. *Strickland v. Washington,* 466 U.S. 668 (1984).

70. *Hill v. Lockhart,* 477 U.S. 52 (1985).

71. *United States v. Glover,* 531 U.S. 198 (2001).

72. Even though the Supreme Court's revolutionary decision in *Blakely v. Washington,* 542 U.S. 296 (2004), imposed a right of jury trial for many aspects of sentencing decisions, it leaves plenty of space for wide and discretionary sentencing ranges, especially in guilty plea cases.

73. *Cuyler v. Sullivan,* 446 U.S. 335 (1980).

74. *Holloway v. Arkansas,* 435 U.S. 475 (1978).

75. In *Mickens v. Taylor,* 535 U.S. 162 (2002), the Court faced the claim that where a trial judge wholly neglected to even inquire about an apparent conflict of attorney interest, the defendant could win reversal without a showing of adverse effect. The Court rejected the claim.

76. *Brecht v. Abrahamson,* 507 U.S. 619 (1993) at 619.

77. *Id.* at 636.

78. *Id.* at 636–37 (quoting *United States v. Mechanik,* 475 U.S. 66 (1986) at 72).

79. *Carey v. Musladin,* 549 U.S. 70 (2006).

80. *Estelle v. Williams,* 425 U.S. 501 (1976); *Holbrook v. Flynn,* 475 U.S. 560 (1986).

81. *Williams v. Taylor,* 529 U.S. 362 (2000) (construing 28 U.S.C. §2254).

82. *Lockhart v. Fretwell,* 506 U.S. 364 (1993).

83. *Collins v. Lockhart,* 754 F. 2d 258 (8th Cir. 1985).

84. *Perry v. Lockhart,* 871 F. 2d 1384 (8th Cir. 1989).

85. *Strickland v. Washington* at 690

86. *Id.*

87. *Teague v. Lane,* 489 U.S. 288 (1989).

88. *Id.* at 306 (quoting *Desist v. United States,* 394 U.S. 244 (1969) at 262–63).

89. *Lockhart v. Fretwell,* 506 U.S. 387 (Stevens, J.; dissenting).

90. Alfred Paul LeBlanc, "Considerations Concerning Harmless Error in Louisiana Criminal," *Louisiana Law Review* 64 (2003): 21.

91. *State v. Gibson,* 391 So. 2d 427 (La. 1980) at 427.

92. LeBlanc, "Considerations Concerning Harmless Error," 31.

93. *Id.* at 32.

94. *Id.* (quoting *Sullivan v. Louisiana,* 508 U.S. 275 (1993) at 284 (Rehnquist, CJ, concurring).

95. *Id.* at 34.

96. *Id.* at 35–36.

97. William Landes and Richard Posner, "Harmless Error," *Journal of Legal Studies* 161 (2001): 161.

98. *Id.* at 182.

99. *Id.* at 163.

100. *Id.* at 175.

101. *Id.* at 164.

102. *Id.* at 174.

103. *Id.* at 179.

104. *Id.* at 177–78.

105. *Herrera v. Collins* at 445 (Blackmun, J., dissenting).

106. *Id.* at 442–44.

107. *McCleskey v. Kemp,* 481 U.S. 279 (1987).

108. *Id.* at 312–13.

109. *Id.* at 315–19 (citations omitted).

110. John C. Jeffries, Jr., *Justice Lewis F. Powell, Jr. and the Era of Judicial Balance* (New York: Scribner's, 1994), 451–52.

Part II

||||||||||||||||||||||||||||||||||||||||||||||||||||||||||||

Miscarriages of Justice and Legal Processes

Chapter 4

IIIIIIIIIIIIIIIIIIIIIIIIIIIIIIIIIIIIIIIIIIIIIIIIIIIIIIIIIIII

Recovering the Craft of Policing
Wrongful Convictions, the War on Crime,
and the Problem of Security

Jonathan Simon

In recent years there have been few more poignant examples of miscarriage of justice than the scores of prisoners exonerated by DNA tests that disprove key aspects of the prosecution's case against them (e.g., that the defendant's semen or blood was found on the victim). Illuminated by DNA evidence,[1] stories of devastation and tragedy have been repeatedly brought before us. Often these involve terrible crimes, frequently rape, followed by the conviction and imprisonment of the wrong person. Years (typically 10 or more) are spent languishing in America's harsh and often overcrowded prisons and with expectations of spending decades more, while the real criminals remain free (perhaps committing new crimes) and the victim is subjected to a new and terrible relationship with pain and violence (now as an unintentional instrument of injustice).

These same cases have yielded insights for legal scholars, psychologists, and criminologists who have developed a broad profile of bad practices that lead to wrongful convictions. The usual litany includes eyewitness identification problems caused or exacerbated by police mishandling (D. Simon forthcoming); coercion applied to vulnerable (young, mentally ill, or grief-stricken) subjects undergoing custodial interrogation; and reliance on jailhouse "snitches" who, by luck or manipulation of the authorities, had been able to share a cell with a suspect in a notorious case (Leo et al. 2006; Saks and Koehler 2005).

Police practices are clearly the major factor producing wrongful convictions, but beyond this broad profile, students of wrongful conviction have had relatively little to say about the social or institutional dynamics that lead police (or prosecutors) to engage in investigatory tactics that can be described at best as high risk (Leo et al. 2006; Saks and Koehler 2005). Nor have they been able say much about whether this kind of high-risk conduct is more or less prevalent today than was the case in the past. Are wrongful convictions a stubborn residue of a once even more common phenomenon? Or is it possible that contemporary policing, however improved in training and in background human capital, is more prone toward error than was true in the past?

No criminologist has the data to answer that question. In this chapter, I aim in the direction of that gap by developing the thesis that police practices might, in fact, produce more wrongful convictions today.[2] Sadly, I cannot offer empirical evidence for this claim (I am as yet unsure of what ascertainable data would constitute proof). Instead, I offer an interpretation of the profile of the exonerations that is consistent with more well-anchored scholarship about the changes in criminal justice produced by the war on crime (and especially drugs) pursued by American political leaders since the 1960s (see generally Scheingold 1991; Simon 1993; Beckett 1997; Zimring, Hawkins, and Kamin, 2001; Garland 2001a; Western 2006; Simon 2007).

The conventional wisdom is that police are much more professional today than they were a generation or two ago, largely as a result of a decline in police discretion and investment in better management, training, and technology. In June 2006, in the case of *Hudson v. Michigan* (2006), the U.S. Supreme Court declined to exclude evidence collected by the police in admitted violation of the "knock and announce" rule that has been held to be a substantive requirement of a Fourth Amendment "reasonable" search of a house. Reasoning that the additional deterrent benefit of applying the exclusionary rule in such a case would not be worth the social cost of losing probative evidence, the Court, per Justice Antonin Scalia, endorsed the view that American police had been much improved over the past few decades and that the law now provides numerous avenues for discouraging police misconduct:[3]

> Another development over the past half-century that deters civil-rights violations is the increasing professionalism of police forces, including a new emphasis on internal police discipline. Even as long ago as 1980 we felt it proper to "assume" that unlawful police behavior would "be dealt with appropriately" by the authorities, . . . but we now have increasing evidence that police forces across the United States take the constitutional rights of

citizens seriously. There have been "wide-ranging reforms in the education, training, and supervision of police officers." . . . Numerous sources are now available to teach officers and their supervisors what is required of them under this Court's cases, how to respect constitutional guarantees in various situations, and how to craft an effective regime for internal discipline. . . . Failure to teach and enforce constitutional requirements exposes municipalities to financial liability. . . . Moreover, modern police forces are staffed with professionals; it is not credible to assert that internal discipline, which can limit successful careers, will not have a deterrent effect. There is also evidence that the increasing use of various forms of citizen review can enhance police accountability. (*Hudson v. Michigan,* 547 U.S. 586, at 598–99)

Academic police experts also argue that many of the demographic features that once divided police from the communities they police (e.g., race, ethnicity, and sexual orientation) have been substantially diminished by affirmative action and other efforts to recruit a more representative police force (Sklansky 2006).

For purposes of this chapter, I assume that police professionalism (screening, training, accountability), and the demographic representativeness of police forces in the United States have in the aggregate[4] improved, perhaps substantially. The thesis explored is that these improvements may have been to an important degree subverted by the profound effects of a long and continuing war on drugs.[5] To state the central claim at the outset, the culture of investigation inside American policing has become reliant on forced confessions and other forms of "junk evidence"[6] as a by-product of its long, dirty war on drugs.

In the first section, I develop a dynamic explanation for why police investigation today might be worse than in the past, notwithstanding significant improvements. This theory is speculative, but it allows us to acknowledge a disturbing feature of our public debate about policing during much of this period that is more grounded. In heated battles over subjects like the exclusionary rule and *Miranda* warnings, both critics and defenders of American policing from the 1960s right up until our present moment largely ignored the issue of wrongful conviction in favor of a concern with rights enforcement and crime control. What this battle between 1965 and 1995 largely replaced was an earlier discourse that did focus on reducing the risks of wrongful conviction by improving the professionalism of police and the craft aspects of policing itself. In the second section, I sketch this earlier discourse and what its implications are for today.

To refocus on what has been missed in this recent history, and what we might seek to build on in imagining an adequate response, I end the chapter by considering a small example of the kind of policing we might have had, and might still demand, beyond the war on crime. In section three, I offer this utopian recovery of a forgotten moment of our past (or future).

I. How the War on Crime Transformed American Policing

In the political landscape left by the war on crime, police have come to stand for the interests of crime victims and, through them, of the public generally (Simon 2007). Almost any criticism of the police is taken to be a betrayal of victims and potential victims. This kind of highly charged power effect is reflected in the recent decision by California Governor Arnold Schwarzenegger to veto a series of bills implementing the recommendations of a commission set up by the California Senate in 2004 to investigate the causes of wrongful conviction in California (Egelko 2006). The governor was lobbied by state law enforcement groups who opposed the measures that would have required police to videotape confessions (at least of violent crime suspects) and established protocols for eyewitness identification procedures. Both are subjects that have been firmly linked to the problem of wrongful convictions (Scheck, Neufeld, and Dwyer 2000).

Police and Victims in the American Political Imagination

One of the most striking features of the current debate engendered by exonerations is the resistance of law enforcement to serious efforts to improve the reliability and visibility of the investigatory techniques that pose serious risks to conviction of the innocent. Perhaps any profession resists outside oversight (but keep in mind this is just what Justice Scalia told us contemporary police are used to), but to understand the extremity of this resistance, we must appreciate the radical shift in public confidence that the police have come to enjoy since the middle of the twentieth century.

From the 1930s through the 1960s, academic experts agreed that the public perceived police as corrupt, inefficient, and capable of brutality.[7] Popular culture, pulp fiction, and movies regularly portrayed the police in precisely the same terms. Consider *The Maltese Falcon* (1941), where Humphrey Bogart and everyone else knows that whole game is to give the police somebody they can blame for the murder of Sam Spade's partner and it does not matter whether that "somebody" did or it not. As the war on crime unfolded beginning in the late 1960s, the crime victim began to emerge as a modern "everyman," a representative or idealized citizen whose needs define the needs of the public (Garland 2001a, 11; Dubber 2002; Simon 2007, 76). Police came to be recast as champions of, and, sometimes, stand-ins for, crime victims. Their public image consequently moved from highly critical to reverential.

This shift is also captured in public opinion surveys. In 1979 (almost a decade into the war on crime), 37 percent of a national sample rated the honesty and ethical standards of the police "very high" or at least "high"; by 2005, 61 percent shared that rating. Asked how much confidence they had in the police in 2005, some 64 percent of a national sample indicated "a great deal or quite a lot." In contrast, only 53 percent said the same of churches and organized religion, 22 percent of Congress, 44 percent of the presidency, and 41 percent of the Supreme Court. Criminal justice overall, by the way, scores even lower than Congress. The only institution that evokes more confidence than the police is even more steeped in symbolic identity with the body politic, i.e., the military, in whom 74 percent of respondents held such high confidence (*Sourcebook of Criminal Justice Statistics* 2007, table 2.20).

Policing Mass Incarceration

While the powerful political linkage between police and victims has provided significant protection from legislative regulation of police, the war on drugs and crime declared by state legislatures in the name of the same victims has produced a surplus population of incarcerated and easily incarcerated people. If most of these people were incarcerated for violent victimization crimes like homicide, robbery, and rape, it would not be surprising if they also generated future arrests for these crimes. Exoneration cases suggest that the dynamic is just the opposite. It is because the war on drugs has created such a large pool of available suspects that so many are wrongfully convicted of violent crimes.

During the 1980s and 1990s, U.S. police departments focused heavily on drug crimes. A war on drugs drove the growth of the prison and jail population in a way that no other crime agenda could have done (Caplow and Simon 1998). Unlike burglary and robbery, drug crime produces an almost limitless population of available arrestees. In most cities, the only constraint on how many drug arrests can be made is how much overtime pay police budgets can produce. Whatever other effect this practice of "mass imprisonment" (Garland 2001b) leads to, it clearly forms a ready-to-hand supply of possible criminal suspects or, in the form of "snitch" testimony, evidence to convict other incarcerated suspects.[8] Even beyond the currently jailed or imprisoned population, the war on drugs has created a vast penumbra of persons on parole or probation who can be easily taken into custody and held without the burdens of proof that would normally fall on the prosecution. In a number of documented cases, this has led police to lock up a suspect who is on parole or probation based on a parole or probation violation (technical violations are never hard to find) without having to show any substantial evidence of a link to a violent crime under investigation. The police often inform the media that a suspect is in custody, allowing them to take some initial credit for solving the case while permitting considerable time for the development of the "facts."

This ease of catching, holding, and blaming facilitates a number of investigative pathologies that have been noted by the wrongful conviction literature. One is the problem of tunnel vision. Having identified a particular suspect and taken him off the streets, police often focus solely on collecting further evidence consistent with that theory of the crime while ignoring anomalies that could lead a less biased observer to follow other leads. A second is the problem of snitch testimony. Once a suspect is in custody, he is likely to be housed with other inmates who may be motivated to provide testimony (including false testimony) against the suspect. The drug war provides additional incentives for this by producing the potential for long prison sentences that can motivate defendants to lie about another inmate in order to win prosecutorial cooperation (few other crimes provide long prison sentences but are a type of crime that does not cause public outcry when leniency is granted, in contrast to crimes of violence).

Another potential causal vector links the drug war to the problem of false confession. False confession experts suggest that "mentally handicapped or cognitively impaired individuals, children, juveniles, and the mentally ill are also unusually vulnerable to police interrogation pressure and are more likely to confess as a result" (Leo et al. 2006, 518). The drug war, by scooping up masses of youth from disadvantaged communities, has almost surely increased the proportionate representation of everyone of these classes among the prison and jail population.

Beyond these specific effects, the war on drugs may have helped reduce internal normative checks on manipulating evidence against suspects by promoting a view that law enforcement is engaged in a wholesale war against a criminal underclass (framed by race, age, and gender) rather than a retail struggle against individual wrongdoers. This stance, in which a vast population of low-level drug criminals is presumed to include the somewhat smaller core of violent repeat offenders, may support cognitive-institutional logics conducive to wrongful conviction along several paths. Police may believe that, regardless of his responsibility for a particular crime, a suspect who fits the profile of the criminal class is a "gang banger" whose relationship to any particular act of violence is one of chance but who exists as a mortal risk and shares the same moral stigma with one who has actually killed or raped.

Police may likewise believe that the only effective way to prevent future violence is to seek the most comprehensively eliminationist punishment available (including the death penalty) against members of the criminal class so as to obtain the maximum overall extent of incapacitation over the group as a group (Feeley and Simon 1992). To this extent, the "guilt phase" of determining whether any particular suspect is guilty of any particular crime is logically subordinated to a "penalty phase" in which those who can most reliably be tagged with the most extensive punishment are "it."

Finally, the experience of drug policing itself, the petty humiliations of "stop and frisks," the revolving door of frequent arrests and releases, and the extensive violence associated with the drug business, tend to support a battlefield ethics in which police may view themselves as engaged in a war with criminal gang members and in which ordinary values of due process need to be set aside to assure victory (essentially the logic of the war on terror).

II. The Craft: A Lost Possibility in American Policing

Justice Scalia's quotation cited above locates the improved professionalism of American policing in the expanded discipline, training, and supervision of police officers. Like other disciplinary exercises of power (Foucault 1977), this top-down model of improvement focuses on reducing misconduct and error by making deviation visible and applying corrective coercion.

Indeed, one way of looking at the Warren Court's criminal procedure jurisprudence is as a judicially led imposition of a "panoptic" regime visibility and accountability on police, long one of the most hidden and discretionary forms of legal authority. Through provision of counsel to indigent criminal defendants (*Gideon v. Wainwright*, 1963), the availability of the exclusionary remedy for Fourth Amendment violations (*Mapp v. Ohio*, 1961), and *Miranda* warnings (*Miranda v. Arizona*, 1966), the Court sought to extend the judicial power to review (literally, to see again) what was actually occurring in police stations, courthouses, and jails. Despite Justice Scalia's confidence that this discipline is working, many experts on wrongful conviction today see improvement of this visibility approach as crucial to making such miscarriages of justice less common—for example, by video-recording all custodial interrogations.

The emphasis on discipline and sanction that has been the focus of police reform since the early 1960s stands in contrast to an alternative approach, promoted by criminology and police sociology, that has long emphasized the reform potential of a "craft" conception of policing. As used by police scholars, the phrase "craft of policing" generally contrasts the practical and experience-based knowledge of the police to the rule-based imperatives of the law and scientific models of policing (e.g., Bayley and Bittner 1984).

While he never used the craft of policing language, no figure in modern police expertise was a more forceful advocate of this view than Fred Inbau (1909–98). Professor of law at Northwestern University, coauthor of the leading textbook on police interrogation, director of the leading forensic crime laboratory of the period (1938–41), and editor and chief of the *Journal of Criminal Law: Criminology and Police Science* (as it was pertinently called in his period), Inbau became the chief advocate of the view that greater police training and skill rather than judicial limitations were the best strategies to eliminate abuse and miscarriages of justice:

> The only real, practically attainable protection we can set up for ourselves against police interrogation abuses (just as with respect to arrest and detention abuses) is to see to it that our police are selected and promoted on a merit basis, that they are properly trained, adequately compensated, and that they are permitted to remain substantially free from politically inspired interference. . . . And once again I suggest that the real interest that should be exhibited by the legislatures and the courts is with reference to the protection of the innocent from the hazards of tactics and techniques

that are apt to produce confessions of guilt or other false information. (Inbau 1961, 20)

In retrospect, we can see how Inbau's interest in the truth value of confessions got lost in the increasingly bitter debate on the Warren Court's criminal procedure jurisprudence.[9] In that context, talk about truth seemed a way of rationalizing the admission of evidence collected in violation of the Constitution (although Inbau did not deny the power of courts to reject such evidence even if probative). Both the Warren Court and its critics increasingly ignored the problem of wrongful conviction. By the time the more conservative Burger Court began to roll back many of the doctrines viewed as hampering the police in the war on crime, it did so with no apparent consideration as to whether the underlying police practices were in fact "tactics and techniques that are apt to produce confessions of guilt or other false information" (Inbau 1961, 20).

The craft conception had a natural fit with the dominance of labor and occupational ideas of governance in the mid-twentieth century. Proponents of professionalizing the police force by raising hiring standards and improving training viewed policing as a body of knowledge and practices best rationalized through the evolution of internal, substantively rational reflection rather than external, judicially imposed rules.

But whatever potential might have existed in the 1960s to reduce abuse and miscarriages of justice through improved training and fostering of the craft of policing was washed out by the war on crime and the transformations of policing to which it led. From the skilled worker, the idealized figure of the police officer was reconfigured in two directions. One was as a symbolic stand-in for the citizen crime victim, the official vigilante (think *Die Hard*), the target of armed assailants facilitated by defense lawyers and liberal judges. The other was as a highly militarized and technologically enhanced cyborg—*Robocop*[10]—who could confront armed and violent criminals in a battlefield-like setting using special weapons and tactics (Kraska 2001). In neither the vigilante nor SWAT mode does the contemporary police officer draw on the kind of craft conception that Inbau championed with its emphasis on the protection of the innocent from wrongful conviction. Ironically, the proponents of a craft approach today are scholars and advocates like Richard Leo, Gary Wells, and Barry Scheck who are precisely the ones calling for taping of all police interrogations. Were Fred Inbau alive today, I suspect he'd be on their side.[11]

III. X-Rays: A Past That Might Have Been,
a Future That Could Be

In the late twentieth century, police experts divided between those who looked to judicially imposed external norms and those who looked to an internal process of craft elaboration. In fact, both were probably necessary for either to have had a chance of succeeding. But the war on crime, and the massive transformation of governance it produced, has led to a security paradox. The police have enough power to resist accountability in most respects but not enough knowledge to effectively deal with violence, community disorder, and now terrorism.

In the hope of going beyond critique and diagnosis to identifying the resources from which a remedy might be fashioned, we must have recourse to history. The success of a particular movement or project often has the effect of burying all memory of possible options that existed in the problematizations of the recent past (Foucault has made this into a key methodological imperative). Without bowdlerizing the past, we need to remain open to imagining possibilities for reconstructing our modern public institutions that have been lost.

The beachfront city of Fort Lauderdale, Florida, is known to many contemporary Americans as the liberal bastion that gave Al Gore hundreds of thousands of votes in 2000. In the 1960s, however, it was still largely a segregated southern city whose police force treated black residents primarily as a source of crime and a target for abuse and violence. In the early 1960s, under pressure from the local NAACP, the Fort Lauderdale Police Department hired two African American college graduates from the city's segregated northwest side, Doug Evans and Ozzie Davenport. Both had been star athletes and strong students at the local Dillard High School. In 1966 or 1967, "the riot years" as Evans recalled them in a recent interview, Chief Robert Johnson, brought together Evans and Davenport, by then detectives, together with several of the best white detectives to form a new unit with the goals of reducing the increasingly violent drug trade in the city and avoiding a major racial conflagration of the sort that had swept major cities in the North. Named the "X-Rays" because of their reputation for "sharp vision," these detectives specialized in deep knowledge of their local communities. Each summer the unit would be re-created to share street knowledge from both the black and white sides of town and to identify conflicts or crimes that might lead to racial violence.

The operation was not a perfect success. In 1969, Fort Lauderdale did suffer a riot along its major black commercial street, albeit a smaller and less violent one than others. But Evans and Davenport were able to intervene in many early-stage conflicts that might have led to other and possibly more violent eruptions. The cooperation with white officers and the imprimatur of the chief probably aided them.

What is especially striking to me about the tactics of the X-Rays is that they form alternatives to two of the major practices of investigation influenced by the war on drugs and which have contributed to miscarriages of justice: the use of informants and interrogation. The war on drugs has promoted the recruitment of professional informants who often have powerful monetary or legal incentives to lie. In contrast, the X-Rays cultivated informants more along the model of anthropological informants: local figures in a position to observe what is going on in a community and who have a relationship of trust and friendship with the detectives. The war on drugs has also made available a large pool of suspects who form a ready supply of suspects in other cases and has encouraged practices of deceptive interrogation aimed at pressuring the most dysfunctional of these suspects to cooperate in convicting themselves. In contrast, the X-Rays sought to obtain confessions by winning the trust of suspects and confronting them with the results of their prior investigations.

For me, the X-Rays represent a model of the craft tradition in a positive confrontation with problems of equality and inclusion posed by the civil rights movement in the 1960s. The story is not one of unblemished progress. Both Evans and Davenport struggled against the continuing racism of the city's (and the police force's) white power structure. Davenport left the force in the early 1970s to become a private detective. Evans had a remarkable career of investigatory triumphs, but he was never promoted to the leadership position he had so richly earned. His health was compromised by frustrations at a law enforcement apparatus that placed minimal priority on the security of people from Evans's own neighborhood of northwest Fort Lauderdale, and Evans retired in the late 1980s.

Evans's most famous case involved his capture of a serial killer and later a series of wrongful convictions produced by flawed police practices. Both aspects illuminate the disciplinary and craft approaches to policing we have discussed. Eddie Lee Mosley was one of the most prolific serial killers in U.S. history. For a decade and half during the 1970s and 1980s, a neighborhood in the northwest section of Fort Lauderdale, little more than a square mile, became a literal killing field for women and girls. Over 20 female victims were killed after being raped, and at least 100 women were raped in similar circumstances. Meanwhile, Americans all over the United States in these years developed an obsession with violent crime, especially sexual attacks and murders (despite stable or declining violence rates for many). This small part of Fort Lauderdale actually experienced something many times more terrifying than even the exaggerated urban crime scene portrayed in popular culture.

In some ways, it was simply unimaginable. In some periods, a body was found every week. Then, just as suddenly, the killings would stop altogether for years at a time. Then the violence would start again. One family actually lost two daughters, not in the same assault but in parallel assaults, one in 1984 and one three years later in 1987. The bodies were found all over the neighborhood. Most were left outside where the hot Florida sun and abundant animal life often made swift work of decomposition. But many were also left lying in their beds. Many times, the bodies were found in or around the dozens of small churches that dot the blocks of the intensely religious African American neighborhood.

While Americans were obsessed with violent crime in these years, they could also be amazingly blind to its presence. In these years, Fort Lauderdale soared as a vacation and relocation magnet. Thousands of tourists flocked to the hotels along Fort Lauderdale's beachfront and riverside, while a murderous rapist or rapists preyed relentlessly a few miles from the yachts and restaurants.

For many Americans, it was enough to know that it was an African American neighborhood—indeed, the heart of "old" Fort Lauderdale's segregated northwest side. Such neighborhoods are often coded high-crime centers to whites who may see such communities only in television news coverage of violence or crime. Perhaps because this extraordinary orgy of violence was concentrated in an African American neighborhood in a city still below the national radar in many respects, it did not draw the fascination that America had in those years for murder streaks in Los Angles, New York, and Atlanta. Other Florida towns had become famous as the targets of serial killers Ted Bundy and Danny Rawlings, but they preyed on pretty white college girls in the kind of photogenic college towns in which slasher movies are always set.

In this context, it is easy to ignore the fact that northwest Fort Lauderdale was a relatively quiet neighborhood in the 1970s and 1980s. Like many traditionally segregated neighborhoods, it contained a wide range of residents from laborers to professionals. The slow decline of Fort Lauderdale's traditional industries has taken a visible toll with closed-up businesses and storefronts scarring many commercial streets and residential areas marked by many abandoned houses and empty lots. But the area was bolstered by its strong multigenerational families (many of them with roots in the Bahamas), ubiquitous churches, and dozens of small businesses that remained full of signs of vitality 30 years later.

The vast majority of the victims were African American. Some were white but were victimized in a neighborhood easily defined as "dangerous." Perhaps fooled by the stereotypes associated with both race and space, most law enforcement officials who even bothered to notice the stunning violence rate against northwest Fort Lauderdale women attributed the killings and rapes to an unknown number of assailants. Indeed, twice in the 1980s, African American men from the community with somewhat similar profiles including marginal intelligence and criminal records were convicted for rape-murders of women in the neighborhood. The killings of women continued, suggesting, perhaps, that the streets still teemed with murderous rapists.

Used to declaring "victories" in a war on crime they never win, few in law enforcement contemplated another, truly shocking possibility: that one person, a serial rapist and killer of extraordinary strength, guile, and ruthlessness, was responsible for most and perhaps all of these rapes and deaths. Perhaps the deepest horror of these nightmarish years is the sense that a criminal justice culture in Fort Lauderdale and elsewhere, imbued with a "tough" but deeply fatalistic view of urban life, failed to pursue the traditional investigatory virtues that in this case were more than ample to lead them to a single man whose insane drives created a one-man crime wave and in whose absence even this very poor community with its share of imperfections would have been far less dangerous.

As a resident of the neighborhood, Evans was not ignorant of the growing number of rapes being reported in the area. But when he took over the rape squad of the investigation department in the summer of 1973, he was outraged to find a list of nearly 150 rapes that had occurred in the last couple of years and which had been allowed to languish unsolved. With partner and friend McKinley Smith and colleague Charlie Tolin, Evans pledged to get out of the office and meet the only people who could solve these crimes—namely, the innocent citizens and victims of the bleeding northwest. The three officers met with rape victims and other neighborhood witnesses they had interviewed who agreed to accompany the detectives as they trolled around the bars and empty lots of the neighborhood one night looking for the suspect.

One afternoon, Evans drove over to consult with a detective at the Broward Sheriff's Office, the sometimes rival police agency responsible for unincorporated portions of Broward County and whose jurisdiction abuts that of the Fort Lauderdale Police Department in the complex ways of municipal boundaries. As he was leaving, Evans spotted two women who had been in the crowds that had gathered around the crime scene of one of the recent victims. One of the two, a 17-year-old, reported that she was on her way to learn what she could about the rape suspect, who she believed was the same man who had earlier raped her. The woman told Evans that she had had a good look at the rapist and, moreover, had seen him twice since. The first time was Thursday night back at the Embassy Club when police had called after a man who looked like the rapist that had been spotted and fled, and a second time walking on Northwest 27th Avenue near 11th Street.

That night, an informal and perhaps unauthorized operation in what a later time would call community policing took place. Three officers— Evans, Smith, and Tolin—accompanied by three female victim witnesses and one male resident of the community who had seen the rapist at the Embassy Club, divided into two cars, a marked patrol car and Smith's personal vehicle. Smith and the three women began to drive around the neighborhood, while Evans and Tolin drove the other volunteer to the Embassy Club where he would keep a lookout in case the rapist reappeared there. Evans and Tolin checked out the Embassy and then went on to Club Down Beat. Smith and the three women continued their own driving tour of the neighborhood.

At around 1:15 A.M., Smith and the women were eastbound on 8th Place in the 2600 block when Linda Haygood began to shout to Smith that the figure walking up the street about three blocks ahead had the rapist's gait. As the car approached the figure, Haygood began to shout "that's the mutherfucker, that's the mutherfucker." According to Evans's arrest report, he was notified about this sighting and advised Smith twice to await his arrival before attempting to approach the suspect.

According to Smith's supplemental report, as he passed the suspect who was southbound on the 900 block of Northwest 25th Avenue, the rapist made a U-turn in the road and disappeared between two houses. Smith then left the vehicle in the hands of one of the female witnesses and ran after the suspect south along 25th Avenue. In the following confrontation, Smith fired his weapon at least twice. In his report, Smith stated that he saw a silver weapon-like object pointed toward him that he took to be a cane gun or a "cane sword." Smith identified himself as a police officer again and demanded that the subject drop the weapon. When it continued to be pointed, Smith fired his weapon in the air once. He identified himself again, and the subject kept pointing the weapon although repeating "it's cool man," "it's cool man." Smith fired again, and this time the subject dropped the weapon and was held spread-eagled on the ground until Evans drove up.

The suspect was a 6'2", 170-pound black male, 23 years old with a date of birth of March 31, 1948. He reported his name as Jesse Jerome Smith, nickname "Skeeter," who claimed to have been born in Kingston, Jamaica. He seemed pleasant but kept repeating the same slang words, "Be cool man, that ain't cool man." Smith/Skeeter was dressed strangely in a "green and white zebra like design shirt brown print trousers that had the fly open" and brown and gray shoes with one-inch crepe soles. Clutched in his hand was a bunch of rags that turned out to be underwear and on his head was a pair of ladies' panties stretched tight over his mid-length, Afro-style haircut. With a beard and mustache, Jesse Smith looked demonic.

By the afternoon following the arrest, the zebra-striped suspect had been identified by three witnesses who had each independently picked him out of a lineup. Two days later, Evans and Smith learned that the rapist's real name was Eddie Lee Mosley and he was the third of 10 children who in his early 20s was still living at home with his parents in the northwest section.

Jessie Jerome Smith was identified as Eddie Lee Mosley by his fingerprints, checked by police aide Robert Knapp, from an application for a handyman job at a hotel on the beach. Further checking of records on Mosley at this time revealed that he had been arrested in 1963 by Jack McFadden on a city charge for kissing a white woman. Based on the lineup identifications, Evans had evidence to charge Mosley for the rapes of the victims who identified him but not for the murder of Naomi Gamble. After the arrest, a file that included all the names of the rape victims was taken to the State Attorney's Office. Evans conferred with Michael Satz, head of the homicide unit, and advised him that additional charges of rape and kidnapping could be added. Satz stated that he would go with what he had because he did not want people to think they were just piling the charges on Mosley.

However, the trial never took place. Deemed incompetent to stand trial, Mosley was sent to the Florida State Hospital for the criminally insane in Chattahoochee.

A few months after taking over the moribund rape unit of the Fort Lauderdale Police Department, Evans and his partner Smith had arrested the man more than likely responsible for most of the perhaps 100 rapes reported in the neighborhood since 1971. In the five years that followed Mosley's arrest, no woman was murdered by a stranger in the northwest side neighborhood, and rapes dropped to a handful per year.

But in the summer of 1979, the bodies started showing up again. Ernestine German was raped and murdered on June 30, Catherine Moore on July 20, Sonia Marion on July 29, and Terry Jean Cummings on August 7. The nightmare was back, and the question was how Mosley got out. Certainly, neither Doug Evans nor the people of the northwest side was so informed. Nevertheless, Mosley's doctors had determined that years of confinement and antipsychotic drugs had rendered him a suitable risk for release. The charges against him had been dropped by the state when it seemed he would be detained indefinitely.

Mosley was back on the streets of Fort Lauderdale, but he was not changed by his years of confinement and treatment. Before, he had raped with an occasional death, perhaps caused when overcoming resistance in his simple but relentless way. Now, death was his modus operandi. There would be no more witnesses.

The four killings in four weeks of July and August 1979 produced a peak of panic in the northwest side. Hope and faith in the police had been dashed. A mob chased and beat a man suspected of being a rapist (King 1988). Evans continued to press for an arrest and prosecution of Mosley. In the meantime, he wanted 24-hour surveillance on Mosley. Evans's supervisors seemed to feel that he was overreacting. Perhaps it was the proximity of so many rapes and murders to the streets where he lived and his own daughters walked to school and work. A few months later, a cousin, Arlene Tukes would become another victim. The leadership of the Fort Lauderdale Police Department began to feel that Detective Douglas Evans had a "fetish" for Eddie Lee Mosley.

Besides, after the terrible frenzy of violence in July and August, in September 1979, the Broward Sheriff's Office announced the arrest of a suspect in the murders and in other rapes and murders going back to 1972. It was Jerry Frank Townsend, another African American man from the neighborhood with a marginal level of mental ability and criminal record. Evans vehemently tried to persuade prosecutors that Mosley not Townsend was the killer, but to no avail. Casting doubt on whether his loyalties were with law enforcement or the people of the northwest section, Evans then went a step further and testified for the defense in the Townsend case.

Although a suspect, Townsend was in custody beginning in September 1979, murder-rape victims began appearing again as early as Christmas Eve 1979, when Susan Boynton never made it home. Jeanette Rogers was found on January 21, 1980, Brenda Carter on February 14, Arnette Tukes on February 21, Gloria Irving on March 16. Nonetheless, Townsend was convicted that July of killing Naomi Gamble and another victim.

Later in 1980, Mosley was charged with another rape-murder and this time was convicted and sentenced to 15 years. His conviction was appealed, in part on the ground that his attorney should have pled him not guilty by reason of insanity. Mosley's mental state again became an issue, and he was held in jail until November 1983, when he was again released after pleading guilty in exchange for the time he had already served.

Another break occurred in May 1984 when one of Mosley's victims escaped. Mosley approached a woman in Bass Park and asked her if she wanted to smoke some marijuana. She followed him to a remote corner of the park to smoke. He demanded sex and began to choke her. This time, Mosley was found competent to stand trial. The defense claimed consent and accused the woman of being a prostitute. On October 25, Mosley was acquitted and released.

The bodies came again: Loretta Young Brown on November 10, 1984; Theresa Giles on December 19, 1984; Shandra Whitehead on April 14, 1985. In 1985, Frank Lee Smith, a paroled two-time killer who wandered the neighborhood selling junk and fishing, was convicted of murdering Shandra Whitehead and sentenced to death. The Broward Sheriff's Office, which handled the investigation, dismissed Mosley early as a suspect on the grounds that he was a cousin of the 9-year-old victim's mother and because he did not murder and rape his victims indoors (a false belief). Some 15 years later, Detective Richard Scheff swore before a Broward circuit judge that he had showed a picture of Mosley to a witness in a photo lineup and that she had failed to identify him.

By February 1987, another woman, Santrail Lowe, was raped and murdered after a three-year hiatus. Evans was preparing to retire, his pioneering career as one of the first African American police officers hired by Fort Lauderdale ended early by his repeated frustrations in winning support from his superiors in combating Mosley and defining an adequate standard of investigation. Rookie Detective Kevin Allen was assigned the Lowe case and was running out of leads; he came to discuss the case with

Evans, who was well known in the department for his crusade against rape-murders in the northwest. Without prompting and never having seen the crime file, Evans described to Allen how the body was found: partially nude, panties pulled down, and bra left pushed up, exposing the victim's breasts. Evans had convinced another detective, a white one, that Eddie Lee Mosley remained the most dangerous threat faced by the Fort Lauderdale Police Department.

Allen's break came several months later when Mosley was arrested pushing a shopping cart loaded with plants that appeared to come from a nearby store that had been broken into. Mosley was interrogated about the rapes and murders that had occurred in 1983 and 1984. For the first and only time, Mosley confessed, saying simply, "you got me." He went on to state, "I had sex with someone and they died while I was having sex with them."

Finally confronted with what they had for so long denied, the top leadership were torn between wanting to take credit for arresting one of the worst killers in U.S. history and admitting that Doug Evans had been right, or keep things quiet. Instead, they tried to compromise. Mosley was charged with the murders of Emma Cook and Theresa Giles, but cases already blamed on prisoners Jerry Frank Townsend and Frank Lee Smith were kept out of the public accounting of Mosley's crime.

The 1990s were different years for Fort Lauderdale and much of the rest of south Florida. Like the nation as a whole, the area enjoyed a historic reduction of crime, including homicides. Development in large parts of the area (but not so much in the northwest section) surged as the national economy and the stock market hit all-time highs. During the nation's confusing end of the 2000 presidential race, Fort Lauderdale and Broward County (along with many other parts of Florida) became the center of national attention, but because of dangling chads and not the bodies of murdered young women.

Then, just as the presidential race was moving to its finale, the first of two echoes of the nightmare years returned to reveal a new and deeper dimension of the horror. Overshadowed by the presidential race, and thus little noticed at first, was the news that Frank Lee Smith, a three-time convicted killer who had died the previous January of pancreatic cancer while on Florida's death row, had been cleared by FBI DNA tests of being the man who deposited sperm on and presumably raped and murdered 13-year-old Shandra Whitehead, whose April 1985 murder had sent Smith to death row.

Smith had spent 14 years asserting his innocence to little avail. His initial lawyer provided a vigorous defense but was apparently not fully aware of the larger string of northwest side rape murders, or of Doug Evans's already 12-year-long quest to bring Eddie Lee Mosley to justice. Like many Florida death row inmates in the 1980s, Smith did not get a new defense lawyer until weeks before his execution date. Investigators for the defense immediately focused on Mosley and received a major breakthrough when the major prosecution witness, northwest side resident Chaquita Lowe, was shown a photograph of Mosley and immediately identified him as the man she had seen outside of the house where Shandra Whitehead was raped and murdered.

The evidence against Smith was actually quite limited. In addition to Lowe, Dorothy McGriff, the victim's mother, had also identified Smith, but on the basis of an admittedly poor glance at the perpetrator climbing out a window to escape the house as she pulled up in her car. McGriff was also a cousin of Eddie Mosley, whose family proved tenacious in protecting him. In addition, Detective Richard Scheff of the Broward Sheriff's Office, who had led the investigation of the Whitehead murder, took the stand and testified that Smith had fallen for an old interrogation trick. When the investigator deceptively told Smith that the victim's brother had been awake and seen the killer, Smith blurted out that he could not have been seen because the house was dark.

Notwithstanding the weak evidence and the recantation of Lowe's testimony, the battle over Smith's conviction dragged on for nearly a decade. When he died, painfully of pancreatic cancer on death row, the Broward State Attorney's Office was still successfully fighting demands by his lawyers that the biological evidence from the Whitehead case be tested with new DNA technologies unavailable in 1985. After Smith's death, the DNA was finally tested, thus clearing Smith of the crimes and identifying Mosley as the rapist and killer.

Spurred by the Smith revelation, Fort Lauderdale and Broward investigators began to test all available materials from cases in which Mosley was a suspect, including the string of rape murders attributed to Townsend. When the tests were completed on two of the Townsend murders, Mosley was once again identified as the source of the DNA. What Evans had learned through careful investigation—that Mosley alone was responsible for the whole series of murders in the northwest that had been blamed on others, including Townsend and Smith—was being proven through the new science of DNA. Evans had put himself in conflict with the law

enforcement culture of Broward County when he took the stand to defend Jerry Frank Townsend, now the newspapers and the top prosecutors
and police officials in the area had to admit what was painfully obvious:
Doug Evans was right.

Yet the real horror of the nightmare years may lie here. After Townsend
was arrested in September 1979, twelve women, up to and including young
Shandra Whitehead, were raped and murdered, very likely by Eddie Lee
Mosley. After Frank Smith was arrested for Whitehead's murder in 1985,
at least one other woman, Santrail Lowe, was probably murdered by Mosley. These 13 victims may have suffered no more horrendously than the
dozen or more other women who probably died at Mosley's hands, but
they did die unnecessarily and through the self-interested connivance of
police officers and officials, primarily in the Broward Sheriff's Office, but
also including those in the Fort Lauderdale Police Department that undermined Evan's investigation.

IV. Technology and Mass Surveillance versus Old-Fashioned Policing in the War on Terror

Doug Evans and the X-Rays were not typical of police officers, let alone
Southern police officers, in the 1970s, and were sadly not modal police
officers, but they offer a precedent for a reflexive, craft-policing approach
that might serve as a model of a different kind of post–war on drugs policing strategy, one aimed at preventing violence in specific communities from all kinds of sources (including both terrorism and reactive hate
crimes) by vigorous local investigation coupled with self-conscious efforts
to guard against racial stereotyping and its analogs.

Two other men were sent to prison, one to death row, for Mosley's
crimes. These miscarriages of justice exemplify the high-risk investigatory
strategies on which contemporary police have come to rely. Doug Evans
solved the crimes using his deep local knowledge of his community and
his willingness to interview dozens of witnesses, but Mosley was released
through the indifference of state officials, and his later crimes were pinned
on men more attractive to prosecute.[12]

As we reflect on the terror attacks of September 11, 2001, it is important
that the debate over security versus liberty (and privacy) not obscure the
debate over how security is to be obtained. Let us start with the blunt fact
that from a policing perspective, the 9/11 plot was highly vulnerable to

traditional suspicion-based surveillance. As documented by the 9/11 Commission, American officials were aware of the presence within the United States of all of the terrorists. Some of these individuals were known by other American officials to be involved in militant Islamist politics in Europe. Famously, our government agencies "failed to connect the dots," but that should not satisfy us. Any close surveillance of these individuals would have raised many deeper reasons for suspicion. Why were they in flight schools? How were they being financed? Even if prior knowledge of the terrorists had not identified them as persons worthy of suspicion, their behavior alone—especially their highly irregular conduct in Miami when Mohammed Atta and one of his associates flew a small private aircraft from their flight school to the very busy Miami International Airport and then left the aircraft on the tarmac after abandoning their take off—should have drawn attention to their suspicious character.

Instead of an effort to improve our law enforcement ability to identify and follow suspicious persons, the Bush administration's war on terror has consisted of issuing intimidating orders to appear for questioning to thousands of Muslim immigrants to the United States, imprisoning for more than five years hundreds of apparently "low-value" suspects in Guantanamo, torturing (or close to it) higher-value suspects in secret prisons around the world, overthrowing governments in Afghanistan and Iraq and replacing them with apparently more democratic governments which continue to survive only with U.S. military (or NATO) life support, and embracing high-technology surveillance of international phone calls.

This is a broader pattern of global security that has fed on the bad example of the American war on crime. While the rhetoric of the war on crime celebrated the heroism of police, the tactics emphasized rounding up low-value suspects through relatively easy low-grade surveillance and seizure. DNA exonerations in recent years and the exposure of police fabrication in the conviction of over 40 mostly black residents of Tulia, Texas, have shown that for more serious crimes coercive interrogation, jailhouse informants, and, if necessary, police perjury became all too common. The minimal concern with the seriousness or even guilt of arrestees reflected a belief that incarcerating large numbers of potentially dangerous criminals would repress crime, making careful investigations superfluous.

We see this concern reflected in an international anti-doping effort in sports that is largely dependent on drug testing rather than police investigation (Alexander 2006). We see it reflected in the preference of many contemporary mayors spending money on high-technology license plate readers and roadside video surveillance cameras instead of on community policing. The reliance on technology and mass surveillance over close police investigation of suspicious individuals is promising only if you like the logic of the war on drugs. We need a new paradigm across a whole set of security problems (from terror to urban crime, white collar crime, and sports), but fortunately we can recover much from an old paradigm—that is, investigation that relies on knowing a community and its residents rather than on broad dragnets or coercive tactics. A community policing approach to, say, doping in sports, would not require harsh prison terms for those found doping or even formal criminalization. Police can seek to discover the source of nuisances that endanger the health and well-being of the community and seek civil measures to restrain the abusive behavior.

What would a "community policing" approach to homeland security look like? First, it would involve direct contacts between law enforcement and Muslim immigrant communities to assure them that they are part of the community being protected. Political scientist David Thacher (2001) has described this kind of approach by the police in Dearborn, Michigan, a city with the highest concentration of Middle Eastern immigrants and their children in the United States. Second, it would involve expanding police staffing to permit permanent site-appropriate surveillance of vulnerable terrorism targets (police departments today are doing this on a limited basis, but at a cost of stretching existing resources). Third, it would require upgrading the communication and command integration of police and other first-responding organizations to assure that rescuers would have the best possible chance of saving lives (including their own).

NOTES

1. Scheck, Neufeld, and Dwyer (2000) use the apt metaphor of a flashlight beam to describe the way in which DNA evidence shines a focused beam on a case that then suggests broader patterns of misconduct, patterns that extend to potentially many more cases where no relevant biological evidence is available for testing.

2. This is a small contribution toward what Richard Leo (2005, 202) has called for—that is, a "criminology of wrongful conviction."

3. One source that Scalia relied on was Samuel Walker's influential study of the increasing rationalization, or bureaucratic control of discretion, within the criminal justice system (see Walker 1993, 51). Walker, however, had other

thoughts, which he published in an op-ed piece in the *Los Angeles Times* noting that police reform remains an incomplete project (Walker 2006).

4. Aggregates may be especially misleading because American policing is overwhelmingly locally controlled.

5. For a parallel that may prove fruitful, consider the discussion in Israel over whether the long involvement of the Israeli Defense Force in the suppression of Palestinian resistance to occupation on the West Bank and Gaza created internal changes, the vulnerabilities of which were on display in the recent and disastrous (from Israel's perspective) Lebanese war.

6. The analogy to junk food is almost irresistible (see Pollan 2006).

7. In the preface to his pioneering book on police, sociologist William Westley had this to say about police in the 1950s when he made his observations: "In 1950, when this study was made, some rookie policemen were so conscious of public disapproval of the police that they refused to wear their uniforms going to and from work" (Westley 1970, xiii).

8. This is especially the case for those in jail who can get access to a suspect detained and awaiting trial.

9. Inbau's manual on police interrogation was the very target of the Chief Justice's ire in the *Miranda* opinion.

10. Robocop, ironically, turns out to be a Warren Court proceduralist, citing his legal mandates, placed in his root program, as preventing him from carrying out the violent acts of repression planned by his corporate masters.

11. Video-recording, as noted above, is an extension of the disciplinary model of police reform, and many of the other wrongful conviction reforms have disciplinary as well as craft aspects. Rather than seeing these as opposites, it might be better to see them as alternatives that can be combined. The craft conception combines discipline with forms of self-fashioning.

12. Doug Evans's role in the case is profiled in the Frontline (PBS) documentary, *Requiem for Frank Lee Smith* (2002).

CASES

Gideon v. Wainwright, 372 U.S. 335 (1963)
Hudson v. Michigan (2006) 547 U.S. ___; 2006 U.S. LEXIS 4677
Mapp v. Ohio, 367 U.S. 643 (1961)
Miranda v. Arizona, 348 U.S. 436 (1966)

REFERENCES

Alexander, Brian (2006) "Tour de Farce: Floyd Landis' Positive Test Shows Why Drug Testing Will Never Work," *Slate*, July 27, at http://www.slate.com/id/2145530.

Bayley, David H., and Egon Bittner (1984) "Learning the Skills of Policing," *Law and Contemporary Problems* 47, no. 4, pp. 35–59.

Beckett, Katherine (1997) *Making Crime Pay: Law and Order in Contemporary American Politics* (New York: Oxford University Press).

Caplow, Theodore, and Jonathan Simon (1998) "Understanding Prison Policy and Population Trends," in *Crime and Justice*, vol. 26: *Prisons*, ed. Michael Tonry and Joan Petersilia, p. 63–120.

Dubber, Markus (2002) *Victims in the War on Crime: The Use and Abuse of Victim's Rights* (New York: New York University Press).

Egelko, Bob (2006) "Governor Vetoes Bills on Wrongful Convictions: Measure to Record Interrogations Called Too Vague," *San Francisco Chronicle* (October 3).

Feeley, Malcolm, and Jonathan Simon (1992) "The New Penology: Notes on the Emerging Strategy of Corrections and Its Implications," *Criminology* 30, pp. 449–74.

Fort Lauderdale Police Department (n.d.) "Photograph Album in Uniform," at http://ci.ftlaud.fl.us/police/photobook5.html (last visited January 4, 2008).

Foucault, Michel (1977) *Discipline and Punish: The Birth of the Prison,* trans. Alan Sheridan (New York: Pantheon).

Garland, David (2001a) *The Culture of Control: Crime and Social Order in a Contemporary Society* (Chicago: University of Chicago Press).

Garland, David (2001b) *Mass Imprisonment: Social Causes and Consequences* (Thousand Oaks, CA: Sage).

Inbau, Fred E. (1961) "Police Interrogation: A Practical Necessity," *Journal of Criminal Law, Criminology and Police Science* 52, no. 1, pp. 16–20.

King, Jonathon (1988) "The Fifteen Year Hunt for Serial Killer," *Sun Sentinel* (October 30).

Kraska, Peter (2001) "The Military-Criminal Justice Blur: An Introduction," in *Militarizing the American Criminal Justice System: The Changing Roles of the Armed Forces and the Police,* ed. Peter B. Kraska (Boston: Northeastern University Press).

Leo, Richard A. (2005) "Rethinking the Study of Miscarriages of Justice: Developing a Criminology of Wrongful Conviction," *Journal of Criminal Law and Criminology* 21, pp. 201–23.

Leo, Richard A., Steven A. Drizin, Peter J. Neufeld, Bradley R. Hall, and Amy Vatner (2006) "Bringing Reliability Back In: False Confessions and Legal Safeguards in the 21st Century," *Wisconsin Law Review* 2006, pp. 479–539.

Pollan, Michael (2006) *The Omnivore's Dilemma* (London: Penguin Press).

Saks, Michael, and Jonathan J. Koehler (2005) "The Coming Paradigm Shift in Forensic Identification Science," *Science* 309, pp. 892–95.

Scheck, Barry, Peter Neufeld, and Jim Dwyer (2000) *Actual Innocence: Five Days to Execution and Other Dispatches from the Wrongly Convicted* (New York: Doubleday).

Scheingold, Stuart A. (1991) *The Politics of Street Crime: Criminal Process and Cultural Obsession* (Philadelphia: Temple University Press).

Simon, Dan (forthcoming) *Judging Blame: Law, Psychology, and Wrongful Convictions* (Cambridge: Harvard University Press).

Simon, Jonathan (1993) *Poor Discipline: Parole and the Social Control of the Underclass 1890–1990* (Chicago: University of Chicago Press).

Simon, Jonathan (2007) *Governing through Crime: How the War on Crime Transformed American Democracy and Created a Culture of Fear* (New York: Oxford University Press).

Sklansky, David (2006) "Not Your Father's Police Department: Making Sense of the New Demographics of Police Departments," *Journal of Criminal Law and Criminology* 96, pp. 1209–42.

Sourcebook of Criminal Justice Statistics at http://www.albany.edu/sourcebook.

Thacher, David (2001) "Conflicting Values in Community Policing," *Law and Society Review* 35, pp. 765–98.

Walker, Samuel (1993) *Taming the System: The Control of Discretion in Criminal Justice 1950–1990* (New York: Oxford University Press).

Walker, Samuel (2006) "Scalia Twisted My Words," *Los Angeles Times* (June 25).

Western, Bruce (2006) *Punishment and Inequality* (London: Sage).

Westley, William A. (1970) *Violence and the Police: A Sociological Study of Law, Custom, and Morality* (Cambridge, Mass.: MIT Press).

Zimring, Franklin E., Gordon Hawkins, and Sam Kamin (2001) *Punishment and Democracy: Three Strikes and You're Out in California* (New York: Oxford University Press).

Chapter 5

||||||||||||||||||||||||||||||||||||||||||||||||||||

Kalven and Zeisel in the
Twenty-First Century
Is the Jury Still the Defendant's Friend?

Daniel Givelber

The Beneficent Jury

We now recognize that our system of determining criminal guilt is fallible. We make both kinds of errors: we acquit the guilty, and we convict the innocent. The latter practice—convicting someone innocent of the crime—has traditionally been identified as the error we strive hardest to avoid. For most of the twentieth century, those who participated in and commented on the criminal justice system were quite sanguine that our criminal process achieved this goal. The concern was whether we paid too high a price in terms of the guilty going free, not whether we had done all we could do to ensure that the innocent were not convicted. Writing in 1970, Henry Friendly asserted:

> The proverbial man from Mars would surely think that we must consider our system of criminal justice terribly bad if we are willing to tolerate such efforts at undoing judgments of conviction. He would be surprised, I should suppose, to be told both that it never was really bad and that it has been steadily improving. . . . His astonishment would grow when we told him that the one thing almost never suggested on collateral attack is that the prisoner was innocent of the crime.[1]

This rosy picture altered dramatically with the emergence of DNA-related exonerations in the early 1990s. Spurred by the results of DNA tests that successfully challenged the outcome of routine criminal cases, there is widespread recognition—at least among scholars[2]—that neither prosecutorial screening nor the requirement of proof beyond a reasonable doubt nor any other adjudicatory rule eliminates the occasional conviction of the innocent. We do not know how often this occurs, but the general view is that it is far from a "freakish" outcome. Commentators, and occasionally legislators, have proposed a range of remedies for this problem, none of which is entirely satisfactory.

Why did it take us until the 1990s to pay serious, systemic attention, to the possibility that the innocent are convicted? The question of whether we convict the innocent had been raised repeatedly since the 1930s by jurists as distinguished as Jerome Frank, authors as well known as Erle Stanley Gardner (author of the Perry Mason stories), and scholars as eminent as Edwin Borchard.[3] One answer is that there was no science comparable to DNA that enabled advocates to "prove" that an innocent person had been convicted of a crime he did not commit. For whatever reason, fingerprints did not generate a comparable response when they were introduced into American law enforcement. Typically, it was the emergence of evidence of guilt against a third party or key witnesses recanting testimony which established that the convicted person was innocent, and the cases in which this occurred were simply too infrequent to support any conclusion other than it was possible (although highly improbable) to come to an inaccurate determination of guilt.

A second answer is that we are committed to a method of determining historical fact in criminal trials—the adversarial presentation of evidence to the jury—which is both secret and beyond challenge. Without a record of its deliberations, there was no possibility of demonstrating that the jury had arrived at its conclusion through flawed reasoning or that it credited the testimony of a witness for inappropriate reasons. Judicial review of jury verdicts focused on the question of whether, given the evidence before them, it was *possible* for the jury to arrive at the conclusion it did. There was no way to know how the jury found facts or understood the law or performed the task of integrating law and fact. Nor could this inquiry even be undertaken if the jury acquitted the defendant.

George Fisher has suggested that these very qualities made the jury a particularly attractive fact-finder. Tracing the history of adjudicatory "lie detection" (to use his term), Fisher argues that the very impossibility of resolving conclusively which of two or more opposing witnesses was telling the truth argued for giving the task to a jury operating in a "black box."[4] Juries were embraced not because their determinations were accurate but because they were secret and definitive. Leaving highly contested determinations of historical fact to the jury shielded judges from the need to make these very difficult judgments.

Those who have examined the jury and its operation in criminal cases have generally evaluated its contributions positively. With respect to the question of whether a system that embraces the jury produces superior justice to one that trusts the disposition of criminal cases exclusively to professionals, the answer has typically been "yes." Different observers focus on different functions. Some observers applaud the jury for its ability to transcend the results that accrue from a literal application of law to fact in order to achieve a higher justice.[5] Others celebrate the jury's role in providing for citizen participation in the vital work of government.[6] The jury also serves as a check on government overreaching.[7] Others like Fisher note that the jury provides legitimacy for a necessarily flawed system of determining historical fact. Critics complain about the institution's inefficiency and the high price we pay in terms of the guilty going free.[8]

Rather than the jury system generating alarm among those who valued a fair criminal process, it has been celebrated. When the Supreme Court decided in 1968 that the Fourteenth Amendment to the United States Constitution required states to provide jury trials in all serious criminal cases,[9] it did not reason that criminal defendants are entitled to a jury trial because juries are more accurate determiners of guilt or innocence than judges. Rather, the jury served as a check on executive and judicial power. The Court pointed to the jury's ability to ignore law and fact and thus acquit the technically guilty as a justification for its view of the jury's centrality in our constitutional scheme of guilt adjudication. The jury was essential precisely because it could constrain governmental overreaching by refusing to convict a person whom the state was pursuing for reasons that the jury might consider inappropriate.

The other side of the coin—that a jury freed from any effective review of its deliberations might also convict the innocent—was not identified as a problem.[10] First, the defendant could always waive the jury if he felt that he was going to be treated unjustly. Second, outcomes unjust to the defendant were improbable because, in the Court's view, Kalven and Zeisel's *American Jury* had demonstrated that juries "do understand the evidence and come to sound conclusions in most of the cases presented to them and that *when juries differ with the result at which the judge would have arrived, it is usually because they are serving the very purposes for which they were created and for which they are now employed*" (emphasis added).[11] Kalven and Zeisel had shown that juries were seven times as likely to acquit when the judge would have convicted as they were to do the opposite—to convict when the judge would have acquitted.[12] They were, in Kalven and Zeisel's terminology, "liberated" in close cases to decide the case in light of their values (sentiments), and this liberation worked overwhelmingly in favor of the defendant. Juries were also more likely to credit the testimony of defendants with no criminal records. Finally, juries demanded more proof than judges before they were prepared to find a defendant guilty. This last feature of the jury identified by Kalven and Zeisel—that jurors had a higher evidentiary threshold for conviction than did judges—was recently affirmed by Eisenberg and his colleagues.[13]

The American Jury was published in 1966, at the height of the Supreme Court's due process revolution in criminal procedure. Its attitude toward accuracy resonated with the Court's embrace of due process values: factual fidelity was neither the only nor, in some circumstances, the most important value to be served by criminal adjudication. Defendants had a right to a lawyer. Relevant evidence could not be considered in determining the defendant's guilt if that evidence had been seized unconstitutionally. The defendant could not be required to speak if he opted for silence, nor could his silence be the basis for the conclusion that he refused to speak because he had something to hide. Although sacrificing accuracy in the name of higher, dignitary values appears at odds with an unwavering commitment to the accurate determination of innocence, no one in any Court majority ever suggested that sacrificing the innocent was an acceptable price to pay in order to protect the rights of the accused. The innocent were simply not at risk. As Learned Hand insisted more than 80 years ago, "The ghost of innocent man convicted" was "an unreal dream."[14] The due process revolution was treated as a single-edged sword: it was appropriate to place other values ahead of accuracy because the result would only be to free the guilty, not to convict the innocent.[15]

How could the Court be certain that its new rules would not harm the innocent? The specter of the falsely convicted innocent dissolves either if there are no innocents to be convicted (only the guilty are charged) or if we can be assured that the few innocents who do go to trial will necessarily be acquitted. Since juries were far more acquittal prone than judges, the defendant's right to invoke a jury provided reassurance that no innocent person would be convicted. And, in the view of no less an observer than Justice Scalia, things have only improved since the days of Kalven and Zeisel.[16]

While their data showed the jury to be the defendant's friend, Kalven and Zeisel resisted making such a claim. Indeed, "we suspect there is little directionality to the jury's response. It is not fundamentally defendant-prone, rather it is non-rule minded: it will move where the equities are. And where the equities are will depend on both the state of the law and the climate of public opinion."[17] They did not explain why "the state of the law and the climate of public opinion" in the America of the 1950s was pro-defendant. Nor did they explain why it was that juries were responding to "the equities" rather than "the facts" when they disagreed with the judge. Although they had no basis for comparing the judge's assessment of what moved the jury with the jury's own assessment and no basis for determining how the judge arrived at his view of the case, Kalven and Zeisel nonetheless concluded that "when the jury reaches a different conclusion than the judge on the same evidence, it does so not because it is a sloppy or inaccurate finder of facts, but because it gives recognition to values that fall outside the official rules."[18]

Liberation: Fifty Years Later

More than 50 years have passed since Kalven and Zeisel undertook their study of the criminal jury.[19] They collected data as to the race and gender of defendants but did not ask about the race or gender of either the judge or the jurors. Nor did they ask whether the defendant was represented by a public defender or private attorney. Apparently, these were not variables that the authors believed were going to be useful in explaining why judges and juries might agree or disagree.

The 50 years since Kalven and Zeisel were marked by sweeping changes in racial and gender diversity on the bench and among juries. In 1975, the Supreme Court ruled that juries had to be drawn from a representative cross section of the community, ending years of practices that made juries virtually all male and very white.[20] The people passing judgment on guilt today are far more representative of the community than those in the Kalven and Zeisel survey. The people on whom they are passing judgment have changed as well: three-quarters of the defendants in the Kalven and Zeisel survey were white. This contrasts to only 10 percent of the defendants in the National Center for States Courts study of 400 criminal trials in four jurisdictions, which was designed, in part, to replicate the Kalven and Zeisel study.[21]

Contemporary juries remain more acquittal prone than judges. Table 5.1 is taken from Eisenberg et al.'s partial replication of the Kalven and Zeisel study of juries.[22] It shows that if one follows Kalven and Zeisel's path of dividing the cases of hung juries between acquittals and convictions, judges and juries today exhibit the same pattern of agreement that they did 50 years before. However, whereas in 1966 juries were *more* likely to agree with the judge about acquittals (14/17 = 82%) than about convictions (64/83 = 77%), now juries are *less* likely to agree with judges about acquittals (13/19 = 68%) than about convictions (62/81 = 78%). The rate at which judges disagree with a jury's guilty verdict has doubled (from 3% to 6%).

Rather than following Kalven and Zeisel and arbitrarily dividing hung juries between convictions and acquittals, it makes more sense to exclude hung jury cases altogether from an analysis of whether we convict the innocent.[23] Table 5.2 does this.

TABLE 5.1
Judge-Jury Agreement: The National Center for State Courts (NCSC) (2002) and Kalven and Zeisel (1966)

	Jury acquittal (%)	Jury conviction (%)
NCSC		
Judge acquittal	13	6
Judge conviction	19	62
Kalven and Zeisel		
Judge acquittal	14	3
Judge conviction	19	64

Sources: Kalven and Zeisel 1966; Hannaford-Agor, Hans, Mott, and Munsterman 2002.

TABLE 5.2
Judge-Jury Agreement, Excluding Hung Juries: National Center for State Courts (NCSC) (2002) and Kalven and Zeisel (1966)

	Jury acquits (%)	Jury acquits (n)	Jury convicts (%)	Jury convicts (n)	Total (%)
NCSC					
Judge acquits	12.4	(36)	5.8	(17)	18.3
Judge convicts	17.0	(49)	64.7	(187)	81.7
Total	29.4		70.6		100
Kalven and Zeisel					
Judge acquits	14.2		2.3		16.5
Judge convicts	17.9		65.6		83.5
Total	32.1		67.9		100

Sources: Hannaford-Agor, Hans, Mott, and Munsterman 2002; Kalven and Zeisel 1966.

Unlike 50 years earlier, judges and juries in the 2000s are more likely to disagree about when an acquittal is appropriate than they are about when a conviction is appropriate.[24] Kalven and Zeisel found the opposite. Juries agreed with judges that the defendant should be *acquitted* 86 percent of the time. They agreed that the defendant should be *convicted* 77 percent of the time. While the rate of agreement between judge and jury as to who is guilty has not changed (78% in the NCSC study as opposed to 77% in the Kalven and Zeisel survey), the rate of agreement as to who is innocent has.[25] It has gone from judge and jury agreeing about innocence in 86 percent of the cases when Kalven and Zeisel did their research to 70 percent agreement in the NCSC study.

Juries still acquit more people whom judges indicate they would convict (17% of cases are "normal disagreements," to use Kalven and Zeisel's terms) than they convict people whom the judges say they would acquit (5.8% of cases are what Kalven and Zeisel termed "crossover disagreements"). However, rather than the Kalven and Zeisel ratio of 7.8:1 cases in which the jury acquits although the judge would convict as opposed to the opposite (see table 5.2), the NCSC data show that ratio now to be 2.9:1. If one were to make the (generous) assumption that the judge's assessments are always correct in that those whom the judge would have acquitted are, at a minimum, legally (and perhaps factually) innocent, this shift would mean that we have gone from a system that generates nearly eight acquittals of the legally guilty for every conviction of a legally innocent to a system that generates slightly more than three acquittals of the legally guilty for every conviction of a legally innocent person. Whatever we mean by the claim that "it is better that ten guilty go free than one innocent be convicted" (which suggests, after all, that the guilty are going free to ensure that no innocent is convicted, and not to justify the occasional conviction of an innocent), a system that operates to convict a possibly innocent person every time three guilty are acquitted does not meet the ideal.

We do not know that the judge's indication of her willingness to acquit in cases where the jury convicts reflects what she would have done had she been sitting without a jury. Since there are (apparently) no cases in which the judge ordered either a judgment of acquittal or granted a motion for new trial,[26] the judge probably felt that the evidence supported the jury verdict, even if she would not have come to this result. This does not mean that judges were particularly troubled when juries convicted

TABLE 5.3
Judge's Level of Satisfaction with Jury Verdict

	Dissatisfied		Equipoise		Satisfied		
	(%)	(n)	(%)	(n)	(%)	(n)	Total n
Liberation	43.5	(20)	34.8	(16)	21.7	(10)	46
Reverse liberation	13.3	(2)	33.3	(4)	53.3	(8)	15

Source: Analysis of data from NCSC study (Hannaford-Agor, Hans, Mott, and Munsterman 2002)
Note: Applies to cases in which the jury acquits a defendant whom the judge believes is guilty ("liberation" cases) as contrasted to cases in which the judge would acquit a person whom the jury acquits ("reverse liberation"). Dissatisfied, 3 or less on a 7-point scale; equipoise, 4 on a 7-point scale; satisfied, 5 to 7 on a 7-point scale.

those whom the judge would have acquitted. Judges who were not sure of the defendant's guilt endorsed a jury conviction far more than judges who were persuaded of the defendant's guilt welcomed a jury acquittal. *They were more than twice as likely to indicate that they were quite satisfied with a jury decision when that decision was to convict even though the judge would have acquitted (53%) than when the jury's decision was to acquit when the judge would have convicted (22%)* (table 5.3). Thus, while the judge's disagreement with the jury in the crossover cases may suggest that the evidence of guilt was, to her eyes at least, equivocal, these satisfaction levels make it difficult to invoke the judge's support for the position that all the defendants in crossover cases are innocent. Kalven and Zeisel's respondents were also more troubled by liberation cases (the jury acquits when the judge would have convicted) as opposed to reverse liberation (the jury convicts when the judge would have acquitted), although at lower rates overall (20% of their respondents thought that jury decisions that were more lenient than the respondent believed appropriate were "without merit" as opposed to only 7% of the cases in which the judge was more lenient than the jury).[27]

If we limit the cases of potential miscarriage of justice to those cases in which the judge both would have acquitted and was somewhere between dissatisfied and in equipoise with the jury's decision to convict, there are nine such cases, or 2.7 percent of the total cases and 3.8 percent of convictions.[28] If we do not limit the inquiry to crossover cases and instead look at the judge's level of satisfaction with guilt determinations in single-count cases (there are 56 such cases in the database), the judge is dissatisfied with four of them, or 7.1 percent of the single-count convictions and in equipoise about the guilty verdict in another five, or 8.9 percent of such convictions (table 5.4).[29]

TABLE 5.4

Judge's Satisfaction with Jury's Verdict in Prosecutions
Containing a Single Criminal Charge

Single-count jury verdict	Dissatisfied (%)	(n)	Equipoise (%)	(n)	Satisfied (%)	(n)	Total n
Guilty	7.1	(4)	8.9	(5)	83.9	(47)	56
Not guilty	13.3	(4)	16.7	(5)	70	(21)	30

Source: Analysis of data from NCSC study (Hannaford-Agor, Hans, Mott, and Munsterman 2002)
Note: Dissatisfied, 3 or less on a 7-point scale; equipoise, 4 on a 7-point scale; satisfied, 5 to 7 on a 7-point scale.

TABLE 5.5

Conviction Rate by Strength of Evidence as Evaluated by Judge and Jury

Judge's view of evidence	Cases judge convicts (%)	Cases jury convicts (%)	Jury's view of evidence	Cases judge convicts (%)	Cases jury convicts (%)
Strong for guilt n = 113	99	87	Strong for guilt n = 97	97	98
Middling for guilt n = 149	78	61	Middling for guilt n = 149	79	61
Weak for guilt n = 26	27	46	Weak for guilt n = 29	41	17
Total	82 n = 235	70 n = 201		82 n = 224	70 n = 191

Source: Percentages are derived from Eisenberg et al. 2005, 186 (table 4).

Assuming that cases in which the judge indicates that she would have acquitted when the jury convicts are, at a minimum, a likely source of wrongful convictions, is there reason to believe that the frequency with which jurors may convict the innocent has possibly increased since Kalven and Zeisel's day?

We have seen a modest increase in the overall percentage of cases in which either the judge or the jury disagree about whether the defendant should be found guilty (from 20.2% to 22.8%, an increase of 13%) and a very large increase in the percentage of cases where judges acquit and juries convict (from 2.3% to 5.8%, a 250% increase). The NCSC juries were readier to convict than were the Kalven and Zeisel juries, and the NCSC judges were readier to disagree with the jury's conclusion that the defendant was guilty. These data do not establish that the danger of an innocent person being convicted has increased or at least not diminished since 1966, but they are consistent with such a conclusion.

These concerns are not alleviated if we compare the judge and jury's assessment of the weight of the evidence with their respective willingness to convict.

Judges decide guilt at the same rate when the evidence is middling, whether or not it is their view of the evidence or that of the jury that one considers. Juries exhibit the same characteristic (although they are considerably less likely than judges to convict):[30] judges react similarly when the jury considers the evidence of guilt to be strong; juries are slightly less ready to convict in the cases in which judges evaluate the evidence as strong. As shown in table 5.5, major differences are found in the cases that either the judge or jury evaluates as weak: juries convict at a higher rate than judges (46% vs. 27%) when the judge evaluates the evidence of guilt as weak (1 or 2 on the Likert scale), and judges convict at a higher rate than juries (41% to 17%) when the jury evaluates the evidence as weak. Despite the requirement of proof beyond a reasonable doubt and despite the jury's ability to be merciful, juries convict defendants almost 20 percent of the time when the jury views the evidence against him as weak and nearly one-half (46%) of the time that the judge views the evidence against the defendant as weak. If the judge's assessment of the evidence is correct, juries are injustice machines, convicting nearly one-half of the likely innocent and acquitting one out of eight of the very likely guilty. If the jury's assessment of the evidence is correct, judges are prepared to convict the likely innocent but not to free the clearly guilty.

Why Are Contemporary Juries Less Likely to Agree with Judges about Acquittals Than about Convictions?

What Has Changed?

Ask how criminal adjudication has changed since 1960, and the answer appears obvious. Due process has been revolutionized. Various commandments of the Bill of Rights have been applied to the states.[31] This process began just as Kalven and Zeisel completed their surveys and continues to the present. One might imagine, then, that the picture of criminal litigation presented in the *American Jury* and the picture reflected in the NCSC study would differ significantly, given the flowering of constitutional criminal procedure beginning in the 1960s. The picture that emerges from the NCSC study is quite different from that presented by Kalven and Zeisel, but the direction of the change is hardly encouraging. As some scholars have suggested might be the case, the emergence of constitutional criminal procedure has not led to a more vigorous factual defense of criminal cases. The trend is in the opposite direction.

Due Process Revolution

Kalven and Zeisel's data were collected during the 1950s,[32] at a time when states were not constitutionally obligated to provide an attorney in all serious cases, much less a constitutionally competent attorney.[33] Nor were criminal defendants entitled to a jury trial in such cases. The right of a prosecutor to impeach the accused with his criminal record was virtually unconstrained, and prosecutors were free to comment on the accused's failure to testify. The protections against racial bias in the selection of those juries that were employed were quite limited. It was an era of white judges and white juries.[34]

Today a defendant has a right to a jury trial conducted by constitutionally competent counsel. He can remain silent, and his silence cannot be treated as an indication of guilt. If he testifies, there are now limits on whether, and to what extent, the prosecutor can question him about this criminal record. The state is obligated to provide the defendant with exculpatory material and to provide him with expert witnesses in the event that their analysis and testimony would be material to his defense. The jury judging the defendant's guilt must be drawn from a pool from which minorities cannot be systematically excluded.[35] Judges are also far more likely to reflect the diversity found in society at large.[36]

These changes have not improved the amount of information available to judges and juries. While one would imagine that the right to both counsel and a jury trial should alleviate the problems of inaccuracy, whether they do so depends on what counsel does and how that affects the jury. The juries determining guilt or innocence in the 1950s and 1960s were considerably more likely to hear from the defendant, to hear from more than one defense witness, and to hear *any* defense witness than the contemporary juries in the NCSC study. In the one area where contemporary juries are provided with more information than those from the mid-twentieth century—expert testimony—the number of cases in which the prosecution employs such experts has more than doubled, whereas defense experts have only increased by 50 percent.[37] The juries in the NCSC study determined guilt or innocence based on considerably less information from and about the defendant than did the juries that Kalven and Zeisel studied. A higher proportion of defendants faced the jury clothed in very little more than the presumption of innocence in the year 2000 than did so in the 1950s (table 5.6).

TABLE 5.6
Percentage of Trials with Particular Forms of Evidence

	Kalven and Zeisel $n = 1,191$	NCSC $n = 313$
Defense presents no witnesses	10	25
Defendant testifies alone	(Not included)	18
Defendant testifies at all	82	50
Defense presents more than one witness	65	42
Defense presents expert witness	6	9
Prosecution presents two or more witnesses	98	97
Prosecution presents expert witness	5	54

Explaining the Change

ROLE OF CRIMINAL RECORD

Why did the defendants in the NCSC study put on less of a defense case? One explanation for the decrease in the defendant's testimony is that contemporary defendants are more likely to have criminal records than did those in the Kalven and Zeisel survey. More than one out of two —53 percent—of the defendants in the Kalven and Zeisel study had no criminal record; only one out of four—26 percent—of the defendants in the NCSC had no record. A higher percentage of the Kalven and Zeisel defendants without a record testified than the NCSC defendants (91% vs. 67%), as did the Kalven and Zeisel defendants who had a record (74% vs. 42%).[38] Thus, even if we control for the presence or absence of a criminal record, contemporary defendants are less likely to testify than were their counterparts over half a century ago.

Defendants in the 1950s, like their contemporary counterparts, faced the dilemma that if they testified and were disbelieved, the sentencing judge might punish them for the act of testifying falsely. They also faced the possibility of being impeached with their criminal record. Both of these practices—punishment for false testimony and impeachment with the prior record—have been legitimized to an extent that did not exist in the 1950s.[39] Perhaps this very circumstance makes counsel more aware of these dangers and leads more often than previously to the advice to a client not to testify. Quite independent of whether the defendant can be punished for the perjury if he takes the stand and denies guilt, courts are also authorized to punish those who go to trial and are convicted more severely than those who plead guilty. Putting the government to its proof can be costly.

TABLE 5.7
Reason for No Plea Bargain, NCSC Study (in percentages; n = 203)

	Defendant claims innocence	Defendant refused to plead	No plea offered	No plea agreement reached	Total
Only defendent testifies	42.9	11.4	14.3	31.4	100
No witness testifies	34.8	19.6	10.9	34.8	100
Overall rate	48.8	10.3	10.3	30.5	99.9

Source: Analysis of data from NCSC study (Hannaford-Agor, Hans, Mott, and Munsterman 2002).

If a defendant has no defense, why not plead in return for a lesser sentence? The NCSC study asked defense lawyers why the case did not end in a plea. The answers with respect to the cases in which the defense either offered no witnesses or the defendant testified alone are instructive. In about one-quarter of the cases in which the defense either puts on no witnesses or the defendant testifies alone, either no plea was offered or the defendant refused to consider it. In about one-third of these cases, the parties could not reach an agreement. In at least another one-third of the cases, however, the defendant claimed innocence and refused to plead for that reason (table 5.7).

ROLE OF COUNSEL

William Stuntz has pointed to what he characterizes as the "uneasy relationship" between the flowering of criminal procedure doctrines and the just resolution of criminal cases. He notes that the public resources available for criminal defense are highly constrained, so that the effect of adding more potential defense claims may change the mix of issues that counsel may pursue but is unlikely to affect the overall number of such claims:

> The picture is of an archery contest, where each contestant is given three arrows and three shots at the target. Just before the contest is to begin, all the contestants receive three more arrows. But while a few contestants are, like the rich defendant, allowed to fire all the arrows they have, the large majority must still make do with only three shots. For most contestants, more ammunition does not mean more shots fired, and (depending on the difference in quality of the arrows) it may have only a slight effect on how particular contestants perform. Its primary effect may be to change which arrows contestants pull from their quivers.

That is a fairly accurate picture of criminal litigation and its relationship to changes in the law of criminal procedure. For defense attorneys paid at an hourly rate up to a low fee cap, the picture captures attorneys' litigation incentives quite well. For public defenders, the story is more complicated, though the essential point remains the same. Recall that salaried public defenders, like prosecutors, must ration their time across a set of cases. If the set is large enough (as it appears to be in most public defenders' offices), the level of litigation is essentially at capacity. Additional claims and arguments in one case must mean less aggressive litigation somewhere else. Once again, the prime effect of more constitutional regulation is not so much to increase the level of litigation as to change its distribution. Some claims displace others.[40]

The interaction of expanding constitutional rights and limited defense resources may do more than simply force counsel to substitute one available claim for another. It may lead the defense to expend its limited resources on pursuing constitutional claims rather than developing a defense on the merits.[41] Darryl Brown suggests that the underfunding of criminal defense (as well as prosecutors and police), combined with the primacy of the adjudicatory goals of legitimacy and dispute resolution, exacerbates the already challenging problem of accurately determining historical fact through the adversary presentation of proofs to a panel of amateurs. He notes that no other enterprise seeking to determine historical fact opts for such an awkward approach.[42]

A defense bar operating with constricted resources might well adopt a strategy of stressing constitutional claims and then negotiating a settlement in the event the claims did not succeed in eviscerating the state's case. By definition, the NCSC trials did not follow this pattern. Eschewing a plea in favor of a trial in which one puts forward no witnesses or only the defendant does not appear to be a rational response to the resource constraints under which criminal defense operates. Resource constraints may explain why defendants so regularly contest cases without any witness other than the defendant (or no witness at all), but they do not explain why these cases go to trial in the first place. We know that in more than one-half of these kinds of cases (either no defense witnesses or only the defendant), the defense lawyer's explanation for the trial is that the defendant insisted on his innocence or simply refused to plead. They may have refused to plead because they were, in fact, innocent.

TABLE 5.8
Case Features by Type of Lawyer (in percentages; n = 300)

Case features	Privately retained	Court-appointed private	Public defender
Claims innocence	52.6	54.2	45.4
No witness	23.7	23.3	23.8
Defendant alone	3.4	17.6	22.7
Any witness but not defendant	39.0	25.8	29.7
Defendant and another witness	35.1	32.1	24.0
Convicted of all counts	23.7	40.7	44.4
Acquitted of all counts	39.0	31.4	25.8

Source: Analyses of data from NSCS study (Hannaford-Agor, Hans, Mott, and Munsterman 2002).

The NCSC data suggest that resource constraints may affect the quality of information available to those who decided guilt or innocence. Table 5.8 sets forth the information. Those defendants with privately retained counsel were more likely to be acquitted than those represented by court-appointed counsel or a public defender.[43] They were less likely to be convicted of all counts. Privately retained counsel were also more likely to present a witness independent of the defendant and slightly more likely to present such a witness in combination with the defendant. They were far less likely to ever try a case using the defendant as the sole witness. At least compared with court-appointed lawyers, they were *not* more likely to represent a defendant who refused to plead because he claimed innocence.

Using a refusal to plead on the grounds of innocence as an indicator (albeit not a guarantee) that the defendant may not be guilty, between 45% and 55 percent of the defendants represented by each type of lawyer made this claim (table 5.8). Yet those defendants represented by private counsel were acquitted of all counts at a higher rate than those represented by court-appointed private attorneys or public defenders. They were also less likely to be convicted of all counts than those represented by court-appointed lawyers or public defenders.[44]

One explanation may reside in the evidence presented: those defendants represented by privately retained lawyers were more likely to offer the evidence of a witness other than the defendant and to offer the testimony of both the defendant and another witness than were defendants represented by court-appointed attorneys or public defenders. All three kinds of lawyers were equally likely to try a case without introducing any defense witnesses. The sharpest disagreement, however, is in their approach to trying a case with the defendant as the sole witness: privately retained attorneys virtually never took this approach (3.4% of the cases), whereas court-appointed attorneys and public defenders tried cases in this manner about one-fifth of the time. Defendants represented by private attorneys presented a witness other than the defendant in almost three-quarters of the cases (74.1%); court-appointed attorneys did so in almost 60 percent of the cases (57.9%), and public defenders did so in slightly more than one-half the cases (53.7%).

This is a depressing picture. Unless we are to imagine that the ability to afford a lawyer makes it more likely that someone is innocent (legally, if not factually),[45] there appears to be a disturbing relationship between wealth and the ability to put forth a defense case and case outcome. Yet if there was a connection between wealth and guilt, one would imagine that it would cut the other way. The police would be more reluctant to arrest and the prosecutor to charge someone with resources because of shared assumptions about the profile of a criminal and because the deployment of resources by the defendant would make it more difficult to secure a conviction. The likelihood is that the cases against the defendants with resources were at least as strong as those against the poor. The better results achieved by retained attorneys probably reflects the quality of the defense rather than the relative inadequacy of the state's case.

Drug cases provide an interesting comparison. A higher percentage of those represented by court-appointed attorneys and public defenders were charged with either drug possession or sale (40% and 26%, respectively) than were those represented by private attorneys (17%). Thus it might appear that retained counsel's greater use of witnesses other than the defendant simply reflects the lower incidence of drug charges against those with the resources to hire counsel. Yet in drug cases, as elsewhere, defendants represented by retained counsel were more likely to introduce the evidence of a witness other than the defendant (60%) than defendants represented by court-appointed counsel (51%) and were much more likely to do so than defendants represented by the public defender (25%). Drug acquittals followed a similar pattern: 40 percent for those represented by retained lawyers, 29.4 percent for those represented by court-appointed lawyers, 23.7 percent for those represented by public defenders. Again, unless one wants to imagine that the people arrested for drug-related offenses who can hire a private attorney are simply more likely to have access to third parties to testify on their behalf than those who are represented by assigned lawyers or public defenders, wealth appears to play an unseemly role in the disposition of criminal cases.

Conclusion

The years since the middle of the twentieth century have witnessed a slight decline in the willingness of juries to acquit criminal defendants and an increase in judge-jury disagreement about who should be found not guilty. During that time, the constitutional rights of criminal defendants have increased while the evidence relating to guilt or innocence presented to the jury by criminal defendants has decreased. There is a substantial argument that these developments are related, as lawyers operating under resource constraints may be tempted to substitute relatively inexpensive constitutional legal claims for more expensive factual investigation and disputation. The data demonstrate that defense lawyers are presenting juries with less evidence on behalf of their clients today than was true when Kalven and Zeisel did their survey. It also demonstrates that the decline in defense cases is uneven: privately retained lawyers present more defense evidence than either court-appointed lawyers or public defenders. Privately retained lawyers are also far more likely than publicly appointed lawyers to eschew a defense resting entirely on the defendant's testimony.

These observations do not provide a definitive answer to the question of whether the conviction of the innocent is a more severe problem today than it was over fifty years ago. If to be charged is to be guilty, these outcomes may reflect nothing more than performance: privately retained attorneys are better at manipulating the factors that move a group of amateurs to conclude that guilt has not been established beyond a reasonable doubt. However, if police and prosecutors are not both omniscient and benevolent so that the innocent are charged and forced to trial, we need to be concerned that defendants with the means to retain an attorney fare so much better than those who lack those means. We need to confront the question of which is the appropriate acquittal rate: that occurring in 20 percent of all trials in which the defendant is represented by a privately retained attorney or that generated by trials in 50 percent of all trials in which the defendant is represented by a public defender. Our ideals suggest that the appropriate rate is the one produced when the defendant presents a vigorous defense. Indeed, unless one assumes that innocence manifests itself so unmistakably that an acquittal follows regardless of the resources, time, or skill of the lawyer, it is hard to conjure an argument that the real measure of innocence (legal and, to an unknowable extent, factual) is what is produced by a jury confronted with an unequal presentation of evidence.

Even if we adopt as appropriate the acquittal rate generated by privately retained attorneys, we cannot be certain that the difference in outcome—39 percent acquittals if the attorney is privately retained versus 26 percent acquittals if the attorney is a public defender—means that the poor who are factually innocent are being convicted. What we can be certain about is that, as Kalven and Zeisel suggested more than fifty years ago, juries follow the evidence, and that those defendants who present witnesses in addition to or other than the defendant fare better than those who do not. We can also be certain that, even after appropriate obeisance to the cynicism that surrounds any discussion of actual innocence, one reason that defendants who present affirmative evidence of their innocence prevail more than those who do not is that some of them are, in fact as well as in law, innocent. When a defendant's resources (as reflected by whether the attorney is private or public) affects the extent to which she can present a defense, justice can and does miscarry. Kalven and Zeisel speculated that juries did not have a pro-defendant bias but were likely to move with the equities of the case.[46] If this is correct, as the defense shrinks, the "equities" move toward the prosecution.

NOTES

1. Henry J. Friendly," Is Innocence Irrelevant? Collateral Attack on Criminal Judgments," *University of Chicago Law Review* 38 (1970): 142, 145.

2. Justice Scalia remains skeptical of claims that the problem is widespread. *Kansas v. Marsh*, 126 S. Ct. 2516, 2532–2539 (2006) (concurring opinion).

3. Jerome and Barbara Frank, *Not Guilty* (Garden City, N.Y.: Doubleday, 1957); Earl Stanley Gardner, *The Court of Last Resort* (New York: W. Sloane, 1952). The seminal work was Edwin Borchard, *Convicting the Innocent* (New York: Da Capo, 1970 [1932]). Perhaps the most influential work is that of Hugo Bedau and Michael Radelet, "Miscarriages of Justice in Potentially Capital Cases," *Stanford Law Review* 40 (1987): 21, which was published on the eve of the DNA revolution.

4. George Fisher, "The Jury's Rise as Lie Detector," *Yale Law Journal* 107 (1997): 575.

5. Norman J. Finkel, *Commonsense Justice* (Cambridge: Harvard University Press, 1995); Harry Kalven and Hans Zeisel, *The American Jury* (Chicago: University of Chicago Press, 1966).

6. Jeffrey Abramson, *We, The Jury* (New York: Basic Books, 1994).

7. *Duncan v. Louisiana*, 391 U.S. 145 (1968) at 156.

8. William T. Pizzi, *Trials without Truth* (New York: New York University Press, 1999).

9. *Duncan v. Louisiana*, 391 U.S. 145 (1968).

10. The facts of *Duncan* did not present this question. The issue was whether Duncan, an African American, who was trying to separate his cousins from a larger gang of white youths, actually slapped a white youth on his elbow or only "touched" him. Under Louisiana law, Duncan was not entitled to a jury for this crime, and the facts were found by a judge, who concluded that Duncan had slapped the victim and that he should be incarcerated for doing so. The unspoken assumption was that a constitutionally drawn jury would necessarily include African Americans, and such a jury would never unanimously agree that Duncan was guilty of battery.

11. *Duncan v. Louisiana* at 156.

12. Kalven and Zeisel, *American Jury*, 56 (table 11).

13. Theodore Eisenberg, Paula Hannaford-Agor, Valerie Hans, Nicole Mott, G. Thomas Musterman, Stephen Schwab, and Martin Wells, "Judge-Jury Agreement in Criminal Cases: A Partial Replication of Kalven and Zeisel's *The American Jury, Journal of Empirical Legal Studies* 2 (2005): 171–206.

14. *United States v. Garsson*, 291 F. 646 (S.D.N.Y. 1923) at 649.

15. There were some doubters. In his dissent in *Miranda*, Justice White called attention to the possibility that giving the *Miranda* warnings might lead an innocent person to refuse to speak to the police, a circumstance that would delay his release. He did not suggest that it might lead to the conviction of an innocent. *Miranda v. Arizona*, 384 U.S. 436 (1966) at 543–44. The Fifth Amendment right to refuse to incriminate oneself can also produce a distinct problem for the innocent. By protecting a witness' right not to testify at trial, it may deprive an innocent defendant of his ability to present a convincing defense. See Peter Tague, "The Fifth Amendment: If an Aid to the Guilty Defendant, an Impediment to the Innocent One," *Georgetown Law Journal* 78 (1989): 1–69.

16. In discussing changes in criminal procedure since 1961, Justice Scalia asserted: "The legal community's general attitude towards criminal defendants, the legal protections States afford, the constitutional guarantees this Court enforces, and the scope of federal habeas review, are all vastly different than what they were in 1961. So are the scientific means of establishing guilt, and hence innocence—which are now so striking in their operation and effect that they are subject of more than one popular TV series." *Kansas v. Marsh*, 126 S. Ct. at 2534 (concurring opinion).

17. The somber side of jury equity became apparent in *McCleskey v. Kemp*, 481 U.S. 279 (1987) (upholding capital punishment in the face of empirical evidence that African Americans convicted of killing white people were much more likely to receive death than white people who killed other whites). Justice Powell invoked the values underlying the liberation hypothesis to explain why the Court would not intervene: "The capital sentencing decision requires the individual jurors to focus their collective judgment on the unique characteristics of a

particular criminal defendant. It is not surprising that such collective judgments often are difficult to explain. But the inherent lack of predictability of jury decisions does not justify their condemnation. On the contrary, it is the jury's function to make the difficult and uniquely human judgments that defy codification and that "buil[d] discretion, equity, and flexibility into a legal system. H. Kalven & H. Zeisel, The American Jury 498 (1966)." *McCleskey v. Kemp* at 311. Justice Brennan, in dissent, cited Kalven and Zeisel's "liberation hypothesis" to make the point that illegitimate factors (e.g., race) are most likely to influence jury decisions in close cases. *Id.* at 325, fn. 4 (Brennan, J., dissenting).

    18. Kalven and Zeisel, *American Jury,* 495.

    19. *Id.,* 12.

    20. *Taylor v. Louisiana,* 419 U.S. 522 (1975).

    21. The survey is described in Paula L. Hannaford-Agor, Valerie P. Hans, Nicole L. Mott, and Thomas G. Munsterman, *Are Hung Juries a Problem?* (Williamsburg, Va.: National Center for State Courts, 2002), 29–33.

    22. Eisenberg et al., "Judge-Jury Agreement in Criminal Cases," 181.

    23. There were 334 cases in the NCSC study that ended in either a conviction of at least one count or an outright acquittal.

    24. Eisenberg and his coauthors state: "Jurors in both data sets are much more likely to disagree with a judge's decision to convict than with a judge's decision to acquit." *Id.* at 181. The data they present demonstrates that, while this was true of the Kalven and Zeisel study, it is not true of the jurors in the NCSC study. The following is derived from table 5.2 in the text and shows the percentage of cases in which the judge and jury agree as to the appropriate outcome (acquittal or conviction) in both the Kalven and Zeisel and NCSC studies:

Judge-jury agreement on acquittal: 86% in Kalven and Zeisel vs.

    70% in NCSC

Judge-jury agreement on conviction: 77% in Kalven and Zeisel vs.

    78% in NCSC

    25. The difference is also present if the question is the verdict that the judge *predicts* the jury will return. Judges are correct in their predictions of convictions about 85 percent of the time and correct in their predictions of acquittals about 65 percent of the time.

    26. The NCSC survey instruments neither asked for the sentence actually imposed nor sought information about whether the judge granted relief following a conviction. It did seek information on the sentencing range for convictions assuming that the jurisdiction had such guidelines. Kalven and Zeisel reported that judges set aside verdicts in 14 percent of the cases in which the jury convicted when the judge would have acquitted. The judge imposed a minimum sentence in another 34 percent of such cases and gave a sentence fully respecting the verdict in the remainder (48%). Kalven and Zeisel, *American Jury,* 412 (table 101).

    27. Kalven and Zeisel, *American Jury,* 431.

28. In a most rigorous attempt to identify the percentage of innocents convicted in a particular class of cases (capital rape-murders during the 1980s), Michael Risinger has derived " an empirical minimum of 3.3% and a fairly likely generous maximum of 5%." D. Michael Risinger, "Convicting the Innocent: An Empirically Justified Wrongful Conviction Rate," *Journal of Criminal Law and Criminology* 97 (2008): 761–800.

29. The analysis is restricted to cases involving a single count in order to deal with the difficulty that a judge's expression of dissatisfaction with respect to a jury result in a multiple-count indictment might have to do with the jury's acquittal on one or more of the counts. Even if we treat the "true" crossovers as only those cases in which the judge is equivocal or dissatisfied with the jury's guilty verdict, there are still a higher percentage of such cases in the NCSC study than in that of Kalven and Zeisel. While Kalven and Zeisel reported a 2.7 percent crossover rate, their discussion of the phenomenon suggests that many judges may have been satisfied with the jury's verdict of guilty. Further, in nearly one-half of the cases, the judge sentenced in a manner indicating "full respect for the verdict." Kalven and Zeisel, *American Jury*, 412. In short, one could readily conclude that the actual rate of substantial judicial disagreement with a guilty verdict was 1.3 percent, not 2.7 percent.

30. Kalven and Zeisel, *American Jury*, 412.

31. One caveat is that Kalven and Zeisel's survey included some federal courts, which would have been bound by the Bill of Rights even before incorporation.

32. The data for *American Jury* was apparently gathered during the 1950s. That is the date on both questionnaires (*American Jury*, 527, 531), and the first book reporting the results of the jury study, *Delaque Court*, appeared in 1959.

33. In 2.7 percent (97) of the cases in the Kalven and Zeisel study, the defendant was not represented by an attorney. Kalven and Zeisel, *American Jury*, 361.

34. Race was only included on the second set of questionnaires which the authors distributed, and here the respondent's choice was to identify the defendant and witnesses as either "white" or "colored." Jack Greenberg, *Race Relations and American Law* (New York: Columbia University Press, 1959), 328–29, provides an indication of the limited range of protections against discrimination in jury selection available at the time of the survey.

35. There was at least one African American present on 72 percent of the juries in the NCSC overall and on 80 percent of juries with African American defendants. Interestingly, there is no difference in conviction rates of African American defendants depending on whether at least one black juror was present. Some 80 percent of black defendants are convicted, regardless of whether they confront a jury with or without an African American juror. African Americans were defendants in 27 percent of the cases studied by Kalven and Zeisel, *American Jury*, 195. They were defendants in more than one-half of the cases in the NCSC study (Hannaford-Agor et al., *Are Hung Juries a Problem?*, 39). Whites (or at least non-

African Americans) were the defendants in 73 percent of the Kalven and Zeisel study, and Caucasians were defendants in 10 percent of the NCSC study. African American defendants do not appear disproportionately in the group that the judge would acquit when the jury convicts.

36. At least 18 percent of the judges in the counties included in the NCSC study were African American, 6 percent were Hispanic, and 2.5 percent were Asian. The distribution of these judges was quite uneven: while 45 percent of the judges in the District of Columbia were African American or Hispanic, this was true of only 11 percent of the judges in Maricopa, 21 percent of the judges in Los Angeles, and 28 percent of those in the Bronx. And there were large disparities between the race of judge and the race of juror in some locations. While 72 percent of the judges in the Bronx were white Caucasians, this was true of only 14 percent of the jurors. 79 percent of the judges in Los Angeles were Caucasian as contrasted to 36 percent of the jurors. Eisenberg et al., "Judge-Jury Agreement in Criminal Cases," 204–5, n.61. The NCSC data do not provide the information needed to link judge to jury.

37. This may reflect the presence of drug-related crimes, which represented 5 percent of the crimes in the Kalven and Zeisel survey and 28 percent of the crimes (and, coincidentally, 28% of the expert witnesses) in the NCSC study.

38. Kalven and Zeisel, *American Jury*, 146.

39. For example, the Federal Rules of Evidence Rule 609 authorizes the impeachment (discrediting) of a witness by questioning him about his prior criminal record. Rules 413 and 414 authorize the introduction of prior crimes of sexual assault or child abuse in any prosecution for those crimes, regardless of whether or not the defendant testifies. The Federal Sentencing Guidelines permit a court to treat those who refuse to plead guilty more harshly than those who "accept responsibility." Daniel Givelber, "Punishing Protestations of Innocence: Denying Responsibility and Its Consequences," *American Criminal Law Review* 37 (2000): 1363.

40. William Stuntz, "The Uneasy Relationship between Criminal Procedure and Criminal Justice," *Yale Law Journal* 107 (1997): 1, 36.

41. *Id.* at 40–42.

42. Darryl K. Brown, "The Decline of Defense Counsel and the Rise of Accuracy in Criminal Adjudication," *California Law Review* 93 (2005): 1585, 1592–1610.

43. Kalven and Zeisel did not "have the foresight" to collect information about whether counsel was privately retained, court appointed, or worked for a defender agency. *American Jury*, 358.

44. Private attorneys were more likely than either public defenders or court-appointed attorneys to represent defendants charged with more than one count, thus increasing the chance for a split verdict. In more than three-quarters (78%) of the cases involving private lawyers, the defendant faced more than one count,

as contrasted to 64–65 percent of the cases in which the defendant was represented by either a public defender or court-appointed attorney. However, private attorneys enjoyed more success in single-count cases as well: their clients were convicted in slightly more than one-half of such cases (53.8%) as opposed to defendants represented by court-appointed attorneys or public defenders (convicted in 70% and 68.5% of all cases, respectively; data not shown).

45. A study of criminal cases in Denver, Colorado, found that private counsel, both retained and appointed, are more effective than public defenders when measured against the success achieved through plea bargaining. Morris B. Hoffman, Paul H. Rubin, and Joanna M. Shepherd, "An Empirical Study of Public Defender Effectiveness: Self-Selection by the "Marginally Indigent," *Ohio State Journal of Criminal Law* 3 (2005): 223. The authors suggest that the results may reflect the decision of the "marginally indigent" who know they are guilty to accept representation by the public defender rather than attempting to raise money for private counsel. However, the Denver data, unlike the NCSC data presented here, reveal no difference in outcome by counsel in the small fraction of cases that actually go to trial. *Id.* at 239, figure 2. Both public defenders and private counsel achieved a 30 percent acquittal rate. This is consistent with a study of nine jurisdictions, which concluded that, although public defenders achieved dismissals or acquittals at a lower rate than other types of attorneys, the differences were not statistically significant. Roger A. Hanson, Brian J. Ostrom, William E. Hewitt, and Christopher Lomvardias, *Indigent Defenders: Get the Job Done and Done Well* (Williamsburg: National Center for State Courts, 1992): 53 (table 15).

46. Kalven and Zeisel concluded that an examination of the three out of every 100 trials that resulted in a crossover verdict led them to " think of the jury not so much as an institution with a built-in protection of the defendant, but rather as a rule that is stubbornly non-rule minded" (375): "[W]e suspect there is little or no intrinsic directionality in the jury's response. It is not fundamentally defendant-prone, rather it is non-rule minded: it will move where the equities are. And where the equities are at any given time will depend on both the state of the law and the climate of public opinion" (495).

Chapter 6

IIIIIIIIIIIIIIIIIIIIIIIIIIIIIIIIIIIIIIIIIIIIIIIIIIIIIII

Extreme Punishment

Douglas A. Berman

The wrongful punishment of the innocent receives considerable academic and public attention. The perceived underpunishment of the guilty not only receives much attention but also frequently prompts new criminal laws or increased sentencing terms. But extreme punishments of the guilty are rarely even noticed by anyone other than those enduring extreme punishment and their loved ones. The potential miscarriages of justice resulting from extreme punishments—especially severe restrictions on liberty that have become pervasive in modern American criminal justice systems—has rarely been the subject of sustained analysis and criticism.

The extraordinary modern growth, scope, and harshness of American punishment systems has started garnering serious academics scrutiny.[1] However, for various legal, political, and social reasons, the extreme punishments that have become pervasive in United States are rarely conceived or perceived as miscarriages of justice. Political and public discourses often frame justice in stark and binary terms: justice is served or injustice endured; few, if any, shades of gray are admitted or even perceived. But extreme punishment of the guilty is necessarily characterized by shades of gray, and this nuanced reality often makes it difficult for those concerned about miscarriages of justice to even appreciate and assesses the problem of extreme punishments. Moreover, and perhaps even more problematic, modern movements to spotlight and remedy "traditional" miscarriages of justice may contribute to, and even exacerbate, the problem of extreme punishments.

In this modest essay, my chief goal is to ensure that extreme punishments are included in any catalogue of miscarriages of justice in the American criminal justice system. In so doing, I hope to spotlight legal and social factors that have contributed to a modern American affinity for extreme punishments and suggest reasons why extreme punishments need and deserve far more sustained political and public attention.

I. Taking Stock of America's Modern Affinity for Extreme Punishment

An account of extreme punishments in America can and perhaps must begin with a brief overview of the extraordinary and unprecedented increases in state punitiveness that has defined and shaped modern criminal justice systems. Franklin E. Zimring, a leading observer and commentator on American penal policies, recently provided this description of modern developments:

> The last quarter of the twentieth century stands out as the most remarkable period of change in American penal policy even when the entire history of the United States is considered. Nothing in the two centuries before 1975 would prepare observers to expect that a long run of stable rates of incarceration would shift to a fourfold expansion of rates of imprisonment in less than three decades.[2]

Though this quote from Zimring spotlights the extraordinary modern increase in imprisonment levels, other forms of direct and indirect state punishment and control have also grown dramatically since the mid-1970s. And, as explained below, America's modern affinity for extreme punishment has notable quantitative and qualitative dimensions.

A. Extreme Punishments: Some Quantitative Realities

The quantitative story of extreme punishment can begin with basic data about the extraordinary modern growth in persons subject to criminal justice control in the United States:

> Between 1970 and 2005, state and federal authorities increased prison populations by 628 percent. By 2005, more than 1.5 million persons were incarcerated in U.S. prisons on any given day, and an additional 750,000 were incarcerated in local jails. By the turn of the 21st century, more than

5.6 million living Americans had spent time in a state or federal prison—nearly 3 percent of the U.S. population.[3]

The overall population of incarcerated individuals nationwide hits record highs nearly every year, and sophisticated projections suggest that the extraordinary number of persons locked behind bars is likely to continue to increase in coming years.[4] As a point of comparison, consider that in 1970, just before the start of the modern era of "get tough" reforms, there were only about 300,000 persons serving time in prison or jail. Barring significant changes in modern American penal policies, the national population of incarcerated individuals could be nearly 10 times as large by 2010.

The extraordinary modern growth in prison and jail populations is also stunning when placed in a global perspective. A far higher proportion of the adult population in the United States is incarcerated than in any other country in the world, and our incarceration rate—which is nearly 750 individuals per 100,000 in the general population—is now roughly 5 to 10 times the rate of most other Western industrialized nations:

> The U.S. imprisons significantly more people than any other nation. China ranks second, imprisoning 1.5 million of its much larger citizen population. The U.S. also leads the world in incarceration rates, well above Russia and Cuba, which have the next highest rates of 607 and 487 per 100,000. Western European countries have incarceration rates that range from 78 to 145 per 100,000.[5]

Significantly, the overall U.S. incarceration rate is only the tip of a massive punishment iceberg. Well over 7 million people in the United States are under the supervision of the correctional system, including jail, prison, parole, probation, and other types of community supervision. As one commentator recently noted, "If one adds up the total number of prisoners, parolees, probationers, employees of correctional institutions, close relatives of prisoners and correctional employees, and residents in communities where jails and prisons are major employers, tens of millions of people are directly affected each day by the carceral state."[6]

These numbers document the overall modern trend of expanding state punishments; drilling a bit deeper into some specifics provides an even more refined and stunning snapshot of extreme punishments in the United States. For example, a recent study by the Sentencing Project documents an extraordinary growth in the number of offenders serving terms of life imprisonment:

> The 127,677 lifers in prison [as of 2003] represent an increase of 83% from the number of lifers nationally in 1992, which in turn had doubled since 1984. During the 1990s the growth of persons serving life without parole has been even more precipitous, an increase of 170%, between 1992 and 2003. Overall, one of every six lifers in 1992 was serving a sentence of life without parole. By 2003, that proportion had increased to one in four. . . .
>
> In addition, the number of long-term prisoners is considerably greater than just the total of lifers, and contributes to the population of what can be considered "virtual lifers." These are persons serving very long sentences, or consecutive sentences, that will often outlast the person's natural life. One 2000 study estimated that more than one of every four (27.5%) adult prisoners was serving a sentence of 20 years or more. And data from the Department of Justice show that as of 2002, state and federal prisons held 121,000 persons age 50 or over, more than double the figure of a decade earlier.[7]

These statistics assembled by the Sentencing Project suggest that there are now more individuals sentenced and nearly certain to die in prison than the total prison population just a generation ago. The Sentencing Project's report also details that nonviolent drug offenders, female offenders, mentally ill offenders, and juvenile offenders have become a significant portion of the population sentenced to life terms.[8]

Relatedly, a report from Human Rights Watch and Amnesty International documented the modern willingness (and international anomaly) of American jurisdictions sentencing juvenile offenders to life without the possibility of parole:

> [T]here are currently at least 2,225 people incarcerated in the United States who have been sentenced to spend the rest of their lives in prison for crimes they committed as children. . . . Before 1980, life without parole was rarely imposed on children. . . .
>
> Virtually all countries in the world reject the punishment of life without parole for child offenders. At least 132 countries reject life without parole for child offenders in domestic law or practice. And all countries except the United States and Somalia have ratified the Convention on the Rights of the Child, which explicitly forbids "life imprisonment without possibility of

release" for "offenses committed by persons below eighteen years of age." Of the 154 countries for which Human Rights Watch was able to obtain data, only three currently have people serving life without parole for crimes they committed as children, and it appears that those three countries combined have only about a dozen such cases.[9]

Though many more statistics could be highlighted to document the quantitative realities of extreme punishment in the United States, these numbers should provide a flavor of the concerns that motivate this essay. Though I cannot here even begin to systematically describe and assess the scope of the phenomenon of extreme punishment in the United States, just these few statistics should spotlight why extreme punishment realities are worthy of considerable attention and concern.

B. Extreme Punishments: Some Qualitative Realities

The modern story of extreme punishments in the United States is about a lot more than increased numbers of persons in prison or otherwise subject to traditional criminal punishments. Over the past few decades, the nature, and not just the numbers, of modern criminal punishment have changed dramatically.

As the number of prisoners has progressively increased, the rehabilitative programming provided to prisoners has decreased and the myriad problems resulting from prison overcrowding has become a facet of nearly every penal system.[10] And while imprisonment is extraordinarily grim and often unsafe for the more than 2 million persons housed in standard prisons and jails, a subgroup of more than 20,000 prisoners are confined to a new kind of "supermax" prisons that involve a deprivation of human liberty that may be unprecedented in human history. Consider this National Public Radio account of the nature of, and realities in, a supermax facility:

> Everything is gray concrete: the bed, the walls, the unmovable stool. Everything except the combination stainless-steel sink and toilet. You can't move more than eight feet in one direction. . . . The cell is one of eight in a long hallway. From inside, you can't see anyone or any of the other cells. This is where the inmate eats, sleeps and exists for 22 ½ hours a day. He spends the other 1 ½ hours alone in a small concrete yard. . . .
>
> One inmate known as Wino is standing just behind the door of his cell.

It's difficult to make eye contact, because you can only see one eye at a time. . . . Wino is a 40-something man from San Fernando, California. He was sent to prison for robbery. He was sent to the [Security Housing Unit] SHU for being involved in prison gangs. He's been in this cell for six years. "The only contact that you have with individuals is what they call a pinky shake," he says, sticking his pinky through one of the little holes in the door. That's the only personal contact Wino has had in six years. . . .

Inside the SHU, there's a skylight two stories up. But on an overcast day, it's dark, and so are the cells. There are no windows here. Inmates will not see the moon, stars, trees or grass. They will rarely, if ever, see the giant, gray building they live in. Their world—24 hours a day, seven days a week, every day of the year—is this hallway.[11]

Significantly, extreme punishments and novel deprivations of liberty are no longer confined to the 2 million persons in cells or the traditional restrictions endured by the roughly 5 million persons serving probation, parole, or some other form of post-release supervision. In addition to the huge number of persons formally subject to criminal justice control in the United States, a massive (and largely uncounted) number of former offenders are subject in virtually every American jurisdiction to a range of punitive collateral consequences. As a recent report explains:

In every U.S. jurisdiction, the legal system erects formidable barriers to the reintegration of criminal offenders into free society. When a person is convicted of a crime, that person becomes subject to a host of legal disabilities and penalties under state and federal law. These so-called collateral consequences of conviction may continue long after the court-imposed sentence has been fully served . . . [and] a criminal record can be grounds for exclusion from many benefits and opportunities, including in employment, education, health care, and transportation. . . . These legal barriers are always difficult and often impossible to overcome, so that persons convicted of a crime can expect to carry the collateral disabilities and stigma of conviction to their grave, no matter how successful their efforts to rehabilitate themselves.[12]

In recent years, the nature and severity of these collateral consequences have become especially severe for certain classes of offenders. Sex offenders in particular have become modern pariahs subject to unprecedented new types of restrictions on their liberties. Hundreds of thousands of sex offenders nationwide not only must register their movements to authorities but also are now literally being banished from ever living or even coming near many regions of the country.[13]

Once again, these examples of some qualitative realities of extreme punishment in the United States provide only a partial account of the concerns that motivate this chapter. I do not hope here to systematically describe and assess all facets of modern extreme punishments in the United States; rather, as suggested before, my goal here is simply to spotlight the modern and unprecedented American affinity for punishment and to encourage conceiving and perceiving extreme punishments in any catalogue of miscarriages of justice.

II. Social, Political, and Legal Dynamics Fostering Extreme Punishments

There are many intersecting social and political dynamics that contribute to the problem of extreme punishment in the United States, and a number of academics and commentators have spotlighted and examined the array of forces that account for modern "tough-on-crime" rhetoric and realities.[14] What has not been generally analyzed or even acknowledged, however, is the way even efforts to identify and address other miscarriages of justice in modern criminal justice systems may contribute in various ways to the extreme punishment problem.

A. How Miscarriages of Justice Are Perceived

The wrongful punishment of the innocent and the perceived underpunishment of the guilty are often showcased in memorable moments of personal horror and societal injustice. Sadly, an all too common, modern photo-op captures the innocent man as he is released from prison after years of wrongful incarceration; this Kodak moment shines a bright light on the fallibility of our criminal justice system. A similar message of criminal justice failure comes through when grieving victims—who often seem eager to appear on 24-hour news programs and at special press conferences—tearfully ask why a repeat offender was released from prison and allowed to victimize the public again.

These extraordinary personal moments documenting miscarriages of justice can, and often do, turn into sustained political action. The innocent man prods elected officials and voters to support DNA testing and new safeguards to avoid wrongful convictions. The grieving family prods elected officials and voters to support tougher sentencing laws, community notification, and other means to keep "us" safe from "them." In these contexts, it is not surprising that social sympathies become political opportunities. When the innocent are wrongfully punished or victimized by repeat offenders, the average citizen (and voter) may often think "there but for the grace of god . . ." Consciously or unconsciously, most observers will consume and process moments of personal horror and societal injustice involving innocents by thinking "that could be me." The next thought, in turn, is that government officials should be doing whatever is needed to make sure innocent persons like me are never again wrongfully convicted and never again needlessly victimized by a repeat offender.

In sharp contrast, there rarely are specific salient moments spotlighting the miscarriage of justice that is extreme punishment. No news program or photo-op can capture the slow agony and continuous extinguishing of hope that mark the progression from just punishment to extreme punishment. On occasion, a judge may speak out at sentencing against a long mandatory imprisonment term he or she is forced by law to impose. But these moments rarely generate sustained media attention. Moreover, the asserted injustice lamented by the sentencing judge is muted by three realities: (1) the defendant being harshly sentenced is necessarily guilty of some (usually serious) crime meriting some punishment; (2) the prosecutor involved has, at least indirectly, endorsed the harsh sentence; and (3) the offender's punishment is not severe enough to prod the sentencing judge to declare it constitutionally excessive under the Eighth Amendment.

The social realities of extreme punishment contribute to a set of political realities that foster extreme punishment. Politicians and the public rarely give thought to the concept of extremely punishing the guilty, and persons guilty of crimes rarely generate much empathy. Most persons perceive themselves and their family as "innocents" and never personally contemplate the prospect of suffering the harm of extreme punishment. Even when extreme punishments are effectively documented, general ignorance of this problem will often just become general indifference.

Ultimately, these dynamics are one part of a broader story of institutional perspective and modern-day criminal justice politics. As Ronald Wright has succinctly explained, "[w]hen it comes to statutes involving criminal punishments, legislators have every incentive to announce more punishment rather than less."[15] Whenever a legislature considers the appropriate sentence for a particular criminal prohibition, it can only contemplate the criminal offender qua criminal offender. Making decisions about crime and punishment ex ante, legislatures have no context for assessing and passing judgments on the actual persons who will come to violate various criminal prohibitions. Rather, legislators only consider criminal offenders as abstract characters—the threatening figure of a killer or a sex offender or a drug dealer—and concerns about innocent victims will always eclipse any regard for these nefarious stick figures. Lacking any understanding or real concern for the harm of extremely punishing the guilty, legislatures' sentencing judgments will tend to be punitive; attention is focused only on the worst aspects of those who will be subject to the criminal sanction and only the problems of underpunishment will resonate.

The responsive nature of the modern legislative process exacerbates legislatures' tendency to be especially punitive when setting sentencing terms. Because criminal codes are rarely created anew, legislatures typically contemplate crime and sentencing laws only in response to a perceived "crime problem." This context necessarily aggravates the punitiveness of enacted crime and sentencing laws; legislators often conclude that a crime problem is the result of "soft" laws that fail to deter potential lawbreakers and fail to sufficiently incapacitate past lawbreakers. Even legislators who may believe deeper social problems are a root cause of crime are hard-pressed to devise politically viable alternatives to the immediate and seemingly straightforward solution of longer sentences. Moreover, while perceived "crime problems" will spur the enactment of severe sentences, any subsequent dips in crime can reinforce legislators' beliefs that severe sentences "work," thereby prompting ever wider use of ever tougher criminal sanctions.

Finally, and of perhaps greatest significance, as a matter of both theory and practice, the majoritarian politics of a democratic society pushes legislators toward enacting ever-harsher sentencing provisions. One need not be fully versed in public choice theory to recognize that legislators will be more responsive to those persons who are most likely to favor punitive criminal sanctions (that is, law-abiding citizens who view themselves as potential crime victims) rather than to those persons who are most likely to oppose such severe punishments (that is, past [and future?] criminals). Indeed, with many jurisdictions still disenfranchising many criminal offenders, those most directly harmed by harsh sentencing laws are often completely excluded from the electoral process.[16] Felon disenfranchisement formalizes the already considerable political incentives for legislators to systematically disfavor the interests of those persons who are affected most by severe criminal sanctions.

Moving from theory to practice, elections at national, state, and local levels have repeatedly demonstrated the political value of supporting ever-more punitive sentencing laws. Since the late 1960s, politicians who can lay claim to being the toughest on crime have been regularly rewarded with electoral success. The symbolic impact of support for harsh sentencing laws is viewed as a key ingredient for victory on election day.[17] These political realities not only fuel the enactment of severe sentencing laws but also thwart efforts to scale back harsh sentencing laws even when it is clear that these laws are ineffective and unjust. Candid elected officials will readily admit flaws in certain harsh sentencing laws passed in the midst of a moral panic about, say, drug or sex offenses, but then will explain that fear of sound-bite "soft on crime" attacks in the next election campaign prevent them and their colleagues from supporting reforms to restrict or eliminate the most harmfully severe sentencing laws.

B. How Miscarriages of Justice Are Addressed

1. THE PROBLEM OF INNOCENCE

Many criminal justice reformers believe—or at least hope—that modern revelations about the extent of, and reason for, wrongful convictions will prompt systemic reforms to the criminal justice system. The bright light that wrongful convictions shine on the failings of our criminal justice procedures and practices should be a catalyst for an array of reforms that could benefit every individual affected by state power through the criminal justice system.

But the relationship between innocence concerns and extreme punishment is more textured. In a recent commentary in the *Washington Post,* law professor David Dow explained why an emphasis on innocence concerns in modern critiques of the death penalty has negatively affected his efforts to resist the death penalty more generally. Here is an extended passage from his commentary:

> [T]he focus on innocence has insidiously distracted the courts. When I represent a client in a death penalty case, judges want to know whether there is any chance that client is innocent. If he isn't, then they are not much

concerned about anything else I have to say. Oh, so blacks were excluded from the jury? So what, he's guilty; any jury would have convicted him. Oh, so police hid evidence? Big deal, there was plenty of other evidence that he did it. Oh, so his lawyer slept through trial? Why does that matter? Clarence Darrow himself couldn't have kept him from the gallows.

This past week the Supreme Court agreed for the second time to hear the appeal of LaRoyce Smith, a death row inmate in Texas, because the Texas courts, convinced of Smith's guilt, believed they could therefore ignore the fact that his right to a fair trial was violated. Yet the Supreme Court itself is partly to blame. In the recent case of *Kansas v. Marsh*, Justices Antonin Scalia and David Souter engaged in an extraordinary debate over . . . whether any innocent person has been executed in the modern death penalty era. Of course, only the most naive person—or perhaps the most disingenuous —would think that we miraculously identify everyone who is innocent just in the nick of time. But what was even more astonishing about this debate was that the arcane legal issue in *Marsh* had absolutely nothing to do with the question of whether Marsh was innocent or even with the issue of innocence in general.

Innocence is a distraction because most people on death row are not in fact innocent, and the possibility of executing an innocent man is not even remotely the best reason for abolishing the death penalty.[18]

Dow's central point is both astute and troubling: an excessive focus on innocence issues in the debate over the death penalty desensitizes criminal justice participants to the many other forms of injustice that pervade the administration of capital punishment. But, critically, this problem of desensitization to injustices other than wrongful convictions permeates all aspects of, and all actors within, the criminal justice system.

As Dow spotlights, courts now seem less concerned about legal "technicalities" if and when a defendant's guilt is not in dispute, and, in my experience, this problem is even more acute outside the context of the death penalty. In all sorts of cases, police and prosecutors will often refuse to address or even admit error when they are convinced of a particular defendant's guilt; emphasis on innocence directly and indirectly reinforces an "ends-justify-the-means" mentality. And because innocence issues have such a salience for politicians and voters across the political spectrum, reforms focused on preventing wrongful convictions are placed at the top of legislative agendas, leaving other needed criminal justice reforms to languish.

I believe our nation's commitment to protecting individual liberty and limiting government power should prompt concerns about extremely punishing the guilty that are comparable to our concerns about wrongfully punishing the innocent. But this sentiment does not typically find expression in our criminal justice policy debates or in our modern legal doctrines. Defendants' pretrial and trial rights have long received much attention, whereas their sentencing rights and the unique sentencing dynamics that affect defendants' interests have not. Defendants at sentencing are situated quite differently from those awaiting trial: by sentencing, a judge or jury has already found the defendant guilty beyond a reasonable doubt or the defendant has admitted guilt through a plea; at issue is how the state will treat the proven wrongdoer. Because safeguards for the innocent are no longer essential and because conviction of the innocent is no longer a hazard, legislatures, courts, and prosecutors tend to feel more comfortable with procedural shortcuts at sentencing. Put simply, as the "distraction" of innocence fades during the transition from trial to sentencing, coercive power starts to favor the state both formally and informally, and even seemingly neutral sentencing rules can tilt the system toward extreme punishments.

2. THE PROBLEM OF THE DEATH PENALTY

Dow's intriguing charge of "insidious distraction" can also be lodged against the death penalty more generally. Of course, the death penalty is the one arena in which extreme punishment of the guilty is regularly spotlighted and lamented: the essence of most abolitionist arguments is that, even for those guilty of the very worst crimes, death is always an excessive punishment. And though I am eager to praise death penalty abolitionists for waging a campaign against extreme punishment of the guilty, I fear that much of the advocacy against the death penalty can often (1) distract would-be reformers from recognizing and assailing broader extreme punishment problems and (2) desensitize moderates and conservatives to broader problems throughout the criminal justice system.

Prodded by abolitionists and as evidenced by its copious and complicated death penalty jurisprudence, the U.S. Supreme Court has itself been quite attentive to extreme punishment concerns in the context of capital punishment. As a result of Supreme Court doctrines requiring state reforms, the modern American death penalty is now only applied to a relatively small group of murderers and only in those cases in which prosecutors, jurors, and numerous judges all have concluded that death is not too severe a punishment. But the somewhat successful capital campaign against extreme punishment has a problematic impact on modern criticisms of the death penalty: abolitionist claims of extreme punishment in the death penalty context are now necessarily raised on behalf of the least sympathetic of all defendants (the worst group of convicted murderers) and are thus likely to ring hollow to persons not categorically opposed to the punishment of death (because many criminal justice actors have decided death is a fitting punishment for these defendants).

By any measure, courts and commentators invest an extraordinary amount of time and attention to death penalty processes and defendants. But all this time and attention is given only to a small group of the very worst murderers and in cases in which the alternative to execution is typically the (arguably more) extreme punishment of life imprisonment in prison without the possibility of parole. Notably, many death penalty abolitionists now embrace and endorse life imprisonment without the possibility of parole as a sound alternative to the death penalty. But there are reasons to fear that modern attacks on the death penalty may actually *increase* the number of defendants serving life imprisonment: a New Jersey commission in January 2007 recommended that the state abolish the death penalty in favor of life imprisonment without parole, and an independent analysis of past New Jersey trials subsequently revealed that "scores of murderers would have been punished more harshly under the life-without-parole bill proposed by the Death Penalty Study Commission."[19] Putting innocence issues aside, abolitionist advocacy against the death penalty in essence is about trying to ensure that a small group of the worst convicted murderers are permitted to spend more time locked in a cage before they die.

Consequently, for those concerned about extreme punishment throughout the criminal justice system, the death penalty is an "insidious distraction" because it draws enormous energy and attention to the project of helping the worst criminals suffer a different sort of extreme punishment. To paraphrase Dow's remarks about innocence as a distraction, I view the death penalty as an extreme punishment distraction because most people enduring unjust sentences are not on death row, and the possibility of unjust capital punishment for murderers is not the best reason for reforming the harshest aspects of federal and state criminal justice systems. In short, as suggested in section I of this chapter, there are so many more extreme punishment concerns throughout American criminal justice systems than what we see in the (overanalyzed) systems of capital punishment.

3. THE PROBLEM OF MODERN SENTENCING RULES
AND THE QUEST FOR UNIFORMITY

Another often-unexplored factor contributing to the problems of extreme punishment emerges from the law, policies, and rhetoric integral to modern noncapital sentencing reforms. By (excessively) shifting sentencing power to ex ante rule-makers and by (over)emphasizing the goal of sentencing uniformity, modern reforms have recast the concepts and culture of sentencing decision-making in ways that have directly and indirectly contributed to the problems of extreme punishment. To understand this part of the extreme punishment story, a bit of modern sentencing history needs to be reviewed.

For the first three-quarters of the twentieth century, vast and virtually unlimited discretion was the hallmark of the sentencing enterprise. Trial judges in both federal and state systems had nearly unfettered discretion to impose on defendants any sentence from within the broad statutory ranges provided for criminal offenses. During this period, punishment decisions and offender treatments were premised on a rehabilitative model. Broad judicial discretion in the ascription of sentencing terms—complemented by parole officials exercising similar discretion concerning prison release dates—was viewed as necessary to ensure that sentences could be individually tailored to the particular rehabilitative prospects and progress of each offender. The rehabilitative ideal was often conceived and discussed in medical terms, with offenders described as "sick" and punishments aspiring to "cure the patient." Sentencing judges and parole officials, making decisions with a focus on individual offenders after they committed their crimes, were thought to have unique insights and expertise in deciding what sorts and lengths of punishments were necessary to best serve each criminal offender's rehabilitative potential. Aided by complete information about offenders and unfettered discretionary authority, judges were expected to craft individualized sentences "almost like a doctor or social worker exercising clinical judgment."[20]

In 1949, the Supreme Court constitutionally approved this philosophical and procedural approach to sentencing in *Williams v. New York*.[21] In rejecting a claim that defendant Williams had a right to confront and crossexamine the witnesses against him reflected in a pre-sentence report, the Supreme Court stressed that "[r]eformation and rehabilitation of offenders have become important goals of criminal jurisprudence," and the

Court spoke approvingly of judges and parole boards exercising broad discretion in the service of the "prevalent modern philosophy of penology that the punishment should fit the offender and not merely the crime." According to the *Williams* Court, the value of "modern concepts individualizing punishments" meant that sentencing judges should "not be denied an opportunity to obtain pertinent information by a requirement of rigid adherence to restrictive rules of evidence properly applicable to the trial." Significantly, the *Williams* Court suggested that the rehabilitative ideal and its distinctive procedures had benefits for offenders as well as for society. The Court stressed that "modern changes" justified by the rehabilitative model of sentencing "have not resulted in making the lot of offenders harder." Rather, explained the Court, "a strong motivating force for the changes has been the belief that by careful study of the lives and personalities of convicted offenders many could be less severely punished and restored sooner to complete freedom and useful citizenship."

While the theory and procedures of the rehabilitative model of sentencing was sanctioned by the Supreme Court, they were eventually questioned in other quarters. Through the 1960s and 1970s, criminal justice researchers and scholars were growing concerned about the unpredictable and disparate sentences that highly discretionary sentencing systems could produce. Evidence suggested that broad judicial sentencing discretion was resulting in substantial and undue differences in the lengths and types of sentences meted out to similar defendants, and some studies found that personal factors such as an offender's race, gender, and socioeconomic status were influencing sentencing outcomes and accounted for certain disparities.

Driven by concerns about disparity and discrimination resulting from highly discretionary sentencing practices, which dovetailed with concerns over increasing crime rates and powerful criticisms of the entire rehabilitative model of punishment and corrections, criminal justice experts and scholars urged reforms in order to bring greater consistency and certainty to the sentencing enterprise. Led by the groundbreaking and highly influential work of Judge Marvin Frankel,[22] many reformers came to propose or endorse some form of sentencing guidelines to govern sentencing determinations and also suggested creating specialized sentencing commissions to develop these guidelines.

Calls for reform were soon heeded. Through the late 1970s and early 1980s, a few states enacted determinate sentencing statutes that abolished parole and created presumptive sentencing ranges for various classes of offenses. During this same period, Minnesota, Pennsylvania, and Washington became the first states to create sentencing commissions to help produce comprehensive sentencing guidelines. Congress soon followed suit with the passage of the Sentencing Reform Act of 1984 (SRA), which created the U.S. Sentencing Commission to develop guidelines for federal sentencing.[23] And throughout the next two decades, many more states adopted some form of structured sentencing; though some states did so only through a few mandatory sentencing statutes, many states created sentencing commissions to develop comprehensive guideline schemes.

An integral component of this "structured sentencing revolution" was a repudiation of rehabilitation as a dominant sentencing purpose and a far greater concern for increased sentencing uniformity. Enhanced concerns about more consistently imposing "just punishment" and deterring the most harmful crimes prompted legislatures and sentencing commissions to embrace more certain and often more severe sentencing outcomes. As suggested before, because legislatures and sentencing commissions make decisions about crime and punishment ex ante, they contemplate criminal offenders as abstract characters—the threatening figure of a killer or a sex offender or a drug dealer—and the sentencing judgments will always tend to be more punitive. Moreover, most structured sentencing reforms formally mandated (or at least informally encouraged) sentencing judges to focus principally on offense conduct and to limit consideration of those aspects of "the defendant's life and characteristics" that might provide a basis for mitigating a harsh response to an offense.

Consider, as but one example, the Pennsylvania Mandatory Minimum Sentencing Act of 1982, which was at issue in the Supreme Court case of *McMillan v. Pennsylvania*.[24] That act provided for the imposition of a five-year mandatory minimum sentence if a judge found, by a preponderance of evidence, that an offender visibly possessed a firearm during the commission of certain offenses. The act clearly was not enacted in service to the rehabilitative model of sentencing; rather, in the words of the Pennsylvania Supreme Court, the state legislature was seeking "to protect the public from armed criminals and to deter violent crime and the illegal use of firearms generally, as well as to vindicate its interest in punishing those who commit serious crimes with guns."[25] Tellingly, the Pennsylvania Mandatory Minimum Sentencing Act required specific sentencing consequences based exclusively on specific offense conduct (i.e., visible firearm possession triggered the mandatory minimum sentence), and the act did not incorporate any consideration of offender characteristics (i.e., an offender's personal history was of no relevance to the mandatory minimum sentence).

Similar dynamics have played out in the federal sentencing system since the 1980s. The new sentencing philosophies and goals reflected in the federal guidelines and mandatory sentencing statutes have brought a new emphasis at sentencing on offense conduct and have limited federal judges' opportunity to consider mitigating offender characteristics. Most of the mandatory sentencing provisions that Congress has enacted since the 1980s are triggered by particular offense conduct—for example, a five-year mandatory sentencing enhancement arises from use of a firearm in certain crimes and mandatory minimum penalties for drug trafficking are pegged to drug quantities. These statutory provisions entail that many federal sentencing outcomes will be driven by one aspect of offense conduct, and they necessarily diminish the significance of offender characteristics in federal sentencing.

The relative roles of offense conduct and offender characteristics within the Federal Sentencing Guidelines are a bit more nuanced but similarly emphasize offense conduct relative to offender characteristics. Since the outset of the Federal Sentencing Guidelines era, the U.S. Sentencing Commission has declared through a series of policy statements that many potentially mitigating offender characteristics—such as a defendant's education and vocational skills, mental and emotional conditions, previous employment record, and family and community ties—are either "not ordinarily relevant" or entirely irrelevant to whether a defendant should receive a sentencing below the guidelines range.

Though there is considerable variation in the form and consequences of structured sentencing reforms, the modern "structured sentencing revolution" has dramatically altered criminal justice practices and outcomes. It is not mere coincidence that, as detailed in section II of this chapter, we have witnessed a massive increase in incarceration during the same period in which jurisdictions have reformed their sentencing structures. Important and largely progressive goals initially fueled modern sentencing reforms; but sentencing power has now been excessively shifted to ex ante rule-makers, thereby contributing to both a legal structure and a social culture that fuels severe sentencing outcomes. Moreover, through emphasis on the goal of sentencing uniformity, modern reforms have enhanced a "leveling up" dynamic: in nearly all efforts to make sentences more consistent, doctrines and decisions have typically sought to make disparately lenient sentences more consistently harsh and have rarely attempted to make disparately harsh sentences more consistently lenient.

III. Conclusion: Brainstorming Responses to Extreme Punishments

Unfortunately, I am far better at spotlighting the basic problem of extreme punishment than I am at suggesting obvious or workable solutions. However, especially from the vantage point of the ivory tower, I think I can —and thus will—begin to outline some theoretical, political, and practical ideas for starting to work against this miscarriage of justice. The arguments against extreme punishment simmer within our nation's traditions and within our current political and social dialogues. But there has been only limited effort to synthesize and energize these arguments in order to help them have real traction and significant impact.

First and foremost, our nation's commitment to protecting individual liberty and limiting government power should prompt profound concerns about extremely punishing the guilty. It is these interests that generate such considerable concerns about wrongfully punishing the innocent, but they have not been carried over into a broader concern for extreme punishment. Criminal justice power is government power, and mass punishments are the most oppressive form of big government. The framers of the Constitution fully understood these realities when they enacted a Bill of Rights that is almost exclusively focused on limiting and regulating the exercise of police power. Arguably, nine of the first ten amendments to the Constitution directly or indirectly establish safeguards against different possible forms of extreme punishment. The framers' commitment to personal liberty and individual freedom is surely undercut by governments with broad powers to lock citizens in small cages for long periods of time and additional power to invasively supervise and regulate citizens' activities after they are let out of these cages.

Sadly, despite a modern rejuvenation of originalist thinking in constitutional law and policy, few leading constitutional scholars speak out against extreme punishment. Notably, in a few recent Supreme Court decisions, Justices Scalia and Thomas have recognized how a serious commitment to the framers' constitutional vision requires affording criminal defendants greater procedural rights. But, in my view, a serious appreciation for and effectuation of our nation's founding principles would lead to many more

voices spotlighting and decrying the modern extreme punishment problem. We rarely hear leading libertarians and constitutional conservatives,
when lamenting government interferences or the problem of big government, express serious concerns about the problems of extreme punishment in modern criminal justice systems. It is disappointing that those
who claim to champion liberty and small government are not leading
campaigns against the problem of extreme punishment.

Moving beyond modern political and social theory to more pragmatic
issues, there is also ample evidence that "tough on crime" policies are
costly and often ineffectual. Even if the objective of sentencing law and
policy is focused only on public safety—on what specific sets of programs
and policies can best promote safe communities—the problematic economics of extreme punishment could and should expand the discussion
to a broad range of different social and criminal justice interventions. The
rapid expansion of the prison system in recent years has created a vicious
cycle involving resource allocation and sentencing options. While three-
fourths of offenders under supervision are currently in the community on
probation or parole, only one-tenth of correctional resources are devoted
to these agencies. The result is high caseloads for supervision of offenders
on probation or parole and relatively little ability to either supervise or
support these offenders as they reenter communities. This, in turn, causes
sentencing judges and parole boards to lose confidence in these nonin-
carcerative options. Greater resources for community-based supervision
would alleviate the imbalance in the system and lead to more effective
sentencing options.

While advocacy for alternatives to incarceration in the abstract is difficult in a harsh political environment, public understanding may be more
readily attained for distinct offender groups. For example, many offenders
have become caught in a cycle of drug addiction and dependency, which
is not readily addressed by harsh sentencing policies. Significant numbers
of offenders are mentally ill or learning disabled and often do not receive
appropriate services or consideration of mitigating factors in the court
process. Analyzing prison populations in this manner helps develop a
policy discussion that is problem-oriented rather than sound bite-driven.

As stressed at the outset, the problem of extreme punishment of the
guilty is rarely even noticed by anyone other than the extremely punished
and his or her friends and family. To my knowledge, this particular kind
of miscarriage of justice—which is arguably the most pervasive problem in modern criminal justice systems—has never been the subject of

sustained analysis and criticism. There has been and will continue to be, of course, attention given by academics to the dynamics of extreme punishment, but my goal in this chapter is to reframe the discussion in terms of a miscarriage of justice and to examine all the challenges that the social and political dynamics present to assail this pervasive problem in modern criminal justice systems.

The problem of extreme punishment has developed rapidly since the 1970s, largely outside of the public eye, and not necessarily according to a common plan. These developments have been an invisible feature of modern American politics, not a direct subject of examination and debate. The underlying political causes of this massive expansion and what might reverse it are not well understood. A more informed and dynamic political and social dialogue may be a critical first step toward needed legal reforms.

NOTES

1. For example, James Q. Whitman, *Harsh Justice: Criminal Punishment and the Widening Divide between America and Europe* (New York: Oxford University Press, 2003); Nora V. Demleitner, "Is There a Future for Leniency in the U.S. Criminal Justice System?," *Michigan Law Review* 103 (2005): 1231; Richard S. Frase, "Historical and Comparative Perspectives on the Exceptional Severity of Sentencing in the United States," *George Washington International Law Review*, 36 (2004): 227.

2. Franklin E. Zimring, "Penal Policy and Penal Legislation in Recent American Experience," *Stanford Law Review* 58 (2005): 323

3. Don Steman, *Reconsidering Incarceration: New Directions for Reducing Crime* (New York: Vera Institute of Justice, 2007), 1.

4. Pew Charitable Trusts, *Public Safety, Public Spending: Forecasting America's Prison Population 2007–2011* (Philadelphia: Pew Charitable Trusts, 2007).

5. Ibid., 1.

6. Marie Gottschalk, "Dismantling the Carceral State: The Future of Penal Policy Reform," *Texas Law Review* 84 (2006): 1694.

7. Marc Mauer, Ryan S. King, and Malcolm C. Young, *The Meaning of "Life": Long Prison Sentences in Context* (Washington, D.C.: Sentencing Project, 2004), 11.

8. Ibid., 1.

9. Human Rights Watch and Amnesty International, *The Rest of Their Lives: Life without Parole for Child Offenders in the United States* (New York: Human Rights Watch and Amnesty International, 2005), 1–2, 5.

10. See generally Commission on Safety and Abuse in America's Prisons, *Confronting Confinement* (New York: Vera Institute of Justice, 2006).

11. Laura Sullivan, *At Pelican Bay Prison, a Life in Solitary*, National Public Radio (2006), available at http://www.npr.org/templates/story/story.php?storyId=5584254.

12. Margaret Colgate Love, *Relief from the Collateral Consequences of a Criminal Conviction: A State-by-State Resource Guide* (Buffalo, N.Y.: William S. Hein, 2006).

13. See generally Corey Rayburn Yung, "Banishment by a Thousand Laws: Residency Restrictions on Sex Offenders" (February 2007), available at http://ssrn.com/abstract=959847; Wayne A. Logan, "Constitutional Collectivism and Ex-Offender Exclusion Zones," *Iowa Law Review* 92 (2006): 1.

14. For just a sample, see Whitman, *Harsh Justice;* Demleitner, "Is There a Future for Leniency," and Frase, "Historical and Comparative Perspectives," as well as William J. Stuntz, "The Pathological Politics of Criminal Law," *Michigan Law Review* 100 (2001): 505; Marc Mauer, "Why Are Tough on Crime Policies So Popular?," *Stanford Law and Policy Review* 11 (1999): 9; and Sara Sun Beale, "What's Law Got to Do with It? The Political, Social, Psychological and Other Non-Legal Factors Influencing the Development of (Federal) Criminal Law," *Buffalo Criminal Law Review* 1 (1997): 23.

15. Ronald F. Wright, "Three Strikes Legislation and Sentencing Commission Objectives," *Law and Policy* 20 (1998): 437.

16. Since the mid-1990s, there have been some encouraging developments in securing the franchise for persons who have completed their criminal punishment, but there are still more than 5 million Americans unable to vote because of felony disenfranchisement laws. See generally Ryan S. King, *A Decade of Reform: Felony Disenfranchisement Policy in the United States* (Washington, D.C.: Sentencing Project, 2006).

17. These forces have all proved particularly problematic at the federal level. A perceived crime problem or simply one headline-grabbing crime arising anywhere in the United States can provide the impetus for new and tougher federal criminal legislation. As documented by the continued enactment of harsh mandatory sentencing provisions, in Congress thoughtful sentencing policymaking now often takes a back seat to popular sentencing lawmaking, with election day results serving only to reinforce this dynamic.

18. David R. Dow, "Death by Good Intentions," *Washington Post,* October 15, 2006, B7.

19. Robert Schwaneberg, "When Life without Parole Is Worse Than Death: Analysis Finds More Than 100 Murderers Who Might One Day Go Free Would Face Certainty of Dying in Prison," *Newark Star-Ledger,* February 4, 2007.

20. *United States v. Mueffleman,* 327 F. Supp. 2d 79 (D. Mass. 2004) at 83.

21. *Williams v. New York,* 337 U.S. 241 (1949). All quotations in this paragraph are from this case.

22. Marvin E. Frankel, *Criminal Sentences: Law without Order* (New York: Hill and Wang, 1973).

23. Sentencing Reform Act of 1984, Pub. L. No. 98-473, 98 Stat. 1987 (1984).

24. *McMillan v. Pennsylvania,* 477 U.S. 79 (1986).

25. *Commonwealth v. Wright,* 494 A.2d 354 (Pa. 1985).

Chapter 7

Miscarriages of Mercy?

Linda Ross Meyer

In 2003, Iraqi General Mowhoush died in American custody after Chief Warrant Officer Lewis Welshofer stuffed him head first in a sleeping bag and sat on his chest. There were also allegations that Welshofer used beating and waterboarding as interrogation techniques. Welshofer was convicted by court-martial of negligent homicide, reprimanded, restricted to base for two months, and fined $6,000. Welshofer's commanding officer, Major Jessica Voss, received a reprimand for the death.[1]

Sergeant Gary Pittman was accused of kicking and beating detainees in 2003, including 52-year-old Nagem Sadoon Hatab, who died after he was beaten and, with diarrhea, left for hours in the sun. Pittman was convicted in 2004, received 90 days, and was demoted to private.[2] Major Clarke Paulus was court-martialed for ordering Pittman to drag Hatab by the neck and dismissed from the service (the equivalent of a dishonorable discharge for officers—he lost all his retirement benefits).[3]

Two prisoners, one of whom was an innocent taxi driver swept into custody along with his customers, died in an American prison in Bagram, Afghanistan, after they were chained to the ceiling and repeatedly beaten and kicked in the common peroneal nerve over several days. Court-martials resulted in sentences of two months, three months, and 75 days for three of the soldiers and reprimands for two of the sergeants involved.[4]

At the now-infamous prison in Abu Ghraib, guards, CIA, and military intelligence officers beat to death, stripped, stepped on, used dogs on, threatened with death and electrocution, sexually assaulted, and humiliated prisoners, and then took jeering photos of them. After court-martial hearings, Spc. Charles Graner received a 10-year sentence and dishonorable discharge; Staff Sergeant Ivan Frederick received 8 years and a dishonorable discharge; Spc. Lynndie England received 3 years and a dishonorable discharge; Jeremy Sivits received one year and a bad conduct discharge; Roman Krol, 10 months and a bad conduct discharge; Armin Cruz, 8 months and a bad conduct discharge; Sabrina Harman, 6 months and a bad conduct discharge; Michael Smith, 6 months; Javal Davis, 6 months and a bad conduct discharge; Santos Cardona, 90 days and a reduction in rank; and Megan Ambuhl, pay forfeiture and a less than honorable discharge. Lt Col. Steve Jordan and Lt Col. Jerry Phillabaum were reprimanded and relieved of command. Cpt Donald J. Reese was reprimanded and relieved of command. Col Thomas Pappas received a nonjudicial punishment and $8,000 fine. Brigadier General Janis Karpinski had her rank reduced to colonel.[5]

Journalists and human rights groups have raised concerns that courts-martial are not tough enough in responding to these crimes.[6] The Human Rights Watch and Center for Human Rights and Global Justice issued a detailed report charging that abuses by service members in Iraq and Afghanistan are far more widespread than Abu Ghraib and that "promises of transparency, investigation, and appropriate punishment for those responsible remain unfulfilled."[7]

It is time to remember that we had similar cases, and similar leniency, in the Vietnam era: Lieutenant Rusty Calley was sentenced to life in prison for the round-up and slaughter of hundreds of women, children, and old men at My Lai. Witnesses told of toddlers gunned down as they tried to crawl away from the pile of bodies and mothers shot trying to retrieve their children. Yet Calley served only four months in prison before he was pardoned by President Richard Nixon, and today he manages a jewelry store in his home town of Columbus, Georgia.[8] Others involved in My Lai were acquitted or not prosecuted. Private Michael Schwartz, sentenced to life at hard labor for shooting 16 Vietnamese women and children as they stood in front of their homes, served only nine months before his sentence was reduced by a military superior.[9] A squad of American soldiers gang-raped and murdered two young Vietnamese girls, 17 and 14, who were suspected to be enemy nurses. Both were brutally raped more than 20 times and forced to engage in oral sex at gunpoint, then, days later, shot. The soldiers tried to cover up the crime by forcing another prisoner to shoot the girls. Two members of the squad were found not guilty, and none of the rest were prosecuted.[10]

During the more than 10 years we were at war in Vietnam, at courts-martial convened in the field, the army convicted 95 soldiers of murder or manslaughter and the Marines, 27.[11] But many of these sentences were later commuted, and many more crimes were never prosecuted at all. Officers and soldiers testifying at the Dellums committee hearings in 1971[12] related widespread, uninvestigated, and unprosecuted beatings of prisoners, old men, old women, and children (sometimes to death),[13] use of dogs (and pythons) to intimidate prisoners,[14] cutting off the ears and other body parts of dead enemy soldiers as proof of body count or as trophies,[15] burning the skin of prisoners,[16] waterboarding,[17] shooting unarmed civilians,[18] routine electrical torture of prisoners,[19] shooting wounded prisoners,[20] shooting groups of women and children,[21] burning occupied dwellings,[22] throwing blindfolded and hooded prisoners into sewage ponds,[23] throwing prisoners out of helicopters to encourage others to cooperate,[24] throwing old men, women, and children into wells with grenades,[25] starving prisoners to death,[26] putting prisoners into coffin-size cages in the hot sun,[27] refusing medical treatment to Vietnamese wounded,[28] forcing prisoners to dig their own graves,[29] and so on. New evidence in recently declassified Pentagon files reveals more instances of unprosecuted war-related crimes against civilians in Vietnam, including unprovoked shootings of women and children, torture, and sexual abuse.[30]

Many questions arise from this shameful and gut-wrenching recital of American brutality and the apparent lack of severe punishment for most of those responsible. How can we fix the system? Should we eliminate the discretion and clemency within the military justice system? institute sentencing guidelines? try these cases before nonmilitary juries? try these cases in international tribunals? beef up our legal doctrines of command responsibility?

All of these questions will and should be asked. However, I would like to ask a prior question: How can we understand leniency—giving less punishment than is "deserved" or "due"—in the context of military courts-martial? Only when we understand the role that leniency plays can we begin to say when it may be a miscarriage of justice or answer any of the "fix-it" questions.

I. When Is Mercy Appropriate?

Some legal theorists answer this question very simply: mercy should never play a role in criminal prosecution or punishment.[31] From this perspective, any evidence of leniency or even discretion is absolutely inappropriate. Mercy is a miscarriage of justice anytime it cannot be recharacterized as justice—that is, understood as a form of "case-to-case equity" or maybe a global distributive justice of pain. Justice, in the form of the rule of law and retributive principles of punishment, should dominate the field of punishment. Mercy is laudable only insofar as it is an emotion of forgiveness at play in the private, but not public, realm.

These court-martial cases present a special challenge for me because my premises are different. First, I cannot accept the easy out that mercy is just an emotional attitude, like compassion, toward another person. Though forgiveness is often given this interpretation, in part to restrict it to the "private" world, the moral worth attributed to forgiveness suggests that there is an active element even in "forgiveness" that is under intentional control.[32] Whatever one calls it, mercy or forgiveness seems to require actions and entail efforts to repair relationships, an important consideration for public officials as well as for families and friends.

Second, I cannot say that mercy is always wrong. Part of my reason for rejecting the "mercy is always wrong" view is that, one, I do not conceive of justice as a set of rules that allow for "like cases to be treated alike," and, two, I have rejected the basic premise of retribution, which requires punishment to be measured by moral desert.

Because human law is in time and general, it allows only for rough justice. Equity, or ideal justice perfectly tailored to the case, calls to us and leads our judgment insofar as we can discern it under conditions of imperfect information and the clumsiness of language, but such justice is impossible to attain: always in a future (we always need more time, more investigation, more research, better technology), just out of our reach. Under conditions of rough justice, mercy may be the better form of error, reinforcing the trust and gratitude that underlie responsible relationships rather than fostering resentment and revenge.

I also call into question the premise of retributive justice that punishment should be the rebound of the crime onto the criminal. Punishment, in this way, is seen as necessary in order to treat the criminal's action with respect, as a universal law set forth by a creature of reason, applicable to the criminal himself. But we cannot treat others with respect, and therefore give them their own law as universal, when their law is a law of disrespect. Either we do not give them the full measure of their "maxim," and fail to treat them as the legislators of universal law and as persons, or we do universalize their disrespect and treat them disrespectfully, failing again to treat them as persons. The "respect" we accord offenders in punishing them, then, is an undeserved respect, not the full measure of the universality of their crime. Inherent in the metaphysics of retribution lurks the undeserved gift of treating the criminal with respect—a necessary mercy.

And here, I contend, is a significant clue to the place of mercy in the metaphysics of justice. Mercy is what is already there, before justice can get a toehold. Without the unfounded, undeserved, disposition of others to respect, to understand, to see themselves as "like" us, to believe us, and to try to make sense of us, neither law nor retribution can get off the ground. This undeserved benefit is foundational: we assume, absent further information, that "the other" we empirically confront is, in fact, a person, worthy of dignity and responsibility. Traditionally, we accord each other this worth and dignity, in Kantian terms, because we assume that the other is a reasonable being (though this empirical assumption is contingent, not required by reason).

But we must recognize that reason, too, is possible for us precisely because we are caught up in the limitations of time that make it possible for us to understand action as meaningful by projecting a past experience on a future one. It is our vulnerability to experience of the world that allows us to see and feel and respond to others and to make sense of their actions—to ground the assumption that the other we empirically confront is reasonable. Assuming the worth, dignity, and sense-making of others, then, is foundational. It is the being-with-others that must precede reason, law, and justice, and this allows us to respond to each other and the world and therefore be "responsible." Mercy is rooted in the undeserved, uncommandable-by-reason gift of experiencing another as a self: vulnerable and therefore reasonable. Without this "given," our hypothetical reasonable person would never come to know another person as reasonable, and the categorical imperative would remain hypothetical: that is, *if* there is another reasonable person, I must treat them with respect.

So there is no foundational, philosophical reason to leave mercy out of the picture, because it neither treats like cases unlike (or at least, no more than we usually do at our best) nor undermines responsibility by giving less than is "deserved" (at least, not any more than retribution itself). Instead, mercy invokes an experience of the other-as-self that grounds both justice and responsibility by allowing us to experience the other as a person who both makes sense and responds to the world.

But that leaves open the harder question: When is leniency inappropriate or not an experience of "being-with"? Does the mercy I describe call for more leniency than merely respecting the disrespectful—which is already a part of the theory of retributive justice as we think of it? How can we ever say that mercy is appropriate or inappropriate? Wouldn't any such distinction presuppose a "reason" and therefore something lawful rather than merciful? If I allow for mercy in some set of "appropriate" cases, am I not just advocating a finer-grained justice or equity rather than mercy?

My view differs from notions of equity in this: equity as a perfect, fine-grained justice is always called for (though never, in the human world, fully accomplished). Mercy, understood as undeserved leniency,[33] is not called for by reason in the same way. It may well be inappropriate in some cases. I would say that leniency is inappropriate, or not fitting, when the relationship experienced between mercy-giver and mercy-receiver is not grounded in a mutual recognition of the already-existing condition of being-with. (In other words, though we are already "with" and "like" each other as human beings, we do not always experience that connection and relationship.)

Appropriate mercy, in contrast, is an experience of recognizing another as a second self. As an experience of an underlying metaphysical truth, it may "show" different aspects of being-with in different circumstances. Mercy, if it comes out of a minimal recognition of the "personhood" of another, may ground the humane treatment of the "monster killer" or "terrorist." This minimal recognition is necessary simply in order to accord an offender justice: we cannot punish nonpersons; we can only confine them or treat them or "dispose" of them.[34] This level of charity is necessary in every meaningful interaction with others, from the simplest conversation to the most profound relationship. Otherwise, we could not make sense of each other at all.

If the mercy experience is grounded in the mutuality of temporal limitation, mercy can extend the recovery of time that is a "second chance." Seeing the other person as one (like us) who is unable to change the past and unable to control the future, locked into a life sentence of self-hatred and remorse, we can offer the arbitrary settlement that allows for a new start to the relationship.

Mercy that comes out of a recognition of mutual vulnerability can be the mitigation of sympathy. Part of our nature is to be open and vulnerable to the impressions and forces acting on us in the world. That passivity is part of our ability to respond to the world. When we see the other as beset by emotional and physical obstacles, our compassion may lead us to forgive, for we experience their vulnerability and the limitations on their power to act in the world.

Mercy that comes out of a recognition of mutual dependency can connote gratitude. Being-with necessarily means being mutually dependent on each other. When we forgive another who has served and helped others, we recognize our mutual dependence and renew our mutual trust.

Finally, when the experience of mercy comes out of a recognition of mutual guilt, it can connote complicity, or lack of standing to judge. We see the connection between our own fault and the defendant's crime, and we judge ourselves complicit, unable to stand apart and judge from outside the crime.

All of these forms of mercy stem from a relationship between the mercy-giver and the mercy-receiver. The possibility of a relationship between mercy-giver and receiver is contingent—sometimes this mutual recognition occurs, sometimes it does not. That experience is one we may have a duty to be open to but cannot summon at will. The experience is a gift, a grace—not something owed, but part of the very vulnerability to experience that is at the heart of being human.

Inappropriate leniency does not rest on a relationship between mercy-giver and mercy-receiver. It may instead be the result of careless indifference (flipping a coin), failure to see clearly the wrong (moral blindness), lack of concern for the victim (racism), considerations external to the case (political trade-offs), or desire for gain (bribery). In such cases, lenity clearly does not arise out of an experience of connection with an offender, and it simply does not "fit"—it is not proper or appropriate to the experience of relationship between the mercy-giver and receiver.

Mercy, then, refers itself to the experience of being-with, not to a judgment of desert. The language varies as well: relationships, as we say, can be appropriate or inappropriate, but not "deserved."[35] Easy cases of "appropriate" mercy might appear to be those in which the mercy-giver is at grave future risk from the offender—we might presume that the experience of mutual relationship here is genuine, for, in the sober language of economics, the mercy-giver is voluntarily "internalizing the cost" of her action.[36] Mercy between companions may often be the most obvious example of the recognition of mutual connection that leads one to trust the other into the future, despite the past.

If mercy is about the particular and unique experience of human connection, then it cannot be fruitfully discussed at this level of abstraction. To understand lenity in courts-martial, to decide whether it is proper or improper, requires looking at the cases and context in which it operates. As always, the story is richer and more complex than one might expect, and it requires a more considered response than simply imposing sentencing guidelines or eliminating discretionary decision-making across the board. The military justice culture is shot through with opportunities for discretionary lenity. As I show in the following discussion, lenity in the military context may often support norms of mutual responsibility and mutual trust, may sometimes be necessary for equity, and may at times be the best way to negotiate the uneasy relationship between the reality of war and individual moral judgment.

II. Lenity in the Military Trial Process

The military justice system, unlike the federal civilian system under the sentencing guidelines, allows for the operation of mercy at every stage of the criminal process. First, "corrective training" may be imposed by a service member's immediate superior, which avoids any official record of wrongdoing and, like community policing at its best and worst, can provide either early correction of wrongful conduct and modeling of good conduct, or harassment, extortion, and cover-up. The need for such discretion is clear, however. For example, technical crimes can be put in context: breaking into a fellow marine's room to watch television need not be treated as burglary; punching a superior in the course of a semi-friendly drinking spree can be overlooked; failing to pay one's bills on time can be corrected by sitting down weekly with the commanding officer and writing the necessary checks.[37] Though placing responsibility for correction at the lowest command level may also lead to cover-up of serious crime, it is necessary for unit cohesiveness and the trust required for teamwork.

Second, a whole range of nonjudicial punishments is available to commanders to avoid the need for formal trial and allow service members to avoid discharge.[38] Nonjudicial punishments are used frequently and at an increasing rate. In 2005, for example, the Army imposed nonjudicial punishments in 45,299 cases, compared with 825 general courts-martial, 700 special courts-martial, and 1,252 summary courts-martial.[39] As one officer put it: "I would nonjudicially punish or correctively train a service member instead of something else more severe. It did build a bond between commander and subordinate. Many well-known leaders, Tommy Franks, Colin Powell, tell stories of officers sparing their careers at an early age."[40]

In this respect, at least, the system of military justice loosely resembles John Braithwaite's regulatory pyramid of restorative justice.[41] Where the emphasis is on restoring the community and teamwork that is so essential to developing a "tight unit" of members able to trust each other under the intense conditions of combat, discretion and mercy help build relationships of gratitude and trust.

Discretion remains in the formal processes. Like prosecutors in civilian cases, the "convening authority" of a court martial has untrammeled discretion to prosecute or not, as well as to determine the charges, regardless of the outcome of pretrial investigation.[42] Additionally, the convening authority has discretion as to which type of court-martial to convene: a summary court-martial, a special court-martial, or a general court-martial. Summary and special courts-martial have abbreviated processes but also cannot impose the most serious penalties, again allowing discretion to play a role in setting a "ceiling" on sentencing.

Before trial, military defendants, like their civilian counterparts, may reach a plea agreement, which can be accepted by the convening authority at any time and can specify a maximum sentence. However, unlike a civilian defendant, the military defendant still has the opportunity to seek a lower sentence from the sentencing authority. Because the military sentences are indeterminate and set by the court-martial panel (or military judge, if the defendant agrees), the military offender will receive the lower of the two sentences, with the pretrial agreement setting a ceiling, but not the floor.[43]

During trial and in sentencing, great importance is placed on the "military character" of the defendant, allowing the full account of a defendant's service to be presented to the panel, regardless of its relevance to the specifics of the crime charged.[44] This evidence may be the basis for compassion or gratitude for prior service by the court-martial panel that provokes an acquittal or reduces a sentence.[45] Again, the practice is very different in our federal civilian courts where military service is rarely an important factor in sentencing.[46]

Another difference during trial is the extent to which evidence of a breakdown in command can serve to exonerate or mitigate sentence. In a military hierarchy, responsibility cuts (at least) two ways. One is personally responsible for one's actions, but one is also responsible for one's comrades and subordinates. An officer is responsible for his soldiers. In the words of one former military lawyer, "you take care of your people on-duty and off-duty."[47]

The "break-down in command" argument lays partial blame for the offense at the door of the commanding officer, who is supposed to know his people so intimately that crimes do not have a chance to occur. The service member's behavior is not separate from the community in which he lives and works, and the community must shoulder some of the blame.[48] A court-martial made up primarily of officers may be especially critical of an officer who did not prevent a subordinate from getting out of line, or who did not recognize a problem and deal with it at an earlier stage.[49]

Like the military character defense, the break-down in command argument can be abused. But it recognizes an important feature of military culture: its interconnectedness and the mutual responsibility it entails. As in the battlefield, the commander cannot leave his soldiers behind but has an obligation to back them up and take responsibility for them and for their actions. This kind of mutual responsibility is not always recognized in criminal law (except perhaps ironically in the law of conspiracy), and when responsibility does not go up the chain of command, the convening authority may be reluctant to punish those on the front line.

In a case in which the penalty is mandatory or severe, the court-martial or military judge may append to its sentence a nonbinding recommendation of clemency to the convening authority.[50] This recommendation must be forwarded to and considered by the convening authority before final approval of the sentence.[51] Individual members of the court-martial also may make more informal recommendations of clemency to the convening authority.

After trial, the defendant has another opportunity for clemency and may file a brief with the convening authority asking for a sentence reduction or dismissal of the charges.[52] The defendant has the right to assistance of counsel in filing this brief, and his sentence must be reconsidered by the convening authority if counsel was ineffective.[53] An experienced military lawyer, a staff judge advocate, advises the convening authority as to the lawfulness of the trial, the legal appropriateness of the sentence, and the clemency application.[54] These two functions—legal advice and clemency advice—may be contradictory.[55] A sentence may be appropriate to the law and culpability of an offender but be commuted nonetheless. The convening authority "may remit, mitigate or commute a sentence as a matter of grace alone. He need not be seized of a reason, nor be required to state one."[56] This opportunity for clemency is not a mere formality, but "the convening authority is an accused's last best hope for clemency."[57]

The importance of the clemency decision is underscored by the fact that a defense counsel will be considered "ineffective" if she fails to advise a client of the opportunity for clemency and aid the client in preparing the application. One former military lawyer estimates that reductions in sentence are granted about 10 percent of the time,[58] and deferral or waiver of pay forfeiture for family circumstances may be more frequent, perhaps 25 percent of the cases.[59]

The Court of Military Appeals for each service (Army, Air Force, Coast Guard, and Navy/Marines), formerly known as a Service Board of Review, has discretion to review the sentence as well as the legal aspects of the case de novo and may reduce, though not increase, a sentence.[60] Sentence review at this stage, however, is for "sentence appropriateness" defined as "the judicial function of assuring that justice is done and that the accused gets the punishment he deserves."[61] By contrast, the convening authority's clemency power "involves bestowing mercy—treating an accused with less rigor than he deserves."[62]

Although sentence review is not available at higher appellate levels, review for legal errors, including procedural errors in reviewing clemency applications, may be sought before the Court of Appeals for the Armed Forces (CAAF, formerly the Court of Military Appeals), a court composed of civilian judges.[63] Review of a CAAF decision may be sought by writ of certiorari from the U.S. Supreme Court.[64] After serving a specified portion of a sentence of confinement, a defendant may also seek a reduction in sentence from the Service Branch's Parole Board[65] and appeal a denial of that decision to the Secretary of Defense.[66] Counsel is not required at this stage, but a defendant may receive aid from his military lawyer anyway.[67] Even if sentenced to confinement, a prisoner may be eligible for a "return to duty program" run by his or her service.[68]

Discretion to be lenient, then, is a procedural option at all levels of the military trial process—by the commanding officer and convening authority at the charging stage; by the convening authority during and after trial; by the court-martial itself in sentencing; by clemency brief; and by seeking parole, pardon, or return to duty. The model allows the services to hold service members responsible for their actions but then to reintegrate and "forgive" them if they are repentant and committed. The discretion built into the system, especially at the posttrial clemency stage, reflects the ideal of mutual trust and obligation built into a hierarchical, interdependent military culture, as I next try to explain.

III. The Military Culture

Family is a metaphor often used in the military to describe the bonds of its personnel.[69] A Marine sergeant puts it this way: "The Marine Corps is like a family, and we teach family values."[70] New recruits write their unit number on their hands and learn first of all to work together. One description of a military training exercise makes the point:

> As the platoon enters its temporary barracks in the receiving building, most of its members remove their "utility hats"—the enlisted Marines' everyday headgear. Several say, "Good afternoon, sir," to a passing civilian. . . . They march to the mess hall for an early dinner, than back to the barracks, where Sergeant Lewis gives them twenty seconds to remove and hang up all their gear—hats, canteens, canteen web belts. The more astute members realize that the only way to do it within that limit is to aid one another. When Daniel Armstrong, a gangling, stork-like road construction worker from Florida, gets tangled trying to remove his canteen belt, Christopher Anderson, a smart, short black recruit who plans to study criminology at the University of Maryland, leans over and helps him. Sergeant Lewis watches in silent approval: They are getting the message.[71]

Marine lore prescribes: "Share everything, even the pound cake and cookies,"[72] and "Remember, if everyone does not come home, none of us can ever fully come home."[73]

Trust of one's comrades and trust of one's leaders is interconnected. The hierarchy of military organizations means that responsibility is always *for someone* and *to someone.* Marine lore puts it this way: "I will never forget that I am responsible to my Commanding Officer for the morale, discipline, and efficiency of my men. Their performance will reflect an image of me." If one's subordinates get into trouble, that will be noted and reflected in the commanding officer's performance review. Officers are expected to "take care of their people."[74] As one officer put it: "My soldiers, by and large, were willing to charge a machine gun nest for me. My duty to them is *tenfold.*"[75]

On the flip side, the subordinate must always have the support of his entire chain of command in order to get permission for leave, vehicle use, various recreational activities, and so on. And, to reenlist, the soldier, sailor, or marine must be recommended by his or her superior officers.

A reenlistment ceremony is a solemn occasion. The reenlisting service member is in full-dress uniform, her family is present, her commanding officer is present, and her senior officer speaks for her. Those up for reenlistment are the first to meet VIPs and are given places of special honor. When your superiors have supported you in all these ways, "you can't let these people down."[76]

Military culture at its best promotes and depends on relationships of teamwork and mutual responsibility. In turn, both are supported by the gratitude and trust created in allowing room for mercy. Reacting to sentences in war-related crimes by eliminating mercy from the military justice system would ignore the fact that mercy extended in soldier versus soldier cases actually promotes, rather than destroys, responsibility for others. Mercy enables the defendants to make a fresh start, reflects the community's gratitude for prior service, and recognizes communal and command responsibility for crime. The mercy-givers are themselves potential future victims, and they accept the risk of the defendant's future conduct. Mercy is not cheap and easy but reflects the mercy-giver's willingness to take risks on the strength of the relationship with the defendant. Defendants are already in close relationship with their victims and their commanding officers, responsible to and for them in the future,[77] and bonds of gratitude, trust, and mutual commitment are formed and strengthened by the mercy-giving. On the other hand, lengthy or harsh punishment in such a community setting may generate resentment and leave "nothing owing," leading to defendants' sense of separation, disaffection, and lack of a sense of responsibility or commitment to others.

IV. When the Victim Is an Outsider

The harder cases of mercy or leniency in the military context are those sentences for war-related crimes committed by American soldiers against "outsiders" or the "enemy" with which this chapter began.[78] How should we think about military mercy when the victim is not an "insider" to the military community but an outsider or, even more problematically, an "enemy"? In that case, the mercy-giver is not a potential future victim —making mercy seem cheap, "risk-free" and all too easy.[79] Lenity may even reflect the opposite of a connection with others: the mercy-giver's own lack of sympathy, or even animosity and racism, toward the enemy-victim. For these reasons, mercy extended to soldiers guilty of crimes against "outsiders" to the military community seems especially problematic and more likely to be "inappropriate" mercy.

The first question is whether there is any reason to believe that courts-martial are more lenient in cases involving crimes against "outsider" victims than they are in cases involving "insider" victims. Though data on military sentences are notoriously hard to come by, because the sentences are not governed by sentencing guidelines and are "moving targets" subject to review and clemency by several layers of authorities, I did make some statistically naive efforts to compare sentences of insiders and outsiders, as well as to compare military and civilian cases. I summarize here:

- Of 35 court-martial sentences of U.S. service members (court-martialed and found guilty) for crimes against Iraqi or Afghani prisoners or civilians (the time period is roughly from 2004 to September 2006) that were reported in American news sources, the average sentence is 26.8 months, and 8 months is the median sentence. This does not include acquittals, nonjudicial punishments, or cases dismissed after Article 32 hearings and only includes sentences I could find as of September 30, 2006, as reported in media sources. These sentences may also be later modified downward by the convening authority, appellate court, or parole authorities.
- Of 35 court-martial sentences during the same period (2004–2006) for violent crimes (excluding sexual assaults, domestic assaults, and crimes against children[80]) against other soldiers or civilians in nonhostile countries, the average sentence was 117.4 months, and the median sentence is 21 months. Again, this does not include acquittals, nonjudicial punishments, or cases dismissed after Article 32 hearings and only includes sentences as reported online by the military newspaper *Stars and Stripes* from 2004 to September 2006. Sentences may also be later modified downward by the convening authority, appellate court, or parole authorities. Some sentences may not reflect any pretrial agreement, though most do.
- Of the 35 sentences in electronically searchable federal cases against guards or police for violence against prisoners or suspects since the advent of the sentencing guidelines (1982–present), the average sentence is 84.4 months and the median is 60 months. Obviously, this problematic sample does not include cases prosecuted civilly,

cases not prosecuted, cases settled by plea, or many sentences not appealed. There is no parole in the federal civilian system, and sentences are rarely modified on appeal for reasons other than mistakes of law.

- According to the U.S. Sentencing Commission report for January 12, 2005, to September 30, 2005 (post-*Booker*), the mean sentence for all civil rights cases (all those sentenced under U.S.S.G. 2H1.1, which includes police and prison guards' crimes against defendants and prisoners, as well as nonofficials charged with depriving others of civil rights—like cross-burnings and deprivations not involving violence or injury) is 53.6 months and a median of 15 months (46 cases).

- Suggested federal guidelines sentences for the following crimes committed by a public official (a factor that raises the sentence) with no criminal history as set forth in U.S.S.G. 2H1.1 would be as follows:

> Unconstitutional assault, no serious injury: 46–57 months
> Serious injury: 57–71 months
> Life-threatening: 70–87 months
> Threatening with a gun, no serious injury: 27–33 months
> Reckless (unintentional) homicide: 27–33 months
> Voluntary manslaughter: 87–108 months

By any of these comparisons (and given the unavailability of reliable data and the obvious sample bias in the information I have collected above, these comparisons are at best only suggestive),[81] sentences for soldiers convicted by court-martial of crimes against prisoners or civilians during wartime *seem* to be more lenient than sentences for either violent crimes against other soldiers or violence against detainees or prisoners by civilian police or guards. Assuming the glimpse provided here is at all reliable, it looks like courts-martial are more lenient in prosecuting and sentencing war-related crimes than crimes against "insiders" and probably more lenient than civilian courts under the federal guidelines (even post-*Booker*).[82]

Is this mercy, giving defendants less than they deserve? The apparent lenity in these cases (if it indeed exists) may be explicable in legal terms. First, crimes are much harder to prosecute under conditions of war for lack of witnesses and evidence, resulting often in lesser charges or acquittals.[83] Especially in a war zone without a "front," bodies cannot be found;

evidence cannot be collected or preserved properly; witnesses flee or hide or simply move away.

Second, the use of violence in combat situations is especially ambiguous. For example, did Ilario Pantano shoot two detainees because they turned and made a sudden move toward him, as he claims, or did he shoot them, as his sergeant testified, because he thought they had been mortaring his men and he believed intelligence units would only release them again? Situation and intention are both constantly shifting in battle; lenity may reflect residual doubts about the appropriate interpretation of the defendant's actions.

Finally, there are ambiguities of law: What exactly were the rules of engagement in effect for intelligence units at Abu Ghraib and Bagram, and how much force is too much force? How closely should prohibitions on torture be parsed? Is it torture to repeatedly kick a prisoner under interrogation in the tender nerve areas of the thigh, or is it only "torture-lite"? There are also ambiguities in orders—sometimes intentional sorts of ambiguities that give unofficial "permission" for atrocities, as in My Lai or Son Thang and perhaps Abu Ghraib. And finally, there is the question: When must a soldier disobey an order of a superior officer? When is such an order "patently illegal"?

The very possibility of the last question, of course, goes to the heart of the nature of law. If law is only how the president parses the Geneva Convention, then there is no "patently illegal" order, for ultimately, the superior's order is law by virtue of being the superior's order. Positive law is law. Taking this view, as we know, would exonerate both Adolf Eichmann and Lieutenant Calley, who both defended themselves on the ground that they were "lawful" in this way.[84] But the fact that we did convict both of these men suggests that we cannot take this position. The aspirational "free" judging self has to be acknowledged at least as an aspiration and a possibility—perhaps even at the price of convicting soldiers for doing as they are told. What "we demand" in trials of this kind is that, as Hannah Arendt puts it, "human beings be capable of telling right from wrong even when all they have to guide them is their own judgment, which moreover, happens to be completely at odds with what they must regard as the unanimous opinion of all those around them."[85] A willingness to exploit legal ambiguities in the Geneva Conventions, rules of engagement, or orders of superiors, in these cases of extreme cruelty, seems to deny the possibility of any law but positive law. Such a position may eliminate convictions of "our" soldiers, but it also destroys the conception of military (or any other) honor. Those who heroically succeed in controlling their fear and rage, who resist orders to butcher and torture, are, under positive law, criminals.

Of course, our willingness to exploit legal ambiguities in these cases may not evince a commitment to positive law but may, instead, be itself generated by sympathy or mercy. Even if we do not legally excuse our soldiers on the ground of following orders, we can yet show mercy, which is not about judgment at all. This separation between liability and clemency accords with the structure of court-martial procedure in general —the court-martial convening authority can choose both to convene the trial and to pardon afterward: to exercise both justice and mercy. But even if both are possible, our original question remains—When is mercy proper?

If we do have mercy operating in these sentences, are the sentences we are seeing in Iraq and Afghanistan to be compared with the trials of Nazi war criminals by German courts—where defendants whose crimes would have provoked the death penalty if tried in the civilian courts of the victim nation received only a few years from German courts, as a token gesture to "obstinate" foreign opinion?[86] Is lenity in these cases only another example of the "thin blue line" where soldiers join ranks to protect their own? Is it only the cases that are internationally notorious that are prosecuted and the notorious defendants that are given stiffer sentences (such as Charles Graner's 10-year sentence for atrocities at Abu Gharib, or the apparent severity with which the crimes in Mahmudiya and Haditha are being treated)?

This is, of course, one possible explanation for the apparent lenity in these cases—a mercy not generated by an experience of mutual recognition between mercy-giver and mercy-receiver, but one based on considerations of personal gain external to the case; that is inappropriate mercy. But if this were the "thin blue line" in operation, why are some of the less spectacular cases being prosecuted? Convening authorities could be using their discretion to avoid prosecution altogether. The very use of a court-martial makes the abuses public and damages the perception of the armed forces. Yet, we are holding courts-martial, even in cases where there has been little publicity. And, in some cases where commanders have tried to hide abuses and avoid courts-martial, they have done so at the expense of their own military careers.[87] It is more likely that the motivations for lenity are mixed here. Given the honor-culture of the military, and the sense that dishonorable conduct reflects on the whole community, once the crime can no longer be "kept in the unit," it is unlikely that lenity would be motivated in every case by a desire to "protect our own." Certainly, many service members expressed revulsion and anger at their colleagues at Abu Ghraib, who tainted the honor of the military, overshadowed the heroic and compassionate acts of others, and compromised the mission.[88]

Assuming (and it is a big assumption) that sentences in these cases cannot be completely explained by problems of proof or by strategic efforts to whitewash offenses and exculpate offenders—assuming, in short, that we are really seeing lenity or mercy that is a response to the facts or nature of the particular case or offender—what sense could we make of it?

A. Recurring Themes: Revenge and Mistrust

Nearly every serious war crime reported in Iraq and in Vietnam involved many of these distinctive factors:

1. Defendants stationed in an extremely dangerous, long, and harsh post in which hostile civilians were routinely involved in tricking, bombing, or booby-trapping soldiers[89]
2. A recent loss of a trusted leader or beloved comrade to guerrilla attacks or explosive devices[90]
3. A disrupted or confused command structure, or one in which a renegade, unbalanced, or a first-time unit leader takes charge[91]
4. Vaguely-worded aggressive orders conveyed along with an atmosphere of anger, desire for revenge, and hatred toward a dehumanized enemy, and little or no attention given to articulating and reinforcing the limits imposed by the rules of engagement[92]

All of these factors played a role in the crimes committed at My Lai, Son Thang, Abu Ghraib, and Mahmudiya, as well as in other horrendous murders of civilians in the Vietnam era.[93] Paradigmatic is the case of Mahmudiya, where service members went on a killing spree after an Iraqi civilian came up to an American patrol smiling and friendly, shook hands with the soldiers, and then shot two of them.

The crimes here are horrendous: gang rapes of young girls; close-range shootings of crying children; obliteration of harmless and helpless toddlers, mothers, blind women, old men. But over and over again, we also see the fear, hurt, and anger of young men who have lost their closest friends without being able to retaliate in a "fair fight" and who explode in random and sickening violence.[94] At some point, retributive justice and punishment may seem only to reinforce and reiterate the revenge-instincts that create these tragedies in the first place, yet lack of punishment can also reiterate revenge. Can mercy be an appropriate response?

In the final section, I suggest that lenity seems to be extended to service members when (1) their moral judgment is perverted by the military's own demand that soldiers suppress their compassion and humane feelings and treat enemies as less than human and (2) when soldiers act out of rage and revenge and grief. Lenity may not be as readily extended to service members who are shown to be less-than-honorable outside the conditions created in a war zone. Mercy in this way recognizes the mercy-giver's own responsibility for the crime and avoids condemning those who lose their honor for the sake of their country. Insofar as this form of mercy deeply implicates the mercy-giver in the crime, it is not easy mercy, caused by a lack of concern for the victim. Instead, mercy here should cause us all to share the shame—for we are the ones who demand that some of our most self-sacrificing citizens cross the lines of humanity and destroy their own nobility on our behalf.

B. War and the Perversion of Moral Judgment

1. ROLE MORALITY

Soldiers are taught to be "tough" and follow orders without question. Moreover, they live in a "total institution," where the power of communal living, uniforms, and teamwork strip the individual of the usual idiosyncratic modes of self-presentation that make him or her different and create a situation in which it is very hard to stand up, stand out, or question the way things are done.[95] Like judging, lawyering, and other institutions where participants are urged to leave the ultimate moral decision-making to others (to the legislature, to the client, to the "process"), service members rely on authorities to set the "rules of engagement." Their job is to follow, not to make, policy. Comments by service members reflect their need to distance themselves from normal moral responses in order to perform their duties.

Military culture extols "ruthless toughness" and prides itself on being

able to set aside emotional reactions so as to follow orders dispassionately and accomplish the mission. Even the Nazis weeded out those who
"enjoyed" killing or killed sadistically. They wanted dispassionate, professional killers. In bureaucratic killer Adolf Eichmann's case, Hannah Arendt points out that Eichmann turned his vice into virtue: in a perversion
of Kantian ethics, he considered his ability to "overcome" his natural, human aversion to killing as a duty and a virtue. He was "tough" and able
to kill (from afar, at least) dispassionately. He even refused to stop sending Jews to their deaths near the end of the war when Himmler ordered
him to, on the ground that Himmler's order was based on selfishness and
greed (hoping to curry favor with the likely victors), not duty. Eichmann's
defense throughout his trial was that he bore no malice or ill-will toward
the Jews; he was a normal, kind person who was doing his duty (facilitat-
ing the killing in the most humane way he could)—and the odious nature
of his duty only made his obedience seem (to him) more noble.[96]

The testimony of Lance Corporal Kenneth Campbell before the Dellums Committee hearings on Vietnam is chillingly similar to Eichmann's
self-justification. Campbell admits that he called for artillery strikes on an
inhabited village from which he had received no enemy fire. When asked
whether he ever thought he was doing wrong, Campbell replied:

> It went through my mind, what am I doing? And it shook me for a while
> and my radioman, who I had become very close to, never said anything,
> but he just stared at me and the look on his face, you know, the idea that
> he conveyed to me was the same question I had, what are you doing, you
> know. And this rattled me, but going back to the old Marine Corps idea
> of being hard, I just pushed it to the back of my mind. I knew I could not
> think about it too long or else I would not be hard anymore, I would not be
> one of the elite killers anymore if I started having feelings. Besides this I ra-
> tionalized it, I mean, this is what they had told me, nobody questioned it, it
> was the thing to do. . . . I just had to put it in the back of my mind, because
> I would have been a weakling.[97]

Over time, the intentional dulling of emotional reaction and humanitarian responses results in a zombie-like numbness toward violence and
death. Often, when war crimes are described, it is the "new guys," still full
of high ideals, chivalry, good intentions, and patriotism who feel the horror and shame of killing women and children and defenseless old men,
not the "old timers."[98] For example, after witnessing the slaughter of 10

Vietnamese women and children in retaliation for a soldier's death, a soldier related: "I was like in a state of shock and these guys did this so systematically like it was something done so many times before, it was easy. It didn't bother them, any of them, at least it didn't appear to bother any of them. Now these guys were old-timers, they had been there for a long time, you know? It was just cut and dried like it was understood that this was going to happen."[99]

In another incident, a first lieutenant described feeling "shocked" when he saw another military intelligence agent put a 38-mm revolver to a prisoner's head. He testified: "Not understanding what military intelligence policy was, being my first patrol, I stopped the man from doing that. . . . But the thing I want to stress is not that I was more moral than the other people involved, but that no other man—and there must have been thirty men around—no other man—all of them seasoned soldiers—moved to prevent that man from being murdered on the spot."[100]

One soldier tried to explain this phenomenon: "After your initiation to the realities of war . . . you just become numb to these things. You are—well, your emotions can't take it. You don't shock any more so you are tempted to just numb yourself and it gets to the point that it doesn't bother you until your buddy gets killed. But Vietnamese getting killed doesn't seem to bother you. You become so dehumanized, you become a stone."[101]

2. RACISM TOWARD THE ENEMY

In the rhetoric of war there is pervasive verbal derogation of the enemy, which creates, feeds, and expands racist categories. From the beginning of military training, recruits are taught (sometimes "officially," but always "unofficially" by the prevailing language used by others) to call the enemy by slurs and slangs—krauts, japs, gooks (a slur orginally used to refer to Nicaraguans in 1912),[102] slopes, slants, dinks—and now, ali baba, johnny jihad, goat fuckers, muhammads, hajjis, cunts.[103]

As one soldier testified during the Dellums commission hearings about his experience in Vietnam:

[T]here was always the attitude—it developed in boot camp, it developed in ITR, it developed in staging battalion before we went over and it developed all of the way through the time we were in Vietnam—we hated these people, we were taught to hate these people, they were gooks, slants, dinks, they were Orientals, inferior to us, they chewed betel nuts, they were ugly, you know, they ate lice out of each other's hair, they were not as good as us. And you could not trust them.[104]

American commercialism, with its tendency to judge people by their possessions and standard of living, contributes to this racism. As a captain in Vietnam put it: "With me, I couldn't help but somehow view these Vietnamese as a little less than human when we went in and destroyed their homes. They weren't really homes, they were just hooches. I wouldn't have had the same zeal if we were destroying red brick homes or split level homes in suburbia."[105]

The same judgments seem to hold today in Iraq: "I don't like to say it, but after a while, when you have the rifle, and you see how the Iraqis look at you and how they live, . . . then some of our guys feel superior—like the people in Haditha or Fallujah aren't quite human like us. You don't think of them the same way. That's not right, but it does happen."[106]

But beyond whatever racism a soldier already brings with him to the battlefield, the "racism" of war is insidious; even service members who have respectful attitudes toward the culture or race of those they are fighting at the beginning of a war succumb to it. For example, Pantano starts his tour in Iraq armed with polite Arabic phrases, many copies of "Islam for Dummies" that he passes out to his men, and a determination not to use terms like "man dress" that he finds "belittling" (referring to the traditional dishdasha robe worn by Iraqi men). By the middle of the battle narrative, however, he is referring routinely to "an Iraqi in a man dress" and using terms like "cunts" and "goat fuckers" to describe the enemy and "Sheik Butt-Fuck" to describe untrustworthy civilian leaders. Instead of the polite greetings and handshakes he exchanges with civilians he meets on his arrival, three months later he is threatening uncooperative civilians with Abu Ghraib in order to get information.[107]

John Crawford writes that, after a year in Iraq, "I went to the gas station yesterday to buy some cigarettes. An Arabic man was working behind the counter. He turned when he heard the door chime and gave me a broad smile. I walked out. I never wanted to hate anyone; it just sort of happens that way in a war."[108] Again there are echoes of Vietnam. Captain Bartek emphasized "the brutalizing [effect] . . . the war has on Americans . . . the subtleties that have crept into our own minds and into our own emotions when we look at a Vietnamese. There is a certain repulsion there. Certainly we are intellectually committed to erasing it, but it is a difficult thing to do. That was again the effect of the policies in Vietnam."[109]

3. RAGE AND REVENGE

In addition to the role-based norm of intentionally silencing one's feelings of humanity and a pervasive war-generated racism, war narratives demonstrate that human responses to enemy civilians as fellow human beings disintegrate after a long period of guerrilla combat, especially in conditions, like Vietnam and Iraq, where civilians hide or help enemy soldiers or simply refuse to warn American soldiers of known dangers. Soldiers' mounting frustration, humiliation, and anger at civilians, in both Vietnam and Iraq, spilled into racism, rage, and violence when their military "family members" are killed by landmines or bombs or ambushes that civilians knew about but failed to warn of.[110]

This rage and revenge, in turn, reinforces racist categories and generates violent retaliation. As one soldier put it during the Dellums commission hearings: "My attitude and feelings were, to the people over there, were exactly—I couldn't care less what happened to any of them because I had buddies and friends shot and killed, wounded, too."[111] Soldiers in Vietnam who began their tour by handing out candy to children and playing ball with them ended by abusing them, kicking them, beating them with rifle butts, and making trophies of their hair.[112] "They slugged every little kid they came across."[113]

The devaluation of victims that pervades these war crimes, especially in wars in which the enemy melts into the civilian population, may not even be at core about race but precipitates out of grief and revenge. Race is then used as a ready vehicle and label for this anger, enabling service members to stifle their feelings of humanity and kill on command. Hence, the "role morality," racism, and revenge in these stories feed and reinforce each other, enabling service members to become "killing machines." The hate, anger, and mistrust of all civilian members of the enemy state is part of a radical breakdown of public trust. Soldiers in Vietnam and perhaps in Iraq report feeling that they operate in a "war of all against all"—a Hobbesian state of nature, in which many of them assert an absence of all law, all justice. Service members articulate lenity sometimes in this way —as an inapplicability of principles of individual responsibility in such a context: "[I]f one can say 'waste dinks,' there no longer is a moral frame of reference, there is no longer a moral judgment."[114]

At least part of the ugly specter here, then, is the possibility that lenity is exercised on the racist grounds, propagated and internalized by methods of war itself, that the lives of the enemy victims are not "worth" as much as the career or honor of an American service member. In Vietnam, this racism even had its own acronym: MGR—the "mere gook rule."[115]

C. Convict and Forgive

It is possible that lenity in war-related crimes is based on racist attitudes generated by the rage of war. Looking at the anecdotal evidence from courts-martial, however, this hypothesis does not seem adequate to explain all the sentences. It seems that some defendants are still treated more harshly than others for the same kinds of war-related crimes against the same enemy victims. A different hypothesis, more consistent with military culture, is that courts-martial are lenient toward soldiers whose moral judgment was perverted by the conditions of war and less lenient toward soldiers whose dishonorable conduct appears to "spill over" —either predating or postdating the combat or war.

The great emphasis in military trials on character evidence and the offender's prior service record, while often mystifying to civilian commentators, may be the framework for a possible noncynical account of appropriate mercy in sentencing war-related crimes. When a soldier has committed a crime, his military record says a lot about who he was "before." If the defendant was honorable and self-sacrificing going in, and yet has become hard, cruel, and full of hate, his very character is a tragic casualty of war[116]—of what we required him to do and become in order to accomplish his mission.[117]

On the other hand, if a defendant's record demonstrates a person already violent or sadistic, or if the defendant later fails to acknowledge responsibility and guilt, fails to see those he killed or harmed as "insiders," or fails to "come clean" to his commanders, sympathy seems less fitting. Spc. Charles Graner's 10-year sentence might be explained this way; perhaps also the life sentence (later reduced to 25 years) given to Sergeant Michael P. Williams for three execution-style killings of Iraqi prisoners.[118] In both of these cases, the defendants' own comrades testified against them; there was no "good military character" defense.[119] On the other hand, in cases like Bagram, where interrogators employed more or less officially sanctioned but ultimately inhumane interrogation techniques, defendants have not received stiff sentences, perhaps because their commanders recognized the sacrifice of honor they made for us and for our purposes.

In showing appropriate mercy in war-related cases, we acknowledge that we cannot expect wars to be fought honorably and that in sanctioning methods of waging war that are likely to bring about the dishonor of honorable service members, we are shamed. Is this cheap mercy, out of racism and a culpable lack of concern for victims? Not necessarily. If we truly see the moral degradation of our own (formerly honorable) service members as our fault, then mercy is a finding of complicity, putting us all on trial.

Ilario Pantano, a veteran of the Iraq war, sums it up: "No real soldier wants their actions recorded for posterity. I didn't want my family to know. I didn't want my children to learn about bloodlust and fear and shit and killing. There was nothing good in it. There was nothing good that came out of war. You didn't come back more. You came back less."[120]

If we see that moral degradation in war is what we ask of our service members, should we go farther and exonerate, rather than merely extend leniency, to service members guilty of war-related crimes but whose records reflect that their moral blindness, racism, rage, and inhumanity was a product of the demands of war?

This point of view is supported by the fact that modern warfare inevitably devastates the civilian population—old and young alike. In the context of modern warfare, fought from computer terminals and remote controls where "you don't have to look at the corpses, you don't have to listen to the women and kids crying,"[121] and no discerning judgment intervenes before violence, "criminal' warfare," if defined as knowing or intentional slaughter of civilians, is "inevitable."[122] Or as Pantano puts it, "chivalry is for museums."[123] The contested question of when an interrogator, a guard, or an infantryman has crossed the line of honor is, for most deaths in war, irrelevant, and in view of the mass destruction and death even "conventional" warfare now causes, worry about holding a "grunt" responsible begins to seem a mere quibble around the edges.[124] Most suffer and die lingering deaths without anyone judging whether they are civilian or soldier, child or adult, armed or unarmed, threatening or friendly. Some veterans even assert that "fighting fair" entails losing. If indeed the law of war has been outstripped, is it madness to call to account the few "grunts" who still have to fight it in all its real gore and danger, rather than those who sit at the joystick?

Certainly it does seem as though we need a better legal paradigm of accountability for commanders (even presidents and citizens), not only for crimes done at our bidding but by our acquiescence.[125] But we cannot eliminate the responsibility of the "grunt." As I said above, to deny the possibility of individual responsibility in this context would be disastrous—for it would also fail to recognize and honor those who manage to resist the temptations of rage and revenge, resist the claimed necessity of illegality, and act with only appropriate force. It would also criminalize the conduct of those whose humanity leads them to disobey "illegal" orders. Hannah Arendt likewise rejects the idea of legal "communal responsibility" in her examination of Nazi butcher-bureaucrat Eichmann: "No matter through what accidents of exterior or interior circumstances you were pushed onto the road of becoming a criminal, there is an abyss between the actuality of what you did and the potentiality of what others might have done."[126] To fail to judge is wrong. But that does not eliminate the possibility of mercy.

So we are left with an apparent futility: to convict and forgive. The oddness of this stance may merely be an echo of a fundamental contradiction of military culture itself. Military honor and self-discipline may be in fundamental conflict with moral honor and may appear only as a perverse shadow of true or natural right action (should it exist). Perhaps this is inevitable, as the military "objective," the purpose of all the fine rhetoric of honor and all the mutual commitment and comradery, is, after all, to win the war through violence (and not just kill those enemies who are an imminent threat). Perhaps in the last analysis, we must see these torturers, killers, and rapists as human tragedies, not inhuman monsters, or we risk losing our own souls, too. Seeing "the enemy" as human, whether inside or outside our ranks—indeed, whether inside or outside our skins—is still humanly possible, in glimpses and moments, and that may be our only redemption:

> Well, there was this kid. I sat there and I had fed the kid all day, and he was walking along the dike, and he said hello to us and while the squad leader—well, he grabbed the kid and started beating him up. He put a .45 up to his head and then he cocked the hammer and he said, "Was there VC in his village last night?" And the kid said, "No, there wasn't." Then we beat him up and then I realized that he wasn't going to tell us that his father was in their village last night. Were they going to tell us that their husbands were there? That's all I have to say.[127]

NOTES

With many thanks to Tom Belsky, Joe Cavo, David Connell, Vern Coverdell, Bryan Haas, Devant Joiner, Joyce Kaneko, John Morgan, Earl "Mitch" Mitchell, and Joe Race for taking the time to teach me about military service—especially

Mitch, who corresponded so generously with me even during his service in Baghdad. They did their best; any remaining mistakes are mine. Thanks also to Leslie Lax, Freda Keklik, Emily Graner, and Tina Delucia for outstanding help with research, to many of my colleagues at Quinnipiac for comments on earlier drafts, and to the other contributors to this volume for their insights and suggestions.

1. John Sarche, "Military Jury Recommends No Jail Time for Officer Convicted in Death of Iraqi General," *Stars and Stripes*, January 25, 2006.

2. Alex Roth, "Bones May Be from Iraq," *San Diego Union Tribune*, September 17, 2006; Mynda Ohman, "Integrating Title 18 War Crimes into Title 10: A Proposal to Amend the Uniform Code of Military Justice," *Air Force Law Review* 57 (2005): 1.

3. Alex Roth, "Marines Involved in Iraqi Abuse Frustrated after Their Convictions," *San Diego Union Tribune*, December 13, 2004.

4. Tim Golden, "In U.S. Report, Brutal Details of 2 Afghan Inmate's Deaths," *New York Times*, May 20, 2005; Tim Golden, "The Bagram File: Revisiting the Case Years after 2 Afghans Died, Abuse Case Falters," *New York Times*, February 13, 2006.

5. Mynda Ohman, "Integrating Title 18"; Eric Schmitt, "Iraq Abuse Trial Is Again Limited to Lower Ranks," *New York Times*, March 23, 2006; Neil Lewis, "Court in Abuse Case Hears Testimony of General," *New York Times*, May 15, 2006; "Abu Ghraib Dog Handler Sentenced," *CBS News*, June 2, 2006.

6. Alex Roth, "U.S. Servicemen Found Guilty of Killings Often End up Serving Little Time," *San Diego Union-Tribune*, June 11, 2006; Russell Carollo, "Soldier Convicted in 2004 Slaying of Iraqi Man Leaves Prison a Year Early: Daily News Probe of Cases Like This Showed Soldiers' Jail Sentences Usually Were Lighter Than in Civilian Courts," *Dayton Daily News*, June 24, 2006; Tim Whitmire, "Short Sentences, Dismissals, Show Wartime Murder Prosecutions Hard," *Associated Press*, June 5, 2005; Golden, "The Bagram File"; Schmitt, "Iraq Abuse Trial"; Josh White, Charles Lane, and Julie Tate, "Homicide Charges Rare in Iraq War: Few Troops Tried for Killing Civilians," *Washington Post*, August 28, 2006.

7. *By the Numbers: Findings of the Detainee Abuse and Accountability Project* (New York: Human Rights Watch and Center for Human Rights and Global Justice, New York University, 2006), 1.

8. Michael Belknap, *The Vietnam War on Trial: The My Lai Massacre and the Court-Martial of Lieutenant Calley* (Lawrence: University of Kansas Press, 2002); Richard Hammer, *The Court Martial of Lieutenant Calley* (New York: CM&G Press, 1971); John Sack, *Lieutenant Calley: His Own Story as told to John Sack* (New York: Viking, 1971).

9. Gary D. Solis, *Son Thang: An American War Crime* (Annapolis, Md.: Naval Institute Press, 1997).

10. *United States v. Goldman*, 43 C.M.R. 722 (Army Bd. of Rev. 1970) (fining soldier for failing to report these crimes). See also Jack Crouchet, *Vietnam Stories:*

A Judge's Memoir (Boulder: University Press of Colorado, 1997), 70–82, 130–35, 174–75. The 1989 film *Casualties of War,* screenplay by David Rabe, is based on this crime. For another acquittal in a rape case during Vietnam, see Solis, *Son Thang,* 103.

11.   Gary D. Solis, "Military Justice, Civilian Clemency: The Sentences of Marine Corps War Crimes in South Vietnam," *Transnational Law and Contemporary Problems* 10 (2000): 59 (arguing that courts-martial in Vietnam treated crimes against the enemy very seriously, though many received clemency later through stateside pardon and parole authorities). By comparison, the *Washington Post* reported that in the first three years we have been in Iraq, 39 service members were formally accused of crimes in connection with civilian deaths; 26 were charged with murder, negligent homicide, or manslaughter; and 12 served prison time. White, Lane, and Tate, "Homicide Charges Rare in Iraq," A1.

12.   After Calley was court-martialed, many Vietnam veterans wanted Congress to hold hearings on the extent of other war crimes in Vietnam. They felt that Calley was being scapegoated for conduct that was pervasive and widespread. Congressional committees refused to hold these hearings, so a junior congressman, Ron Dellums of California, decided to chair informal hearings, attended by other members of Congress who were against the Vietnam War. These hearings are a remarkable read, for the soldiers' testimony is graphic, detailed, and moving, and they testify without any apparent concern for incriminating themselves. Citizens Commission of Inquiry, ed., *The Dellums Committee Hearings on War Crimes in Vietnam: An Inquiry into Command Responsibility in Southeast Asia* (New York: Vintage, 1972).

13.   Ibid., 32, 41, 85–86, 89, 93, 95, 144, 212, 231, 236, 240, 241, 248–49, 250, 252.

14.   Ibid., 213, 135.

15.   Ibid., 10, 40.

16.   Ibid., 90.

17.   Ibid., 32, 67 (part of training).

18.   Ibid., 112–13, 218–19, 234, 238.

19.   Ibid., 29, 32, 68, 92–93, 136–37, 144–46. One standard practice was to use a field telephone, which had two "hot" wires. This was known as "ringing up" a prisoner or "Bell Telephone Hour."

20.   Ibid., 41, 168, 228, 251.

21.   Ibid., 188–90, 211 (recounting retaliatory killing of civilian women and children after a favorite platoon member was killed by a booby trap).

22.   Ibid., 60.

23.   Ibid., 135.

24.   Ibid., 111, 133–34, 232.

25.   Ibid., 166, 178.

26.   Ibid., 129.

27. Ibid., 137.

28. Ibid., 16, 146–47.

29. Ibid., 149.

30. Nick Turse and Deborah Nelson, "Civilian Killings Went Unpunished: Declassified Papers Show U.S. Atrocities Went Far beyond My Lai," *Los Angeles Times,* August 6, 2006.

31. Dan Markel, "Against Mercy," *Minnesota Law Review* 88 (2003): 1421.

32. Joanna North, "The "Ideal" of Forgiveness: A Philosopher's Exploration," in *Exploring Forgiveness,* ed. Robert D. Enright and Joanna North (Madison: University of Wisconsin Press, 1998), 5.

33. I could define mercy as appropriate leniency, but that would beg the question. With the term mercy, I am trying to capture the idea of giving less than the punishment ideally deserved in a perfectly just world.

34. Herbert Morris, "A Paternalistic Theory of Punishment," *American Philosophical Quarterly* 18 (1981): 266 (arguing that we cannot punish nonpersons and we have a "duty" to punish persons rather than "treating" them).

35. We do sometimes say "they deserve each other" or "I don't deserve him." But these metaphors only highlight the contingency of desert to relationships. We don't have obligations to befriend or love others; sometimes it happens, sometimes it does not.

36. Even in such cases, however, it is still possible that the experience of "relationship" is not one of mutual recognition but is about (or, at least is a perception of) personal gain. The mercy-giver may be so dependent on the offender that even future crime seems better than no relationship at all—as when an abused child forgives a parent or an abused wife forgives a husband (though, again, it is not impossible to have appropriate mercy in such cases, just more difficult to know).

37. Interview with R. All the interviews cited in this article took place in September 2004 with the author, at Quinnipiac University in Hamden, Connecticut. Interviewees were former members of the armed services, speaking about their personal experiences. Some asked that their comments not be attributed. See also Lieutenant Colonel W. G. "Scotch" Perdue, "Weighing the Scales of Discipline: A Perspective on the Naval Commanding Officer's Prosecutorial Discretion," *Naval Law Review* 46 (1999): 83.

38. Article 15, Uniform Code of Military Justice (UCMJ), 10 U.S.C. §815.

39. *2005 Annual Report to the Committees on Armed Services and Secretary of Defense,* appendix, at http://www.armfor.uscourts.gov/annual/FY05AnnualReport.pdf.

40. Interview with H. See also Elizabeth Lutes Hillman, *Defending America: Military Culture and the Cold War Court Martial* (Princeton: Princeton University Press, 2005), 25–26: "The centralized authority that military officers sought to preserve [under the new UCMJ] was not necessarily wielded in malevolent fashion;

commanders could use their discretion to excuse as well as to punish. After a court-martial concluded the UCMJ permitted the officer who ordered the trial to unilaterally reduce, but not enhance, the sentence of a convicted service member. An accused person who had served in combat, performed well in an elite unit, or had a long record of meritorious service was likely to benefit from the intervention of a senior officer, even if convicted of a crime under the UCMJ."

41. John Braithwaite, *Restorative Justice and Responsive Regulation* (New York: Oxford University Press, 2002), 30–31: "The idea of the pyramid is that our presumption should always be to start at the base of the pyramid, then escalate to somewhat punitive approaches only reluctantly and only when dialogue fails, and then escalate to even more punitive approaches only when the more modest forms of punishment fail."

42. The convening authority may not be the same commander who brought or "preferred" the charges. The convening authority is usually at least two steps up the chain of command from the defendant. The convening authority does not have any role as investigating officer, judge, or prosecutor and takes no part in the trial itself. Lower-ranking commanders may convene summary or special courts martial but do not have the authority to convene a general court-martial. If a lower-ranking commander believes a general court-martial is appropriate, he or she must send the case up the chain of command. Service members can elect a general court-martial instead of more summary dispositions, if they choose, though the sentencing risks are much greater. David A. Schleuter, *Military Criminal Justice, Practice and Procedure*, 5th ed. (Charlottesville, Va.: Matthew Bender, 1999), 288–311.

43. For example, *United States v. Bauer,* 1998 CCA LEXIS 44 (Navy Marine Ct. Crim App. 1998) (sentence given by judge after plea was reduced to reflect pretrial agreement reached with convening authority); *United States v. Muse,* 1995 CCA LEXIS 87 (1995) (sentence of 20 years reduced to 13 per pretrial agreement with convening authority); *United States v. Washington,* 1996 CCA LEXIS 475 (Navy Marine Ct. Crim App. 1996) (pretrial agreement suspended all but three years of a 25-year sentence for raping stepdaughter; defendant had 21 years of "stellar" performance as a chief petty officer). In some circumstances, a pretrial agreement may be reached without a plea of guilty, if the defendant agrees to stipulated facts, for example. Schleuter, *Military Criminal Justice,* 376: "Promises by the convening authority usually relate to withdrawing charges, referring less serious charges, referring charges to a particular court, instructing the prosecutor not to present evidence on certain charges, or providing some sort of sentence relief such as suspension of a portion of the sentence. . . . Although pretrial agreements usually involve a promise by the accused to plead guilty, there is nothing to prevent the parties from reaching an agreement involving a plea of not guilty or even a conditional plea of guilty."

44. *United States v. Clemons,* 16 M.J. 44 (Ct. Mil. App. 1983) (Everett, C.J.,

concurring) (arguing that military character and record should be more generally admissible even under the new rule, because, citing *Wigmore*, military personnel are subject to closer supervision and more record-keeping than civilians
are); *United States v. Kahakauwila*, 19 M.J. 60 (Ct. Mil. App. 1984) at 61 (error to
exclude military character as evidence in conviction for drug sale: "The military
rule is taken from the Federal Rules of Evidence. However, the peculiar nature of
the military community makes similar interpretation inappropriate." Opinion for
the Court by Everett, C.J., citing with approval the more expansive good character
rule of common law); *United States v. Weeks*, 20 M.J. 22 (Ct. Mil. App. 1985) (error
to equate military character with general good character—former is admissible
in drug sale case); *United States v. Belz*, 20 M.J. 33 (Ct. Mil. App. 1985) (holding
that general military character could be admissible in defense of a drug charge,
since it had been held admissible in defense of "conduct unbecoming" based on
similar facts); *United States v. Court*, 24 M.J. 11 (Ct .Mil. App. 1987) (error to restrict introduction of entire military record, especially when charged with "conduct unbecoming an officer"); *United States v. Hurst*, 29 M.J. 477 (Ct Mil. App.
1990) at 481–82 (error to restrict introduction of officer effectiveness reports in
child abuse case because "the location of the offenses on base, their abusive and
degrading nature and their deleterious impact on the military family clearly call
into question appellant's character as a military officer"). See also "Symposium on
the Military Rules of Evidence," *Military Law Review* 130 (1990): 1, 3 (Comments
of Retired Justice Robinson O. Everett: military courts "obliterated" the civilian
limitation on character evidence to a relevant "trait," despite the intention of the
drafters and the language of the rule, because of unique circumstances of military
culture).

45. One very interesting example of mercy-as-gratitude involved a soldier
who refused to chamber a round in response to a direct order to do so whenever he was assigned to work outside the base perimeter. The soldier's tour of
duty was almost over; the soldier had served well but had had his fill of death.
The commander was reluctant to court-martial this soldier, and other soldiers in
the unit were sympathetic, too. Instead of convening a court-martial, the commander chose to assign the soldier to duties within the perimeter for the rest of
the soldier's tour, a mercy that recognized the soldier's "good military character"
and prior service and which would not have been possible otherwise. Interview
with H.

46. Military service is a "discouraged factor" for sentencing departures under
the guidelines. U.S.S.G. 5H1.11. I have found no pre-*Booker* federal criminal case
that granted a departure on this ground, and several that overturned departures.
United States v. Booker, 543 U.S. 220 (2005). For example, *United States v. Miller*,
94 Fed. Appx. 121 (3d Cir. 2004) (overturning downward departure for military
service); *United States v. Jared*, 50 Fed. Appx. 259 (6th Cir. 2002) (reversing a
downward departure for military service); *United States v. Coble*, 11 Fed. Appx.

193 (4th Cir. 2001) (same); *United States v. Given,* 164 F.3d 389, 395 (7th Cir. 1999) (same); *United States v. Miller,* 146 F.3d 1281 (8th Cir. 1998) (military performance not relevant though defendant had received a Bronze Star in Vietnam); *United States v. Lawrence,* 1997 U.S. App. LEXIS 3849 (4th Cir. 1997) (overturning departure); *United States v. Winters,* 105 F.3d 200, 209 (5th Cir. 1997) (same); *United States v. Ellis,* 1997 U.S. Dist. LEXIS 7362 (E.D. Penn. 1997) (refusing to depart for military service); *United States v. Rybicki,* 96 F.3d 754 (4th Cir. 1996) (reversing departure for a Vietnam veteran who had saved a civilian during My Lai); *United States v. Pittman,* 1993 U.S. App. Lexis 21851 (4th Cir. 1993) (not showing military service was extraordinary, so no error in failing to consider it). *United States v. Pipich,* 688 F.Supp. 191 (D. Md. 1988) granted a downward departure for military service, based on a long history of respect for those with exemplary military service, but this case was decided before the Sentencing Commission amended the guidelines to make military service a discouraged factor.

Post-*Booker,* some courts are finding a conflict between the guidelines' rule discouraging departures based on military service (U.S.S.G. §5H1.11) and the guidelines-enabling statute that directs courts to consider a defendant's history and circumstances. 18 U.S.C. §3553(a)(1). See also *United States v. Ranum,* 353 F.Supp. 2d 984 (E.D. Wisc. 2005); *United States v. Long,* 425 F.3d 482, 488–89 (7th Cir. 2005) (post-*Booker,* district courts can consider "discouraged factors," including military and community service). One case, *United States v. Nellum,* 2005 U.S. Dist. LEXIS 1568 (N.D. Ind. 2005), granted a downward departure based, in part, on military service ("The defendant is also an Army veteran, who was honorably discharged. Under the guidelines, Nellum's military service is not ordinarily relevant in arriving at an appropriate sentence. See U.S.S.G. §5H1.11. Yet, this Court finds it very relevant that a defendant honorably served his country when considering his history and circumstances. [18 U.S.C. §3553(a)(1)]."). Other courts continue to deny these departures. For example, *United States v. Tabor,* 365 F.Supp.2d 1052, 1061–62 (D. Neb. 2005); *United States v. Turner,* 2005 U.S. Dist. LEXIS 6368 (N.D. Ind. 2005).

47. Interview with B. See also interview with J: "If you are willing to volunteer and you have a good attitude, the Marines takes care of you, they reward you."

48. For example, *United States v. Thomas,* 38 C.M.R. 655 (Army Bd. of Rev. 1968) (court-martial appended clemency recommendation to life sentence in part on ground that "idea of committing the offenses concerned originated with the accused's patrol leader, . . . and probably would not have occurred without his encouragement and guidance").

49. Interview with B.

50. *United States v. Weatherspoon,* 44 M.J. 211, 213 (C.A.A.F. 1996) ("for over 4 decades, the President has provided for, and this Court has recognized, the power of a court-martial to recommend clemency to the convening authority, contemporaneously with announcement of the sentence."); *United States v. Strom,*

5 C.M.R. 769 (Air Force Bd. of Rev. 1952) (members of court-martial appended recommendations of clemency to the sentence).

51. *United States v. Smith,* 20 C.M.R. 477 (Army Bd of Rev. 1955).

52. Schleuter, *Military Criminal Justice,* 777–81.

53. *United States v. Raistrick,* 1998 CCA LEXIS 268 (Air Force Ct. Crim. App. 1998) (defendant convicted of sodomy with his 10-year-old stepson; court sent the case back for clemency reconsideration by convening authority because counsel failed to ask for full extent of clemency options defendant wanted; court held that counsel's failure met standard of "colorable showing of possible prejudice" because appellant "had many years of good service, had shown remorse for his actions and believed individuals at Lajes Field and his family would have requested clemency consideration if contacted"); *United States v. Frueh,* 35 M.J. 550 (Army Ct. Crim. App. 1992) (setting aside convening authority's approval of the sentence because defense counsel failed to submit clemency application: "A defense counsel has a responsibility to review a case after the trial and to raise all legal issues and clemency matters with the convening authority which may assist his client"; waiver of right to submit matters regarding clemency should in future be signed by both lawyer and client); *United States v. Washington,* 1996 CCA LEXIS 475 (Navy Marine Ct. Crim. App. 1996) (defense counsel must submit clemency petition even if unlikely to result in more clemency than pretrial agreement, especially where clemency requested was reduction to E-3 rather than E-1 in order to help support family); *United States v. Washington,* 1996 CCA LEXIS 483 (Navy Marine Ct. Crim. App. 1996) (case returned to convening authority even though "relatively lenient sentence" because counsel did not submit fiancee's letter asking for clemency on the ground that she has no support for defendant's newborn child).

54. For example, *United States v. Manibo,* 1990 CMR LEXIS 252 (Navy Marine Ct. Crim. App. 1990) (staff judge advocate recommended clemency, but convening authority did not grant it); *United States v. Guerrero,* 2001 CCA LEXIS 131 (2001) (staff judge advocate on behalf of convening authority offered clemency if defendant would take polygraph); *United States v. Clear,* 34 M.J. 129 (Ct. Mil. App. 1992) (convening authority's decision set aside because staff judge advocate did not advise convening authority of trial judge's recommendation of clemency).

55. *United States v. Tu,* 30 M.J. 587 (Army Ct. Crim. App. 1990) ("When taking final action on the findings and sentence, the convening authority considers legal error in his quasi-judicial capacity and must therefore apply appropriate legal standards of review. . . . Clemency is a matter of executive grace and the convening authority therefore acts in his executive capacity. . . . When serving in this latter function, the convening authority's discretion is plenary and he has complete discretion to disapprove findings of guilty and any portion or all of an adjudged sentence. . . . Thus, the convening authority's final action in a court-martial may require him to apply independent and ofttimes inconsistent standards" [citations omitted]).

56. *United States v. Myers,* 46 C.M.R. 719 (Army Bd. of Rev. 1972) at 720.

57. *United States v. Cook,* 46 M.J. 37 (1997) at 39. See also *United States v. Wilson,* 9 U.S.C.M.A. 223, 26 C.M.R. 3 (Ct. Mil. App. 1958) at 6 ("it is while the case is at the convening authority level that the accused stands the greatest chance of being relieved from the consequences of a harsh finding or a severe sentence"); *United States v. Sorrell,* 47 M.J. 432 (1998, Sullivan, J., dissenting) at 434 ("Our clemency process is too important a step in our military justice system to have even the hint of anything irregular as part of the process").

58. Interview with B. Published and "unpublished" but electronically available examples of posttrial grants of clemency by a convening authority include *D'Agnese v. United States Naval Clemency and Parole Board,* 2006 US District Lexis 33284 (D. Kans. 2006) (noting that convening authority had reduced sentence from 20 years to 12 years); *United States v. Rocha,* 2005 CCA Lexis 361 (Navy Marine Ct. Crim. App. 2005) (convening authority reduced nine-month sentence to 200 days, but staff judge advocate's delay forced defendant to serve out entire sentence; court of appeal further reduced confinement to 100 days so that defendant could seek an adequate monetary remedy from another court); *United States v. Fagan,* 29 M.J. 238 (C.A.A.F. 2004) (convening authority had reduced 30-month sentence to 20 months in case involving distribution of marijuana, larceny, and forgery); *United States v. Jenkins,* 62 M.J. 582 (Navy Marine Ct. Crim. App. 2005) (convening authority reduced 12-year sentence for rape to 9 years); *United States v. Phillips,* 2006 CCA Lexis 61 (C.A.A.F. 2006) (convening authority reduced fine); *United States v. Rountree,* 2005 CCA Lexis 347 (Navy Marine Ct Crim. App. 2005) (convening authority disapproved hard labor without confinement); *United States v. Gaines,* 61 M.J. 689 (Navy Marine Ct. Crim. App. 2005) (convening authority reduced two years to 12 months); *United States v. Griggs,* 2005 CCA Lexis 183 (Navy Marine Ct. Crim. App. 2005) (reducing 90-day sentence to time served); *United States v. Robbins,* 60 M.J. 607 (Navy Marine Ct. Crim. App. 2004) (convening authority disapproved one month of confinement and one month of pay forfeiture); *United States v. Myers,* 46 C.M.R. 719 (Army Bd. of Rev. 1972) (convening authority reduced bad-conduct discharge to four months of confinement at hard labor); *United States v. Huggins,* 1998 CCA LEXIS 93 (Navy Marine Ct. Crim. App. 1998) (convening authority reduced bad-conduct discharge and reduction to pay-grade E-1 by suspending bad-conduct discharge for 12 months and reducing pay grade only to E-3); *United States v. Sorrell,* 47 M.J. 432 (1998) (convening authority reduced sentence by six months); *United States v. Freeman,* 2000 CCA LEXIS 199 (Air Force Ct. Crim. App. 2000) (convening authority reduced sentence from bad-conduct discharge, confinement for 10 months, forfeiture of 1,000 per month for 10 months, and reduction to E-1 to bad-conduct discharge, confinement for 8 months, forfeiture of $959 per month for 10 months, and reduction to E-1); *United States v. Strom,* 5 C.M.R. 769 (Air Force Bd. Rev. 1952) (convening authority suspended a dishonorable discharge and all but six months

of confinement and forfeitures); *United States v. Rogers,* 1998 CCA LEXIS 244 (Air Force Ct. Crim. App. 1998) (convening authority allowed defendant to enter Return to Duty program instead of receiving immediate bad conduct discharge); *United States v. Henson,* 58 M.J. 529 (Army Ct. Crim. App. 2003) (larceny; convening authority reduced 18 months to 10 months); *United States v. Lentz,* 54 M.J. 818 (Navy Marine Ct. Crim. App. 2000) (wife and child abuse, adultery; convening authority reduced 18 years to 12 years). One examination of sentences and clemency for service members in the Vietnam era is Gary D. Solis, "War and the United States Military: Military Justice, Civilian Clemency: The Sentences of Marine Corps War Crimes in South Vietnam," *Transnational Law and Contemporary Problems* 10 (2000): 59 (arguing that stateside parole boards exercised more clemency than military panels convened abroad during wartime). His statistics show that court-martial sentences were reduced by the convening authority in 14 of the 27 cases he examined. The most dramatic exercise of clemency was reducing a life sentence to one year. Five other life sentences were approved, and nine others were reduced to between 20 and 40 years.

59. For example, *United States v. Baur,* 1998 CCA LEXIS 44 (Navy Marine Ct. Crim. App. 1998) (plea bargain included waiving automatic forfeitures "with the understanding that the funds would be used for the benefit of appellant's wife and two children."); *United States v. Craft,* 1999 CCA LEXIS 226 (Air Force Ct. Crim. App. 1999) (convening authority disapproved adjudged forfeitures and waived for three months the mandatory forfeiture for appellant's spouse and children "based on a letter written by appellant's wife"). See also Solis, *Son Thang,* 278–79: "Here was the hidden price of a court-martial conviction and perhaps its cruelest cost. In punishing the serviceman his family is penalized as well. . . . It is a matter that every military judge considers when deciding upon a sentence."

60. 10 U.S.C. Sec. 866 c requires Courts of Appeals to affirm only that sentence which should be approved. *United States v. Craft,* 1999 CCA LEXIS 226 (Air Force Ct. Crim. App. 1999) (reducing confinement by one month because convening authority did not consider clemency materials); *United States v. Griffith,* 2000 CCA LEXIS 253 (Navy Marine Ct. Crim. App. 2000) (reducing dishonorable discharge to bad conduct discharge because convening authority did not have opportunity to act on clemency petition); *United States v. King,* 21 C.M.R. 365 (Army Bd. of Rev. 1956) (reducing dishonorable discharge, total forfeiture, and confinement at hard labor for one year to bad conduct discharge, total forfeitures, and confinement at hard labor for nine months, for sleeping on guard duty; no error below, but "we do not foreclose ourselves at this appellate level from our duty and obligation to make our own independent evaluation and determination of the appropriateness of the sentence"); *United States v. Haynes,* 44 C.M.R. 713 (Navy Bd. of Rev. 1971) (eliminating bad conduct discharge for attempted larceny, on ground that court-martial was misinformed of its right to recommend an administrative discharge "both in law and in grace"); *United States v. Chollet,* 30 M.J. 1079 (Coast

Guard Ct. Crim. App. 1990) (eliminating bad conduct discharge for wrongful co-caine use on ground that record not clear and that court really thought an admin-istrative discharge more appropriate); *United States v. Triplett*, 56 M.J. 875 (Army Ct. Crim. App. 2002) (reducing confinement from 15 to 10 years because sentence was disproportionately more severe than co-accuseds); *United States v. Doss*, 57 M.J. 182 (C.A.A.F. 2002) (court of appeals had reduced sentence because lawyer failed to present evidence of mental distress at sentencing, but CAAF reversed because court of appeals should have remanded instead). But see *United States v. Ransom*, 56 M.J. 861 (Army Ct. Crim. App. 2002) (sentence of co-accused was highly disparate but difference was rational.) The court may not consider a civil-ian sentence in determining appropriateness. *United States v. Hutchinson*, 57 M.J. 231 (C.A.A.F. 2002).

61. *United States v. Healy*, 26 M.J. 394 (Ct. Mil. App. 1988) at 395. See also *United States v. Fagan*, 59 M.J. 238 (C.A.A.F. 2004) (overturning Army court of appeals' reduction of sentence from 20 to 19 months because court had not held the required fact-finding hearing to determine whether the defendant's claims of ill treatment in prison were valid—court had no general clemency authority ab-sent a finding of legal right); *United States v. Miller*, 18 M.J. 599 (Navy Marine Ct. Crim. App. 1983) (trial judge's recommendation for clemency does not under-mine the appropriateness of the sentence; the two are distinct—a sentence may be considered not excessive, even when the trial judge believes clemency should be recommended); *United States v. Johnson*, 58 M.J. 509 (Navy Marine Ct. Crim. App. 2003) at 514 (refusing to reduce sentence because it was appropriate for the crime, "appellant's argument on appeal is simply a plea for clemency, which is the prerogative of the convening authority and not the appellate courts"); *United States v. Emerson*, 20 C.M.R. 434 (Army Bd. of Rev. 1955) (refusing to change dis-honorable discharge (suspended) to bad conduct discharge in order to give effect to convening authority's desire to keep appellant from losing all his pay during confinement; appellate court cannot give effect to illegal attempts at clemency by altering a sentence without a basis in justice) Other examples are found in Crouchet, *Vietnam Stories*, 197–205, esp. 57–69 (remembering two cases in which service members were extended clemency by the appellate process—one for re-fusing to go into combat after having served faithfully in other firefights and the other for taking part in a prison riot).

62. *United States v. Healy* at 395.

63. Again, there is a significant difference here from civilian practice. The ci-vilian courts will generally not inquire into the pardon process. *Ohio Adult Parole Authority v. Woodard*, 523 U.S. 272 (1998).

64. Schleuter, *Military Criminal Justice*, 33–34.

65. James D. Johnston, "Military Parole: The Final Steps toward Responsible Citizenship," *Corrections Today* (December 2003): 88–91.

66. Dennis L. Phillips, "The Army's Clemency and Parole Program in the Correctional Environment: A Procedural Guide and Analysis," *Army Lawyer* (1986): 18.

67. Interview with B.

68. Department of Defense Instruction 1325.7, as amended June 10, 2003: "6.10.4.3. Return-to-Duty Programs. Each Service is authorized to establish policies and procedures for prisoner return-to-duty programs. The scope of these programs shall be determined by available resources, facilities, personnel, and the needs of the Service. Prisoners shall be evaluated under their Service regulations for suitability for the program and provided appropriate opportunities to improve potential for return to duty." The Air Force Return-to-Duty Program is at Bolling Air Force Base, Washington, D.C. "Candidates must attend individual and group counseling plus develop a personal rehabilitation plan. A treatment team, comprised of a social worker, a psychologist, substance abuse and mental health technicians, military training leaders and a chaplain, regularly evaluates candidates. They meet each week to assess each candidate's progress in individual and group therapy, seminars, military training and other treatment programs. When a candidate completes all phases of the program, a board is convened from among the Air Force members at the Charleston Brig. They consider each candidate's judgment, impulse control and coping skills, acceptance of responsibility, potential for future misconduct and promise to contribute to the Air Force." A. J. Bosker, "CSAF Witnesses Air Force Return-to-Duty Program," *Air Force Military News*, October 28, 2002, available at http://findarticles.com/p/articles/mi-prfr/is_200210/ai_1570588739.

69. *American Military Culture in the Twenty-First Century: A Report of the CSIS International Security Program* (Washington, D.C.: Center for Strategic and International Studies, 2000), 13 (quoting Lt. Gen. Paul Van Riper and noting that the Marines have the "strongest service culture" in the armed forces).

70. Thomas E. Ricks, "Making the Corps," in *Semper Fi: Stories of the United States Marines from Boot Camp to Battle*, ed. Clint Willis (New York: Thunder's Mouth Press, 2003), 11. Gary Solis states: "The essence of the Marine Corps is family" (*Son Thang*, 65). See also Jill Schachner Canen, "JAG Edge: Proposed Changes for Military Lawyers Have Critics at Attention," *ABA Journal* (2003): 26: " 'Most people do not understand how family-oriented the military and the JAG corps are,' [Lee Schinasi] says. 'The thing people really need to consider is the culture. It's what keeps good JAG officers on active duty.' " Interview with J, explaining how a father's court-martial will affect the military career of his daughter: "You have to understand how family-oriented the service is."

71. Ricks, "Making the Corps," 19.

72. Marion F. Sturkey, *Warrior Culture of the U.S. Marines* (Plum Branch, S.C.: Heritage Press International, 2002), 155.

73. Ibid., 162.

74. *American Military Culture in the Twenty-First Century,* survey question, 85 (item 70).

75. Interview with H.

76. Interview with K.

77. A service member who does not want to remain in service is not as likely to receive clemency. For example, *United States v. Hundley,* 56 M.J. 858 (Navy Marine Ct. Crim. App. 2002) ("although appellant's desire for a discharge cannot transform an inappropriate sentence into a just one, it is 'a strong indication of a lack of rehabilitative potential and a significant factor for consideration'").

78. I do not use the technical term "war crimes" here because "war crimes" carrying the death penalty under domestic law are not and cannot be prosecuted under catch-all provisions of the Uniform Code of Military Justice (UCMJ). Ohman, "Proposal to Amend the Uniform Code of Military Justice" (the UCMJ does not contain its own category of war crimes, and though it allows prosecution of any federal crime through a catch-all provision, crimes carrying the death penalty must be defined within the UCMJ itself).Moreover, I wish to avoid the knotty legal questions of just when a murder or assault crosses over to the technical definition of "war crime."

79. That was my view before I looked closely at these cases. Linda Ross Meyer, "The Merciful State," in *Forgiveness, Mercy, and Clemency,* ed. Austin Sarat and Nasser Hussain (Stanford: Standford University Press, 2006), 112 n.89: "I would insist that an authority only has the power to pardon crimes of the community in which he or she moves. An authority must be, in that respect, a potential victim."

80. I excluded domestic abuse, child abuse, and sexual assault from my "control group" because of my sense that "women" and the "private crimes" are still likely to be "outsiders" and outliers. Sexual and domestic crimes have a problematic history in military courts. For example, Elizabeth Lutes Hillman, *Defending America: Military Culture and the Cold War Court Martial* (Princeton: Princeton University Press, 2005).

81. The military services report to Congress the numbers of courts-martial and nonjudicial punishments and the rate of convictions, but they do not report sentences. Sentencing data are hard to come by. Hillman, *Defending America,* 156 n.74. Responses to my requests under the Freedom of Information Act confirm that the Navy and the Marine Corps do not currently compile centralized sentencing data, though a database of sentencing information is being developed and may be available in the next few years. I am currently analyzing data from the Army that I received after this article had to be completed. The data I have, however, do not follow the cases posttrial, so I do not have disaggregated information about convening authority clemency or parole.

82. This trend may be changing, however. In late 2006, in the Mahmudiya

rape/murder/arson and the Haditha house-to-house shootings, the military sentenced one defendant to life and two others to 18 years each. Moreover, four officers in the Haditha case were charged with serious crimes for their failure to clarify the rules of engagement and failure to report the facts up the chain of command. Paul Von Zielbauer, Carolyn Marshall, and Archie Tse, "Marines Charge 4 with Murder of Civilians," *New York Times,* December 22, 2006; Paul von Zielbauer, "Soldier to Plead Guilty in Iraq Rape and Killings," *New York Times,* November 15, 2006.

83. Ilario Pantano explains that the bodies of the Iraqis he killed were buried in the middle of a combat zone; they could not at first be exhumed for examination. Ilario Pantano with Malcolm McConnell, *Warlord: No Better Friend, No Worse Enemy* (New York: Simon and Schuster, 2006). See also Tim Whitmire, "Short Sentences, Dismissals, Show Wartime Murder Prosecutions Hard," *Associated Press,* June 5, 2005. On the many difficulties in finding and transporting witnesses and preserving evidence in Vietnam, see Gary D. Solis, *Marines and Military Law in Vietnam: Trial by Fire* (Washington, D.C.: History and Museums Division, U.S. Marine Corps, 1989).

84. American jurisprudence for qualified immunity has already made this "positive law" choice, granting qualified immunity to any officer whose actions do not violate "clearly established law." Ironically, those officers guilty of outrageous acts of cruelty that are so beyond the pale as to have no precedent may be the ones who are exonerated. See Linda Ross Meyer, "When Reasonable Minds Differ," *New York University Law Review* 71 (1996): 1467, 1518–21.

85. Hannah Arendt, *Eichmann in Jerusalem: A Report on the Banality of Evil* (New York: Penguin, 1961), 14–16.

86. Ibid.

87. For example, Dexter Filkins, "The Fall of the Warrior King," *New York Times Magazine,* October 23, 2005.

88. Interview with H. Pfc. Justin Watt, whose concerns began the investigation into the Mahmudiya rape/murders, "felt obligated to say something . . . out of a sense of loyalty to the friends who had fought in Iraq and died. 'We'd come through hell together and there were a lot of good men who died. . . . And this happened for what? We're just trying to do a little good over here.'" Paul von Zilbauer, Qais Mizher, and Ali Adeeb, "Soldier Who Testified on Killings Says He Feared for His Life," *New York Times,* August 8, 2006. See also the letter of reprimand issued in *United States v. Islas,* 2000 CCA LEXIS 239 (Navy Marine Ct. Crim. App. 2000) ("the extent of your selfishness is nothing less than an embarrassment to the Naval service, the Marine Corps and to your family"); *United States v. Court,* 24 M.J. 11 (Ct. Mil. App. 1987) (Cox, J., dissenting in part as to remand for harmless error finding) ("Because of my strong feelings, I am simply unwilling to allow the concept of 'an officer and a gentleman' to erode on my watch"); *United States v. Brisky,* 2001 CCA LEXIS 68 (Navy Marine Ct. Crim. App.

2001) (no judicial bias shown by judge's reference to "our Marine Corps' ethics" and "our ethics").

89. Son Thang: "[T]he infrantrymen of 1/7 contended with considerably more than forty-two identified enemy battalions. The Marines' opponents included a Vietnamese civilian population that was not exactly sitting out the war—the civilians often were the enemy. According to Marine historians, it was a war 'of snipers, ambushes, and old women who planted booby traps. . . . Throughout the summer of 1969, 1/7 was engaged in virtually continuous heavy combat." Solis, *Son Thang*, 12.

Xuan Ngoc: Testimony of a Navy psychiatrist: "War in Vietnam is one where the enemy is usually unseen until he chooses to make himself known, while the Marines are forced to repeatedly expose themselves to attack and ambush. Civilians often shelter and aid the enemy and give rise to very strong resentment from the Marine troops, especially when it is clear that the civilians can prevent the death of numerous Marines by providing information about the presence of enemy troops and the location of booby traps and mines. This is a situation that caused PFC Potter to feel appropriately angry and frustrated and to look forward to raiding a village." Solis, *Marines and Military Law in Vietnam*, 54.

Mahmudiya: "In February, soldiers were ordered to spend up to 30 days at a time at the checkpoint—eating and sleeping there—instead of the routine three-to-five-day rotation. . . . The checkpoints south of Baghdad are deadly, and the one the accused men were at was among the worst. . . . On December 10, about three months before the rape, an Iraqi man in civilian clothing walked up to it, greeting and shaking hands with one of the soldiers on duty, according to relatives and lawyers of men in the unit. The Iraqi then raised a pistol and shot two sergeants in the head, fatally wounding them. Seconds later, Private Spielman shot and killed the attacker. Mr. Green, who was also at the scene, threw one of the wounded sergeants onto the hood of a Humvee and struggled to keep him alive during a frantic ride back to base." Robert F. Worth, Carolyn Marshall, and Kirk Semple, "The Reach of War: Accusations; G.I. Crime Photos May Be Evidence," *New York Times*, August 5, 2006, A8.

Haditha: Haditha was an area of intense insurgent activity, where on August 8, 2005, a roadside bomb killed 14 Marines. On November 19, the day the Marines allegedly killed 24 civilians in their homes and car, including seven women and three children, a lance corporal was killed by another roadside bomb. Gayle S. Putrich, "A Dozen Marines May Face Courts-Martial for Alleged Iraq Massacre," *Marine Times*, May 25, 2006.

Abu Ghraib: The brigade was "severely underresourced" because it "had to conduct tactical counter-insurgency operations while also executing its planned missions." Fay-Jones Report, August 23, 2004. "In addition to being severely undermanned, the quality of life for Soldiers assigned to Abu Ghraib (BCCF) was extremely poor. . . . There were numerous mortar attacks, random rifle and RPG attacks, and a serious threat to Soldiers and detainees in the facility. The Prison complex was also severely overcrowded." Taguba Report, 38. Both the Fay-Jones and Taguba reports are reprinted in Karen J. Greenberg and Joshua L. Dratel, eds., *The Torture Papers: The Road to Abu Ghraib* (New York: Cambridge University Press, 2005). See also Marian Blasberg and Anita Blasberg, "The Prisoner and the Guard: A Tale of Two Lives Destroyed by Abu Ghraib," *Der Spiegel*, English ed., September 26, 2005: "Abu Ghraib felt like living in hell; it was over 100 degrees, there was constant shelling, prisoners were abusive, guards were abusive, it was filthy and rat-infested, hours were long and there was no place else to go."

90. My Lai: "When Calley arrived in Vietnam, he had had forty-five men in his platoon; by the eve of the attack on My Lai (4), he was down to twenty-seven men, and of his casualties, 'I would say ninety-five per cent with mines, booby traps." Hammer, *Court Martial of Lieutenant Calley*, 245.

Son Thang: "Any combat death affects the entire company to some degree. The loss of Sgt. Jerry E. Lineberry [killed along with 12 others in an enemy ambush] was particularly disheartening. Lineberry, an eight-year Marine and the platoon sergeant of B Company's second platoon, was competent and well-liked, a spark plug around whom younger Marines rallied." Solis, *Son Thang*, 23.

Abu Ghraib: Violence escalated after prisoners with weapons injured a female soldier and a prisoner shot at a guard. Blasberg and Blasberg, "Prisoner and Guard."

Mahmudiya: Civilians had recently murdered two sergeants, and the defendants had tried to keep them alive—see note 89: "All told, between September and June, at least 17 members of the battalion were killed, 8 of them from Company B, and dozens more were seriously wounded. In February, morale took another hit when a fire broke out in the abandoned factory being used as makeshift barracks . . . fire destroyed most soldiers' personal items." Worth, Marshall, and Semple, "Reach of War."

Haditha: Some 14 marines had been killed there by a roadside bomb three months before the alleged murders, and a lance corporal had been killed by a roadside bomb just before the murders. Bing West, "The Road to Haditha," *Atlantic Monthly*, October 2006, 98.

91. Mahmudiya: "At the time, the men's squad leader and the overseeing platoon commander—both highly respected leaders—were on leave . . . 'I know none of that would have happened if he was around,' [a fellow sergeant told reporters]. Worth, Marshall, and Semple, "Reach of War."

Son Thang: A recently demoted private, Herrod, was put in charge of the "killer team," even though he had never commanded before and even though he was outranked by another member of the team. Solis, *Son Thang*, 36–37.

Abu Ghraib: Lines of command were confused; no one wore any insignia, so no one knew who was supposed to give orders and who was supposed to follow them. Military police were under the impression that military intelligence wanted the abuse to happen. "[The] MI Brigade Commander did not assign a specific subordinate unit to be responsible for interrogations at Abu Ghraib and did not ensure that a military intelligence chain of command at Abu Ghraib was established. The absence of effective leadership was a factor in not sooner discovering and taking actions to prevent both the violent/sexual abuse incidents and the misinterpretation/confusion. . . . The perception that non-DOD agencies had different rules regarding interrogation and detention operations was evident." Fay-Jones Report, 5. "There was chaos in the camp, a state of lawlessness." Blasberg and Blasberg, "Prisoner and Guard."

92. Son Thang: The company commander, Ambort, "reminded [Herrod and his team] of the nine people that we had killed on the 12th of Februrary and I reminded him of Whitmore, who had died that day. I said, 'Don't let them get us any more. I want you to pay these little bastards back.'" Solis, *Son Thang*, 27.

Quang Nam: February 8, 1968. The company had lost five men in a firefight the night before, then rounded up 19 women and children and shot them all. Turse and Nelson, "Civilian Killings Went Unpunished."

My Lai: "Medina started out with words similar to, you all know what happened in a mine field a couple of miles from here. Well, tomorrow you're going to have a chance to get back at them. . . . When we came through the next day he didn't want to see anything living but GIs." Hammer, *Court Martial of Lieutenant Calley*, 189.

Haditha: House-to-house shooting was preceded by an explosion that killed American soliders; the soldiers who responded had been in a similar attack before in Falluja. West, "Road to Haditha."

Abu Ghraib: Violence against prisoners began before, but escalated after, prisoners with weapons injured a female soldier, and riots and shooting occurred. Taguba Report.

93. Citizens Commission of Inquiry, *Dellums Committee Hearings*, 165–66: "These men were rather bitter, like their friends had been killed, and they went back and threw the old woman and the child down the well and threw two grenades in on top of them." Also, 186–92: Soldiers killed 30 women and children in a village near where a favorite member of the platoon had just been blown up by a hidden explosive device.

94. For a moving article comparing the experience of war criminal and victim, see Blasberg and Blasberg, "Prisoner and Guard."

95. Erving Goffman, *Asylums: Essays on the Social Situation of Mental Patients and Other Inmates* (New York: Anchor, 1961).

96. Arendt, *Eichmann in Jerusalem*, 135–37.

97. Citizens Commission of Inquiry, *Dellums Committee Hearings*, 277.

98. Ibid., 161.

99. Ibid., 188.

100. Ibid., 98.

101. Ibid., 198.

102. Solis, *Son Thang,* 103.

103. Pantano, *Warlord,* 46.

104. Citizens Commission of Inquiry, *Dellums Committee Hearings,* 273.

105. Ibid., 51.

106. Quoted in West, "Road to Haditha," 98.

107. Pantano, *Warlord,* 110–13, 268, 223, 199, 256.

108. John Crawford, *The Last True Story I'll Ever Tell: An Accidental Soldier's Account of the War in Iraq* (New York: Penguin, 2005), 154.

109. Citizens Commission of Inquiry, *Dellums Committee Hearings,* 68–69.

110. Sack, *Lieutenant Calley,* 74–75; Pantano, *Warlord,* 255–56; Crawford, *Last True Story,* 197. "Someone who supposedly wears one face during the day, and agrees with us, and feeds us, and then at night he tries to kill us. You know, who is the enemy? Apparently the whole Vietnamese people are the enemy. That's the way I saw it and that's the way I was trained to treat them, and that's the way it was." Citizens Commission of Inquiry, *Dellums Committee Hearings,* 192. "I realized, I've been foolish. I had been asking everyone where the VC were: I had been talking to VC myself! That is why everyone said: 'I don't know.' They weren't about to tell me, 'I surrender.' At last it had dawned on me, 'These people, they're all the VC.'" Sack, *Lieutenant Calley,* 78–79. See also Belknap, *Vietnam War on Trial,* 57 (morale of Charlie company just before My Lai).

111. Citizens Commission of Inquiry, *Dellums Committee Hearings,* 252.

112. Sack, *Lieutenant Calley,* 28, 74.

113. Belknap, *Vietnam War on Trial,* 57.

114. Citizens Commission of Inquiry, *Dellums Committee Hearings,* 56.

115. Solis, *Son Thang,* 103.

116. Ironically, even Adolf Eichmann was concerned when he saw German soldiers shooting down women and children. He told the local SS commander: "Well, it is horrible what is being done around here; I said young people are being made into sadists. How can one do that? Simply bang away at women and children? That is impossible. Our people will go mad or become insane, our own people." Quoted in Arendt, *Eichmann in Jerusalem,* 88–89.

117. Pantano argues that no war can be fought "clean" and our insistence that it be clean is hypocritical: "You are paid to follow orders, to do what you are told. You are paid to accomplish the mission. No, we don't care how, just get out there and do it. Well, we didn't really mean, 'we don't care how.' We just meant we didn't want to know how. Because if we know how, then we have to do something about it." Pantano, *Warlord,* 357. See also Blasberg and Blasberg, "Prisoner and Guard"; C. J. Chivers, "Medic Tends a Fallen Marine, with Skill, Prayer, and Anger," *New York Times,* November 2, 2006, A1 ("I would like to say that I am a good man . . . but seeing this now, [his friend felled by sniper fire] what happened to Smith, I want to hurt people. You know what I mean?")

118. White et al., "Homicide Charges Rare in Iraq War." It looks as though Williams tried to falsely implicate his commander in order to reduce his own sentence, then later recanted. "Soldier Recants Iraq Accusation," *New York Times*, November 18, 2005.

119. David Finkel and Christian Davenport, "Records Paint Dark Portrait of Guard: Before Abu Ghraib, Graner Left a Trail of Alleged Violence," *Washington Post*, June 5, 2004, A1.

120. Pantano, *Warlord*, 220.

121. Citizens Commission of Inquiry, *Dellums Committee Hearings*, 196.

122. Arendt, *Eichmann in Jerusalem*, 256.

123. Pantano, *Warlord*, 44.

124. Calley's counsel made this point at his trial: "It's all right for the air corps to bomb cities; it's all right for the artillery to tear down houses and wreck the lives of the inhabitants. But it is wrong for the infantry." Hammer, *Court Martial of Lieutenant Calley*, 337.

125. An analysis of the theories of command responsibility is beyond the scope of this chapter. Suffice to say that actual prior knowledge or actually illegal orders (our present scheme) is too little; vicarious responsibility is too much. Perhaps we could draw on the innovations of tort law—a presumption of vicarious responsibility with a burden of proof on the defendant to prove affirmative efforts to prevent atrocities. I leave all of that for another day.

126. Arendt, *Eichmann in Jerusalem*, 278.

127. Citizens Commission of Inquiry, *Dellums Committee Hearings*, 236.

Chapter 8

_{IIIIIIIIIIIIIIIIIIIIIIIIIIIIIIIIIIIIIIIIIIIIIIIIIIII}

Memorializing Miscarriages of Justice
Clemency Petitions in the Killing State

Austin Sarat

Legal interpretation demands that we remember the future.

> —Drucilla Cornell, "From the Lighthouse:
> The Promise of Redemption and the
> Possibility of Legal Interpretation"

I had no evil intent when I taught the tricks of pleading, for I never meant them to be used to get the innocent condemned but, if the occasion arose, to save the lives of the guilty.

> —St. Augustine, *Confessions*

Turning a terrible action into a story is a way to distance oneself from it, at worst a form of self-deception, at best a way to pardon the self.

> —Natalie Zemon Davis, *Fiction in the Archives:*
> *Pardon Tales and Their Tellers in*
> *Sixteenth-Century France*

The 1990s brought increased attention to the problem and prevalence of miscarriages of justice in capital cases in the United States.[1] Dramatic exonerations from death row,[2] rigorous empirical studies,[3] and judicial decisions acknowledging failures in the death penalty system[4] have made a compelling case that, where the stakes are highest, the law fails with alarming frequency. Yet, at the same time, the Supreme Court and Congress have grown impatient with the complex legal process used in the administration of law's ultimate penalty.[5] Thus the Court has gradually cut back on the availability of federal habeas corpus relief in death penalty cases,[6] and Congress has passed legislation to curb what it sees as "abuses" in the habeas process in capital cases.

Court decisions dealing with procedural default,[7] exhaustion,[8] and abuse of the writ through the filing of successive habeas petitions[9] have made it increasingly difficult for federal courts to reach the merits of a defendant's habeas claims. Almost 20 years ago, in the most significant of these cutbacks, the Supreme Court declared that defendants must generally base their habeas petitions on asserted violations of the federal law as it existed at the time of the original state proceedings.[10] In a follow-up case, it held that if the federal law was unclear at that time, any reasonable, "good faith" interpretation of the federal law by the state courts immunizes the conviction and sentence from later habeas attack.[11] It then extended the same principle to the method of application of the federal law to the facts of a particular case; if the state courts' method of application of the federal law was proper in view of the precedents that existed at that time, then federal habeas relief is unavailable (even if those precedents are later overruled or changed).[12]

Reacting to the bombing at the Alfred P. Murrah Federal Building in Oklahoma City, in 1996 Congress enacted stringent new limits on habeas review in the Anti-Terrorism and Effective Death Penalty Act (AEDPA).[13] Among its key provisions, AEDPA established a one-year deadline within which state prisoners must file their federal habeas petitions and modified the "exhaustion" doctrine to permit federal courts to dismiss "groundless" petitions, notwithstanding the fact that state courts have not been afforded the opportunity to find them without merit.[14] In addition, it barred repetitious habeas petitions by state and federal prisoners and instructed federal judges not to grant relief on any claim adjudicated on the merits in state court unless the adjudication (1) is contrary to, or involved an unreasonable application of, clearly established federal law as determined by the Supreme Court of the United States, or (2) resulted in a decision that was based on an unreasonable determination of the facts in light of the evidence presented in the state court.[15]

Because of what the Supreme Court and Congress have done, a defendant who receives a death sentence now often finds it very difficult to obtain federal habeas review of the merits of whatever decisions or rulings

might have been made by the judge during his capital trial.[16] So hostile
have the courts become to extended litigation in capital cases that in one
case where there had been repeated last-minute requests for a stay of execution in several different courts, the Supreme Court, usurping the legal
prerogatives of the lower courts, took the unprecedented step of ordering
that no further stays be granted.[17] And, even new evidence of actual innocence has been found to be inadequate as the basis for challenging a
death sentence.[18]

Due to the imposition of these procedural bars and default rules, and
the resulting limits on judicial review of convictions and sentences in
death cases, gubernatorial clemency has become, in essence, the court of
last resort, providing what Justice Rehnquist in *Herrera v. Collins* called
a "fail safe" mechanism in the death penalty system.[19] As Rehnquist observed:

> Clemency is deeply rooted in our Anglo-American tradition of law, and
> is the historic remedy for preventing miscarriages of justice where judi-
> cial process has been exhausted. Executive clemency has provided the "fail
> safe" in our criminal justice system. It is an unalterable fact that our judi-
> cial system, like the human beings who administer it, is fallible. But history
> is replete with examples of wrongfully convicted persons who have been
> pardoned in the wake of after-discovered evidence establishing their inno-
> cence. . . . Recent authority confirms that over the past century clemency
> has been exercised frequently in capital cases in which demonstrations of
> "actual innocence" have been made.[20]

While much has been said and written about the power to kill within
the confines of modern law,[21] that sustained focus on the right to impose
death sometimes eclipses its essential corollary—the sovereign right to
spare life.[22] As Rehnquist reminds us, in a modern political system this
power to spare life remains in the form of executive clemency.[23] Executive
clemency in capital cases is distinctive in that it is the only power that can
undo death: the only power that can prevent death once it has been prescribed and, through appellate review, approved, even if erroneously, as a
legally appropriate punishment.

Clemency is a general term referring to the authority of an executive
to "intervene in the sentencing of a criminal defendant . . . It is a relief
imparted after the justice system has run its course."[24] Clemency is the
reduction of a punishment authorized by law. That clemency provides

"relief" from legal justice reminds us that not only has clemency traditionally been an important element of sovereign power, but also it has
often been a vivid expression of mercy.[25] Long ago William Blackstone
described the relation of clemency and mercy by noting that the power to
spare lives was "one of the great advantages of monarchy in general; that
there is a magistrate, who has it in his power to extend mercy, whenever
he thinks it is deserved: holding a court of equity in his own breast, to
soften the rigour of the general law, in such criminal cases as merit an
exception from punishment."[26]

At the same time that it has assumed increased importance as a process
for rectifying miscarriages of justice in the killing state, clemency in capital cases has, despite Rehnquist's claim about its "frequency," in fact become quite rare. With the exception of an unusual dramatic gesture, like
Governor George Ryan's mass commutation in Illinois in January 2003,
the long-held constitutional right of chief executives to spare life seems
to have "died its own death, the victim of a political lethal injection and
a public that overwhelmingly supports the death penalty."[27] During the
1990s, from one to eight death row inmates had their sentences commuted
every year—out of approximately 20 to 90 executions.[28] This represents a
radical shift from several decades ago, when governors granted clemency
in 20 to 25 percent of the death penalty cases they reviewed.[29]

In Florida, for example, one of the states most firmly in the "death
belt," between 1924 and 1966, there were 59 commutations and 196 executions in capital cases, but between 1983 and 2000, the clemency requests
of all 161 Florida prisoners on death row were denied.[30] Yet the rarity of
capital clemency is not just a southern, death-belt phenomenon. Thus
"since at least 1965, no Washington Governor has intervened to overturn
a death sentence, and in only one instance was an execution postponed
by a Governor's action."[31] From 1964 to 2003, the year of Governor Ryan's
clemency, it was granted in only one Illinois capital case. And, in Pennsylvania, another state with a large death row population, the last death
penalty commutation took place in the early 1960s.[32]

Some speculate that capital clemency has fallen into disfavor because
of increased public support for the death penalty. Thus Richard Dieter,
executive director of the Death Penalty Information Center, observes that
capital punishment is "the answer to the public's fear of crime, so (clemency) just goes against the grain."[33] Even as crime rates declined during
the 1990s, fear of crime persisted and, in this climate, mercy fell into disfavor as compassion went out of style.[34]

Others suggest that capital clemency has been a victim of the rejection of rehabilitation as the guiding philosophy of criminal sentencing and the increasing politicization of issues of crime and punishment since the 1960s. In this climate, governors seek, in Jonathan Simon's evocative phrase, to "govern through crime," to turn crime fighting, tough-on-crime policy into a strategy for building coalitions and strengthening the state.[35] Many have used the death penalty in their campaigns, promising more and quicker executions.[36] Simon's work suggests that the political power of governors depends

> in large part on their power to mobilize the state around crime fears. In numerous states and on many occasions the death penalty has been the venue for the assertion of a governor's power by campaigning for, or signing into law, a new death penalty statute . . . or signing a death warrant authorizing the execution of a particular prisoner. Clemency provides another occasion when, in effect, the Governor can assert his or her support for the death penalty (and empathy with ordinary citizens) by rejecting clemency.[37]

Rejecting appeals from the pope, Mother Teresa, televangelist Pat Robertson, former prosecutors, and even judges and jurors in death cases, today governors reserve their clemency power largely for cases where there is *indisputable* proof that someone has been erroneously convicted and no other remedy is available.[38] Thus, at the outset of his administration, Texas Governor George W. Bush embraced a standard for clemency that all but ensured that few if any death sentences would be seriously examined. Writing about Bush's views, Alan Berlow noted,

> "In every case," [Bush] wrote in *A Charge to Keep,* "I would ask: Is there any doubt about this individual's guilt or innocence? And, have the courts had ample opportunity to review all the legal issues in this case?" This is an extraordinarily narrow notion of clemency review: it seems to leave little, if any, room to consider mental illness or incompetence, childhood physical or sexual abuse, remorse, rehabilitation, racial discrimination in jury selection, the competence of the legal defense, or disparities in sentences between co-defendants or among defendants convicted of similar crimes. Neither compassion nor "mercy," which the Supreme Court as far back as 1855 saw as central to the very idea of clemency, is acknowledged as being of any account. . . . During Bush's six years as governor 150 men and two women were executed in Texas—a record unmatched by any other

governor in modern American history. . . . Bush allowed the execution to proceed in all cases but one.[39]

Similarly, then-Governor Bill Clinton explained his reluctance to grant clemency by saying, "The appeals process, although lengthy, provides many opportunities for the courts to review sentences and that's where these decisions should be made."[40]

The Bush and Clinton views are today the norm.[41] This may be, in part, a consequence of structural changes in the post-*Furman v. Georgia* death penalty process.[42] Since the mid-1970s, juries in capital cases have been required to consider *any* mitigating evidence that the defendant wishes to present, thus ensuring that consideration of mercy is part of every death penalty sentencing decision.[43] As a result, governors can say that the question of mercy already has been addressed by the time a clemency petition reaches their desk. In addition, while before 1976 there was relatively little appellate review of death sentences, since then there has been a substantial expansion of appellate review, and, until recently, of federal habeas proceedings in those cases,[44] again allowing governors to say that the person seeking clemency has already had a full adjudication and review of their case.

Whatever the reason, governors are reluctant to substitute their judgment for those of state legislators and courts, and, in death cases, to use clemency much at all.[45] Rehnquist's description of clemency as a "fail safe" in the killing state may do more to help legitimate judicial dismantling of various procedural protections than to point toward an efficacious device for correcting law's failures in the killing state.[46]

Despite the reluctance of governors to grant clemency and despite the difficulty of rectifying miscarriages of justice through the clemency process, petitions seeking commutation or pardon still are regularly filed with chief executives. With so little chance of success, filing them may seem to be nothing more than an empty ritual, meaningful, if at all, as a way for lawyers to satisfy the desires of desperate death row inmates to leave no stone unturned. Or, they may appear to be occasions to rehash arguments previously made to, and rejected by, the sentencing jury or appellate courts. Or, they may look like efforts to move beyond the law, deploying arguments imagined to have more resonance in a political rather than a legal forum.

Yet those petitions may serve another function and take on meaning in another way, even as they seek to appease desperate clients, rehash old arguments, or reframe legal into political appeals, and even if they are unable to persuade governors to stop executions. This function I label "memorialization." These pleas provide an archive of stories of law's failures, of alleged breakdowns in the legal process, and of a legal process in disrepair, as well as of racial prejudice, of lives shattered by violence and neglect, of remorse, rehabilitation, and redemption.

In this chapter, I analyze the memorialization function of stories told by the condemned and their advocates in their petitions for clemency, as well as the narrative conventions and cultural assumptions that frame their pardon tales.[47] I treat those petitions as cultural artifacts, documents that address both governors and an indeterminate audience beyond them and as documents that memorialize miscarriages of justice. While they reveal the importance of religion, family, and good works in American thinking about remorse, redemption, and mercy at the end of the twentieth century, they also should be seen as histories of the present, documenting the breakdowns and inequities in the death penalty system along with the tragic circumstances of lives shaped and shattered by poverty, abuse, and neglect.[48]

Through this analysis I mean to highlight an account of the clemency process that previously has not been addressed in the scholarly literature. My work is theoretically driven and interpretive, trying to unearth previously neglected meanings in the clemency process. As a result, in my discussion of that process I focus neither on the motivations of the lawyers who file clemency petitions (or the persons on whose behalf they are filed) nor on explaining why those petitions are filed or why they tell the stories they tell. In this sense, I do not seek to test and refute rival plausible hypotheses. Whether the motivations of lawyers, or their death row clients, are base or noble, whether they understand and consciously seek to speak to the future or intend their petitions to have no such audience, I seek to provide a frame within which scholars might interpret those petitions, understand at least one of their meanings, and assess part of their significance.[49]

Making a Record and Calling on the Future to Remember

The petitions I examine were filed during slightly different, though overlapping, 10-year periods in two of America's leading killing states, Texas and Virginia.[50] (Appendix A provides a description of data and methods used in this chapter.) From 1990 to 2000 in Texas, there were 206 executions and one successful clemency petition. From 1990 to 2002 in Virginia, 74 people were put to death and 5 people had their death sentences commuted. Expanding the time frame from *Gregg v. Georgia*'s reintroduction of capital punishment in the United States to 2005, there were 369 executions in Texas and 95 in Virginia.[51] During that same almost 30-year period, 229 clemencies were granted nationwide in capital cases. Of these, Texas governors granted only 1, and Virginia governors granted 7.[52] Thus in these two states as elsewhere, filing clemency petitions is a bit like buying a lottery ticket in a contest for a multimillion-dollar payoff. Filing them, death row inmates participate in this lottery for life, hoping against long odds that they will draw the winning number.[53]

Yet, as Drucilla Cornell reminds us, "Legal interpretation demands that we remember the future."[54] In that phrase, Cornell suggests that legal processes fix their gaze temporally, not just on the possibilities (or impossibilities) of the present but on a future promise of justice; legal scholars should attend to the way law speaks to that future. She reminds us that there are, in fact, two audiences for every legal act: the audience of the present (to which one might appeal to spare the life of the condemned) and the audience of the future (which stands as a figure of law's redeeming promise of justice). In this sense, processes like clemency also may be seen as offering the chance to record a history of the present, and, in that history, preserve the present's pained voice. In Robert Cover's words, they provide "a bridge to alternity."[55]

Taking Cornell's and Cover's perspective, one might say that clemency petitions, which have so little chance of immediate success, nonetheless participate in the logic of what Cover called "redemptive constitutionalism."[56] While they may serve many purposes, those documents refuse to recognize the violence of the present moment as the defining totality of law and carry a vision of a future in which justice prevails over that violence. Whatever the intentions of those who draft them, they conjure a world, borrowing Cover's formulation, in which "[r]edemption takes place within an eschatalogical schema that postulates: (1) the unredeemed character of reality as we know it, (2) the fundamentally different reality that should take its place, and (3) the replacement of one with the other."[57]

Cover uses the example of an abolitionist struggle of another era—namely, antislavery activism in the mid-nineteenth century—to suggest that the work of "redemptive constitutionalism" reveals "a creative pulse that proliferates principle and precept, commentary and justification, even in the face of a state legal order less likely to hold slavery unconstitutional than to declare the imminent kingship of Jesus Christ on Earth."[58] In this view, clemency petitions speak in a prophetic voice, even as they supply the argumentative and interpretive resources to bridge the gap between the violence of the present and the beckoning possibility of justice.[59]

But there is perhaps a second way of understanding the meaning of those petitions in the contemporary killing state. In this second understanding, Cover's image is reversed, and redemption gives way to judgment. As redemption gives way to judgment, the future is called on to remember the injustices of the present.[60] Given this imperative to remember, those who ask for clemency serve as witnesses testifying against those injustices. Their petitions supply

> the testimonial *bridge* which, mediating between narrative and history, guarantees their correspondence and adherence to each other. This bridging between narrative and history is possible since the narrator is both an *informed* and an *honest* witness. . . . All the witness has to do is to *efface himself,* and let the *literality of events* voice its own *self-evidence.* "His business is only to say: *this is what happened,* when he knows that it actually did happen."[61]

Like the mitigation stage of a capital trial or the habeas process,[62] clemency provides a chance to take advantage of one of the legitimating promises of law: its commitment to giving everyone a hearing.[63] The clemency process creates a record that serves as the materialization of memory and creates an archive of unnecessary, unjust, and undeserved pain and death.[64] Clemency petitions record history by creating narratives of present injustices and call on an imagined future to choose justice over the jurispathic tendencies of the moment.[65] Doing so ensures that, even when no one (including the governors to whom they are addressed) seems willing to listen, the voices of the "oppressed" will not be silenced.

The movement from giving testimony to writing history is a movement from the immediacy of the eyewitness report to the mediation produced through narrativization.[66] In this movement, clemency petitions may, as Robert Gordon indicates, frame the stories they seek to record in what he calls "legalist" style. This narrative treats the injustices of the present as wrongs "done by specific perpetrators to specific victims."[67] It stays within the frame of liberal-legalism and describes present injustice in terms of the remedies that governors, should they be willing, could easily supply.

Alternatively, the petitions may speak about "bad structures rather than bad agents. . . . This historical enterprise takes the form of a search for explanations rather than a search for villainous agents and attribution of blame."[68] In this narrative style, pardon tales broaden the scope of inquiry by linking the particular stories of the condemned inmate with broader patterns of injustice and institutional practice.

The ability to use the clemency process to speak to the future and memorialize the present, to both give testimony and write history, to this point has been ignored in the scholarly literature. By focusing on the possibilities and problems of the present moment, those who write about clemency portray its value exclusively in terms of its most immediate effects. But, as Cornell reminds us, legal processes, like clemency, are as much about the future as the present, and as much about the possibilities of memory as the current prospects of success. Thus clemency petitions

> posit the very ideal . . . [they] purportedly find "there" (in those processes) . . . as [they] posit the ideal or the ethical [they] promise to remain true to it. [Their] promise of fidelity to the ethical or to the ideal is precisely what breathes life into the dead letter of the law and provides a barrier against the violence of the word. . . . To heed the call to responsibility within law is to remind . . . [ourselves] of the disjuncture between law and the ideal and to affirm our responsibility to make the promise to the ideal, to aspire to counter the violence of our world in the name of universal justice.[69]

Clemency petitions in capital cases represent one method of "remembering the future," of memorializing miscarriages of justice, and of ensuring that the future remembers. They are both a kind of testimony and a way of recording a history of injustice. The stories they tell put state killing in a narrative context that juxtaposes it to the good, and preserve "the versions of legal meaning created by groups outside the mainstream of American law."[70] They turn clemency boards and governors' offices into memorials to present injustice. Perhaps by paying attention to this function of the clemency process, we can gain a new perspective on its value in the contemporary killing state.

Narrative Conventions and Cultural Assumptions in Contemporary Pardon Tales

Writing about so-called letters of remission in sixteenth-century France, historian Natalie Zemon Davis called attention to their " 'fictional' " qualities: namely, "their forming, shaping, and molding elements: their crafting of narrative." She described the letter of remission as a "mixed genre: a judicial supplication to persuade the king and the courts, a historical account of one's past actions, and a story."[71]

Today, clemency petitions in capital cases remain mixed genres. Typically, each of them raises several claims and tells many stories. However, given the prevailing Bush-Clinton understanding of clemency, they are predominantly tales of legal woe—stories of errors made in the legal process. As such, they position governors, exactly as Rehnquist imagined (as courts of last resort unburdened by law's rules of relevance, procedural bars, and default rules), able, finally, to rectify injustices left uncorrected in earlier stages of the legal process. Thus while the condemned and their advocates can appeal to a broader set of narrative conventions than those available to lawyers in the guilt phase of a death penalty trial, or those pursuing redress through the appellate or the habeas process,[72] in the clemency process they tend to frame their stories narrowly, in what Gordon described as the "legalist mode."

Moreover, few contain outright acknowledgments of guilt or extended narratives of the crime for which the condemned was sentenced. As a result, they have relatively little to say about mercy or about the place of grace in the killing state, and when they do make appeals for mercy, they do so in the most conventional terms, appealing to the twin pillars of American cultural conservatism: religion and family life.

In what follows, I describe five stories that play key roles, either in whole or in part, in the memorialization of miscarriages of justice in clemency petitions. I examine the way these stories appear in five "exemplary" cases in Texas and Virginia.[73]

1. "You Got the Wrong Man": Innocence

The specter of executing the innocent haunts the system of capital punishment in the United States and has helped to transform the national debate about the death penalty. As Lawrence Marshall notes, the so called "innocence revolution . . . addresses a value that everyone shares: accurate determinations of guilt and innocence. Put another way, the innocence revolution is born of science and fact, as opposed to choices among a competing set of controversial values. . . . [I]t is safe to conclude that our newfound appreciation of the system's fallibility is destined to make a lasting mark on criminal law."[74] At the heart of this innocence revolution is DNA, which is now admissible as evidence in criminal trials in almost every state.[75]

Preventing gross miscarriages of justice of the kind revealed by DNA testing,[76] as I suggested earlier, has become the almost exclusive grounds on which governors will today grant clemency. Thus, many clemency petitions aim to raise doubts about the guilt of the condemned on whose behalf they are filed. Mistaken eyewitness identification, the corrupt jailhouse snitch, newly discovered evidence—all are marshaled to serve that end. A few request DNA testing, or present DNA evidence, to prove that someone scheduled to die is, in fact, innocent. One such petition was filed in Virginia by two large-firm lawyers working pro bono on the case of Michael Satcher, who had been convicted of stabbing a 23-year-old girl to death after raping her during an assault on March 31, 1990.

In their clemency petition, his lawyers wasted no time before stating the heart of Satcher's case for clemency:

> Michael Satcher is a loving father of two small boys, respected within his church, and, prior to 1990, had no history of violent behavior. He was also convicted of the cold-blooded killing of a young Arlington, Virginia woman in March 1990 and sits on death row with a fast approaching execution date of December 9, 1997. This contradiction of character could have a simple explanation—innocence—which has not yet been fully explored by the Commonwealth despite the strong reasons presented post-trial for doing so. We implore the Governor to rectify this situation before allowing Michael to be put to death.

Using the conditional, "could have," the petition seeks to raise doubt, rather than resolve it. It asks the governor to stop the execution to allow time to investigate and resolve that doubt In this sense its narrative strategy follows a familiar model: namely, the trial strategy of many criminal defense lawyers.

"Michael has consistently maintained his innocence," the petition notes. Moreover:

All of the evidence presented at trial supports his innocence except one piece—a deoxyribonucleic acid (DNA) test. As discussed below, however, that evidence is now in grave doubt. We did not become involved as Michael's counsel until after his state court remedies were exhausted and the time had come to pursue federal habeas corpus relief. As of that point, no attorney for Michael had done anything to check the accuracy of the critical DNA test introduced at trial in 1990 (the "1990 test"). Because the physical evidence found at the crime scene was in the custody of the Commonwealth, we did the only thing we could to double-check the 1990 test before filing a federal habeas petition. We ran a new DNA test on Michael's blood, the only relevant DNA to which we had access.

We arranged with the Lifecodes Corporation in Stamford, Connecticut to conduct this test (the 1995 test) and then compared the results to those of the 1990 test on the crime scene evidence. (We replicated the 1990 test as closely as possible; in fact Lifecodes was selected as the laboratory to do the test because it was capable of using the same procedures as the laboratory that conducted the 1990 test.) The results were stunning: the DNA from Michael's blood did not match the DNA extracted from the 1990 crime scene evidence.

This narrative moves from circumstantial evidence (the anomaly of the good, churchgoing father, with no history of violence being charged with murder), to testimonial evidence (the fact that the condemned has consistently maintained his innocence), to scientific evidence (the new DNA test). The authority of science is deployed to verify conventional cultural assumptions associated with family and religion and the legal assumption that consistency is an indicator of credibility. DNA is presented as the trump, the showstopper.[77]

But the new test does little more than create a mystery—"Why did Michael's blood match the crime scene evidence in 1990 but not in 1995?" —to which the petition suggests there is a straightforward answer: "The most obvious explanation is that the 1995 test supports Michael's persistent claim of innocence and the 1990 test was flawed." Yet that answer, the petition acknowledges, has not persuaded the courts that have heard it. "Neither the federal district court nor the United States Court of Appeals for the Fourth Circuit," Satcher's lawyers concede, "determined the reason for the conflict between the two tests; instead, both federal courts held that a 'battle of experts' was an insufficient reason to grant a writ of habeas corpus." In the Bush-Clinton paradigm, the fact that courts had already considered the new evidence would be dispositive, as it eventually was in this case.

Knowing this, Satcher's lawyers concede that, at this point, the situation is indeed a "battle of the experts," a battle, they argue, that can be resolved by yet *another* DNA test, one that would put the battle to rest and definitively establish their client's innocence:

> We respectfully submit that it would be irresponsible to execute Michael before this "battle of experts" is resolved, especially when a clear and simple means to resolving it exists—a new test. In fact, Michael has . . . authorized us to request the crime scene evidence from the Commonwealth. . . . We urge the Governor to order a new DNA test of the crime scene evidence and Michael's blood before Michael is executed.

To bolster their "reasonable doubt" strategy, Satcher's lawyers present an extended account of the crime and the evidence tying their client to it. They note that many of the traditional, and most important, pieces of evidence were lacking: "No eyewitness placed Michael at the crime scene. No murder weapon was ever found. . . . Neither motive evidence nor evidence that Michael had any violent history was introduced at trial." Suggesting that he had nothing to hide, they state that "[a]t the time of his arrest, Michael voluntarily gave the police blood, saliva and hair samples" and that the prosecution failed to "match these samples with hair and semen samples found on Ms. Borghesani's clothing and taken from her body." All that tied their client to the crime was DNA. The petition says: "The prosecution's only direct evidence linking Michael to the murder was DNA evidence."

They try to undermine the credibility of that evidence by raising questions about the laboratory in which the DNA testing was done, noting along the way that the "laboratory . . . was not subject to accreditation or licensing requirements, was not operated under uniform standards, and often did not conduct confirmatory testing of initial test results."

A large portion of their narrative consists of a rather technical description of the 1995 DNA test and a point-by-point refutation of the state's attack on it. Speaking scientific language, they assure the governor of this new test's reliability and validity:

> Because the Tidewater Lab's 1990 testing procedures were based on Life-codes' procedures, and because Lifecodes was equipped to conduct a new

test using those procedures, a retest by Lifecodes was the best and only way to replicate the Tidewater Lab's test. (The Tidewater Lab is available only to the police and, in any event, no longer uses the same procedures and protocols it used in 1990.) The sample was sent to Lifecodes anonymously —nothing was done (or could have been done) by Michael or the defense team to affect the results of the 1995 test.

The results of this new test, they remind the governor, "fully support Michael's claim of innocence." Satcher's lawyers concede, however that

> whether or not such a comparison is scientifically sound boils down to scientific judgments. In the judgment of Michael's experts, such a comparison is scientifically sound. In the judgment of the Commonwealth's experts, such a comparison is not. However, at the end of the day, relying on expert judgments is unnecessary because a better way to resolve this dispute exists—conducting a new DNA test on the crime scene DNA and Michael's blood at the same time and in the same laboratory.

This argument, as Culbert suggests in another context, places "faith in a new authority-DNA . . . (and) undermines the distinction between how things appear to us and how they really are."[78] They argue that a new test will provide the kind of certainty that no set of human judgments can provide while, at the same time, expressing "a sense of futility at the possibility of ever determining for ourselves what is true."[79]

Indeed, Satcher's petition concedes as much in that it does not rest its entire case on the request for a new test. Arguing in the alternative, it again appeals to Satcher's family, religion, and community as it presents a mitigation case and urges the governor to choose a sentencing option that was not available to Satcher's jury:

> Furthermore, even if there were no new DNA evidence demonstrating his innocence, Michael should not be executed. Rather, as one of the jurors from Michael's trial has stated in an affidavit accompanying this Petition, life without the possibility of parole would be the more appropriate punishment for Michael. Since word that the Commonwealth has set an execution date has spread, there has been an outpouring of community support for Michael, not only from friends and family, but from others who have known Michael throughout his life. A District of Columbia corrections officer, a high school principal, the owner of a beauty shop, church choir

members, people from all walks of life have written and called to tell us that they do not believe that Michael should be executed. All state their belief that Michael could not have committed these crimes. And all unanimously describe Michael as a good father, a family man, a quiet man, a religious man, and a peaceful man. Michael's conduct during incarceration also demonstrates that he is not the type of person the Commonwealth should execute. His record is devoid of a single instance of violent behavior. Indeed, there is nothing to suggest that he poses a future danger to others within the prison community.

The jury that determined Michael's sentence did not have the option of choosing life without the possibility of parole because Virginia did not offer that option at the time of Michael's trial. The Governor does. Thus, we respectfully urge the Governor to consider that option.

This petition, like many others, gives pride of place to religion.[80] His lawyers state:

One additional fact about Michael is mentioned over and over again by almost everyone who knows him: his dedication to God and the church. Michael was brought up in the New Macedonia Baptist Church in Southeast Washington, a large church with numerous active members. Michael did not just passively attend church, he actively participated in it: he sang in the church choir from the age of 6 and belonged to the Junior Usher Board. Michael remains committed to God.

Satcher's lawyers suggest that these facts should make a difference to the governor by noting that they would have made a difference to some of those who served on his jury:

Jurors who sentenced Michael to death would seriously have considered the alternative of life in prison without parole had they had the opportunity to do so. Three jurors have submitted affidavits stating as much. Moreover, one juror, Rubye Baumgardner, has sworn in an affidavit that she would have voted for life imprisonment without parole had she been given the option. This is all the more significant because, to impose the death penalty, the jury had to be unanimous.

Ms. Baumgardner's affidavit creates a substantial question as to whether such unanimity would have been possible among the jurors. Indeed, on the basis of this affidavit, it is likely that the jury would have decided that life without the possibility of parole was more appropriate for Michael.

In the end, DNA testing, Satcher's lawyers contend, points the way to a solution and provides the governor the chance "to correct two grievous errors." The first could be addressed

> simply by providing Michael access to whatever crime scene evidence still exists so that the 1990 test can be redone. If the retest proves a non-match, the Commonwealth will know it has the wrong man in prison and a great injustice will be avoided. If the new test turns out to be a match . . . the Governor can consider the second question presented by Michael's application. The Governor has the power to heed these jurors and sentence Michael to a life behind bars, a life where he can continue, in a limited way, to be a father to his children, a son to his parents, and a brother and friend to those who love him. His life before 1990 and his behavior in prison since his conviction warrant this sentence.

While Satcher's petition did not succeed in saving his life (he was executed by lethal injection on December 9, 1997), it memorializes the tragic possibility of executing the innocent. It calls on the future to recall, and judge, the unreliability of today's killing state.

2. "It Ain't Fair": Legal Error

Clemency petitions in capital cases read like catalogs of legal mistakes and misconduct. As Burnett demonstrated in her study of Missouri, those petitions highlight police and prosecutorial misconduct, mistaken eyewitness identifications, problems in jury selection, and failures of appellate courts to remedy cognizable legal errors. Moreover, 74 percent of the cases she studied contained allegations of ineffective assistance of counsel.[81] Rather than duplicating her treatment of the full range of legal errors documented in pardon tales, in what follows I focus on one case, centering around an ineffective assistance claim, to exemplify this genre.

The 53-page petition of Joe Louis Wise Sr. was submitted to Governor L. Douglas Wilder of Virginia in 1993. His petition, concentrating on what his lawyers called "Death by Default: The Unrepresented Defendant" was written in a highly legalistic style, marshaling facts, affidavits, exhibits, and case law to prove that his lawyer's performance at trial and on appeal was so poor that it was as if he had no lawyer at all:

> On November 9, 1984, Joe Louis Wise, Sr., alone and unrepresented in all but appearance, faced the jury that would decide whether he lived or died. Joe, a young black man, was facing death for a crime he committed when he was 21 years old. He was borderline mentally retarded and had dropped out of school in the ninth grade, after being held back at least once. Joe had been raised in wretched poverty, never consistently living in a house with indoor plumbing until he made the upward move into a public housing project at age twelve. Moreover, Joe had been raised by corrupt and cruel parents who beat him horribly, threatened to put him in foster homes, introduced him to sex, drugs, gambling, and crime, and in short provided him with the worst possible upbringing. None of these facts were known to the jury.

The petition continued,

> Though practically alone, Joe did not face the jury without the semblance of representation. Standing next to him was William Bryant Claiborne, whom the Mecklenburg County court had appointed to be Joe's lawyer. Claiborne was unprepared and unqualified to represent Joe in the fight for his life. The 28-year-old Claiborne was just over two years out of law school, had never tried a murder case, had never tried a jury trial, had never received any capital defense training, had not consulted with any experienced capital defender, and had undertaken little or no investigation of Joe's life. When his, and Joe's, turn came to present evidence that would convince the jury that Joe should receive a sentence of life imprisonment rather than death, Claiborne offered absolutely nothing, because he had looked for nothing. . . . 22 sentences are all Claiborne said to the jury that had just convicted Joe and was about to determine his fate. The jury returned in 42 minutes with a verdict of death.

This argument is straightforward and assertive, highlighting the idea that having an unqualified capital defense lawyer is equivalent to having no lawyer at all. The word "nothing"—offering nothing, looked for nothing—does much of the rhetorical work here. And, the story presented is less one of malevolence on the part of Claiborne than of his being asked to do a task that was way beyond him. In this manner, the petition offers a parallel between the uneducated defendant and the unprepared lawyer. Both, it seems, are victims: Wise was a victim of his lawyer, and his lawyer was a victim of a system of capital representation that put him in such a position.

Claiborne's mistakes were only compounded by the ineffectiveness of Wise's next set of lawyers. Like Caliborne, his state habeas lawyers were inexperienced in the world of capital litigation. The petition claims:

> They failed to offer evidence of the prejudice Joe suffered from Claiborne's ineffectiveness. Second, his lawyer neglected to file Joe's notice of appeal from the Circuit Court's denial of relief. Not only did this default eliminate appellate review of Joe's habeas, it precluded federal review of virtually all of Joe's claims, including his claim that Claiborne gave him ineffective assistance. . . . In order to present his ineffectiveness claims to the federal habeas court, Joe had to preserve them against a procedural bar—a technicality that prevents a court from considering many claims, no matter how meritorious—while passing through state habeas. One necessity for preserving Joe's claims was an appeal to the Virginia Supreme Court from the Circuit Court's denial of his state habeas. The first, mandatory step to appealing was the simple filing of a notice of appeal in the Circuit Court within 30 days after that court issued a decision. . . . That turned out to be too much for Hawthorne, who missed the date, not by a day or a week, but by 2½ months. . . . The consequence of these attorneys' mistakes was that no jury and no court, state or federal, ever considered Joe's compelling case in mitigation.

The argument for clemency contained in this petition came down to this:

> Because Joe has been abandoned at every step by his appointed lawyers, Joe's case constitutes a complete failure of our system of justice. . . . Because of the inexperience, lack of zeal, and other derelictions of his trial and state habeas attorneys—deficiencies matched in no other capital case tried in Virginia in the post-*Furman* era—barely a moment passed in Joe Wise's trial when his trial had true adversarial character. . . . Accordingly, we petition the Governor to commute Joe's death sentence to life imprisonment.

Indeed, the petition goes to the heart of this failure by conceding Wise's guilt at the outset. "Joe," it says matter of factly, "shot (the victim) with a

.25 caliber pistol, beat him over the head with a rifle, breaking the stock, put him in a wastewater-filled hole, and shot him in the chest with a shotgun." Claiborne's incompetence is also narrated in a matter-of-fact tone: "The defense case during Joe's guilt trial consisted of seven witnesses. Six of the defense witnesses had testified for the prosecution, and they repeated and expanded on their prosecution testimony when called by the defense."

But the real focus of the story was Claiborne's performance during the sentencing phase of the trial. "Claiborne compressed the case for Joe's life," the petition notes, "into the 'one or two minutes' required to speak the 22 sentences of his closing argument. Two of the 22 sentences alluded to mitigating evidence and suggested, curiously, that the jury knew what the mitigating evidence was, though Claiborne had not called a single witness during the sentencing trial."

Claiborne's failure, according to the petition, was the result of a failure by the appointing court, for which the petition offers no explanation. Just as Wise was, in effect, made to stand alone before the bar of justice, so, too, did the court abandon Caliborne to his own devices. "There was no shortage of experienced trial lawyers in Mecklenburg County," the petition notes:

> But for whatever reasons, the court did not choose a Mecklenburg attorney. Instead, the court looked toward Halifax County and chose Claiborne. At that time, courts usually appointed two attorneys to represent capital defendants. . . . Indeed, of the 30 trials resulting in death sentences that took place between 1975 and 1985, in fewer than eight did the trial court appoint only one lawyer. . . . The Mecklenburg court opted not to follow this practice, despite Claiborne's inexperience. The court appointed 28-year-old Claiborne and left him on his own. In terms of Claiborne's utter lack of experience and seasoning, the court's choice was unprecedented at the time, and fortunately has not been equaled since.

Wise's petition continues its legalist narrative by presenting expert testimony and carefully parsing the American Bar Association Code of Ethics to bolster its contention that "[n]ot only should the Mecklenburg courts have respected more Joe's entitlement to minimally competent counsel, Claiborne himself owed a duty both to Joe and to the court to decline the appointment." It portrays Claiborne as negligent in, once having accepted the appointment, failing to seek help that the petition contends was readily available. It departs from its earlier tone as it catalogs the errors Claiborne made and notes the severe consequences of those mistakes. Thus, it insists:

> The opportunity to offer mitigating evidence during the penalty phase of a capital trial is not a nicety of law provided to capital defendants by the good graces of the Commonwealth. Rather, it is a constitutional imperative: the Eighth and Fourteenth Amendments require that the sentencer, in all but the rarest kind of capital case, not be precluded from considering, *as a mitigating factor,* any aspect of a defendant's character or record and any of the circumstances of the offense that the defendant proffers as a basis for a sentence less than death. . . . Given that the imposition of death by public authority is so profoundly different from all other penalties, we cannot avoid the conclusion that an individualized decision is essential in capital cases. The need for treating each defendant in a capital case with that degree of respect due the uniqueness of the individual is far more important than in non-capital cases. . . . The non-availability of corrective or modifying mechanisms with respect to an executed capital sentence underscores the need for individualized consideration as a constitutional requirement in imposing the death sentence. *Lockett v. Ohio,* 438 U.S. 586, 605, 606 (1978). Thus, Joe Wise had a constitutional right and Claiborne had a constitutional duty to present to the jury any and all relevant mitigating evidence tending to show that Joe deserved a sentence less than death. That Claiborne failed to grasp this fundamental precept of capital jurisprudence is truly *astounding.* (emphasis added)

The metaphor of solitude, of being alone, reappears throughout the petition, sometimes spoken in the voice of Joe's advocates and sometimes attributed to outside experts: "Joe effectively faced the sentencing jury alone. Professor Bonnie believes that Claiborne's abandonment of Joe at the sentencing trial represents a failure of the justice system."

As if addressed to an appellate court, the petition carefully follows the form required in ineffective assistance cases, first documenting the unreasonable performance of Joe's lawyers and then the substantial prejudice that resulted from it. As to his habeas claim, "Had Joe gotten to litigate, with competent counsel, his claims of ineffective assistance of counsel in federal court, there is a great probability—more nearly a certainty—that he would have received a new sentencing trial." Here the petition's legalistic style comes to the fore, offering as it does a "summary of 26 state and federal cases in which courts have reversed death sentences because counsel failed to properly investigate and present the mitigation available on behalf of a capital defendant."

In addition, it describes in some detail the mitigation case that the jury in Joe's original trial never heard, highlighting a long family history of violence, abuse and neglect, poverty, unaddressed problems at school, and borderline mental retardation: "The jury that sentenced Joe to death knew none of these facts. Claiborne's decisions prevented the jury from achieving a better understanding of who and what shaped Joe into the person he was. . . . The facts were horrible and horrifying." Citing another expert, it states, "Their mitigating force would have been powerful."

The petition concludes again in the mode of a legal argument, drawing an analogy between Joe Louis Wise's case and the famous Supreme Court case of Clarence Gideon. And, like any good legal argument, it presents Joe as making modest, but important, claims, claims that it is very much within the governor's power to recognize and address. Unlike pardon tales that advance structural claims, this petition goes out of its way to present the condemned as seeking redress within a capital sentencing system about which he has no complaint. Yet, in its detailed rendering of the ineffectiveness of Wise's lawyers, it offers to the future another story of a death penalty system in default:

> In *Gideon v. Wainwright,* the United States Supreme Court held that under the Sixth Amendment to the Constitution, an indigent defendant facing criminal prosecution in state court has the right to have counsel appointed for him. The Court stated for all of us that: The right of one charged with crime to counsel may not be deemed fundamental and essential to fair trials in some countries, but it is in ours. From the very beginning, our state and national constitutions and laws have laid great emphasis on procedural and substantive safeguards designed to assure fair trials before impartial tribunals in which every defendant stands equal before the law. This noble ideal cannot be realized if the poor man charged with crime has to face his accusers without a lawyer to assist him.
>
> In a very real sense, this is a fundamental clemency case in the same way that *Gideon v. Wainwright* was a fundamental constitutional case. Joe Wise does not seek relief from this office because he claims innocence. Rather, he seeks commutation of his death sentence because, like Clarence Earl Gideon, he was denied his constitutional right to the assistance of counsel. Unlike Gideon, however, Joe was on trial for his life. And unlike

Gideon, Joe was unable to present his constitutional claim to the federal courts of the United States. As a consequence, Joe faces a September 14, 1993 execution date. Joe does not complain about Virginia's capital sentencing system or its system of appointing counsel to represent those charged with capital murder. Rather, Joe requests commutation because, in his case, these systems have failed completely, in a way that could not now be repeated. Joe's death sentence is a true miscarriage of justice. It is wholly unreliable, because for all these years it has gone untested by the crucible of our adversarial system. Under these unique circumstances, it would be appropriate for the Governor to commute Joe's sentence of death to one of life imprisonment.

Governor Wilder refused to do so, and Wise was executed as scheduled, one of the last inmates in Virginia to be put to death by electrocution.

3. "If You'd Led My Life, You'd Understand": Mitigation

Some clemency petitions do not focus primarily on legal errors of the kind raised in the Satcher and Wise cases; instead, they revisit and sometimes expand the mitigation case that was, or should have been, presented during the original trial. They put the crime in context and highlight aspects of the life circumstances of the condemned that explain why he did what he did or suggest reduced culpability for his offence.

One such petition was submitted in 1992 to Governor Ann Richards and the Texas Board of Pardons and Paroles in the case of Billy White. Authored by an all-star lineup of death penalty lawyers—Richard Burr, Steve Hawkins, Eden Harrington, and Mandy Welch—the 38-page petition puts their expertise and commitment on display on every page. Throughout, they meticulously present facts, marshal expert testimony, and carefully craft arguments. Yet they were unable to save White; he was executed on April 23, 1992.

White's plea for clemency worked in two genres, combining a legalist frame with an appeal to psychological understandings. White's petition centered on his mental retardation, which it claimed meant that he was "less culpable than non-retarded persons for the crime that led to his death sentence." The petition noted that White "has mild mental retardation, not severe mental retardation, but even mild mental retardation is a severe disability." Much of its argument was framed in the language of psychology and relied on the authority of that discipline. Thus early on, it cited "one of the leading mental retardation specialists in the country," who submitted an expert opinion that "[h]is mental retardation affects every dimension of his life."

White's petition went to great lengths to educate its readers about the meaning and significance of retardation. It described mental retardation as combining "(1) significantly sub-average general intellectual functioning (IQ of 70–75 or lower), (2) existing concurrently with impairments in adaptive behavior, and (3) manifested during the developmental period (before one's eighteenth birthday)." As to the first of these elements, it reports:

> "On April 15, 1992, psychologist Windel Dickerson . . . conducted a battery of psychological tests with Mr. White. He determined that Mr. White's full scale IQ is 66. . . . Finding that IQ score consistent with a public school measure of Mr. White's IQ as 69 in 1966, and with Mr. White's school history, Dr. Dickerson found that Mr. White has had "significantly sub-average general intellectual functioning" "during the developmental period."

As to second part of the definition, the petition invoked another psychologist:

> Professor Luckasson obtained and reviewed data with respect to the nine areas of adaptive behavior that are deemed most important by mental retardation professionals: communication, self-care, home living, social skills, community use, self-direction, health and safety, functional academics and leisure and work. She found that Mr. White's behavior was impaired in nearly all these areas.

Using "everyday terms," White's lawyers translated this psychological evidence to provide a picture of how White's retardation affected his day-to-day life. White, they claimed, was extremely dependent on other people. Again seeking to provide a context for his crime and to bolster their argument about reduced culpability they noted:

> Tragically, the direction into which these people led Billy was negative. Roy Charles introduced Billy to heroin and before long he was heavily involved in shooting up heroin and in taking a variety of other street and prescription drugs. . . . The other direction into which Billy was led was criminal

activity. Gradually Billy was transformed from a meek, frightened teenager into a person who was not afraid to break into houses, steal property, and commit robberies.

Seemingly concerned that this portrait of White might make him seem to be a dangerous, out-of-control individual, they contextualized his disability, and, in so doing, tried to humanize him. They continued:

> While Billy White's life has been severely circumscribed by his mental retardation, he remains a complex human being like any other human being. As Professor Luckasson has cautioned, there is "[a] risk in attempting to describe the disabilities and their impact on [Mr. White's] life that [one] might inadvertently stereotype him as a mentally retarded person, rather than fully describe his uniqueness as a complex person who has mental retardation. Mental retardation is a serious disability, and it affects every dimension of Billy's life. He has, however, other attributes and characteristics that make him Billy White." To all who know Billy White, his most striking characteristics beyond mental retardation are his sweetness of spirit, his kindness, and his generosity.

Only after this complex narrative—which joins psychology and the vernacular, White's disability and his redeeming human characteristics —was in place did the authors of his petition discuss his crime: "On August 23, 1976, at approximately 6:00 P.M., Martha Laura Spinks was killed by a single shot from a .38 caliber gun in the office of the furniture store owned and operated by her and her husband, Alge Spinks. Ms. Spinks was shot during the course of an incident involving Billy White." Framing this description in the passive voice works to diminish White's agency in the crime.

Then, the petition returns to a theme noted earlier—White's extreme dependence on others:

> What took place on the day of the crime was significantly the product of other people's shaping of Billy White's behavior. He was only nineteen years old when Ms. Spinks was killed. He was fundamentally dependent upon people like Henry Wyatt at that time in his life. Because of Billy's mental retardation, people like Henry Wyatt and Roy Charles Baines had been able to shape Billy in their image. He did not have the internal capabilities

necessary to question them or resist their influences. Even if he could appreciate that the criminal activities they led him into were wrong, his whole life history revealed that he would have tremendous difficulty changing his behavior. Further, the chance that Billy would accidentally kill someone in the course of an armed robbery was high. Unless Billy was closely guided, he often failed to do what he set out and intended to do.

At this point, the petition provides an extended description of White's trial, highlighting inadequacies in the representation provided by his lawyer and noting the availability of evidence that could have been presented to raise "substantial questions about whether the shooting of Ms. Spinks was intentional, and even if these questions were resolved against Mr. White, whether he was culpable enough to deserve a sentence of death." White's clemency lawyers argued that "[t]he most important evidence omitted from the trial was the evidence that Mr. White had mental retardation. Had the jury known this and come to appreciate the effects of mental retardation in Mr. White's life, it would have viewed Mr. White as less culpable even if Mr. Spinks' version of the crime was accepted without reservation."

It is noteworthy that this clemency petition contains no statements by jurors testifying to this fact. This absence is notable because other petitions, like Satcher's, often present such statements. They provide affidavits from prosecutors, judges, prison officials, and occasionally even the relatives of those killed to bolster their argument for relief.

After a lengthy description of evidence that could have been, but was not, presented White's petition states:

> It is manifest that Billy White's trial was a sham. Lasting little more than a day, dealing with none of the evidence about Mr. White's life and disabilities that had obvious bearing on the crime and his culpability for it, failing to explore in any meaningful way the evidence that bore directly on whether Ms. Spinks was killed accidentally during a struggle, Mr. White's trial cannot engender confidence that reliable judgments were made about his culpability. Clemency must be available for a case like this, where the criminal justice process has failed so miserably to provide a reliable vehicle for arriving at true and just results.

This petition moves toward its conclusion by departing from the genre of the mitigation tale or the tale of legal woe to raise, albeit briefly, the issue of White's post-sentencing conduct in prison. Here it deploys the kind of authority—in the affidavits of prison guards—that was not used elsewhere:

> Perhaps the best proof that death was not the appropriate sentence for Billy, and that his trial resulted in an incorrect and unjust sentence, is the picture of who Billy is today. That picture shows us a human being who possesses attributes which we are taught to value and which enhance the quality of life for others. These attributes were apparent to Professor Luckasson during the several hours she spent with Billy. . . . "In my opinion, his most striking characteristics beyond the mental retardation are his gentleness, kindness, and generosity of spirit. Although his ability to fully actualize that basic goodness is limited by his deficient abilities to understand, express, communicate and have logical understanding of cause and effect or strategic problem solving I believe the goodness is there." . . . The prison officers and guards who are in the best position to know Billy describe him in the same way. They see Billy as a "gentle, friendly person who gets along well with everyone." They consistently remark that "Billy treats people with respect, and is outgoing and friendly with the officers and inmates." Billy has been on death row for almost fourteen years, and he is known as a person who has never caused any problems for the officers or inmates. One officer described Billy as "a model inmate in the prison."

White's clemency petition ends in an almost lyrical and uplifting manner, conjuring Billy in a new role, not simply as "a human being whose life is worth saving" but as a person who

> gives you special insight into that remarkable human spirit which enables a human being to overcome limitations and hardships beyond his understanding without developing bitterness or cynicism. Billy is remarkable in his warmth, his gentleness, his respectfulness, and his kindness. Billy's trial was remarkable in its failure to provide his jury with the information necessary for a fair and just response to his crime. Billy's appeals have been remarkable in their failure to reveal the injustices of Billy's trial. At this point, the Governor of the State of Texas is the only hope Billy has that fairness and justice will prevail in his case.

Despite its lyricism and uplift, another absence is noteworthy: namely, the fact that there is no reference to God, spirituality, or religion of the kind that is ubiquitous in petitions that seek to show that the condemned has been transformed and now has those human qualities that make his a life worth sparing

4. "Accept My Contrition, Grant Me Mercy, Spare My Life": Spirituality and Religion

God, spirituality, and religion are central elements in the 1998 clemency petition of Ronald Watkins. While this petition, like most others, was written by a lawyer, it breaks from the standard narrative of legal injustice and the memorialization of law's failure by beginning with an admission of Watkins's guilt and making a straightforward appeal for mercy. It announces its difference in the way it is titled—"A Plea for the Life of Ronald Watkins"—as well as in its epistolary form. Written as a letter to the governor, it distances itself from legal form, saying in its first sentence: "Insofar as possible, this will not be a legal document. It is a plea for an act of executive grace."

Throughout, Watkins's petition grounds itself in appeals to shared religious beliefs and commitments to family values. This is "an appeal from fellow Christians," it says, "to exercise that grace in recognition of the power of God's grace in the life of Ronald Watkins and the worth of that life to others. . . . We pray that God will guide our hands as we undertake that task." Moreover, the petition's author disclaims his own narrative authority, saying, "I intend to let much of Ron's story be told in this petition through his own words to us. From literally hundreds of letters, I have included excerpts that reveal who Ron is now. I assure you these words were not written with any thought of clemency in mind, but that will certainly be apparent from the writings themselves." This personal assurance seems to come out of a different era in which a man's word was his bond and frames the petition's creation of a vicarious audience between Watkins and the governor. It does so by presenting, in allegedly unmediated form, the voice of the condemned, a voice that is clear, articulate, and revealing enough to need no interpretation.

Like other petitions for mercy, this one is structured as a story of transformation in which religion and family play key roles:

By any test you could formulate, Ron is a different person from the man sentenced to death years ago; he is now a redeemed child of God. He has made every effort to be a good father to his sixteen-year-old son, David. He has reached out to repair the relationship with his own father, who abused him. . . . During his first three years on death row, the abused angry man had time to reflect and accept responsibility for his actions. He also found Christ. For six years, in hundreds of small ways, he has reached out to his family and to others, and has been a helper.

Watkins's willingness to express remorse for his crime and the authenticity of words spoken and actions taken with no thought of their consequences are presented as evidence of the sincerity of his transformation:

> During one of our visits with Ron, he expressed his great remorse over the death of his victim, William McCauley. It was difficult for him to say these things to us face-to-face. Although he had written many times over the years how much he regretted his actions, and told us the same over the phone, his sincerity was evidenced by his actions that day. At his request, we tried to find the McCauley family to convey his remorse. . . . In Ron's case, the redeeming power of God rebuts the death penalty's assumption that, once condemned, he could have no human qualities, particularly remorse. Typical of the person he had become, Ron expressed his humanity and remorse years ago in a poem he never expected anyone but us to read.

In addition, Watkins's petition presents a chronicle of good works, of a once seemingly wasted life now made useful:

> He has been a peacemaker and a keeper of order in the prison. He has helped to keep another Danville teenager from going down the wrong road. He has not done these things out of some hope that you would one day see fit to spare his life, Governor. That he has done them is witness to the magnificent power of Christ to take the unclean vessel and use it to advance the work of the Kingdom on earth. Please let that work continue within the prison walls, where it is so badly needed.

Here the appeal is made in the form of a supplication, an entreaty. "Please . . ." takes the place of the language of grievance or injustice that characterizes many of the petitions in Texas and Virginia.

Yet, as is the case in almost every clemency petition, genres get mixed as new arguments get marshaled. Thus the narrative of this petition, the purest appeal to mercy among the Texas and Virginia petitions I read, proceeds like other genres in its contextualization of Watkins's crime, to broaden the interpretive frame within which it should be understood. The petition states:

> For many of his early years, Ron lived in a situation where he could not escape the constant threat and reality of violence. Outside the door in New York City lay violence and death. Inside the home, he was singled out and subjected to violent and humiliating forms of physical abuse. A summary of this frightening history is attached as Exhibit 1. The reason I detail these events, which are documented in the court records but were never heard by the jury, is that they are not at all offered as an excuse for what he did in 1988. Rather, they are relevant to an explanation and understanding of the young man that emerged from that environment. What would have been the extent of the damage to you, or to me, if, in our youth, there had been week after week with no escape or rest from violence, inside and outside our home? It was after his family moved to Virginia that Ron committed his only other serious offense. It was a serious offense, abduction, and I do not wish to minimize it. But it was also not a random crime.

Several things stand out in this narrative. One is that traces of the very legal language that its author initially disclaimed begin to appear (e.g., "Exhibit 1") as do narrative elements found in other kinds of petitions ("documented in the court records but were never heard by the jury"). In addition, we see some of the rhetoric of the skilled advocate in the penalty phase of a capital trial—"Not at all offered as an excuse" and "It was a serious offense"—and an appeal to empathy through identification.

Furthermore, the petition makes a direct equity appeal, comparing Watkins's case with one of the few recent cases in which clemency was granted in Virginia, the 1997 commutation of the sentence of William Saunders. "In the case of William Saunders," the petition suggests,

> Virginia recognized the relevance of reformation and a changed life to the clemency decision. To be sure, there are many ways to distinguish the cases if one is of a mind to do so. . . . But the record shows that Saunders' post-sentence conduct was an important factor, if not the only factor. It is to be assumed that if doubts about guilt were the primary factor, Saunders' sentence would have been commuted to something less than life without possibility of parole, the commutation sought by Ronald Watkins. The post-sentence record of Ronald Watkins is superior to that of William Saunders. That is not to say that Mr. Saunders did not deserve this act of executive

grace. It is to say that Ronald Watkins has shown himself equally worthy and has demonstrated that he is no danger to anyone.

At the end, Watkins's petition returns to its central narrative elements, again personalizing its appeal, grounding it in shared religious commitments, and concluding not with an appeal to the governor's majestic, sovereign powers but with a request that he seek divine guidance. It concludes:

> We are unashamed to make this plea for mercy to you in the name of Christ. That is because we search in vain in His gospel for examples of the good being taken and made better. But we see story after story of the wretched and sinners being transformed into instruments of God's will. At the end of the day, redemption is what the gospel story is about. Please ignore your lawyers, your political advisors, get on your knees and seek God's will in this case. That is all we can ask, but we do ask it. Please spare the life of our friend.

In the end, the governor refused to heed this plea, and Ronald Watkins was executed on March 25, 1998.

5. "The Death Penalty Is a Tool of Racism": Structural Critique

Even rarer than straightforward appeals for mercy are petitions that embed their appeals in a broad structural critique of the legal system or of the death penalty system, petitions that are, I would contend, the most direct in memorializing injustice and appealing to an imagined future. If the narrative style in appeals for mercy is submissive, the style of the structural genre is declarative and accusatory. Take, for example, the Virginia petition of Johnny Watkins, Jr.[82] The alliterative title—"Danville, Death, and Discrimination"—both proclaims its conclusion and initiates an argument that Watkins is a victim of racism.

The petition's bold opening paragraph states: "For over one hundred years, the death penalty has been a tool of racism in Virginia." It backs up its this claim by reminding its readers that "[b]lack people have been sentenced to death far more often than white people, and they have been sentenced to death for crimes for which white people have not faced death." Only after making those assertions does it connect them to the particulars of Watkins's case:

Now Danville seeks to have carried out the death sentences of Johnny Watkins, Jr., a black man. The process by which those sentences were procured was shot through with the impermissible factor of race. Two separate juries, from which the prosecutor had struck every qualified black person, sentenced Mr. Watkins to death. Significantly, both victims were white. Indeed, virtually everyone involved in the case other than Mr. Watkins—the judge, the jury, the prosecutor, the police investigators, even the court clerk —was white. This was no isolated occurrence: since 1977, Danville capital prosecutions reflect an unmistakable under-representation of black people as anything but defendants. Indeed, Danville's post-*Furman* pattern of capital punishment is indistinguishable from Danville's antebellum, Reconstruction, and Jim Crow pattern. That pattern is one of racism.

This is a narrative of structural inequity and unfairness, one that emphasizes historical continuity, one that names its target "racism."

This train of logic is, of course, hardly one that an elected official would likely embrace. Yet the petition calls on the governor to commute Watkins's sentence and in that gesture to "repudiate" that history. And, if the tone of Ronald Watkins's petition tended toward a kind of intimacy in which petitioner and governor were connected as speaker and listener, here the narration is impersonal. Johnny Watkins is given no agency, no role, in constructing the story ostensibly designed to save his life.

So eager is the author of this petition, a Richmond attorney, to get to the large matters of race and race prejudice that he spends but two lines describing the crime for which his client was sentenced to death: "Johnny Watkins, Jr., was convicted in 1984 of the capital murders and robberies of two convenience store workers, Betty Barker and Carl Buchanan, in separate incidents in the City of Danville. One of the victims was shot three times, the other four. At the time, Mr. Watkins was 22 years of age and had no significant criminal record." He then weaves a description of a single town's history of racial prejudice together with an indictment of the entire state and nation:

> The evidence that race is a factor in Danville capital prosecutions is historic, extensive, and irrefutable. For the past 100 years, race surely has been the best predictor of who gets the death penalty in both Virginia and Danville. Danville has a long history of racial strife, extreme among Virginia cities, which lasted well into the Nineteen Seventies. The widespread perception

among black Americans that systems of justice treat them more harshly than whites is held by black citizens in Danville just as elsewhere. More to the point, capital prosecutions in Danville unmistakably display a pattern of racism.

The petition continues:

> In the post-*Furman* era, Danville has sentenced more men to death than any other jurisdiction in Virginia; every one of those men is black. In all but one case, their victims were white. But in Danville, black capital defendants are not judged or sentenced by juries with anything resembling a representative number of black persons on them. Black citizens are under-represented in the venires from which Danville chooses its juries, black citizens are stricken from those juries by the prosecution in excessive numbers, and black citizens often are completely absent from the petit juries that result. In a city whose population is over 30% black, black citizens have been shut out of any role in the administration of capital justice. In short, Jim Crow's tool remains in the hands of white people in Danville.
>
> Virginia's record in capital punishment from 1908–1962 is one of unadulterated racism. Virginia executed 236 prisoners in that time. Of these, 201 were black, an astounding 85%. The first person Virginia electrocuted was black, the last person Virginia electrocuted before *Furman* was black, and virtually all the ones in-between were black. During this period, Virginia executed 57 black men for crimes less than murder, including attempted rape and robbery. No white man was executed for a crime less than murder during this time. Virginia executed one woman—predictably, she was black. Danville's record is similarly egregious.

Finally, broadening its indictment to the entire nation Watkins's lawyer suggests:

> There can be little doubt that the death penalty process in the United States is heavily influenced by the issue of race. In a famous Georgia study, researchers determined that a black defendant who killed a white victim was 22 times more likely to receive the death penalty than a black defendant who killed a black victim, and 7 times more likely to receive the death penalty than whites who kill blacks. *McCleskey v. Kemp*, 481 U.S. 279, 326–27

(1987). While there is no comparable Virginia study, the Commonwealth's history, and Danville's history in particular, certainly do not suggest that a contrary result would be found here.

Sprinkled throughout the petition are tables documenting these assertions, as well as a long narrative of Danville's tainted history. These tables and this history provide background for an argument about the exclusion of blacks from jury service and its impact in the Watkins case:

> It should come as no surprise that Danville is excluding blacks from jury service, because Danville has been doing so for virtually all its history. Of course, it goes without saying that Danville excluded black citizens from jury duty through most of the Jim Crow era. But Danville's recent history is little better. On at least three occasions, federal courts have found as a fact that Danville was systematically excluding blacks from jury service. . . . What Danville is doing is procuring death sentences against black defendants by means of a racially discriminatory system. What Danville is doing is intolerable. . . . It . . . falls to the Governor to consider whether, in light of all those circumstances, Johnny Watkins, Jr., a young black man, has been sentenced to death by a process tainted by racism, and if so, whether, in 1994, the Commonwealth is still so indifferent to the reality of racism that it is prepared to carry out those sentences regardless of that fact.

It is indeed only on page 16 of this 27-page petition that it returns to the petitioner. When it does so it proceeds in a rather perfunctory fashion, highlighting the impact of the exclusion of blacks from the jury, of what Watkins's clemency lawyers call prosecutorial misconduct, and of the poor quality of his trial lawyer. It briefly recounts the nature of Watkins's crime before devoting a single paragraph to the mitigation evidence presented in the penalty phase of his first trial:

> In the first trial, the evidence created the portrait of a severely dysfunctional family. The evidence established that Mr. Watkins, along with his brother, was abandoned by his mother due to unemployment and ill health. Mr. Watkins was only three years old when he was brought to Virginia by her, where his elderly aunt raised him. The aunt's husband was himself ill, however, and remained in the hospital for years before dying. Mr. Watkins's aunt, therefore, raised him and his brother by herself. There was never a father figure in Mr. Watkins's life. The jury in the first trial had

the opportunity to observe for itself the extraordinary indifference of Mr. Watkins's mother to the very question of whether he lived or died. After she and Mr. Watkins's stepfather had testified, they asked to be excused, because they had to leave early to return to New York! The jury thus had a dramatic first hand demonstration of the fact that Mr. Watkins's mother, who had devoted precious little of her time to him over the years, thought it more important to return home than to see if her son was sentenced to die in the electric chair.

The crimes, while providing a basis for imposition of the death penalty if the jury so chose, were not so horrifying that they mandated it. The mitigating evidence, on the other hand, demonstrated that Mr. Watkins had grown up under difficult circumstances, having been emotionally and physically abandoned by his parents. While this evidence did not compel a life sentence, it did provide a substantial basis for such a result. In fact, a fair jury, one that reflected the entire community and could, therefore, more likely reach a decision unfettered by racial bias, had ample reason not to sentence Mr. Watkins to death despite the nature of the crimes.

This clemency petition vividly describes Watkins's trial lawyer, suggesting that he was so intimidated by the racism of the trial that, in effect, he provided no argument at all that Watkins should not be executed. The petition contends:

In closing arguments, defense counsel vouched for what a wonderful person the victim was, based upon what they had heard about him "outside this trial and in this trial." He told the jury that "the killing of Miss Barker was senseless, brutal, uncalled for, and running entirely against the grain of everything that you and I and perhaps all of us were brought up and raised to believe in"; that his own client had breached a "sacred trust to honor the life and property of others"; that the question "why should we give him mercy when this man probably has shown none" is a "difficult one" that he "could argue to [the jury] all night" and not know if he could convince them or even give them a satisfactory answer. He posed the question "If we take another life will that improve matters any?" and incredibly answered the question "Arguably." Thus, not only did counsel do nothing to object to the prosecutor's excesses, but he gave the jury precious little reason not to follow the Biblical mandate that Mr. Fuller had foisted upon them. Indeed, counsel virtually admitted to the jury that even he did not believe that there was a good reason not to follow Mr. Fuller's agenda.

This pardon tale concludes by returning to its overall theme—Danville, Death, and Discrimination—and by framing its plea less as an appeal to the governor than as a challenge to him. "This petition raises no question whether Mr. Watkins deserves punishment for his crimes," it suggests:

> Instead this petition questions whether the discriminatory manner in which Danville set the level of his punishment should be validated or repudiated. Hundreds of years of harsh and inequitable treatment of black defendants in America's courts provide the answer. Whether overt or subconscious, Danville's latter day banishment of upright black citizens from the criminal justice process in capital murder trials should be rejected, and Johnny Watkins's death sentences should be commuted to life imprisonment.

Here Watkins's fate is linked to a large moral and political question— namely, whether the governor will ally himself with Danville and its history of racism or take the political risk of repudiating it. Clemency in this case would be one small but significant step on the road toward undoing that history. In the end, the governor chose to side with Danville and refused to take that step. Johnny Watkins was executed on March 3, 1994.

Conclusion

Speaking in different genres, telling different stories, clemency petitions in capital cases should be read, I contend, not just as pleas to spare the life of someone condemned to death but as calls to the future to attend to injustices of the present moment, cumulating, despite their often narrow legalist frames, in a broad indictment of the inequities and injustices of America in the late twentieth century. In the present moment, these memorializations of miscarriages of justice appeal to the shared values of a community of imagined readers, values like fairness and equality, Christian compassion, and family connection.[83] How they will be heard and read in the future is, of course, impossible to know.

Yet, through their narratives, the condemned and their advocates give content both to the possibility of justice, as well as to its deferred presence in law.[84] While justice, what Cornell calls the "good," is, on her account, always present *to* law, it is never completely realized *in* law:[85] "[T]he law posits an ideality . . . that it can never realize, and . . . this failure is constitutive of existing law."[86] Law exists both in the "as yet" failure to realize the good, and in the commitment to its realization. In this failure and this commitment, law is two things at once: the social organization of violence through which state power is exercised in a partisan, biased, and sometimes cruel way,[87] and the arena to which citizens address themselves in the hope that law can, and will, redress the wrongs which are committed in its name.[88]

In this same vein, Cover compellingly called our attention to law's "jurisgenerative" and "jurispathic" qualities:

> Law may be viewed as a system of tension or a bridge linking a concept of reality to an imagined alternative. . . . Thus, one constitutive element of a *nomos* is the phenomenon George Steiner has labeled "alternity": the "other than the case," the counterfactual propositions, images, shapes of will and evasions with which we charge our mental being and by means of which we build the changing, largely fictive milieu for our somatic and our social existence. But the concept of a *nomos* is not exhausted by its "alternity"; it is neither utopia nor pure vision. A *nomos*, as a world of law, entails the application of human will to an extant state of affairs as well as toward our visions of alternative futures.[89]

Cover used the word *nomos*, "normative universe," to argue that law is crucially involved in helping persons "create and maintain, a world of right and wrong, of lawful and unlawful, of valid and void."[90] The *nomos* that law helps create, Cover believed, always contains within it visions of possibility not yet realized, images of a better world not yet built. But, he reminds us, law is not simply, or even primarily, a gentle, hermeneutic apparatus; it always exists in a state of tension between a world of meaning in which justice is pursued, and a world of violence in which "legal interpretation takes places on a field of pain and death."[91]

In this chapter, I have shown how clemency petitions in capital cases confront this tension. As they do so, these memorializations of miscarriages of justice are haunted by the specter of an all-but-impossible to stop death, the death of those in whose name they are authorized to speak about the legal failures and injustices of the present. The condemned are suspended in a place between life and death: living, breathing, but with a rapidly closing horizon of possibility. Because everyone knows that their pleas for clemency most likely will be denied, they become rhetorical and political stand-ins for various of law's failures and symbols of martyred innocence, victims of legal incompetence, or of racial discrimination.

Appendix: A Note on Data and Methods

There is no comprehensive, nationwide archive of clemency petitions. Like the death penalty itself, clemency varies state by state in its procedures and in the ways records are kept. After initial inquiries in several places, including Texas and Virginia, I concluded that getting petitions directly from the states would be extremely costly (since most are not kept in electronic form) and difficult, if not impossible. As a result, I turned to the clemency petitions collected by the National Death Penalty Archive (NDPA) at the State University of New York at Albany. Theirs is the largest and most comprehensive single collection in the United States.

At the time of my research, the archive contained 150, machine-readable clemency petitions filed, between 1990 and 2002, in 13 states (Alabama, Florida, Georgia, Indiana, Illinois, Mississippi, Missouri, North Carolina, Ohio, South Carolina, Tennessee, Texas, and Virginia), as well as in the federal system. Of these, 28 were filed in Texas from 1990 to 2000 and 53 in Virginia covering the period 1992 to 2002. Because the petitions were collected from attorneys around the country who represented death row inmates in clemency proceedings, I have no way of knowing whether they are representative of the universe of petitions filed between 1990 and 2002 or, if not, the ways they might be systematically biased.

A research assistant and I began the analysis by separately reading all of the 150 petitions and listing each of the issues/allegations/claims raised in the petitions. Where we disagreed about how an issue/allegation/claim should be classified, we discussed and resolved our disagreement. That exercise resulted in the identification of the following issues/allegations/claims: factual error or innocence; police misconduct; prosecutorial misconduct; false or unreliable witness testimony; incompetent or unethical expert witness; ineffective assistance of counsel; jury bias; errors or omissions in the mitigation phase of the original trial; unavailability of life without parole as an option at the time of sentencing; equity; error or procedural bar in the appellate or postconviction process; remorse or religious conversion or post-sentencing rehabilitation or mercy.

When this first pass was completed, each of us reread the petitions from Texas and Virginia, this time trying to identify the main story, or the predominant genre, of each petition. Where we disagreed or were uncertain, we again discussed and resolved the disagreement or uncertainty. Through this procedure, we identified the five stories and genres discussed in this article.

Once all of the Texas and Virginia petitions had been classified by story or genre, we each did yet another pass to select "ideal types" or "primary exemplars" of those stories and genres. As a result of that exercise, three of the cases that I discuss in this article were initially tagged by both me and my research assistant. One or the other of us nominated six other cases for possible inclusion. Subsequently, we each reread and discussed those six cases, agreeing ultimately on two other cases to be included in the article.

NOTES

I am grateful to Nasser Hussain, Ruth Miller, Adam Sitze, and participants in the Making Sense of Miscarriages of Justice workshop for their helpful comments on an earlier version of this chapter. An earlier version of this chapter appeared in *Law and Society Review* 42, no. 1 (2008), reprinted by permission.

1. Richard A. Rosen, "Innocence and Death," *North Carolina Law Review* 82 (2003): 61.

2. Samuel R. Gross, Kristen Jacoby, Daniel J. Matheson, Nicholas Montgomery, and Sujata Patil, "Exonerations in the United States 1989 through 2003," *Journal of Criminal Law and Criminology* 95 (2005): 523. See also Hugo Adam Bedau and Michael L. Radelet, "Miscarriages of Justice in Potentially Capital Cases," *Stanford Law Review* 40 (1987): 21, and Michael L. Radelet, William Lofquist, and Hugo Adam Bedau, "Prisoners Released from Death Rows Since 1970 Because of Doubts about Their Guilt," *Thomas.M. Cooley Law Review* 13 (1996): 907.

3. For example, James Lieberman, "The Overproduction of Death," *Columbia Law Review* 100 (2000): 2030. See also James Lieberman, Andrew Gelman, Alexander Kiss, and Valerie West, "A Broken System: The Persistent Patterns of Reversals of Death Sentences in the United States," *Journal of Empirical Legal Studies* 1 (2004): 209.

4. A federal district court judge recently threw out a death penalty sentence because of the risk of executing an innocent, but this decision was quickly and summarily reversed on appeal. *United States v. Quinones,* 205 F. Supp. 2d 256 (S.D.N.Y. 2002), rev'd, *United States v. Quinones,* 313 F.3d 49 (2d Cir. 2002).

5. Jack Greenberg, "The Capital Punishment System," *Yale Law Journal* 91 (1982): 908, and Franklin Zimring, "Inheriting the Wind: The Supreme Court and Capital Punishment in the 1990s," *Florida State University Law Review* 20 (1992): 7. Congress has also acted to limit habeas relief. See the 1996 Anti-Terrorism and Effective Death Penalty Act, at http://www.fas.org/irp/crs/96–499.htm.

6. The Court has long viewed itself as having the authority to alter the scope of federal habeas, even without new legislation. *Wainwright v. Sykes,* 433 U.S. 72 (1977) at 81 (referring to the Court's "historic willingness to overturn or modify

its earlier views of the scope of the writ, even where the statutory language autho-
rizing judicial action has remained unchanged").

7. *Id.*

8. *Rose v. Lundy,* 455 U.S. 509 (1982).

9. *McCleskey v. Zant,* 499 U.S. 467 (1991)

10. *Teague v. Lane,* 489 U.S. 288 (1989). The portion of Justice O'Connor's lead opinion in *Teague* referenced in the text garnered only three other votes and thus is technically only a plurality opinion. However, in the subsequent case of *Penry v. Lynaugh,* 492 U.S. 302 (1989), Justice O'Connor picked up the additional vote of Justice White, who had refused to join the relevant portion of her opinion in *Teague,* making hers the view of a majority of the Court.

11. *Butler v. McKellar,* 494 U.S. 407 (1990).

12. *Stringer v. Black,* 503 U.S. 222 (1992) at 226.

13. Charles Doyle, "Antiterrorism and Effective Death Penalty Act [AEDPA] of 1996: A Summary," (June 3, 1996), at http://www.fas.org/irp/crs/96-499.htm.

14. According to Doyle, "The period of limitations begins with the latest of: the date of final completion of direct state review procedures; the date of removal of a government impediment preventing the prisoner from filing for habeas relief; the date of Supreme Court recognition of the underlying federal right and of the right's retroactive application; or the date of uncovering previously undiscoverable evidence upon which the habeas claim is predicated. The period is tolled during the pendency of state collateral review." *Id.*

15. In *Felker v. Turpin,* 518 U.S. 651 (1997), the Supreme Court held that these limitations and provisions of AEDPA did not unconstitutionally suspend the writ.

16. James Liebman, "More Than 'Slightly Retro': The Rehnquist Court's Rout of Habeas Corpus Jurisdiction in *Teague v. Lane,*" *New York University Review of Law and Social Change* 18 (1990–91): 357; Steven Goldstein, "Chipping Away at the Great Writ: Will Death Sentenced Federal Habeas Corpus Petitioners Be Able to Seek and Utilize Changes in the Law?" *New York Review of Law and Social Change* 18 (1990–91): 357; Steven Goldstein, "Expediting the Federal Habeas Corpus Review Process in Capital Cases: An Examination of Recent Proposals," *Capital University Law Review* 19 (1990): 599.

For assessments of the consequences of AEDPA, see Andrew Hammel, "Diabolical Federalism: A Functional Critique and Proposed Reconstruction of Death Penalty Federal Habeas," *American Criminal Law Review* 39 (2002): 1; Bryan A. Stevenson, "Confronting Mass Imprisonment and Restoring Fairness to Collateral Review of Criminal Cases," *Harvard Civil Rights–Civil Liberties Law Review* 41 (2006): 339, 349; Eric Freedman, "Symposium: Further Developments in the Law of Habeas Corpus: Giarratano Is a Scarecrow: The Right to Counsel in State Capital Postconviction Proceedings," *Cornell Law Review* 91 (2006): 1079. As Freedman says about the provisions of the AEDPA, "In today's legal environment the effect of this system is that some prisoners may literally be left to die of neglect" (1090).

For a different perspective see J. Richard Broughton, "The Second Death of Capital Punishment," *Florida Law Review* 58 (2006): 639. Broughton notes that "[i]n the five years since the Court first articulated its approach under the AEDPA, in both capital and non-capital cases, the Court has given substantial deference to state courts, consistent with the AEDPA's scheme and with the expressions of those who crafted the statute. Notably, however, the Court has proven less deferential (though certainly not undeferential) in capital habeas cases. Over the past five years, only death-sentenced inmates have prevailed in challenging a state court's decision as objectively unreasonable under 2254(d). Interestingly, three of those cases involved ineffective assistance of counsel claims, which are ordinarily among the most difficult to prove on collateral review, given the combination of the AEDPA's deference scheme and the high threshold for relief established in *Strickland v. Washington's* requirement that such challenges demonstrate both deficient performance and actual prejudice. . . . The Court also has ruled against the government, and in favor in the death row inmate, in several recent capital habeas cases from Texas that did not all involve AEDPA deference, but that signaled a budding doctrinal feud with the Fifth Circuit in the capital habeas arena" (653–54).

Today, sweeping new limitations on habeas in capital cases have been incorporated into the proposed Streamlined Procedures Act of 2005. Marcia Coyle, "More Fuel Added to Debate over Federal Habeas Review: New Data, New Bill Intensify the Exchange," *National Law Journal* (October 20, 2005) at http://www.law.com/jsp/article.jsp?id=1129712711507, and Dale Baich, "Stones in the Pathway of Justice," *Arizona Republic* (September 18, 2005) at http://www.nacdl.org/public.nsf/legislation/habeas003.

As Vivian Berger explains, "Overruling a long line of Supreme Court precedent, it removes jurisdiction from habeas courts to consider claims that a state court refused to hear on the ground of some procedural error committed by the prisoner or his lawyer—even if the lawyer's inadequate assistance caused the default or the state court's action was unreasonable. To overcome this global barrier to review, a petitioner would generally have to show that 'the factual predicate for the claim could not have been discovered previously through the exercise of due diligence; and . . . the facts underlying the claim . . . would be sufficient to establish . . . that, but for constitutional error, no reasonable fact-finder would have found the applicant guilty of the underlying offense.'" Vivian Berger, "Streamlining Injustice," *National Law Journal* (August 8, 2005) at http://www.nacdl.org/public.nsf/legislation/habeas001.

17. *Vasquez v. Harris,* 503 U.S. 1000 (1992). See also Stephen Reinhardt, "The Supreme Court, the Death Penalty, and the *Harris* Case," *Yale Law Journal* 102 (1992): 205.

18. *Herrera v. Collins*, 506 U.S. 390 (1993). In response to *Herrera*, Justice Blackmun charged the Court with coming "perilously close to murder." Joseph Hoffmann, "Is Innocence Sufficient? An Essay on the United States Supreme Court's Continuing Problems with Federal Habeas Corpus and the Death Penalty," *Indiana Law Review* 68 (1993): 817.

19. *Herrera v. Collins*, 414.

20. *Id.*, 411–12.

21. For example, Austin Sarat, *When the State Kills: Capital Punishment and the American Condition* (Princeton: Princeton University Press, 2001).

22. For important discussions and illustrations of this prerogative, see Natalie Zemon Davis, *Fiction in the Archives: Pardon Tales and Their Tellers in Sixteenth-Century France* (Stanford: Stanford University Press, 1987); Douglas Hay, "Property, Authority, and the Criminal Law," in *Albion's Fatal Tree: Crime and Society in Eighteenth-Century England*, ed. Douglas Hay, Peter Linebaugh, John Rule, E. P. Thompson, and Carl Winslow (New York: Pantheon, 1975); and Robert Turrell, *White Mercy: A Study of the Death Penalty in South Africa* (Westport, Conn.: Praeger, 2004). See also Daniel Kobil, "Chance and the Constitution in Capital Clemency Cases," *Capital University Law Review* 28 (2002): 567; Michael Radelet and Barbara Zsembik, "Executive Clemency in Post-*Furman* Capital Cases," *University of Richmond Law Review* 27 (1992–93): 289; Michael Heise, "Mercy by the Numbers: An Empirical Analysis of Clemency and Its Structure," *Virginia Law Review* 89 (2003): 239; Beau Breslin and John J.P. Howley, "Defending the Politics of Clemency," *Oregon Law Review* 81 (2002): 231; Alyson Dinsmore, "Clemency in Capital Cases: The Need to Ensure Meaningful Review," *UCLA Law Review* 49 (2002): 1825; Elizabeth Rapaport, "Staying Alive: Executive Clemency, Equal Protection, and the Politics of Gender in Women's Capital Cases," *Buffalo Criminal Law Review* 4 (2001): 967; Stephen Garvey, "Is It Wrong to Commute Death Row? Retribution, Atonement, and Mercy," *North Carolina Law Review* 82 (2004): 1319; Margaret Colgate Love, "Fear of Forgiving: Rule and Discretion in the Theory and Practice of Pardoning," *Federal Sentencing Reporter* 13 (2000–2001): 125; Kathleen Dean Moore, *Pardons: Justice, Mercy, and the Public Interest* (New York: Oxford University Press, 1989); Austin Sarat, *Mercy on Trial: What It Means to Stop an Execution* (Princeton: Princeton University Press, 2005).

23. Executive clemency is, of course, not coterminous with "sparing life." Pardons are used for the most mundane of crimes. Moreover, it could be argued that the potential to "spare life" is not exclusively reserved to executive clemency: a jury that declines to impose capital punishment when it has the choice to do so could equally be considered as sparing life, as, indeed, could an appeals court that overturns a death sentence. "As a matter of fact," James Barnett contends, "many others exercise virtually the same function-judges, juries, prosecuting attorneys, informers, police officers, victims of the offense." James Barnett, "The Grounds

of Pardon," *Journal of the American Institute of Criminal Law and Criminology* 17 (1927): 490.

24. *Clemency for Battered Women in Michigan: A Manual for Attorneys, Law Students and Social Workers* at http://www.umich.edu/~clemency/clemency_manual/manual_chapter02.html.

25. As law professor Robert Weisberg puts it, "the commutation of a death sentence [is] the most dramatic example of mercy." Robert Weisberg, "Apology, Legislation, and Mercy," *North Carolina Law Review* 82 (2004): 1421.

26. William Blackstone, *Commentaries on the Laws of England: A Facsimile of the First Edition of 1765–1769* (Chicago: University of Chicago Press, 1979), 4:389. As Montesquieu notes, "So many are the advantages which monarchs gain by clemency, so greatly does it raise their fame, and endear them of their subjects, that it is generally happy for them to have an opportunity of displaying it." Baron de Charles de Secondat Montesquieu, *The Spirit of the Laws* [*1748*], ed. and trans. Anne M. Cohler, Bria Carolyn Martin, and Harold Samuel Stone (Cambridge: Cambridge University Press, 1989), Bk. 6:21

27. Robert Salladay, "Clemency: Slim Chance These Days," *San Francisco Examiner,* November 29, 1998, at http://www.sfgate.com/cgi-bin/article.cgi%3Ff=/examiner/archive/1998/11/29/NEWS8622.dtl&type=printable.

28. Looking at 1998, for example, reveals that 68 people were executed. Only one death row inmate was granted clemency, a Texas man who "confessed" to 600 murders but was found to be in Florida during the one killing for which he received a death sentence.

29. Stuart Banner notes: "For centuries governors commuted death sentences in significant numbers. That pattern continued for the first two-thirds of the twentieth century. Florida commuted nearly a quarter of its death sentences between 1924 and 1966; North Carolina commuted more than a third between 1909 and 1954. Those figures dropped close to zero under new sentencing schemes." Stuart Banner, *The Death Penalty: An American History* (Cambridge: Harvard University Press, 2002), 291–92.

30. Sarat, *Mercy on Trial,* appendix B.

31. Washington State Office of the Attorney General, *Reprieves, Pardons and Commutations in Death Penalty Cases,* at http://www.atg.wa.gov/deathpenalty/pardons.shtml.

32. Sarat, *Mercy on Trial,* appendix B.

33. Quoted in Salladay, "Clemency: Slim Chance These Days." As Magnus Fiskesjo puts it: "In light of 'domestic' opinion, it is very often not the decision to pardon but the decision not to pardon that best furthers the political standing of the power-holder." Magnus Fiskesjo, *The Thanksgiving Turkey Pardon, the Death of Teddy's Bear, and the Sovereign Exception of Guantanamo* (Chicago: Prickly Paradigm Press, 2003), 46.

34. Paul Cobb argues that "[p]olitical considerations have figured promi-nently in the unwillingness of many governors to be merciful. The popularity of the death penalty suggests to these officials that the safest course of action is to avoid the exercise of their clemency powers." Paul Cobb, "Reviving Mercy in the Structure of Capital Punishment," *Yale Law Journal* 99 (1989): 394.

This is not to say that capital clemency has completely disappeared. It has not. For example, in 2002, "[h]ours before Charlie Alston was scheduled to be exe-cuted in North Carolina, Governor Mike Easley commuted Alston's sentence to life without parole. Although Easley did not give a specific reason for the reprieve, he stated, 'After long and careful consideration of all the facts and circumstances of this case in its entirety, I conclude that the appropriate sentence for the defen-dant is life in prison without parole.' Alston's commutation marks the 2nd time Easley has granted clemency, and the 5th time a North Carolina governor has done so since 1976. During that same time, 47 death row inmates nationally have had their sentences commuted for humanitarian reasons." In Oklahoma, Gover-nor Brad Henry recently granted a request for clemency in the case of Osvaldo Torres, a Mexican foreign national on Oklahoma's death row, in part because of a recent International Court of Justice decision ordering the United States to review the cases of 51 Mexican foreign nationals because they were denied their right to seek consular assistance after their arrest. Henry's "decision to commute Torres' sentence to life in prison without parole marks the first time that the Governor has granted clemency to an individual on death row. In his statement, Henry said the International Court of Justice ruling is binding on U.S. courts, and that the U.S. State Department had contacted his office to urge that he give careful consid-eration to the fact that the U.S. signed the 1963 Vienna Convention on Consular Relations, which ensures access to consular assistance for foreign nationals who are arrested. 'The treaty is also important to protecting the rights of American citizens abroad,' Henry noted." Both quoted in Death Penalty Information Center, "Clemency News and Developments," at http://www.deathpenaltyinfo.org/article. php?scid=13&did=850.

35. Jonathan Simon, *Governing through Crime: The War on Crime and the Transformation of American Governance, 1960–2000* (New York: Oxford Uni-versity Press, 2007). See also Joseph E. Kennedy, "Monstrous Offenders and the Search for Solidarity through Modern Punishment," *Hastings Law Journal* 51 (2000): 829. Kennedy argues that "[t]he breadth and depth of the political con-sensus behind . . . increases in the severity of criminal sentences may be without parallel in contemporary political history" (832).

36. Simon, *Governing through Crime,* chapter 5.

37. Letter from Jonathan Simon to author, June 17, 2004.

38. James Acker and Charles Lanier, "May God—Or the Governor—Have Mercy: Executive Clemency and Executions in Modern Death-Penalty Systems," *Criminal Law Bulletin* 36 (2000): 200.

39. Alan Berlow, "The Texas Clemency Memos," *Atlantic Monthly,* July/August 2003, at http://www.theatlantic.com/issues/2003/07/berlow.htm.

40. Quoted in "Clemency Becoming Rare as Executions Increase," *Corrections Digest* (July 8, 1987): 2.

41. These views have a long history, reaching back at least to the early nineteenth century. However, "the actual record of gubernatorial pardons . . . [in that period] shows that in practice the pardon process was not so cut and dried." Richard Brown, *The Hanging of Ephraim Walker: A Story of Rape, Incest, and Justice in Early America* (Cambridge: Harvard University Press, 2003), 191.

42. *Furman v. Georgia,* 408 U.S. 238 (1976).

43. *Lockett v. Ohio,* 438 U.S. 586 (1978). See also Dahlia Lithwick, "The Crying Game: Should We Decide Capital Punishment with Our Hearts or Our Heads?," *Slate* (December 2, 2004), at http://www.slate.com/id/2110567/.

44. The importance and significance of appellate review is discussed in Anthony J. Casey, "Maintaining the Integrity of Death: An Argument for Restricting a Defendant's Right to Volunteer for Execution at Certain Stages in Capital Proceedings," *American Journal of Criminal Law* 30 (2002): 75. Casey notes: "The restriction most commonly imposed upon waivers of capital proceedings is the mandatory appellate review. According to the Department of Justice, 37 of the 38 states where the death penalty is on the books provide non-waivable mandatory appellate review. The federal government does not provide for non-waivable appellate review. In some of these states the mandatory review is of sentencing only; however, most states have included review of the entire case in their mandatory appeal. . . . .Thus the conviction, as well as the sentence, is normally subject to the mandatory non-waivable appellate review" (87–88). For a more complete discussion of the reasons for the decline of clemency in capital cases, see Sarat, *Mercy on Trial.*

45. Breslin and Howley, "Defending the Politics of Clemency," 239. See also Dinsmore, "Clemency in Capital Cases," and Kobil, "Chance and the Constitution in Capital Clemency Cases," 567, 572. Love notes a similar reluctance at the federal level. Beginning with the Reagan Administration, she says, "the number of pardons each year began to drop off." Love, "Fear of Forgiving," 125, 126. Rita Radostitz, codirector of the Capital Punishment Clinic at the University of Texas and an attorney for Henry Lee Lucas, who was granted clemency in Texas, says about clemency: "I think that clearly a miscarriage of justice should be raised, but in other cases, mercy could also come into play . . . [t]hat's what clemency has historically been about—mercy." Quoted in Salladay, "Clemency: Slim Chance These Days."

46. Imagined as fail safe, clemency may provide the judicial system with an alibi for its fallibility. For more, see Vivian Berger, "*Herrera v. Collins:* The Gateway of Innocence for Death-Sentenced Prisoners Leads Nowhere," *William and Mary Law Review* 35 (1994): 943.

47. Here I am following in the footsteps of Cathleen Burnett's study of clemency in Missouri. See Cathleen Burnett, *Justice Denied: Clemency Appeals in Death Penalty Cases* (Boston: Northeastern University Press, 2002). However, my work differs from hers in several ways. First, instead of Missouri I examine two other states: Texas and Virginia. Second, while Burnett's work concentrates on the way errors at various stages in the legal process are described in clemency petitions, my work provides an account of the narrative conventions and cultural assumptions that they contain and reveal. Third, while Burnett analyzes these documents for their value in pointing out problems in the clemency process ("This study demonstrates that the clemency process is non-functional"; Cathleen Burnett, "Petitions for Life: Executive Clemency in Missouri Death Penalty Cases," *Richmond Journal of Law and the Public Interest* (Spring, 2001), at http://law.richmond.edu/rjolpi/Issues_Archived/2001_Spring_Issue/Burnett.html, 9) and highlighting needed reforms in the death penalty system, I treat them as addressing the present and the future. For another examination of clemency petitions focusing on their value in present-day struggles over capital punishment, see Ayse Bertenthal, Elizabeth Hess, and Clare Pinkert, "Clemency Petitions Show Deep Flaws in Death Penalty," *Chicago Sun-Times,* December 21, 2002.

48. While I have not undertaken a systematic comparison of the pre-clemency litigation of capital cases with the clemency process, other stages in the litigation of those cases may also serve a similar function. For a discussion of that pre-clemency litigation, see Austin Sarat, "Narrative Strategy and Death Penalty Advocacy," *Harvard Civil Rights–Civil Liberties Law Review* 31 (1996): 353.

49. Thus my work is not designed to say anything about the way lawyers or their clients *do or should* think about the clemency process.

50. These periods were the time frame of the data available on clemency petitions in Texas and Virginia in the National Death Penalty Archives at SUNY-Albany (see appendix A in this chapter).

51. Since *Gregg v. Georgia,* 428 U.S. 153 (1976), Oklahoma with 81, Missouri with 66, and Florida with 60 were the closest competitors in this race to execute. Death Penalty Information Center at http://www.deathpenaltyinfo.org/article.php?scid=88did=100.

52. Illinois with 172 and Ohio with 9 were the only states to grant more clemencies than Virginia.

53. Clemency procedures in Texas and Virginia are quite different. While in Virginia the governor has the sole and exclusive authority to grant clemency, Texas is one of eight states in which the governor must have a recommendation of clemency from a board or advisory group before he can act. Nonetheless, in both states, during the period in which the clemency petitions I analyze were filed, the chances of receiving a favorable outcome were slim.

The data on executions are from the Death Penalty Information Center at http://www.deathpenaltyinfo.org/article.php?did=414&scid=8. For the clemency data, see Death Penalty Information Center at http://www.deathpenaltyinfo.org/article.php?did=126&scid=13.

54. Drucilla Cornell, "From the Lighthouse: The Promise of Redemption and the Possibility of Legal Interpretation," *Cardozo Law Review* 11 (1990): 1697. In addition, Jules Lobel argues that "[e]ven when prophetic litigation loses in court, it often functions . . . as an appeal to future generations." Jules Lobel, "Losers, Fools and Prophets: Justice as Struggle," *Cornell Law Review* 80 (1995): 1347.

55. Robert Cover, "The Supreme Court, 1982 Term-Forword: Nomos and Narrative," *Harvard Law Review* 97 (1983): 9.

56. *Id.*, 34.

57. *Id.*

58. *Id.*, 39.

59. Lobel explores the utility of the idea of prophecy to the work of lawyers who serve losing causes. Lobel, "Losers, Fools and Prophets," 1337.

60. Jacques Le Goff, *History and Memory*, trans. Steven Randall and Elizabeth Clamon (New York: Columbia University Press, 1992).

61. Shoshana Felman and Dori Laub, *Testimony: Crises of Witnessing in Literature, Psychoanalysis, and History* (New York: Routledge, 1992), 101. Treating the lawyer for a losing cause as a witness giving testimony suggests that he addressed his work to the community of the future as much as the law of the present. "To testify-before a court of law or before the court of history and of the future," as Felman and Laub contend, "is more than simply to report a fact or an event or to relate what has been lived, recorded and remembered. Memory is conjured here essentially in order to address another, to impress upon a listener, to *appeal* to a community." *Id.*, 204

62. For a discussion of the work of those lawyers, see Austin Sarat, "Between (the Presence of) Violence and (the Possibility of) Justice: Lawyering against Capital Punishment," in *Cause Lawyering Political Commitments and Professional Responsibilities*, ed. Austin Sarat and Stuart Scheingold (New York: Oxford University Press, 2001), 317–48.

63. As Martha Minow suggests, legal rights matter not just because they provide dignity to law's victims, or because they help to mobilize them to undertake political action, but because they provide an opportunity to tell a story that might not otherwise get to be told. Martha Minow, "Interpreting Rights: An Essay for Robert Cover," *Yale Law Journal* 96 (1987): 1860.

64. Pierre Nora, "Between Memory and History: Les Lieux de Memoire," *Representations* 26 (1989): 7. Nora argues: "Modern memory is, above all, archival. It relies entirely on the materiality of the trace, the immediacy of the recording, the visibility of the image" (15).

65. Cover, "Supreme Court, 1982."

66. Felman and Laub, *Testimony.*

67. Robert Gordon, "Undoing Historical Injustice," in *Justice and Injustice in*

Law and Legal Theory, ed. Austin Sarat and Thomas Kearns (Ann Arbor: University of Michigan Press, 1996), 36.

68. *Id.*, 36–37.

69. Drucilla Cornell, "Post-Structuralism, the Ethical Relation, and the Law," *Cardozo Law Review* 9 (1988): 1587, 1628.

70. Lobel, "Losers, Fools and Prophets," 1337.

71. Davis, *Pardon Tales and Their Tellers*, 3, 4.

72. As Burnett puts it: "Clemency petitions are different from other legal appeals in that the statements are neither limited by evidentiary rules of admissibility nor defined by the procedural requirements of jurisdictional precedent." Burnett, "Petitions for Life," 2.

73. Elements of each of these stories are often combined in a clemency petition. Below I describe the central narrative lines and the key cultural assumptions of the petitions I studied. Each of the cases I discuss represents a kind of "ideal type." For a discussion of the procedures used in classifying the petitions, see appendix A in this chapter.

Limiting the analysis to these five cases permits a more in-depth examination of the rhetorical strategies and narrative techniques used in different types of clemency petitions, as well as the way those strategies and techniques are combined in an effort to make a persuasive case for clemency.

74. Lawrence Marshall, "The Innocence Revolution and the Death Penalty," *Ohio State Journal of Criminal Law* 1 (2004): 573–74.

75. Edward Connors, Thomas Lundregan, Neal Miller, and Tom McEwen, *Convicted by Juries, Exonerated by Science: Case Studies in the Use of DNA Evidence to Establish Innocence after Trial* (Washington, D.C.: National Institute of Justice, 1996), 6.

76. In fact, DNA has played a relatively small role in preventing executions of the innocent. Of the 199 people freed from death row between 1973 and 2005, only 14 are attributable to the use of DNA technology. See http://www.deathpenaltyinfo.org/article.php?did=412&scid=6. See also James Liebman, "The New Death Penalty Debate: What's DNA Got to Do With It?" *Columbia Human Rights Law Review* 33 (2002): 541–42.

77. Jennifer Culbert explains that, in the era of DNA, "[j]udgment becomes the legal acknowledgment or recognition of what is simply always already the case. . . . With DNA testing human fallibility is authenticated. Human susceptibility to err is *apparent.*" Jennifer Culbert, *Dead Certainty: The Death Penalty and the Problem of Judgment in Modern Society* (Palo Alto: Stanford University Press, 2008), 112 and 122.

78. *Id.*, 114 and 138.

79. *Id.*, 112.

80. In doing so, it joins two domains that, as Giorgio Agamben suggests, are

conjoined in the present moment, the sacred and the biological. Giorgio Agamben, *Homo Sacer: Sovereign Power and Bare Life,* trans. Daniel Heller-Roazen (Stanford: Stanford University Press, 1998).

81. Burnett, "Petitions for Life," 4.

82. He was not related to Ronald Watkins.

83. While I have no data on clemency petitions in earlier eras, it seems that two things may be produced by the recent decline in the chances of success and narrowing of the grounds on which governors are willing to commute or pardon those sentenced to death. First is an increased legalization and juridification of the discourse of clemency. If governors are going to act as courts of last resort, it is not surprising that petitions speak in and through the language of law rather than displaying a more personal or emotive rhetoric. Second, given the political climate that, at least until recently, surrounded the death penalty, it is not surprising that the discourse of mercy for the condemned has fallen into disfavor.

84. Lobel notes: "Law . . . arises from the clash between the state seeking to enforce its rules and . . . activist communities seeking to create, extend, or preserve an alternative vision of justice." Lobel, "Losers, Fools and Prophets," 1333. See also Anthony Alfieri, "Mitigation, Mercy, and Delay: The Moral Politics of Death Penalty Abolitionists," *Harvard Civil Rights–Civil Liberties Law Review* 31 (1996): 352.

85. Cornell, "Post-Structuralism, the Ethical Relation, and the Law," 1587. Justice, Cornell argues, "is precisely what eludes our full knowledge." We cannot "grasp the Good but only follow it. The Good . . . is a star which beckons us to follow." See also Cornell, "From the Lighthouse," 1697.

86. Judith Butler, "Deconstruction and the Possibility of Justice: Comments on Bernasconi, Cornell, Miller, Weber," *Cardozo Law Review* 11 (1990): 1716. Butler contends that "this horizon of temporality is always to be projected and never fully achieved; this constitutes the double gesture as a persistent promise and withdrawal. . . . Cornell argues that it is necessary to repeat this gesture endlessly and thereby to constitute the posture of vigilance that establishes the openness of a future in which the thought of radical alternity is never completed" (1716).

87. "[L]aw is simultaneously a denial of the ethical in the name of the political and a denial of the political in the name of the ethical." Alison Young and Austin Sarat, "Introduction to 'Beyond Criticism: Law, Power and Ethics,'" *Social and Legal Studies: An International Journal* 3 (1994), 328.

88. Sally Merry, *Getting Justice and Getting Even: Legal Consciousness among Working Class Americans* (Chicago: University of Chicago Press, 1990). See also Austin Sarat, "'. . . The Law Is All Over': Power, Resistance and the Legal Consciousness of the Welfare Poor," *Yale Journal of Law and the Humanities* 2 (1990): 343.

89. Cover, "Supreme Court, 1982," 4, 9. For a collection of Cover's work, see

Martha Minow, Michael Ryan, and Austin Sarat, eds., *Narrative Violence and the Law: The Essays of Robert Cover* (Ann Arbor: University of Michigan Press, 1993).

90. Cover, "Supreme Court, 1982," 4.

91. Robert Cover, "Violence and the Word," *Yale Law Journal* 95 (1986): 1601.

Part III

||||||||||||||||||||||||||||||||||||||||||||||||||||

Reconceptualizing
Miscarriages
of Justice

Chapter 9

||||||||||||||||||||||||||||||||||||||||||||||||||||||

Miscarriage of Justice as Misnomer

Markus D. Dubber

As state action, the penal process might usefully be analyzed from two perspectives, police and law.[1] From the standpoint of police, the penal process is a system for the identification and elimination, or at least reduction, of human risks to the state's police, understood in the traditional sense of good order or welfare.[2] As a species of police, penality is rooted in the state's "police power." By contrast, if one regards the penal process from the perspective of law, it appears as a "criminal justice system" designed to do justice, meting out punishment to offenders for injuries inflicted on victims. Penality as a species of law is derived from the state's power to manifest and protect the essential rights of its constituents.

The notion of a miscarriage of justice (or its apparent synonyms, wrongful conviction and criminal justice error)[3] makes sense only within the context of the latter view of the penal process. The Police Power Model of the penal process does not seek justice; it seeks efficiency, obedience, order.[4] To the extent that the penal process is in operation—if not in ideology—a police institution, talk of miscarriages of justice is beside the point.

What is more, to the extent that the Law Model of the penal process obscures the operation of the penal process as a police system, a focus on miscarriages of justice may perpetuate the alegality, and alegitimacy, of that process.[5] The power to police has always been, and has been designed to be, free from principled constraint. The myth of criminal law as law has cloaked the process in a false pretense of seeking justice. Complaints about miscarriages of justice may contribute to this charade of penal legality.

At the same time, however, appeals to justice may be seen as taking the penal process at its word. Taking the claim to criminal justice at face value, pointing out miscarriages of justice may be seen as subjecting the penal process to the norms it pretends to accept as binding. As part of a general principled critique designed to transform the penal process into the criminal justice system it pretends to be, talk of miscarriages of justice may serve to legitimate penality rather than perpetuate its alegitimacy.

Here it might be useful to consider the relationship between the rule and the exception in the penal process.[6] As long as miscarriages of justice are regarded as exceptions to the rule of justice delivery, then their exposure does little to challenge the legitimatory complacency of the penal process.[7] The problem with miscarriages of justice is not that they are miscarriages or even miscarriages of justice. They are not miscarriages at all because the system does not seek to do justice in the first place. At best, they are miscarriages of police: false positives in a system of risk incapacitation. The problem of mistaken identity thus is not a subsidiary problem within the realm of miscarriages of justice, in that false eyewitness identification may lead to wrongful conviction; misidentification is the problem itself, as labeling (as offensive, or dangerous) is the core task of the penal police process.

Of course, one might strip the inquiry into miscarriages of justice of all normative content. False labeling might then be treated as an administrative problem, with the attendant concerns about the identification of reliable risk factors, the implementation of these factors in various institutional settings, quality control, reliability testing, and so on. The problem with getting the "wrong man," however, is not simply that someone has been mistakenly identified as an offender. The problem is that his conviction and punishment is an injustice, or "wrongful." Wrongful convictions are not simply wrong convictions; they constitute a wrong, qualitatively comparable with the wrong of crime (and, in fact, should give rise to criminal liability absent an applicable defense).[8]

Prescribed solutions for the problem of miscarriages of justice that generate lists of reliability-enhancing proposals in the bureaucratic mode thus are entirely consistent with the view of the penal process as a police system. As a result, they do nothing to challenge the alegality of that system and, in fact, may help perpetuate it.

Taking a broader view of the relationship between rule and exception might lead one not only to challenge the assumption that miscarriages of justice are exceptions within a system dedicated to doing justice but also to reconsider the relationship between the Police Power and Law Models of the penal process. From this perspective, it may appear that the vast majority of cases processed by the system are treated as matters of police, while a small minority of show trials celebrates the legality of the American criminal justice in full bloom. This view, however, also would not be inconsistent with one that regarded the system as a whole as a Police Power system, for once again the theatrical celebration of rules of law in a minuscule proportion of highly visible cases might serve merely to prop up the Law Model as a cover for an essentially alegitimate system.

Just how out of place talk of miscarriages of justice is will depend on just how irrelevant considerations of justice are in the operation—as opposed to the ideological apparatus—of the penal process. Let's have a look.

I. Law, Police, Punishment

Paradoxically, regarding the penal process as a police system is a simple black-letter affair. Whenever American criminal law treatises—or judicial opinions—make a passing reference to the origins of the power to make criminal law, they inevitably hit on the"police power," a term long familiar from American constitutional history.[9] States, we can read again and again, make criminal law (and here little distinction is drawn between the general part and the special part of criminal law—that is, the general principles of criminal liability and the definition of specific offenses) as an exercise of their police power, a power they retained in the federalist system of government as essential markers of their continued sovereignty. States must have the police power, it is said, because without that power they would cease to exist as independent sovereigns. At the same time, the federal government must not have the power to police, because that would identify it as an independent sovereign, as opposed to a government that derives all of its power by delegation from the sovereign member states. The power to police is by definition inherent, essential to the very notion of government itself (which is why, in the end, the federal government, as we'll see shortly, had to end up with the police power, too, if not in name).

The police power is not just essential; it is also essentially unlimited, in means as well as in ends. It encompasses any measure that might be appropriate to advance the goal of good police, where the assessment of appropriateness is a matter for the discretion of the entity wielding the power. Scores of American texts, including judicial opinions and treatises, invoked William Blackstone's definition of "public police and oeconomy" as "the due regulation and domestic order of the kingdom: whereby the individuals of the state, like members of a well-governed family, are bound to conform their general behaviour to the rules of propriety, good neighbourhood, and good manners: and to be decent, industrious, and inoffensive in their respective stations."[10]

Remarkably, and as a testament to the ingrainedness of the notion of police, this view of the police power survived the American Revolution unchallenged. Blackstone's prerevolutionary and very English definition of royal prerogative was quoted verbatim—including its reference to "the kingdom"—well into the twentieth century.[11] The U.S. Supreme Court repeatedly went out of its way to emphasize the vastness of the police power. The *Slaughter-House Cases* announced that the police power "is, and must be from its very nature, incapable of any very exact definition or limitation," a power that safeguards "the security of social order, the life and health of the citizen, the comfort of an existence in a thickly populated community, the enjoyment of private and social life, and the beneficial use of property" and as such "extends to the protection of the lives, limbs, health, comfort, and quiet of all persons, and the protection of all property."[12]

In American constitutional law, identifying a state action as an exercise of the police power amounted to shielding it from principled constitutional scrutiny. With few exceptions—notably the soon disavowed *Lochner v. New York*[13]—the history of American police power jurisprudence is the history of judicial restraint. Pace *Lochner*, by the 1930s, the police power was firmly established as "an idiom of apologetics."[14]

At the same time as state legislation was protected from federal constitutional scrutiny by the application of the "police power" label, federal legislation was doomed by it. The federal government, after all, was not supposed to have any such power, lest the fragile federalist compromise collapse. And so different labels took its place; for example, the commerce power fulfills a similar inoculating function for federal legislation.[15] Nonetheless, observers soon realized that the federal government came to exercise a de facto police power while vehemently denying the de jure possession of that power.

To understand the nature of the police power, and its function in American political and legal discourse, it is helpful to consider its roots in the householder's ancient discretionary power over members of his household.[16] Blackstone's reference to state constituents as "members of a well-governed family" hints at a long tradition of police as a mode of governance that can be traced throughout the history of western government, alongside the parallel, and distinct, mode of governance that eventually gave rise to the modern concept of law.

Aristotle already distinguished between the householder's government of his household in the private sphere—the subject of oeconomics—and the government of householders by other householders in the public sphere—the subject of politics.[17] Household governance was essentially heteronomous, hierarchical, discretionary, efficiency-driven. The householder decided (hopefully wisely) what was best for the household and then (hopefully skillfully) implemented his decisions as he saw fit. Members of the household, be they human, animal, plant, or thing, were resources to be used more or less efficiently. Within his private household, the householder-father enjoyed virtually unlimited discretion. The state's interest was limited to having him prepare private resources for public use, notably in the form of younger males who one day would head households of their own and, as householders, join the public forum of politics.

Politics was defined not by power but by persuasion. It was autonomous where oeconomics was heteronomous; it was egalitarian, formalized, and concerned with right and justice. Householders sought to convince one another, rhetoric was a prized skill, and brute force was an inappropriate means of government, except under conditions of emergency (when an appointed dictator would suspend what later came to be called the rule of law).

Patriarchal household governance continued in Rome, with its highly developed doctrine of *patria potestas,* and throughout the middle ages (with its concept of the householder's peace, or *mund,* which the householder protected by any means he deemed necessary). In the public sphere, householders would represent their household as they deliberated on matters of justice. In this realm, householders were liable for the misdeeds of their household (animate and inanimate alike) insofar as they affected other households.

At home, householders enjoyed virtually unlimited authority to discipline household members, including—in ancient Rome—the power of life and death over members of his *familia.* In the middle ages, the lord's power over his servant was limited only insofar as it deprived the servant of life or limb. Permanent serious injuries or death so minimized the servant's value as a human household resource that their infliction was thought to indicate the householder's unfitness for his position as the maximizer of the welfare of his household. Moreover, and this already marks the emergence of a central governmental household (the royal *familia*), rendering a servant useless through harsh discipline also deprived the macro householder of a human resource, as did homicide (including homicide *se defendendo*, which required an exercise of royal mercy) and aggravated assault (which deprived the victim of a limb, rendering him incapable of military service).

The concept of police marks the point of convergence between the private and political realms of government, or, rather, the transference—or expansion—of one onto the other. The prince who wields the power of police over his subjects rules the state as the Athenian *oikonomos* ruled his *oikos* and the Roman *dominus* his *domus*. The autonomous model of government disappears as an independent mode of governance and instead is integrated into the patriarchal governance of the macro household.

The evolution of a science of police in early modern Europe reflects the consolidation of quasi-patriarchal power in the prince, whose government is subject to scientific rules rather than to principles of justice or right.[18] Of course, the patriarchal prince is free to ignore these scientific rules; they are generated by his advisors, who serve at his discretion and cloak their counsel in scientific authority (a novel source of authority that seeks to supplement and, eventually, to replace divine guidance).[19] Nonetheless, traditional economics—as the science of governing the household (*oikos*) —helps to rationalize discretionary government, notably through the use of statistics (which transform household resources, human or not, into figures, much like William's Domesday Book transformed his newly conquered subjects into taxable entities) and budgets (*Haushalt* in German).

The rise of the project of "political economy"—which comes to encompass even, and especially, Anglo-American political discourses that often resisted the concept of police as foreign—nicely illustrates the combination of the two basic modes of governance, politics and economy. Political economy, as Rousseau pointed out, "is derived from oikos, a house, and nomos, law, and meant originally only the wise and legitimate government of the house for the common good of the whole family." "The meaning of the term," Rousseau continues, "was then extended to the government of that great family, the State."[20]

Note that political economy is a species of economy; politics is integrated into economics, rather than vice versa. The science of police simply transferred the science (or art) of micro economics to the realm of macro government and renamed it "police." Political economy does not simply ignore the political element of state government but places it within the overall context of economic government writ large. Politics does not disappear; it simply is reduced to a version of economics.

In the end, then, political economy differs from police only on the surface. The political in political economy serves only to distinguish macro from micro economics, the governance of the state household from that of the private family. Police retains the concept of economy for private governance and renames it police for public governance.

The Enlightenment then launched a critical enterprise that scrutinized the very foundations of state power, including the power to punish—that most awesome of state powers. The Enlightenment can be seen as a radical revival and expansion of the autonomistic project associated with ancient Athenian politics. This time around, however, every person was autonomous as such; autonomy was privatized, even internalized; householder status was no longer the prerequisite for the capacity for autonomy. Every person, including members of households and quasi-households (the military, churches, schools, estates) was entitled to govern himself (in fact, women, along with the poor, were denied the right to autonomy).

In Europe, the Enlightenment's critical project was brought to bear on the state's power to punish; the critique of criminal law attracted the attention of major enlightenment figures, such as Beccaria, Bentham, Kant, Voltaire, and P. J. A. Feuerbach. In the United States, by contrast, the power to punish escaped scrutiny. Instead, the revolutionary generation accepted without serious scrutiny the traditional notion that the power to punish was inherent in the power to police, a power that was essential to the notion of sovereignty itself and as such was simply passed on from one sovereign (the king) to another (the people, in theory, and largely the executive, in fact).[21]

While European thinkers struggled to legalize the police power—notably, the police power in its most intrusive form, the power to punish —Americans saw no reason to challenge the state's authority to deprive some of its citizens of the very life, liberty, and property it ostensibly existed to protect. Consequentialist and deontological theories of punishment (represented by Beccaria and Bentham, on one hand, and Kant and Hegel, on the other) presented different efforts to develop a penal process that was consistent with the notion of the punished as fundamentally similar to the punisher (and the nonpunished, more generally). In Bentham's system, the pain and pleasure experienced (or anticipated) by the object of punishment deserves as much consideration, and weighs as heavily, as that experienced by the punisher (or the victim). The consequentialist balance of costs and benefits is radically uninterested in distinctions among persons, except insofar as they affect a person's experience of pleasure or pain. Likewise, the deontological insistence on treating every person (including those charged and convicted of a criminal offense) with equal dignity, and not merely as the means to an end, is driven by the Enlightenment's insistence on the fundamental equality of persons, regardless of their status as householder or household member.

In the United States, by contrast, the power to punish remained an instance of the power to police and, as such, beyond principled scrutiny. The only federal constitutional amendment (mimicked in state constitutions throughout the land) that might be, but in the end was not, interpreted as a limitation on the state's power to punish—the Eighth Amendment's proscription of "cruel and unusual punishments"—was not inconsistent with the traditional view of punishment as police. Cruel and unusual punishments had long been beyond the scope of the householder's traditional power to discipline recalcitrant or otherwise offensive household members because they reflected a character that rendered the punisher unfit for his patriarchal position. Cruelty revealed a malignant heart, a meanness of spirit that also marked the murderer and, more generally, the felon (originally, someone who violated his obligation of fealty to his lord). The cruel disciplinarian thus was better suited to receive discipline than to inflict it; as a slave to his passions, he lacked the very discipline he claimed to instill.

To this day, the foundation of the power to punish in that idiom of apologetics, the power to police, has not been seriously questioned, or for that matter, examined. No constitutional law of crime and punishment has ever developed.[22] U.S. penal policy has remained relentlessly consequentialist, despite occasional scholarly urgings to the contrary ("just deserts"), which are then promptly integrated into an incapacitationist discourse about eliminating human risks. Some of these consequentialist programs appear more benign than others (rehabilitationism vs. incapacitationism), but none of them treats the object of punishment as a person capable of self-government. Instead, the object of deterrence, rehabilitation, or, most bluntly, incapacitation is the potential offender who is scared, treated, or restrained into submission to state authority.

The Enlightenment spirit of Bentham's consequentialist project (which merely works out the broad program sketched by Beccaria in *Of Crimes and Punishments*) is nowhere to be found in the offense and offender elimination schemes that have characterized American penality and that today leave the United States with over 6 million persons under penal supervision. As an exercise of patriarchal police power, the United States today claims the Roman householder's power of life and death over household members, relying primarily on a paradigmatic instrument of household discipline—imprisonment as a form of close household supervision that infantilizes inmates in the very act of discipline.

II. Penal Police and Criminal Justice

The police roots of American punishment manifest themselves throughout the penal process. While the Law Model continues to drive the ideology of the penal process—domestically as well as globally, as the cornerstone of the dogma of American superiority in criminal justice[23]—the Police Model captures much of the actual operation of that process, as well as many of its less reflective, lower-order norms.

To begin with the formal prerequisites for criminal liability, the concept of jurisdiction remains firmly rooted in the police notion that the paradigmatic victim of crime is the state. Territorial jurisdiction is the jurisdiction of the householder over his household, which in the case of the macro householder (the king, the people, the state) is defined by territory, just as that of the micro householder (the slave owner, the medieval lord, the Roman *paterfamilias*) was spatially defined by the borders of the plantation, the estate, or the house, where the householder acted to protect and enforce his peace. Little attention is given to the question of the applicability of another jurisdiction's penal norms; the peace of the relevant territory has been disturbed and the state-householder is entitled, though of course not obligated, to use his disciplinary power.

The police concept of crime as offense against a sovereign, rather than against an individual, also drives the doctrine of double jeopardy, both within and across jurisdictions. Across jurisdictions, the doctrine of dual sovereignty respects the police power of each state. The violation of a state-issued norm amounts to an act of disobedience: literally, an offense against the sovereign (so that the prohibition of placing someone twice in jeopardy for "the same offense" does not apply). Each state is free to punish any offense against its householder authority; to suggest that only one state may discipline offenders against its sovereignty when another state's norm also has been violated would fly in the face of the latter state's power to police its territory.

The notion of the king or state as the ultimate victim of crime is central to police penality. All offenses in the end are police offenses. Rather than hovering on the outskirts of criminal law as exceptions to the rule of traditional crime, police (or regulatory or malum prohibitum) offenses are the rule of police penality. There are no victimless crimes under a police regime, not because every offense can be connected to the possibility of someone suffering some harm sometime in the future but because every offense is a victimful crime for the simple reason that the notion of a victimless crime is an oxymoron in a system of penality that regards every crime as an offense against the state insofar as it violates a state command.

The idea of a "victims' rights movement" is therefore entirely inconsistent with a Police Power model—the model is not concerned with protecting victims' rights; it is, instead, concerned with disciplining disobedients.[24] Thus, the victims' rights movement serves to perpetuate the fiction that the penal process is a criminal justice system concerned with protecting individual rights, of victims and defendants alike (though there may be disagreement about whether the protection of rights is a zero sum game and whether victims' rights deserve more protection than defendants', or vice versa).

Under the Police Power Model, victimless crimes in fact are preferable to victimful ones, since they remove an obstacle to the assertion of state authority. The penal process can operate far more efficiently without personal victims, who may be, and often enough are, unreliable and even unsympathetic. Victims gum up the process, through their insistence that they stay informed of criminal proceedings against "their" offender, that they be consulted on plea negotiations, that they provide victim impact statements, through their memory lapses, and so on.

The paradigmatic crime of modern American police penality is possession, the victimless crime par excellence, which replaced vagrancy as the policing offense of choice (though vagrancy is attempting to stage a comeback; see *Chicago v. Morales*).[25] Possession offenses—individually and in their totality—provide state officials with a powerful and convenient device for the identification and elimination of individuals deemed offensive.[26] Easy to detect, easy to prove, and potentially devastating in effect (with punishments up to life imprisonment without parole for simple possession),[27] possession offenses are the ideal threat elimination tool in the Police Power Model of the penal process. (Possession offenses, as we'll see shortly, also operate under the radar screen of traditional principles of criminal liability, such as actus reus, mens rea, and defenses, removing formal obstacles to conviction.)

The legality principle—the most explicit attempt to "legalize" state punishment by bringing it under "the rule of law"—has no place in the Police Power Model. At best, the components of the legality principle—specificity, prospectivity, and, more generally, notice—are guidelines for more efficient government. Specific commands are easier to obey; commands that are not prospective cannot be obeyed at all (though they can be useful in eliminating undesirables, at least in states too weak to do so openly), nor can commands given without sufficient notice.

Possession replaced vagrancy as the police sweep offense when vagrancy ran afoul of the specificity requirement, or so it seems. While possession offenses on their face appear to be specific enough, they merely expose the hollowness of the specificity requirement. To begin with, vagrancy was problematic, not because it was vague but because it was broad and, most important, because it was blunt. Vagrancy was explicit about its policing function—it did not pretend to comply with traditional principles of criminal law (though just how traditional these principles are seems doubtful, given that vagrancy traces itself back at least to the fourteenth century and, in fact, the text of the vagueness ordinance in question in the best known vagueness case, *Papachristou v. City of Jacksonville*,[28] was taken verbatim from an old English statute). Vagrancy listed types, rather than conduct; it listed vagrants. Moreover, it listed many different types of vagrant, casting a deliberately wide net that invited charges of overbreadth (charges that were never substantiated and instead cloaked in unconvincing vagueness arguments):

> rogues, vagabonds, dissolute persons who go about begging, common gamblers, persons who use juggling or unlawful games or plays, common drunkards, common night walkers, thieves, pilferers or pickpockets, traders in stolen property, lewd, wanton and lascivious persons, keepers of gambling places, common railers and brawlers, persons wandering or strolling around from place to place without any lawful purpose or object, habitual loafers, disorderly persons, persons neglecting all lawful business and habitually spending their time by frequenting houses.

Possession offenses are more subtle, but no less broad, or vague, or sweeping than vagrancy. They speak not in terms of types; they tend to be short, and they soberly set out the elements of the offense. But, in fact, possession also turns on types, though in a less blatant way. Types enter not into the definition of possession offenses (with the notable exception of felon-in-possession offenses) but in the myriad status-based "exemptions" that exclude certain types (e.g., "persons in the military service of the state of New York," "police officers," "peace officers," "persons in the military or other service of the United States," "persons employed in fulfilling defense contracts with the government of the United States or agencies thereof," etc.) from the scope of the technical definition of a given possession offense,[29] including compound possession of a weapon with the intent to use it unlawfully against another.[30]

Moreover, the true policing power of possession offenses lies in the concept of constructive possession, which is variously defined as having, or being in a position to exercise, dominion or control over contraband (i.e., an object possession of which is prohibited).[31] The notion of constructive possession is so vague (in the sense of not giving sufficient notice to potential offenders as to the scope of the prohibition *and* in the sense of not providing state officials with meaningful guidance regarding its implementation) and so broad as to run afoul of the spirit of the specificity requirement, if not its letter. While vagrancy wore its breadth on its sleeve (listing any number of vagrant types), possession offenses are differentiated into a complex system of offenses, which add up to a vast possession prohibition far wider and finer than the net even the single most imaginative vagrancy statute could hope to weave.

Possession offenses criminalize actual and constructive possession, simple and compound possession (including an element of intent to use); there is unlawful possession and criminal possession; there is possession of weapons (guns, knives, clubs, etc.), dangerous instruments, drugs (and drug paraphernalia), stolen property, forged checks, burglary tools, and so on. At the same time, possession is an evidentiary tool; simple possession may be presumptive evidence of compound possession (with intent to use),[32] as well as larceny. Possession itself may be established through broad presumptions based on presence near contraband.[33]

Vagueness, in a police regime, in fact may prove expedient. Much of modern federal criminal law is driven by vague criminal statutes applied by courts that view themselves as participants in a concerted effort to eliminate criminal threats that otherwise would escape penal discipline.

Prime examples are RICO and the federal mail fraud statute. Their very vagueness makes them the sort of flexible measure that the holder of the power to police must be free to wield in the name of crime control.[34]

In a police regime, one would expect that prospectivity is treated as cavalierly as specificity, as both are but guidelines that serve the ends of government rather than principles rooted in minimum requirements of legitimacy.[35] In fact, the prohibition of retroactivity is said not to apply to judicial criminal lawmaking (which remains subject merely to a largely illusory notice requirement associated with the due process clause),[36] changes in once-mandatory and now-advisory sentencing guidelines,[37] or intrusive exercises of state police power labeled civil, rather than criminal, including the indefinite incarceration of offenders classified as "sexually violent predators"[38] and the registration and notification requirements triggered by the classification as a certain category of sex offender.[39]

The general notice requirement amounts to a constructive notice requirement, abandoning a meaningful publicity requirement and, in effect, imposing an impossible duty to keep tabs on the continuous production of penal norms in all branches of government[40]—including assessing the continued precedential force of prior judicial decisions.[41] Ignorance of law is no defense: even a good-faith effort to identify and apply the applicable norms does not preclude criminal liability, or rather the state's authority to impose penal discipline.[42]

The discretion to choose the proper response, if any, to a norm violation plays an important role in the operation of the penal police regime.[43] The penal police system has no room for a meaningful principle of proportionate punishment (in quality or quantity)[44] or for a legality principle in the strict, continental, sense of a duty to prosecute all provable cases.[45] The American penal process is essentially discretionary. Ignorance of law, then, is not a defense as of right, but a matter of police; that is, it applies only to those whom the state identifies as insufficiently disobedient to require penal discipline.[46]

Ignorance of law is not the only "defense" that amounts to a mere discretionary guideline. So does every traditional ("common law") principle of criminal liability.

The act requirement, as a requirement rather than a guideline, is out of place in a police regime. Events, including acts, are significant only insofar as they manifest offensiveness that requires—or may require—penal discipline. There is no need, however, to await the acting out of a recalcitrant attitude; any sufficiently reliable evidence of a recalcitrant attitude will do.

If a police regime is to have an act requirement at all—so as to maintain the veneer of legality, to the extent keeping up that veneer proves useful to a state that fosters an ideology of legality for the sake of stability—a broad definition of act, perhaps as a "bodily movement," would do.[47] In this way, any offensive act (disrespectful behavior toward, or disobedience of, a state official, suspicious or "furtive" movements) can be cited as a ground of penal interference.

Nothing better illustrates the fluidity of the act requirement than possession, the paradigmatic policing tool. Possession does not fit even within the broadest definition of act, as a bodily movement. Possession is a status, a relation between a possessor and the possessed. It is not an act. Code drafters who insisted on retaining the act requirement solved the problem of actless possession offenses by codificatory fiat: they declared possession to be an act (usually either by recasting it as the act of receiving or retaining, or failing to discontinue possession of the object in question).[48] Possession thus once again demonstrates its superiority to vagrancy as a policing tool; it remains within the traditional principles of criminal liability, if only in form, but not in substance. Being a vagabond flies in the face of the act requirement; being in possession does not, provided being in possession is defined as acting.

Insofar as possession offenses are cast as failure-to-dispossess offenses, they also illustrate the irrelevance of the distinction between act and omission, another line the act requirement is often said to guard.[49] For purposes of detecting individuals offensive to the state who might require penal discipline—"offenders," for short—the distinction between act and omission is no more pertinent than that between act and status. In fact, it is the status of offensiveness that generates the need to interfere; likewise, it is the failure to comply with state commands that manifests offensiveness. Unlike traditional omission liability, which insists on clearly defined duties before their violation might be criminalized, a police regime sees no need to identify specific duties, the violation of which might trigger penal sanctions. The entire penal system is designed to enforce the duty to obey state commands. It is this duty that every offense violates; so obvious and fundamental is this duty that anyone claiming not to be familiar with it thereby identifies herself as someone in need of penal discipline. Moreover, to require the state to spell out the duty to obey its commands would undermine the very authority that punishment for violations of this duty seeks to reassert.

A penal police regime likewise has little use for that other bulwark of traditional Anglo-American criminal law doctrine, mens rea. The "disappearance" of mens rea has long been bemoaned by criminal law commentators, but inquiries into mens rea as modes of culpability are simply irrelevant in a system unconcerned with culpability. Offensiveness might be measured in degrees, so that the various types of mens rea—represented, since the Model Penal Code, as a progression from negligence through recklessness and knowledge to purpose or intent—might be reinterpreted as increasing levels of offensiveness, from the clueless norm violator to the brazen intentional offender. But already the insistence on a predefined mens rea element interferes with the discretion typical of a penal police regime. The objective norm violation itself identifies the violator as presumptively offensive and therefore in need of discipline treatment; it is then up to the state to determine whether penal disciplinary is appropriate and, if so, what quality and quantity of sanction is indicated.

Even when some mens rea element is retained in the offense definition, the state's burden of proof on that element can be eased through evidentiary presumptions (recall the use of presumptions to transform proof of presence to proof of constructive possession and then to proof of knowing constructive possession) or by simply declaring certain types of evidence out of bounds (insanity[50] or intoxication[51]).

Inchoate offenses (attempt, solicitation, conspiracy, facilitation, possession) place particular emphasis on mens rea—since they do not require the commission of the actus reus specified in the crime definition. In a penal police regime, inchoate offenses proliferate as early interference—long before the infliction of harm against another person—may be necessary to assert the state's authority. After all, conduct may be offensive to the state long before it harms another person. The harm under a penal police regime has already been done; in this sense, inchoate offenses are no more inchoate than victimless offenses are victimless.

The doctrine of inchoate offenses, at least since the Model Penal Code, has been remarkably, and unusually, explicit about its focus on the elimination of threats.[52] In this regard, inchoate offenses are the rule in a penal police regime, rather than the exception, just as, notwithstanding the act requirement, status and omission liability are the rule, not the exception, and notwithstanding the old saw, *actus non facit reum nisi mens sit rea* —strict liability is the rule, not the exception.

Similar reversals of the pattern of rule and exception also appear in the realm of criminal procedure. There the celebrated feature of the American criminal process, the jury trial, in fact appears in only a small minority of cases.[53] The American criminal process is a plea bargaining process dominated by the prosecutor, a state official with unlimited discretionary power to decide whether and what to charge. Whatever guidelines may inform the prosecutor's actions are self-generated and self-enforced, informal, unwritten. Plea bargaining may be subject to local and historical patterns, but it is not governed by legal rules. Following the guilty plea, the convicted defendant faces another state official, the judge, whose sentencing discretion is unconstrained by legal rules, though it may be subject to advisory guidelines.

Once sentenced, the convict enters the final stage of the penal process, the infliction of punishment, which—in the United States—is dominated by the sanction of imprisonment. The 2 million prison inmates—with another 4 million parolees and probationers on the verge of imprisonment in case of a violation of the conditions of their supervised release—occupy institutions that traditionally followed a quasi-familial model, with the warden serving as either father, military superior, spiritual leader, factory supervisor, or plantation owner. The state, having failed to police offenders sufficiently in the macro household within its jurisdiction, assigns them to smaller household units, so as to better supervise and discipline them through its designees, the warden and his representatives, the prison guards. It makes no difference whether these designees are themselves state officials or deputized private individuals or entities; the prison's mission is to eliminate human threats, by removing and putting them (literally) in their place. Neither the public nor the private prison is concerned with doing justice; either will do as a warehouse.

For some offenders, merely putting them in their place (i.e., humiliating them) may suffice. Here the state may choose to use explicit public shaming sanctions (as opposed to implicit and private ones, as in prison).[54]

Then again, some offenders are so offensive in their violation of key state norms—notably the norm against intentional killing and treason as a direct intentional act of disloyalty toward the state itself (a macro version of the abominable offense of petit treason)[55]—that no removal is long and strict, and no humiliation complete, enough. These ultimate offenders must be eliminated altogether to reassert the state's superior authority. So foreign is the notion of autonomy to the state's execution of capital punishment (execution of punishment in its purest and bluntest form), the modern manifestation of the Roman householder's *vitae necisque potestas* (power of life and death)[56] over members of his household, that it cannot countenance death row inmates' attempts to hasten their own demise by abandoning appeals. In a penal police regime, the condemned man cannot be permitted to transform the act of execution into an exercise of his right to choose the time and manner of his death, and thereby to transform the ultimate act of humiliation into the ultimate act of self-determination.[57]

III. Miscarriages of Justice as False Positives

Once the penal process is seen as a police regime, miscarriages of justice are either impossible or irrelevant. There can be errors, of course, but they are not errors of justice since the system does not seek to mete out justice. Put another way, all errors are "harmless" insofar as harm is understood as a violation of some right on the defendant's part not to be "wrongly" convicted or punished, or even mislabeled.[58] An error of penal classification is harmful only insofar as it is so egregious as to undermine the state's effort to assert its authority because the only relevant harm is harm to the state, the paradigmatic victim of the penal police process.

Let's assume, however, that false positives are undesirable even in a police regime (or no more desirable than false negatives). Miscarriages of justice as false positives (or negatives) are errors of bureaucratic misclassification. It might be prudent to minimize classification errors, but even with a few errors of classification here and there, the accurary of the classification system as a whole is still close enough for government work. A good-faith classification effort is all that is required; consider as a model the classification system for sex offenders set out in registration and notification statutes.[59]

Now, as with any discretionary police system, even miscarriages of justice as false positives are at least theoretically significant at the extreme margin. The medieval lord was not entitled to destroy his servant's value as a human resource (also to the macro householder) by depriving him of life or limb. Likewise, a prosecutor has unlimited discretion when it comes to deciding whether and how to respond to offenses against the state's sovereignty, but malicious prosecution might reveal him as incapable of self-government in the face of overwhelming malice and therefore unfit for his disciplinary—and classificatory—post.[60]

Without a fundamental reorientation of the penal process, pointing out miscarriages of justice nibbles at the irrelevant margins of an ajust police regime. Within the framework of a penal process aimed at doing justice (to suspects, offenders, and victims), a thorough analysis of miscarriages of justice would extend not only to wrongful convictions but also to wrongful acquittals and, more broadly, to all aspects of the penal process (or at least the criminal process narrowly speaking, including the imposition of norms and the infliction of sanctions for their violation), including decisions to investigate (or not) and to prosecute (or not).[61]

Moreover, critical analysis must extend beyond the criminal process to reach substantive criminal law as well, encompassing the entire penal process.[62] For a focus on miscarriages of justice might otherwise reinforce the process fetishism common in American legal and political discourse; the elimination of wrongful convictions does not, by itself, transform the penal process into a criminal justice system. Procedural perfection cannot cure substantive illegitimacy.

NOTES

1. On the concept of police in general, and the distinction between police and law in particular, see Markus D. Dubber, *The Police Power: Patriarchy and the Foundations of American Government* (New York: Columbia University Press, 2005). The place of the police concept in various disciplinary discourses—including Michel Foucault's concept of governmentality and Giorgio Agamben's recent work on sovereignty—is explored in Markus D. Dubber and Mariana Valverde, eds., *The New Police Science: The Police Power in Domestic and International Governance* (Stanford: Stanford University Press, 2006), and Markus D. Dubber and Mariana Valverde, eds., *Police and the Liberal State* (Stanford: Stanford University Press, 2008).

2. For a classic definition of police in American jurisprudence, see *Slaughter-House Cases*, 83 U.S. 36 (1873) at 49–50 ("the security of social order, the life and health of the citizen, the comfort of an existence in a thickly populated community, the enjoyment of private and social life, and the beneficial use of property").

3. These concepts tend to be used interchangeably; for example, Richard A. Leo, "Rethinking the Study of Miscarriages of Justice: Developing a Criminology of Wrongful Conviction," *Journal of Contemporary Criminal Justice* 21 (2005): 201.

4. The Police Power and Law Models are compared with Herbert Packer's Due Process and Crime Control Models in Markus D. Dubber, "The Possession Paradigm: The Special Part and the Police Power Model of the Criminal Process," in *Defining Crimes: Essays on the Criminal Law's Special Part*, ed. R. A. Duff and Stuart Green (Oxford: Oxford University Press, 2005), 91–93.

5. The police power discourse may be alegitimate, but it needn't be arational. Compare Markus D. Dubber, "Recidivist Statutes as Arational Punishment," *Buf-*

falo Law Review 43 (1995): 689 (arational penal policy), with Dubber, *Police Power,* 180–89 (internal rationality of police governance).

6. See also Patricia Ewick, chapter 10 in this volume.

7. On the long pedigree of this complacency, see Markus D. Dubber, "'An Extraordinarily Beautiful Document': Jefferson's Bill for Proportioning Crimes and Punishments and the Challenge of Republican Punishment," in *Modern Histories of Crime and Punishment,* ed. Markus D. Dubber and Lindsay Farmer (Stanford: Stanford University Press, 2007), 115.

8. It is typical of the American penal police system that the criminal liability of state actors is rarely, if ever, explored. Consider also the example of entrapment, which functions as a discretionary, controversial, and awkward defense for the entrapped rather than as the foundation of criminal liability for the (official) entrapper. Jacqueline E. Ross, "Impediments to Transnational Cooperation in Undercover Policing: A Comparative Study of the United States and Italy," *American Journal of Comparative Law* 52 (2005): 569.

9. For example, *Foucha v. Louisiana,* 504 U.S. 71 (1992) at 80; Wayne R. LaFave and Austin W. Scott, Jr., *Substantive Criminal Law,* 2nd ed. (St. Paul, Minn.: West, 1986), § 2.10.

10. William Blackstone, *Commentaries on the Laws of England,* vol. 4 (Oxford: Oxford University Press, 1769), 162.

11. In criminal law, the police power was cited as the *courts'* authority to recognize "common law misdemeanors." See, for instance, the criminal law textbook standard *Commonwealth v. Keller,* 35 D. and C.2d 615 (Pa. Ct. Com. Pleas 1964) (indecent disposition of a dead body), which quotes Blackstone's definition of police.

12. *Slaughter-House Cases* at 49–50.

13. *Lochner v. New York,* 198 U.S. 45 (1905).

14. Walton H. Hamilton and Carlton C. Rodee, "Police Power," in *Encyclopedia of the Social Sciences,* vol. 12 (1933), 190 (quoted in William J. Novak, "Common Regulation: Legal Origins of State Power in America," *Hastings Law Journal* 45 (1994): 1082 n.58).

15. Unless the Supreme Court decides—and this is a recent development— that an apparent exercise of the commerce clause is, in fact, an exercise of the nonexistent police power. See *United States v. Lopez,* 514 U.S. 549 (1995).

16. For a detailed version of this story, see Dubber, *Police Power.*

17. See generally D. Brendan Nagle, *The Household as the Foundation of Aristotle's Polis* (Cambridge: Cambridge University Press, 2006).

18. See generally Dubber and Valverde, *New Police Science*; Dubber, *Police Power,* 47–62.

19. Pasquale Pasquino, "Spiritual and Earthly Police: Theories of the State in Early-Modern Europe," in *The New Police Science: The Police Power in Domestic*

and International Governance, ed. Markus D. Dubber and Mariana Valverde (Stanford: Stanford University Press, 2006), 42.

20. Jean-Jacques Rousseau, *Discourse on Political Economy* in *On the Social Contract with Geneva Manuscript and Political Economy,* ed. Roger D. Masters and trans. Judith R. Masters (New York: St. Martin's, 1978 [1755]), 209.

21. Dubber, "Extraordinarily Beautiful Document."

22. Markus D. Dubber, "Toward a Constitutional Law of Crime and Punishment," *Hastings Law Journal* 55 (2004): 509.

23. Cf. Mary L. Dudziak, chapter 1 in this volume (U.S. rights ideology nurtured internationally, despite deviations in the American South).

24. Markus D. Dubber, *Victims in the War on Crime: The Use and Abuse of Victims' Rights* (New York: New York University Press, 2002).

25. *Chicago v. Morales,* 527 U.S. 41 (1999); see also Tracey Meares and Dan Kahan, "The Wages of Antiquated Procedural Thinking: A Critique of *Chicago v. Morales,*" *University of Chicago Legal Forum* 1998 (1998): 197.

26. Markus D. Dubber, "Policing Possession: The War on Crime and the End of Criminal Law," *Journal of Criminal Law and Criminology* 91 (2002): 829.

27. *Harmelin v. Michigan,* 501 U.S. 957 (1991).

28. *Papachristou v. City of Jacksonville,* 405 U.S. 156 (1972).

29. N.Y. Penal Law § 265.20.

30. *People v. Desthers,* 73 Misc. 2d 1085, 343 N.Y.S.2d 887 (Criminal Court of the City of New York 1973) (N.Y. City police officers immune from prosecution for possession of a blackjack with intent to use unlawfully against another).

31. N.Y. Penal Law § 10.00(8).

32. *Id.,* § 265.15.

33. *Id.*

34. *United States v. Maze,* 414 U.S. 395 (1974) at 405 (Burger, C. J., dissenting); Dan M. Kahan, "Three Conceptions of Federal Criminal-Lawmaking," *Buffalo Criminal Law Review* 1 (1997): 5. On the flexibility of vagueness's interpretive/judicial cousin, the "rule" of lenity, see Dan M. Kahan, "Lenity and Federal Common Law Crimes," *Supreme Court Review* 1994 (1994): 345.

35. Dan M. Kahan, "Some Realism about Retroactive Criminal Lawmaking," *Roger Williams Law Review* 2 (1997): 95.

36. *Rogers v. Tennessee,* 532 U.S. 451 (2001).

37. *United States v. Demaree,* 459 F.3d 791 (7th Cir. 2006).

38. *Kansas v. Hendricks,* 521 U.S. 346 (1997).

39. *Smith v. Doe,* 538 U.S. 84 (2003).

40. *United States v. Casson,* 434 F.2d 415 (D.C.Cir.1970).

41. *Rogers.*

42. *People v. Marrero,* 69 N.Y.2d 382 (1987).

43. One of the more explicit instances of discretionary judgment is the sovereign's exercise of the pardon power. Cf. Austin Sarat, chapter 8 in this volume.

44. Dubber, "Toward a Constitutional Law," 536–40; Douglas A. Berman, chapter 6 in this volume.

45. German Code of Criminal Procedure § 152; see generally Markus D. Dubber and Mark Kelman, *American Criminal Law* (New York: Foundation Press, 2005), 102–7.

46. Cf. Dan M. Kahan, "Ignorance of Law Is a Defense—But Only for the Virtuous," *Michigan Law Review* 96 (1997): 127.

47. Model Penal Code § 1.13(2). On the Model Penal Code as policing tool, see Dubber, *Victims in the War on Crime*.

48. Model Penal Code § 2.01(1) and (4); N.Y. Penal Law §§ 15.00(2), 15.10.

49. Dubber and Kelman, *American Criminal Law*, 256–77.

50. *Clark v. Arizona*, 548 U.S. (2006).

51. *Montana v. Egelhoff*, 518 U.S. 37 (1996).

52. *People v. Dlugash*, 41 N.Y.2d 725 (1977).

53. The problem of miscarriages of justice in these few, but symbolic, cases is explored in Daniel Givelber, chapter 5 in this volume.

54. *United States v. Gementera*, 379 F.3d 596 (9th Cir. 2004); see also Dan M. Kahan and Eric A. Posner, "Shaming White-Collar Criminals: A Proposal for Reform of the Federal Sentencing Guidelines," *Journal of Law and Economics* 42 (1999): 365.

55. Dubber, *Police Power*, 26–30.

56. John Crook, "Patria Potestas," *Classical Quarterly* 17 (1967): 113.

57. See *Comer v. Schriro*, 463 F.3d 934 (9th Cir. 2006), rev'd en banc, 480 F.3d 960 (2007).

58. See the judicial soliloquy on harmless error doctrine captured in Robert Weisberg, chapter 3 in this volume.

59. Wayne A. Logan, "Liberty Interests in the Preventive State: Procedural Due Process and Sex Offender Community Notification Laws," *Journal of Criminal Law and Criminology* 89 (1999): 1167. On earlier efforts to develop comprehensive classification schemes for purposes of selective incapacitation, see Franklin E. Zimring and Gordon Hawkins, *Incapacitation: Penal Confinement and the Restraint of Crime* (New York: Oxford University Press, 1995); William Spelman, *Criminal Incapacitation* (New York: Plenum Press, 1994).

60. A prison guard similarly enjoys wide latitude in disciplining inmates, unless he displays "malice or sadism." *Hudson v. McMillian*, 503 U.S. 1 (1992). The formalized system of military discipline may provide a useful illustration of the guidelines structuring the exercise of discretion in a complex quasi-patriarchal police regime (so-called military law). Linda Ross Meyer, chapter 7 in this volume.

61. For example, Brian Forst, *Errors of Justice: Nature, Sources, and Remedies* (Cambridge: Cambridge University Press, 2004); see also Richard Nobles and David Schiff, *Understanding Miscarriages of Justice: Law, the Media, and the*

Inevitability of Crisis (Oxford: Oxford University Press, 2000); Berman, chapter 6 in this volume (calling for critique of "over-punishment" as miscarriage of justice).

62. Dubber, "Toward a Constitutional Law of Crime and Punishment."

Chapter 10

||||||||||||||||||||||||||||||||||||||||||||||||||||||

The Scale of Injustice

Patricia Ewick

And what of everyday life? Everything here is calcu-
lated because everything is numbered: money, minutes, meters, kilogram's, calories . . . ; and not only objects but also living thinking creatures, for there exists
a demography of animals and of people as well as of
things. Yet people are born, live and die. They live well
or ill; but they live in everyday life, where they make or
fail to make a living either in the wider sense of surviving or not surviving, or just surviving or living their
lives to the full. It is in everyday life that they rejoice
and suffer; here and now.
    —Henri Lefebvre, *Everyday Life in the Modern World*

Some (infra-state, local) legal orders are too close to
everyday reality to be viewed as a fact of law. Other
(supra-state, world) legal orders are too remote from
everyday reality to be viewed as a law of fact.
    —Boaventura de Sousa Santos, "Law:
            A Map of Misreading. Toward a
            Postmodern Conception of Law

The phrase "miscarriage of justice" connotes a failing of monumental
scale. First, the phrase suggests an event—a decision, a verdict, an act
—that is exceptional, a singular betrayal of the established ideals and
practices of law. The word "miscarriage" suggests an untoward event, an

unexpected interruption in an otherwise unfolding of a process. A "miscarriage of justice" is a derailment, as if justice is the default category. The phrase also conveys the gravity of this failing or derailment. When we speak of a "miscarriage of justice" we imagine lives are shattered and destroyed, freedoms lost, and cherished ideals undermined: an innocent man is condemned; another is stopped and searched solely because of his race; a victim of sexual abuse is ignored or shunned.

Tragically, such monumental failings occur regularly. But the spectacular, singular, and exceptional failings indexed by that phrase do not exhaust the universe of injustices. Particularly, in the contemporary world of neoliberal law, hyperrationalized governance, and global economies, power often operates both from a distance and yet, at the same time, through the finer circuitries of social life.[1] In this world, individuals are part of shifting and overlapping networks rather than role-based relationships. Law exists at multiple, parallel planes.[2] As a result, injustices often occur from a distance and, simultaneously, at a smaller scale; and responsibility for redressing systemic injuries is shifting and vague. Woven into the operation of markets and bureaucracies, embedded into protocols and standard procedures, the scope of such injustices is wide and deep. Such injustices are frequent, systemic, and impersonal. Their consequences are often erosive rather than violent; they are cumulative rather than singular. In other words, as the scalar resolution of power shifts, the ability to apprehend its operation from the ground of everyday interaction diminishes. Finally, because it becomes increasingly difficult to name an event as unjust, to attribute agency or motive, or even calculate injury, these mundane injustices often go unrecognized and thus unremedied, although not unfelt. In this essay, I explore the shape and effects of such mundane and unrecognized injustices.

Justice, Injustice, and Power

The connections that exist among law, power, and justice are abundant, obvious, and complex. Whereas in many social institutions, power lurks, submerged within dominant and often competing discourses of enlightenment, love, or benefaction, within legal institutions the operation of power is rarely disguised or denied by those who deploy it. In acts of surveillance, confiscation, detention, incarceration, reformation, and execution, the law claims for itself the right to commit acts of violence and transgression that would otherwise be forbidden. Yet its power is not limitless. Within the official discourse, justice demarcates the limits of legal power by defining standards against which that power can be held accountable. A commitment to distributive justice, for instance, demands that like cases be treated alike. Similarly, standards of justness require that punishment be reasonable, not cruel, unusual, or excessive To the extent that it contains and regulates the law's power to punish and afflict pain, justice legitimates that power.

The capacity of justice to impart legitimacy to penal power depends, at least in part, on these ideals of fairness and justness construed as stable and transcendent, or "beyond culture and outside of history; a kind of absolute which is unaffected by change or by convention."[3] Justice may be breached, violated, or miscarried in specific situations, but these events are to be understood as distortions of what are essentially the unchanging ideals of justice.

Despite the transcendent quality that has been claimed for justice, David Garland, writing about criminal justice, observes:

> Even if past generations believed that their invocation of justice was an appeal to an absolute value, it is clear that the conceptions of what this value demands, and of what justice implied, have changed over time in important ways. Precisely because justice was understood as unchanging, any changes in the conventions whereby justice was enacted have tended to be gradual and unannounced.[4]

Following Garland, I aim here to historicize the ideas of justice, and injustice, by describing the processes through which injustice is collectively named and recognized. Despite the tendency of these changes to appear "gradual and unannounced," changes in our understanding of what constitutes an injustice are often the result of purposive collective action seeking a cultural revision in knowledge, citizenship, and sovereignty.

Recognizing Injustice

In her influential collection of essays, *The Faces of Injustice*, Judith Shklar points out that moral philosophers tend to conceive of injustice as simply the absence of justice.[5] Construed as such, the meaning, causes, and consequences of injustice are inferred from our notion of justice—that is, from the thing it is *not*. Justice, in what Shklar calls the "normal model" of moral philosophy, is largely a matter of

> the primary rules settling what is due to whom, . . . effective, specific laws and institutions designed to maintain these rules in the course of private exchanges and to punish those who violate them. And no legal system can be just unless it is managed by officials who are fair, impartial and committed to the task of maintaining the legal order that gives the society its whole character. When these norms are not followed, there is injustice.[6]

In this "normal model of justice," injustice is reduced to "a prelude to or a rejection and breakdown of justice, as if injustice were a surprising abnormality." Equating injustice with "*not* justice" has, thus, underwritten a longstanding and nearly exclusive preoccupation of moral philosophers with justice: with defining it, depicting it, seeking it, and celebrating it. By contrast, injustice, conceived of as absence and aberration, remains relatively unexamined.

While moral philosophers have failed to adequately examine the meaning of injustice, sociolegal scholars have been curiously silent in regard to the meaning of justice.[7] Several reasons for this inattention have been suggested. Most often the neglect is explained by the fact that defining justice requires a moral assessment of the meaning of some behavior, decision, or state of affairs. It requires a judgment rooted in values: Was an act or decision fair? Was it appropriate? Did it achieve some measure of "justness?" To engage in such assessments requires leaving the value-free realm of so-called objective social science. To avoid such epistemological exile, the concept of justice is often deployed by sociolegal scholars as a vague but unspecified standard for some set of equally unspecified value commitments having something to do with the distribution of costs and benefits.[8]

In most sociolegal research, the notion of power serves as the conceptual understudy of justice. There are several reasons for this conceptual displacement. One conventional explanation is that power, as a concept, is more compatible with the methods and epistemology of social science. For instance, Bryant G. Garth and Austin Sarat have noted that, "[w]hile avoiding discussions that directly address justice, most law and society researchers have no such qualms about the concept of power. One reason is an assumed academic division of labor. The study of power is relatively easy to frame as legitimate social science."[9] Power leaves a mark: it maims, it diminishes, it injures, it can be known by the trail it leaves. In short, power avails itself of being observed, recorded, and measured. By focusing on the operation of power as the proxy for justice, law and society researchers thus avoid wading into the murky value-laden waters of moral philosophy or social policy.

Indeed, whereas moral philosophers equate justice with the law and conceive of injustice as the aberration of the two, contemporary sociolegal scholars perceive of law as power and of injustice as the inevitable consequence. Injustice, in this framing, rather than a "surprising abnormality," follows from the very exercise of law.[10] In either case, injustice has remained in the conceptual wings of both moral philosophy and social science. Shklar reminds us of what is obscured by conceptualizing injustice as either simply "*not* justice" or as a corollary of power: "The sense of injustice, the difficulties of identifying the victims of injustice, and the many ways in which we all learn to live with each other's injustices tend to be ignored, as is the relationship of private injustice to the public order."[11]

Acknowledging that the phenomenon of injustice exceeds our formal apparatus for naming, monitoring, or redressing such claim, Shklar suggests that we turn to "the self-understanding of victims" if we are to "give injustice its due." According to Shklar, this requires that we trace the relationship between "private injustice and the public order." She insists that we "should concern itself with both *formal* and *informal* victims, both those who are legally or conventionally recognized as such and *those who do not show up in even the best of social inventories of injustices.*"[12]

One way of exploring this relationship is to examine the factors that determine which victims show up in our "social inventories of injustice" (the public order) and which remain private and unrecognized.

The Politics of Injustice

A preliminary step in giving injustice "its due" consists of recognizing the ambiguity of distinguishing injustice from misfortune.[13] Misfortunes are the work of fate, or nature, or whatever nonhuman engine of human misery and suffering we happen to believe in. As victims of misfortune, we are pathetic (in the classical sense) beings insofar as we inspire sympathy and charity from others who are not responsible for our plight but who nonetheless may intervene to alleviate our suffering. Injustice, by contrast, implies a human agent who commits an act that causes the pain, indignity, or injury. Since hurricanes, or floods, or other sorts of natural disasters are rarely, if ever, a result of human action, they are rarely labeled "unjust." These are "acts of God," by which we mean "random" or "uncontrollable" and, perhaps, "inevitable." In a modern, secular world, when we refer to such events as "acts of God," we seem, then, to be exonerating human responsibility more than we are actually assigning divine agency.[14]

Yet, the definition of an event as unjust entails more than simply identifying an agent who is responsible. We do not typically call a murder "unjust," for instance, no matter how unwarranted, unprovoked, or heinous. While we may condemn such an act as immoral, depraved, tragic, or evil, we are unlikely to see it as an injustice. An injustice posits a particular *type* of relationship between the sufferer and another who is responsible for the pain or injury. It is based on a sense of mutually acknowledged obligation, expectations, and responsibilities as they are embodied in social roles. An injustice consists of a violation of these legitimate expectations. Injustice, therefore, is inherently a social phenomenon. Outside of a constellation of roles, and the relationships and responsibilities they define, injustice could not exist.

The recognition of an injustice thus names and locates the victim in relation to the person or persons who caused the harm or injury. The naming of something as an injustice imparts meaning to what might otherwise be understood to be meaningless. The victim is no longer the casualty of randomness, senselessness, or even evil. In this way, the recognition of an injustice restores humanity to the victim by situating him in relation not just to other persons but to a normative, as opposed to a probabilistic, universe as well.

Furthermore, by interpolating the victim in this way, he or she is no longer pathetic, worthy of sympathy or charity, and little else. In this way, the naming of an injustice empowers the victim. As a result of this empowerment, the victim of an injustice can make a claim on the responsible party, a claim warranted by the relationship, rather than the harm per se. As Ralph H. Turner notes:

> The sense of misfortune and the sense of injustice can be distinguished by the difference between *petition* and *demand*. The victims of misfortune petition whoever has the power to help them for some kind of aid. The victims of injustice demand that their petitions be granted. The poor man appealing for alms is displaying his misfortune. The Poor People's March

on Washington to demand correction of their situation expressed a sense of injustice.[15]

Obviously, as Turner's example suggests, the same condition or event—poverty, illness, indignity, or the deprivations of freedom—can be defined differently. This variability is a result of the fact that roles and relationships are themselves constantly being reconfigured and redefined, and as a result of these redefinitions, the scope of injustices expands or contracts.

Indeed, Turner argues that at the heart of all modern social movements has been a demand for redress of some condition or state of affairs that had previously been seen as a misfortune. In the modern era, the sorts of claims that have been made by social movements can be divided roughly into one of three types: the liberal humanitarian movements of the late eighteenth and early nineteenth centuries, such as the French and American Revolutions; the socialist movements of the late nineteenth and early twentieth centuries, such as the labor movements, international communism, and the New Deal; and the liberation or identity movements of the last half of the twentieth century (gay, women's, and black liberation). In each of these periods, a new set of conditions was redefined and a new conception of injustice asserted.

The liberal humanitarian movements were based on the asserted right to self-rule. In seeking freedom of speech, religion, assembly, and so forth, these movements were demanding the institutional apparatus for participating in self- government. Poverty and economic inequality were not the central focus of these movements, nor was their eradication or redress part of the outcomes sought. The social welfare movements built on the liberal humanitarian movements by retaining the commitment to freedom and self-rule, but they expanded those claims to define economic and material insecurity as unjust. "Freedom from want" was now added to the political freedoms secured by earlier movements. Institutional arrangements, such as social welfare, the right to unionize, and the demand for economic security, were put into place to prevent or redress such misfortunes as destitution, exploitation, or unemployment. Turner contends that the identity movements subsumed both the political and economic conceptions of injustice articulated during earlier periods and added to these a new injustice focused on the self and identity. The various liberation movements since the mid-1960s have demanded the right of self-expression, human dignity, and pride in identity.

Turner's analysis illustrates that the process of naming injustices is essentially a discursive process involving the revision of meaning. Such claims for cultural revisions of misfortune represent penetrations insofar as they entail a denaturalization of some state of affairs—political subordination, poverty, or psychosocial repression—that had previously been understood to be inevitable and natural.

An attention to the politics of injustice suggests that the preoccupation of social scientists with power, rather than justice, is more than methodological feint or a way of avoiding the entailments of morality or value. In this framing, injustice is not simply a casualty of power; it is a measure of power, as well. The naming of an injustice is the result of political contest in which some claims are recognized and redressed. By fixing responsibility and the obligation to make institutionalized reforms, definitions of injustice reposition victims vis à vis those conditions or persons that are responsible for their suffering or loss. By reframing misfortune within the hegemonic discourse of agency and responsibility, claimants insinuate themselves into a broader cultural, political, and institutional sphere. In recognizing a claim of injustice, society incurs a debt to misery.

What is necessarily involved in achieving these revisions of misfortune is the linking of misery or injury as it is experienced in everyday life with the ideas, institutions, and material capacities that generate it.[16] In short, such revisions necessitate the formulation of counterhegemonic accounts of action and responsibility. By contrast, the key to understanding the basis of hegemonic power is the maintenance of what Antonio Gramsci called "contradictory consciousness," an experience of the world in which a unbridgeable chasm exists between the experience of everyday life, in which people encounter the conditions of work and lived social relations, and official accounts of how things work.[17] There are ever-present two forms of consciousness:

> [O]ne which is implicit in his activity and which in reality unites him with all his fellow-workers in the practical transformation of the real world; and one superficially explicit or verbal, which he has inherited from the past and uncritically absorbed. But this verbal conception is not without consequences. It holds together a specific social group, it influences moral conduct and the direction of will, with varying efficacy but often powerfully enough to produce a situation in which the contradictory state of consciousness does not permit of any action, any decision or any choice, and produces a condition of moral and political passivity.[18]

Gramsci's notion of contradictory or divided consciousness complicates what often appears to be the acquiescence of relatively powerless groups to conditions of their own exploitation. Hegemonic discourses operate not by top-down social control, imposition of a single vision of the world, but by disqualifying the significance of everyday experience through processes of reification, a process wherein historically specific processes and behaviors are misrecognized as having a temporal and spatial transcendence. Social life appears to be framed by forces and processes that exist "outside of" the daily lives of individuals.[19]

The *contradictory* character of consciousness refers, however, to the fact that persons are not merely ideological dopes, compliant because they are mystified or duped by ideological formulations. Sociological research has consistently shown that relatively powerless persons are able to express critical views of dominant values as they encounter them in their daily lives but are less able to translate that skepticism more generally, no less convert it into a politic of protest. Michael Mann, for instance, found that working class individuals were more likely to express resistant or nonhegemonic attitudes in concrete experiences and to accept the hegemonic as it is expressed in broad abstractions, concluding that "[i]t is not value consensus which keeps the working class compliant, but rather a lack of consensus in the crucial area where concrete experiences and vague populism might be translated into radical politics."[20]

Sociolegal scholars who have studied legal consciousness have also found evidence of such contradictory or divided consciousness in which the internal connection between legality and particular experiences is severed in ways that insulate legal institutions from critique, thereby leaving injustices unnamed. After strongly condemning particular actors or practices of a particular court, police department, or government agency, citizens will often conclude their accounts by observing that "the system" or "the courts" or "the police" are "just," "effective," or "honest." The malfeasance, incompetence, bias, or injustice they encounter are attributed to the particular actors, office, or agency.[21]

The most significant consequence of such contradictory consciousness is a reversal in the moral and causal relationship that is understood to exist between conduct and its reified form ("the system"). The reified version of power becomes the standard of objective reality against which the subjective, concrete, and immediate is assessed and interpreted. Patricia Ewick and Susan Silbey found that American citizens often locate legality in rules and regulations that seem to produce effects independently of human action. One man they interviewed explained his failure to take any action in a situation in which he believed he had been discriminated against by alluding to such a reified view of law. Having worked for a food service management company for many years, he claimed that he was not paid the same as others who had preceded him in the position. Yet, he claimed, "There was not a lot I could do. I spoke to them about it, and you know, they said, they came up with a grading system or grade unit or operation . . . and [said] the most you could get in an increase is a certain amount."[22] This man expressed the futility in challenging the discrimination in the face of the "grading system," an impersonal metric that seemingly justified what he felt to be an injustice.

Yet, as this example illustrates, hegemony is not total. It is, rather, "a process of continuous creation which, given its massive scale, is bound to be uneven in the degree of legitimacy it commands and to leave some room for antagonistic cultural expressions to develop."[23] Indeed, within the "contradictions" of consciousness lie the possibilities for challenge and resistance.[24]

According to Marc Steinberg, we must examine the possibilities of counterhegemonic challenge by focusing on how prevailing cultural meanings are appropriated and reinterpreted as collective actors attempt to depict their understandings of justice, order, and equity. This process of creation and re-creation is relational and dynamic. Each new claim—even while it hopes to innovate cultural understandings of injustice—must invoke existing and recognizable elements of the discursive field. In his study of nineteenth-century English cotton spinners attempting to procure a "living wage," Steinberg observed:

> Contentious discourses are structured not so much by independent grammars of meaning, issue cultures, or some system of beliefs exterior to conflict; rather, they are determined by the ways challengers can combine genres, in particular, social struggles and the discursive fields often dominated by power holders, in which this strategic action occurs.[25]

In other words, discourses that were employed successfully by earlier movements are appropriated by successive claimants and used inventively to underwrite a substantially different sense of what constitutes an injustice. For instance, the nineteenth-century English working-class efforts to obtain a "living wage" "constructed the logic of righteous contention

. . . through metaphorical appropriation and analogy, as the overthrow of aristocratic and theocratic tyranny provided the logic for the overthrow of economic tyranny." Labor movements in the twentieth century also applied the idea of "democracy" to the workplace, invoking the concept in a way that exceeded the liberal humanitarian movements' uses of that notion.

Similarly, beginning in the 1960s, various identity movements appropriated the discourses of "alienation," wresting it out of the materialist context in which the socialist movements had deployed it and invoking the idea in a more existential, psychological, and therapeutic way. Nick Crossley has described such a strategy of discursive borrowing in his analysis of the British mental health movement in the 1970s. The activists, in seeking rights for mental health patients, initially described their group as a "union" and their protest as a "strike," borrowing heavily from the already legitimated discourses of the labor movement.[26]

Counterhegemonic challenges to injustice requires more than discourse, however. The political vehicle for these counterhegemonic redraftings can be traced to what Gramsci referred to as a "historical bloc": allied groups with cross-cutting interests, whether economic, religious, or political. Thus, in order to formulate a persuasive counterhegemonic account of injustice requires the ability to create coalitions with other groups. The formation of such blocs requires, in itself, a measure of political and economic power. Turner writes:

> In each major era the fundamental circumstance that has made possible the development of a revised sense of justice has been the rise in power and general standing of some major class. None of the great movements has been the product of groups who were moving downward nor of groups in abject powerlessness, poverty, or despair.[27]

In the liberal-humanitarian movements, it was a rising industrial and business class who were prevented from more fully realizing their rising status within the framework of the traditional power of the aristocracy and landed gentry. The specific ideological revision reflected their predicament: "They already had the economic resources: all they needed was the freedom to capitalize on them. Hence they had no occasion to think of economic deficiencies as a matter of injustice. The solution to their problem lay in undermining the monopoly of political power in the hands of the aristocracy."[28]

Turner similarly argues that the socialist movements were provoked by the rising prospects of labor in an expanding industrial economy, but one that was premised on a fundamental economic insecurity linked to workers' dependence on large corporate interests. Demands for unionization and other forms of social welfare were a result not just of the relative powerlessness of workers but of their escalating status as well.

Notably, the more recent identity movements, unlike the previous eras, lack a clear class-based constituency. Rather, Turner links these movements to an age cohort that experienced their own type of status inconsistency. On one hand, beginning in the latter half of the twentieth century, young adults and adolescents were given greater autonomy from adult authority. They were often better educated than their parents, and, due to better public health and nutrition, were maturing sexually at earlier ages. According to Turner, "The problem of alienation and the sense of worth is most poignantly the problem of a youthful generation with unparalleled freedom and capability but without an institutional structure in which the capability can be appropriately realized."[29]

The chief problem with this account of Turner's politics of injustice lies in its depiction of a progressive, ever-expanding social inventory of injustice. With each successive period, ever more diverse forms of misery and misfortune are transformed into injustices. As suffering is converted into legitimate political claims, it would appear that certain issues (such as political exclusion or economic insecurity) become "settled matters," allowing us to move on to make the world an ever-better place.

Shklar suggests a similar process through which our sense of and responses to injustice continually escalate and expand:

[T]he very existence of juridical institutions contributes to our awareness of many of the injustices in our midst. Official justice has a built-in paradox. The better it performs, the greater public consciousness of injustice becomes, and with such awareness come increased demands for effective revenge as well as for more juridical services. It is a political race that judicial institutions can never win.[30]

Although Shklar attributes the generation of public consciousness of injustice to the routine operation of law rather than to political contest, both accounts present a picture of an ever-expanding inventory of injustice, with a correspondingly increasing collective obligation to redress.

The historical record challenges this model of expansion and progress. There are a number of factors that derail or prevent such progress.

First, precisely because changes in cultural understandings of injustice entail a shift in power and responsibility, such definitions are continually contested, so that what appears to be "settled" is, in fact, always open to challenge itself. Second, in securing victory over some injustice lies the possibility that the victim of an injustice will, somewhat perversely, become institutionalized as a victim. In part, this perverse outcome is linked to the dialogical necessity of employing a recognizable and resonant discourse. This, as we have seen, increases the persuasiveness of claims, but it may do so at the expense of limiting their reach. Available discursive fields impose their own limits on what can be spoken. Wendy Brown cautions that "[t]he first imaginings of freedom are always constrained by and potentially even require the very structure of oppression that freedom emerges to oppose." In other words, the experience of oppression by workers (or blacks or women, and so forth) shapes their very imagination of and demands for justice. Brown's point is that the images of freedom or justice that are articulated by challenger groups always mirror injury without necessarily "transforming the *organization of the activity through which the suffering is produced* and without addressing the *subject constitution that domination effects,* that is the constitution of the social categories, "workers," "blacks" "women," or "teenagers."[31]

In sum, research on the politics of injustice and social movements suggests a number of things about the process of achieving cultural and institutional recognition of injustice. Most important, the ability to articulate conditions of injustice necessarily entails the bridging of what Gramsci called "contradictory consciousness" linking the conditions of lived oppression to the social processes that generate them. This achievement is inherently discursive, its success being linked to the appropriation of resonant meaning and the employment of legitimate discursive genres. This dialogic approach to collective action suggests that injustice discourses do not emerge de novo: success is linked to the employment of prevailing, hegemonic, discourses in counterhegemonic registers. Yet, because it is an open-ended discursive process, vulnerable to retakings, reinterpretations, and refashionings, the possibilities of injustice once again falling off of our "social inventories of injustice" are ever present. Moreover, because the success of claiming an injustice is contingent on some measure of organizational resources, what Gramsci called a historic bloc, the structural bases for creating and sustaining such alliances will vary historically. With these stipulations in mind, we now turn to the cultural and structural conditions for holding power accountable in the late modern era.

The Politics of Injustice in the Late Modern Era

> One of the greatest challenges to law and governance is the lack of accountability inherent in the capabilities now deployable by powerful actors.[32]

> Justice long named the way persons encountered the world through law. The practices of law are changing, such that modern law often seems silent as to justice.[33]

At the heart of hegemonic, then, is the maintenance of the contradictory consciousness such that the epistemological authority of everyday experiences is unequipped to mount a challenge to the world as it is presented and "inherited from the past."

Gramsci realized, however, that the ascendance of the hegemonic is unstable and variable. He claimed that because the hegemonic is multivocal, containing various contradictions, it could become the foundation for challenge. Yet many of the conditions of late modern era make such counterhegemonic claims of injustice increasingly difficult to generate or sustain. In particular, the possibilities of successfully engaging a politics of injustice has been compromised under conditions of late modernity wherein much social, economic, and political power is exercised at a scale that is incommensurate with the scale at which it is felt. The terrain on which power operates has changed under conditions of globalization and employment of techniques of governmentality.

Globalization connotes a particular configuration of nation-state and capital such that the source and reach of power is extended to overcome both time and space.[34] This means, among other things, that power can be exercised remotely and in such a way as to exceed the contours of ordinary life. As the flows of capital accelerate and the boundaries of nations become more permeable and unstable, the constellation of roles and relationship that underwrite claims of injustice crumble as well. As Arjun Appadarui has written: "Global capital in its contemporary form is characterized by strategies of predatory mobility (across time and space) that have vastly compromised the capacity of actors in single locations even to understand, no less anticipate, or resist, these strategies."[35]

To speak of the "scale" of social action is to delimit the context within which phenomena are perceived and understood. It is also, as its cartographic metaphor suggests, to represent events at a certain level of visibility. In short, what can be seen at one scalar resolution disappears at another. Moreover, because of its ideological purchase in making some events visible and rendering others invisible, the scale of social action is strategically produced and negotiated by actors. As Boaventura de Sousa Santos has observed: "Power represents social and physical reality on a scale chosen for its capacity to create those phenomena that maximize the conditions for the reproduction of power. The distortion and concealment of reality is thus a presupposition of the exercise of power."[36]

In short, the scale at which actions occur reflects the relative assets, power, information, and scope of actors. According to Erik Swyngedouw, changes in scale always reflect shifts in power. In the 1990s, he contends, capital "jumped" upward to the global scale, while the regulation of labor moved downward toward the local. Swyngedouw refers to the double rearticulation of political scales (upward to the global and downward to the increasingly local and even individual) with the awkward term "glocalization."[37] Bob Jessop characterizes it as a "hollowing out of the state."[38]

Both terms attempt to capture the simultaneous processes of the increasing power of global and supranational actors (such as the European Union, the North American Free Trade Association, and the World Trade Organization) and the governance or regulation of labor at the local level. Thus, transnational corporations, mobilizing a discourse of free enterprise, competition, and consumption, are able to obtain favorable trade laws from states, thereby allowing them to move with great velocity across space and time. Global actors such as the World Trade Organization operate with no equally global counterpart among the nongovernmental organizations or transnational advocacy networks (TANs) who work on behalf of oppressed or impoverished citizens.[39] At the same time, these impoverished peoples are "localized" by an array of international immigration laws and regulations that inhibit political organizing across state boundaries.[40]

Globalization itself has become the dominant discourse describing and legitimating these processes. As it is used by politicians, academics, economists, and even challenging groups, it holds up the inevitability, the implacability, and in some cases the desirability of transnationalization of capital and its consequences on local labor markets.[41] Adoption of this discourse by potential challenging groups has operated much like Brown predicted: to rearticulate without revising the processes that produce domination. Thus David Harvey writes of the unintended consequences of the "globalization" discourse by those who would challenge it: "The more the left adopted this discourse as a description of the state of the world (even if it was a state to be criticized and rebelled against), the more it circumscribed its own political possibilities."[42] In short, the adoption of the discourse, with its emphasis on the free market and free competition, by challengers has delegitimated nonmarket alternatives; consequently, more and more aspects of everyday life are "premised on and pervaded by market values, representations and symbols."[43]

Forms of postmodern power not only incapacitate ideological revisions by effacing the everyday through the diminishment of scale, they simultaneously operate by *enlarging* the scale of local action such that the everyday, the mundane, the personal, and the immediate myopically conceal the context in which power operates. Beginning in the last decades of the twentieth century, for instance, citizenship has become increasingly "privatized" through processes linked to mass consumerism, individualism, and a deliberate shrinking of the public sphere.[44] The emergence of what Garland has called "moral individualism"[45] has replaced the constraints and limitations previously exercised by family, community, and state and thus the possibilities of injustice defined by the roles and relationships that they define.

Under the guise of neoliberalism, market-based solutions to previously defined social problems have reversed or compromised many of the rights and protections secured earlier in the century. The demise of labor unions and the privatization of everything from security to health care to Social Security demonstrate the fragility and vulnerability of such rights. Moreover, as a result of an intensifying penality associated with neoconservatism, millions of citizens have become disenfranchised, losing the fundamental rights of liberal democracy secured during the liberal-humanitarian revolutions of eighteenth century.[46]

While globalization is a phenomenon linked to processes of spatialization, at the local level control is also largely accomplished through the use of space: how it is designed, distributed, and inhabited.[47] Michel Foucault, who has been called a cartographer of power, conceptualized modern transformations in social control as a movement from bodies to minds to space. He invoked two powerful, but distinctive, spatial images to represent and contrast exclusionary and disciplinary modes of power. In the former case, he described the leper and his separation into an excluded, disqualified mass. In the case of discipline, he evoked the image of the city under siege by the plague, where the enclosure and meticulous partitioning of space allowed for the distribution of individuals to be contained and supervised. Each of these modalities of regulation relies on space. In the case of the expelled leper, space is used to produce the pure community leached of the unredeemable. In the case of the ordered city, it is used to produce a regimented society where no one was excluded from the regulatory machinery.[48]

In his later essays, Foucault outlined a third form of regulation, governmentality.[49] Space figures most centrally and complexly in this form of regulation. If exclusion and discipline are animated by the dreams of purity and order, this third mode of power seeks a different dream, that of freedom, or to be more precise, a subject who can be governed through his or her freedom. The dream of a free but governable subject is necessitated by the paradox that lies at the heart of liberal regimes: that is, governments create zones of privacy and autonomy to which they, by their own authority, are denied access. Governmentality is a response to this paradox. Through an array of discursive and material practices and technologies, liberal subjects are increasingly governed through, rather than against, their freedom. This trick is achieved in part by the retreat and dispersal of power. We are, to use Nikolas Rose's term, governed "at a distance."[50] This distance is both constitutional, in that regulation is achieved through a variety of nonpolitical experts and authorities, and spatial, in that these operations are located and practiced in dispersed sites.

Ironically, the terminus of these distant and dispersed vectors of regulation and control, the point at which they all converge and reach their fullest expression, is the individual subject. For governmentality to succeed as a mode of regulation, it must realize or produce subjects who are actively engaged in the very same technologies of governance as the political, scientific, medical, and ethical experts. In this sense, governmentality is both distant and, at the same time, very close. Capturing this contradiction, Mariana Valverde has described the result of the process as the "despotism of the self."[51]

The dream of individual freedom and expression has effectively tied people to the project of their own identities, which, in turn, are increasingly managed through consumption of goods and services. According to

Aihwa Ong, "Neoliberalism can be conceptualized as a new relationship between government and knowledge through which governing activities are recast as non-political and non-ideological problems that need technical solutions."[52] Through the production of need and the ordering of choice, the market, advertising, and a culture of consumption operate to regulate not only the behavior but also the imagination and identities of citizens.[53]

It is fitting that the freedom offered by governmentality has been increasing, as it is protected through the purchasing of forms of security that have reinforced privatized forms of life within alarmed homes, gated communities, and heavily patrolled shopping malls and office buildings. It has also fueled an increasingly repressive criminal justice system that, by focusing on individual victims and their relationship to offenders, deflects attention from the larger economic, political, and social context. According to Brown, one of the consequences of this hyperindividualism is an evisceration of politics of injustice and a return to a politics of revenge:

> Social injury such as that conveyed through derogatory speech becomes that which is "unacceptable" and "individually culpable" rather than that which symptomizes deep political distress in a culture; injury is thereby rendered intentional and individual, politics is reduced to punishment and justice is equated with such punishment on one hand and protection of the courts on the other.[54]

Thus, as power becomes increasingly global (operating with greater scale, mobility, and dispersement), subjects' dreams of "empowerment" become ever more individual, emotional, and privatized. Rather than seeking cultural and structural change that would remedy injustice, citizens turn to the law to obtain a measure of revenge. The debt to misery is served, not to the collective whose responsibility it is to make changes that would redress conditions that generate injustice but to individual transgressors who are themselves powerless to make changes.

Postmodern power, fashioned along the lines of the market, is promotive rather than reactive, voluntary rather than coercive, and is based more on choice than on constraint. Most important, power, eclipsed by the promotion of individual choice and freedom, seems to disappear altogether. Yet, as Rose notes, these new forms of regulation are no less powerful for being decoupled from public power: they are simply less visible and less accountable.[55]

Conclusion

Globalization is a process in which some things (information, capital, good, services) move with great reach and velocity, while others (individuals, communities, even states) are stabilized or contained at the local level, Accordingly, James N. Rosenau contends that since the late twentieth century we see "an endless series of distant proximities in which the forces pressing for greater globalization and those inducing greater localizations interactively play themselves out."[56] Governmentality, through technologies of subjectivity, mimics this scalar divergence by entrapping citizens within their own freedom while it removes and disperses power. Both processes work in tandem to inhibit the naming of misfortunes as injustices. The incommensurability between the scale at which injuries are felt and the scale at which power operates incapacitates the sorts of ideological revisions that activated most modern injustice movements. Globalization and governmentality have seemingly effaced power by removing it from the "here" and "now." The apparent evacuation of power from everyday life has profound consequences for the development of a counterhegemonic consciousness or the formation of historic bloc capable of challenge.

Paradoxically, at the same time that globalization and governmentality eclipse power, and thus prevent the naming of injustice, some have argued that these same processes may make the *experiences* of injustice more acutely felt. The flow of information, ideas, and images of economic well-being, along with discourses of human rights and gender equality, circulate freely in a world in which the possibilities of achieving such conditions are limited by repressive local states (which, as Appadurai notes, are themselves sustained by global arms and capital flows). In short, as persons become part of a global interlegality, yet continue to live their lives on the ground of everyday life, they are increasingly unable to hold power accountable.

The possibilities for a politics of injustice under these conditions require a reconsideration of the very discourse of globalization, a discourse that achieves, rather than merely describes, that evacuation of power. As many critics have pointed out, the discourse of globalization operates ideologically to establish the inevitability and implacability of the processes that produce inequality and injustice. Moreover, the championing of the local to oppose global power contributes to the ascendancy of this view by locating the global outside of and impervious to the political agency of actors. What needs to occur in order for a realignment of power and a recognition of injustice is not to oppose the local with the global but, rather, to understand the ways in which they are mutually produced as an ongoing concern. Rather than conceive of the local and the global as two opposable entities, scholars and activists need to recognize that the idea of scale connotes apprehending the *same thing* but from different perspectives.[57] This recognition would enable bridging that epistemological divide that prevents the reconciliation of everyday misery with the structures that produce it. Thus Anna Lowenhaupt Tsing has suggested that we adopt the metaphor of "friction" rather than that of scale in thinking about of globalization.[58] Whereas conventional discourses of globalization inflect the notion of mobility (i.e., capital *flows* freely), the idea of "friction" reminds us that movement of any sort can only occur with engagement. The abstractions that disqualify the everyday (structures, markets, law and justice) must, in reality, find material and symbolic expression "on the ground" of daily life. We must, Tsing insists, ask about such universals "not as truths or lies but as sticky engagements." Thus, rather than project their political agency into the etherized "global," activists must envision the global from below where, as Lefebvre reminds us, people rejoice or suffer. Doing so opens up conditions of possibility for retaining the idea and ideals of justice—rather than efficiency, or security, and, thus, ultimately, the possibilities of calling in our debts to misery.

NOTES

1. Kevin R. Cox, "'Globalization,' the Regulation Approach," and the Politics of Scale," in *Geographies of Power*, ed. Andrew Herod and Melissa W. Wright (Oxford: Blackwell, 2002); David Harvey, *The Condition of Postmodernity: An Enquiry into the Origins of Cultural Change* (Oxford: Blackwell, 1991); James N. Rosenau, *Distant Proximities* (Princeton, N.J.: Princeton University Press, 2003).

2. Boaventura De Sousa Santos, "Law: A Map of Misreading. Toward a Postmodern Conception of Law," *Journal of Law and Society* 14 (1987): 279.

3. David Garland, *Punishment and Modern Society* (Chicago: University of Chicago Press, 1990), 21.

4. Ibid., 205.

5. Judith N. Shklar, *The Faces of Injustice* (New Haven, Conn.: Yale University Press, 1990).

6. Ibid., 18.

7. Marianne Constable, "Reflections on Law as a Profession of Words," in

Justice and Power in Sociolegal Studies, ed. Bryant G. Garth and Austin Sarat (Chicago: Northwestern University Press, 1997), 19; Marianne Constable, *Just Silences: The Limits and Possibilities of Modern Law* (Princeton, N.J.: Princeton University Press, 2005); Patricia Ewick, "Punishment, Power and Justice," in *Justice and Power in Sociolegal Studies,* ed. Bryant G. Garth and Austin Sarat (Chicago: Northwestern University Press, 1997), 36; Bryant G. Garth and Austin Sarat, "Justice and Power in Law and Society Research: On the Contested Careers of Core Concepts," in *Justice and Power in Sociolegal Research,* ed. Bryant G. Garth and Austin Sarat (Chicago: Northwestern University Press, 1997), 1.

8. Despite the reluctance of sociolegal scholars to analyze justice, there is, somewhat ironically, general agreement that there are different *sorts* of justice. The term is often preceded by an adjective connoting the various distinctions that have been drawn: procedural, substantive, or distributive. Unfortunately, there is less agreement regarding the precise practices or values to which these dimensions refer or regarding what relationships might exist among the various dimensions of justice. Although on the surface, these qualifiers would appear to represent ever-finer distinctions of justice, they are actually evasions. These distinctions allow us to focus on particular kinds of justice, having to do with process or with outcomes, for instance, without ever clearly defining the concept of justice itself.

9. Garth and Sarat, "Justice and Power in Law and Society Research," 2.

10. Robert Cover, "Violence and the Word," *Yale Law Journal* 95 (1986): 1601.

11. Shklar, *Faces of Injustice,* 15.

12. Ibid. at 36.

13. William Felstiner, Richard Abel, and Austin Sarat, "The Emergence and Transformation of Disputes: Naming, Blaming and Claiming," *Law and Society Review* 15 (1980–1981): 631. See also Ralph H. Turner, "The Theme of Contemporary Social Movements," *British Journal of Sociology* 20 (1969): 390.

14. The merely rhetorical character of the phrase "act of God" has not, obviously, always been the case; nor is the phrase always used rhetorically today. Some fundamentalist Christian leaders have imputed God's intentionality to such events as Hurricane Katrina. John Hagee, Pastor of Cornerstone Church, San Antonio, Texas, has claimed that the destruction of New Orleans was God's way of punishing the (entire) city of New Orleans for hosting a Gay Pride parade that had been scheduled for the Monday the disaster struck (*Fresh Air,* NPR, September 18, 2006). Similar attributions were made in regard to the AIDS epidemic and, ironically, the terrorist attacks on the World Trade Center.

15. Turner, "Theme of Contemporary Social Movements," 391.

16. Patricia Ewick and Susan Silbey, "Subversive Stories and Counter-hegemonic Tales: Toward a Sociology of Narrative," *Law and Society Review* 29 (1995): 197. See also Patricia Ewick and Susan Silbey, *The Common Place of Law: Stories from Everyday Life* (Chicago: University of Chicago Press, 1997).

17. Gramsci's use of the word "consenso" in this context has generated considerable confusion. Many scholars, relying on different translations, use the term "consensus" rather than "consent" in discussing hegemony. This semantic replacement is not trivial in that it implies a vastly different process through which power is secured. Consensus suggests a process in which information is exchanged and considered, and then some degree of "agreement" is reached among interacting parties. While such processes certainly do occur, in every interaction there is a prior, and largely unacknowledged, realm of meaning that grounds the communicative and deliberative processes. This grounding elaborates on the realm of intersubjective meaning:

> [C]onvergence of belief or attitude or its absence presupposes a common formulation that can be opposed. Much of this common language in any society is rooted in its institutions and practices. It is part of the intersubjective meanings. To put the point another way, apart from the questions of how much people's beliefs converge is the question of how much they have a common language of social and political reality in which these beliefs are expressed. This second question cannot be reduced to the first, intersubjective meanings as it is not a matter of converging beliefs or values. When we speak of consensus we speak of beliefs and values which could be the property of a single person, or many, or all; but intersubjective meanings could not be the property of a single person because they are rooted in social practice. Meaning is what makes consensus, as well as dissensus, possible.

Charles Taylor, "Interpretation and the Science of Man," *Review of Metaphysics* 25 (1971): 351. Gramsci's "consenso" refers to this nonreducible realm of meaning rather than to the consensus or dissensus that it enables. The point is that even in cases of contest, consent may be present insofar as the conflict entails an acceptance of the fundamental categories of thought that make the expression of dissensus possible.

18. Antonio Gramsci, *Selections from the Prison Notebooks,* ed. and trans. Quentin Hoare and Geoffrey Nowell Smith (New York: International Publishers, 1971), 326–327 (cited in T. J. Jackson Lears, "The Concept of Cultural Hegemony: Problems and Possibilities," *American Historical Review* 90 (1985): 567.

19. Timothy Mitchell, "Everyday Metaphors of Power," *Theory and Society* 19 (1990): 545.

20. Michael Mann, "The Social Cohesion of Liberal Democracy," *American Sociological Review* 35 (1970): 423.

21. Ewick and Silbey, *Common Place of Law.* See also Dorothy Smith, *The Conceptual Practices of Power: Toward a Feminist Sociology* (Toronto: University of Toronto Press, 1990). According to Smith, the relationship between the local and everyday to general social relations is not merely a conceptual or a methodological issue. Rather, the relationship between concrete and particular experience and

general experience is a property of social organization of knowledge and, as such, reflects what Smith calls "ruling." Through various objectifying practices (e.g., textualization) peoples' experiences are abstracted and transformed into ways of knowing that enable domination and control.

22. Ewick and Silbey, *Common Place of Law*, 90.

23. Walter L. Adamson, *Hegemony and Revolution: Antonio Gramsci's Political and Cultural Theory* (Berkeley: University of California Press, 1983), 174.

24. Ewick and Silbey, *Common Place of Law*; Austin Sarat, "'The Law Is All Over': Power, Resistance and Legal Consciousness of the Welfare Poor," *Yale Journal of Law and Humanities* 2 (1990): 343–79.

25. Marc W. Steinberg, "The Talk and Back Talk of Collective Action: A Dialogic Analysis of Repertoires of Discourse among Nineteenth-Century English Cotton Spinners," *American Journal of Sociology* 105 (1999): 750.

26. Nick Crossley, "Habitus, Capital and Repertoires of Contention in Recent Mental Health Processes," presented at the Fifth International Conference on Alternative Futures and Popular Protest, Manchester Metropolitan University, March 1999. Cited in Steinberg, "Talk and Back Talk," 749.

27. Turner, "Theme of Contemporary Social Movements," 397.

28. Ibid., 398.

29. Ibid., 399.

30. Shklar, *Faces of Injustice*, 49.

31. Wendy Brown, *States of Injury: Power and Freedom in Late Modernity* (Princeton, N.J.: Princeton University Press, 1995), 7.

32. Saskia Sassen, "Digital Networks and the State: Some Governance Questions," *Theory, Culture and Society* 17 (2000), 19.

33. Constable, *Just Silences*, 7.

34. The practice of "extraordinary rendition" as it is being used in the war on terror exemplifies such global practices of control. Unlike extradition or deportation, rendition is nonterritorial; suspected terrorists may be detained anywhere in the world and "rendered" to a country where torture is practiced. Meg Satterthwaite stressed the differences between renditions and extraordinary renditions, noting that extraordinary renditions should be specifically defined: "The difference . . . is that an extraordinary rendition involves a transfer in the face of the risk of torture. "The reason we created this definition was so that we could [consider] it as an analytical category and talk about a set of transfers that have started to happen in the wake of 9/11." International Gramsci Society at www.amnesty.org.au/Act_now/campaigns/hrs-int/features/getting_away_with_torture.

In 2002, while he was changing planes in New York on his way back from a family vacation, Maher Arar, a Canadian citizen who was born in Syria, was taken into custody on suspicion of being affiliated with al Qaeda. After being held in the United States for six days, Arar was deported to Syria and held for ten months, during which time he was tortured.

35. Arjun Appadurai, "Grassroots Globalization and the Research Imagination," in *Globalization*, ed. Arjun Appadurai (Durham, N.C.: Duke University Press, 2005), 17.

36. Sousa Santos, "Map of Misreading," 284.

37. Erik Swyngedouw, "Neither Global nor Local: 'Glocalization' and the Politics of Scale," in *Spaces of Globalization*, ed. K. R. Cox (New York: Guilford, 1997), 137.

38. Bob Jessop, "The Crisis of the National Spatio-Temporal Fix and the Tendential Ecological Dominance of Globalizing Capitalism," *International Journal of Urban and Regional Research* 24 (2000): 323.

39. Appadurai, "Grassroots Globalization," 2001.

40. Andrew Herod and Melissa Wright, " Theorizing Scale," in *Geographies of Power*, ed. Andrew Herod and Melissa Wright (Oxford: Blackwell, 2002).

41. Stephen Gill, "Gramsci, Modernity and Globalization," International Gramsci Society at www.italnet.nd.edu/gramsci/resources/online_articles/gi1101.shtml.

42. David Harvey, *Spaces of Hope* (Berkeley University of California Press, 2000), 13.

43. Gill, "Gramsci, Modernity and Globalization."

44. Laura Berlant, *The Queen of America Goes to Washington City: Essays on Sex and Citizenship* (Durham, N.C.: Duke University Press, 1997). See also Robert Putnam, *Bowling Alone: The Collapse and Revival of American Community* (New York: Simon and Schuster, 2000).

45. David Garland, *The Culture of Crime Control: Crime and Social Order in Contemporary Society* (Chicago: University of Chicago Press, 2001).

46. Christopher Uggen and Jeff Manza, "Democratic Contraction? Political Consequences of Felon Disenfranchisement in the United States," *American Sociological Review* 67 (2002): 777.

47. Ewick, "Punishment, Power and Justice." See also Susan Silbey and Patricia Ewick, "The Architect of Authority: The Place of Law in the Space of Science," in *The Place of Law*, ed. Austin Sarat (Ann Arbor: University of Michigan Press, 2003).

48. Michel Foucault, *Discipline and Punish: The Birth of the Prison* (New York: Vintage, 1995).

49. Michel Foucault, "The Ethics of the Concern for Self as a Practice of Freedom," in *Ethics*, vol. 1 of *The Essential Works of Foucault, 1954–1984*, ed. Paul Rabinow (New York: New Press, 1994). See also Michel Foucault, "Governmentality," in *Power*, vol. 3 of *The Essential Works of Foucault, 1954–1984*, ed. Paul Rabinow (New York: New Press, 2001).

50. Nikolas Rose, *Governing the Soul: The Shaping of the Private Self* (London: Routledge, 1989). See also Nikolas Rose, *Powers of Freedom: Reframing Political Thought* (Cambridge: Cambridge University Press, 1999).

51. Marianna Valverde, *Diseases of the Will: Alcohol and the Dilemmas of Freedom* (Cambridge: Cambridge University Press, 1998).

52. Aihwa Ong, *Neoliberalism as Exception: Mutations in Citizenship and Sovereignty* (Durham, N.C.: Duke University Press, 2006), 3.

53. Ironically, efforts to legitimate market-led globalization have claimed that trade liberalization would lead to greater specialization and economies of scale, resulting in greater efficiency and producing lower prices for consumers. Thus it is that the dual processes of globalization and governmentality converge around the citizen qua consumer. Mark Rupert, "Globalization and the Reconstruction of Common Sense in the United States," in *Innovation and Transformation in International Studies,* ed. Stephen Gill and J. Mittleman (Cambridge: Cambridge University Press, 1997).

54. Brown, *States of Injury,* 27.

55. Rose, *Governing the Soul,* 255.

56. James N. Rosenau, *Distant Proximities: Dynamics beyond Globalization* (Princeton: Princeton University Press, 2003), 4.

57. J. K. Gibson-Graham, "Beyond Global vs. Local: The Economic Politics outside the Binary Frame, in *Geographies of Power,* ed. Andrew Herod and Melissa Wright (Oxford: Blackwell, 2002), 26.

58. Anna Lowenhaupt Tsing, *Friction: An Ethnography of Global Connection* (Princeton: Princeton University Press, 2005).

Contributors

Douglas A. Berman is the William B. Saxbe Designated Professor of Law at the Ohio State University Moritz College of Law.

Markus D. Dubber is Professor of Law at SUNY Buffalo School of Law and author of *The Sense of Justice: Empathy in Law and Punishment* (NYU Press).

Mary L. Dudziak is the Judge Edward J. and Ruey L. Guirado Professor of Law at the University of Southern California School of Law. She is the author of many books, including the forthcoming *Exporting American Dreams: Thurgood Marshall's African Journey.*

Patricia Ewick is Professor of Sociology, Clark University, and coeditor (with Austin Sarat) of *Social Science, Social Policy, and the Law.*

Daniel Givelber is Professor of Law at Northeastern University School of Law.

Linda Ross Meyer is Professor of Law at Quinnipiac University School of Law.

Charles J. Ogletree, Jr., is the Jesse Climenko Professor of Law at Harvard University and the Founding and Executive Director of the Charles Hamilton Houston Institute for Race and Justice. He is coeditor (with Austin Sarat) of *From Lynch Mobs to the Killing State: Race and Death Penalty in America* (NYU Press) and author of *All Deliberate Speed: Reflections on the First Half-Century of* Brown v. Board of Education.

Austin Sarat is Professor of Law, Jurisprudence, and Social Thought and Political Science at Amherst College. He is coeditor (with Charles J. Ogletree, Jr.) of *From Lynch Mobs to the Killing State: Race and Death Penalty in America* (NYU Press) and the author of many books, including *Mercy on Trial: What It Means to Stop an Execution.*

Jonathan Simon is Professor of Law and Associate Dean of Jurisprudence and Social Policy Program at the University of California, Berkeley, Boalt Hall School of Law. He is the author of *Governing through Crime: How the War on Crime Transformed American Democracy and Created a Culture of Fear.*

Robert Weisberg is the Edwin E. Huddleson, Jr., Professor of Law at Stanford Law School and coauthor (with Guyora Binder) of *Literary Criticisms of Law.*

Index